THE LATER NOVELS OF VICTOR HUGO

The Later Novels of Victor Hugo

Variations on the Politics and Poetics of Transcendence

KATHRYN M. GROSSMAN

OXFORD
UNIVERSITY PRESS

OXFORD
UNIVERSITY PRESS

Great Clarendon Street, Oxford, OX2 6DP,
United Kingdom

Oxford University Press is a department of the University of Oxford.
It furthers the University's objective of excellence in research, scholarship,
and education by publishing worldwide. Oxford is a registered trade mark of
Oxford University Press in the UK and in certain other countries

First Edition published in 2012

Impression: 1

British Library Cataloguing in Publication Data
Data available

Library of Congress Cataloguing in Publication Data
Library of Congress Control Number: 2012930336

ISBN 978–0–19–964295–3

Printed in Great Britain
on acid-free paper by
MPG Books Group, Bodmin and King's Lynn

For John T. Harwood

Acknowledgements

A project that has spanned several decades requires its share of acknowledgements. I am grateful, first of all, for the sustained support of my family, friends, and colleagues as conference papers turned into chapters and articles that eventually led to bigger ideas—and so to multiple drafts of the present volume. With sabbatical leaves from Penn State in 2001–2 and 2008–9, as well as a 2002 fellowship from the Camargo Foundation, I was fortunate to conduct research and to write under ideal conditions. The ability to gain access online to an entire world of scholarly works through Penn State's Pattee Library greatly accelerated my ability to pursue from time to time massive quests for information. My spouse and colleague, John Harwood, provided constant encouragement and material assistance as reader, editor, sounding board, and technical consultant. Tony James, Jean and Sheila Gaudon, Victor Brombert, Isabel Roche, Stéphanie Boulard, and Bradley Stephens sustained long-term conversations with me about matters Hugolian. Suzanne Nash and the late Larry Schehr graciously supported my research efforts in France and the writing of the earliest chapters. Mem Stahley ensured that I stayed on schedule for producing the first full draft of the book; Tess Crossen likewise persisted in eliciting frequent progress reports; and Larry Porter's critical commentary, following an extended discussion about Hugo's fiction over the years, was invaluable in working out the last kinks in argumentation and expression.

I owe a huge debt for producing the book itself to Tom Minsker, maestro of technology, and to Brandy Brown, indexer *extraordinaire*. I must also thank the faculty and staff of the Department of French and Francophone Studies for their patience during the long maturation of my thinking and the occasional moments of high stress along the way, as well as several generations of bright and enthusiastic students who have shared the pleasures of Hugo's texts and indulged my passion for poetic prose.

Finally, I wish to express my appreciation to the editors of the following journals and presses for permission to use, in revised form, material published in a number of earlier essays: Francis Cairns Publications ('"Angleterre et France mêlées": Fraternal Visions in *Quatrevingt-Treize* and *A Tale of Two Cities*', in A. R. W. James (ed.), *Victor Hugo et la Grande-Bretagne*, Vinaver Studies in French, 3, 1986); Éditions Pleins Feux ('Le Shakespeare de la France? sur la trace du Barde dans *Les Travailleurs de la mer*', in Yann Jumelais and Dominique Peyrache-Leborgne (eds), *Victor Hugo ou les frontières effacées*, Collection 'Horizons Comparatistes', 2002);

the Legenda series of the Modern Humanities Research Association, formerly at the European Humanities Research Centre ('"Pleine mer, Plein ciel": The Wave of the Future in *Les Travailleurs de la mer*', in J. A. Hiddleston (ed.), *Victor Hugo,* Romancier de l'abîme*: New Studies on Hugo's Novels*, 2002); University of Nebraska Press, publisher of *Nineteeth-Century French Studies* ('Trading Places: Public and Private Transport in *Les Travailleurs de la mer*', 26/3–4, 1998; and 'Grotesque Desires in Hugo's *L'Homme qui rit*', 33/3–4, 2005); Presses de l'Université de Paris-Sorbonne ('Hugolian Endings: Back to the Future in the Novels and their Adaptations', in David Ellison and Ralph Heyndels (eds), *Les Modernités de Victor Hugo*, Transatlantique, 1, 2004; and 'La Fin de l'histoire? Variations cinématiques sur les dénouements hugoliens', in Léon-François Hoffmann and Suzanne Nash (eds), *Hugo et l'histoire*, Transatlantique, 2, 2005); Presses Universitaires de Valenciennes ('Fictions Fractales dans *L'Homme qui rit*', in Claude Millet, Florence Naugrette, and Agnès Spiquel (eds), *Choses vues à travers Hugo: Hommage à Guy Rosa*, 2007); and *Revue des sciences humaines* ('Hugo, Ricœur et le roman historique poétique', special issue on 'Égo Hugo', Stéphanie Boulard (ed.), 302, 2011).

Contents

Abbreviations

WORKS BY VICTOR HUGO

Unless otherwise noted, references are to:

OC	Victor Hugo, *Œuvres complètes*, ed. Jean Massin, 18 vols (Paris: Club Français du livre, 1967–70)
BJ	*Bug-Jargal*
CHAT	*Châtiments*
CONT	*Les Contemplations*
DJC	*Le Dernier Jour d'un condamné*
HI	*Han d'Islande*
HQR	*L'Homme qui rit*; references are to part, book, and chapter
LS	*La Légende des siècles*
MIS	*Les Misérables*; references are to part, book, and chapter
NDP	*Notre-Dame de Paris*; references are to book and chapter
TM	*Les Travailleurs de la mer*; references are to part, book, and chapter
QVT	*Quatrevingt-Treize*; references are to part, book, and chapter
WS	*William Shakespeare*

OTHER WORKS

EN	Kathryn M. Grossman, *The Early Novels of Victor Hugo: Towards a Poetics of Harmony* (Histoire des idées et critique littéraire, 241; Geneva: Librairie Droz, 1986)
FT	Kathryn M. Grossman, *Figuring Transcendence in* Les Misérables*: Hugo's Romantic Sublime* (Carbondale: Southern Illinois University Press, 1994)
MHF	Paul Ricoeur, *Memory, History, Forgetting*, trans. Kathleen Blamey and David Pellauer (Chicago, IL: University of Chicago Press, 2004); orig. pub. as *La Mémoire, l'histoire, l'oubli* (Paris: Seuil, 2000)
OA	Paul Ricoeur, *Oneself as Another*, trans. Kathleen Blamey (Chicago, IL: University of Chicago Press, 1992); orig. pub. as *Soi-même comme un autre* (Paris: Seuil, 1990)
PL	John Milton, *Paradise Lost*, ed. John Leonard (London: Penguin, 2000) (first pub. 1667)
RM	Paul Ricoeur, *The Rule of Metaphor: Multi-disciplinary Studies of the Creation of Meaning in Language*, trans. Robert Czerny (London: Routledge & Kegan Paul, 1978); orig. pub. as *La Métaphore vive* (Paris: Seuil, 1975)

TN Paul Ricoeur, *Time and Narrative*, trans. Kathleen McLaughlin Blamey and David Pellauer, 3 vols (Chicago, IL: University of Chicago Press, 1984–8); orig. pub. as *Temps et Récit* (Paris: Seuil, 1983–5)

TTC Charles Dickens, *A Tale of Two Cities*, ed. Edward Wagenknecht (New York: Random House, 1967) (first pub. 1859)

Introduction

In this era of instant gratification, Victor Hugo's self-sacrificing heroes might well seem a strange anomaly. Two hundred years after the birth of the celebrated poet, playwright, and novelist, what lessons and pleasures can the culture of clicks derive from his sprawling *œuvre*? After all, today it is Disney 'qui fait rêver', largely about buying spin-offs from films such as *The Hunchback of Notre Dame* (1996), whereas Hugo's pensive protagonists—Bug-Jargal, Quasimodo, Bishop Myriel, Jean Valjean, Marius, Gilliatt, Gwynplaine, Gauvain—all reject their fifteen minutes of fame to operate long, patient labours of love. They traverse interminable wastelands, plunge into murky abysses, and soar in imagination to the constellations; today we seek such sensations, for example, at the movies, on YouTube, and at the mall. Digital and 3-D enhancements create stunning vistas and thrilling action scenes on the silver screen. The massive footprint of our *hypermarchés*, their towering shelves stacked to the brim with an apparently endless variety of goods, likewise simulates Hugo's vertical and horizontal sublime, the feeling of unlimited possibilities in every direction. The illusion of empowerment is, for many of us, almost complete.

Rarely is self-abnegation required in such pursuits, and rarely is it granted. Until the events of September 11, the downside looked so finite—except, perhaps, in vertiginous movie graphics—that we had all but forgotten about mortal risk and death-defying, much less death-embracing, heroism in our day-to-day lives. In our relatively comfortable existence, it had been easy to ignore or to downplay the epic battles raging in the less-developed world until they reached our doorstep. Now they are our battles as well. In *The End of History and the Last Man*, Francis Fukuyama posits that 'a directional and coherent historical process'—one that involves even the great evils of the modern age—is inevitably establishing 'universal republican government' throughout the globe. The spread of liberal democracy has, in the critic's view, created a world 'divided between a post-historical part, and a part that is still stuck in history',[1] between those who have arrived at the political ideal and those who still struggle under more repressive forms of government. But we have been invited down from the relative safety of our 'post-historical' perch to expedite the rites of passage elsewhere. The plastic sublime has given way to true fear—and genuine valour. As in post-Revolutionary France, the experience of terrorism/*la Terreur* has created psychological rifts that foster a renewed apprehension of both the grotesque and the Romantic sublime.

Terror, it has been claimed, leads to delight in the sublime moment.[2] Similarly, for Hugo, leaps of conscience, conversions, and social revolutions generate more highly integrative modes of human interaction and (self-)governance. Fukuyama's aim of seeking a 'meaningful pattern in the overall development of human societies'[3] thus recalls the poet's reflections on individual and collective progress in his historical fiction. In the universe of *Notre-Dame de Paris* (1831) or *Les Misérables* (1862) or *Les Travailleurs de la mer* (1866) or *Quatrevingt-Treize* (1874), for example, the stakes for daring action are characterized as immensely high—to the point that giving up one's life in the quest for the ideal constitutes an oddly tragic but *happy* ending. At the same time, the multi-layered historical allusions that bridge the gap between past, present, and future, between historical reality and a post-historical ideal, inevitably tie the fate of each character to that of the nation itself. The confrontation of dynamic movement and utopian stasis, beginnings and endings, past and future, creates a fictive world as intricate and as stirring as the one in which we live. The utopian overtones of the later novels in particular project the moral actions of the protagonists into the political sphere, offering ways to read both mid-nineteenth- and early-twenty-first-century history. As Hugo's future—the here and now—looks back at his past, we are invited to reflect anew not only upon nineteenth-century France but upon our own time as well.

In this Introduction, I highlight several keys to my argument: the lack of closure and futuristic bent of Hugo's later fiction; the intertwining of poetics and politics in the exiled writer's prolific literary production; the evolution from harmony to transcendence of his artistic and social ideal; and my critical methodology. I end with an overview of the questions that frame my current study and of each of the four chapters that follow.

[1] Francis Fukuyama, *The End of History and the Last Man* (New York: Free Press, 1992), 59, 130, 276.

[2] See Immanuel Kant, *Critique of Judgment*, trans. J. H. Bernard (New York: Hafner, 1968), 99–104, and Thomas Weiskel, *The Romantic Sublime: Studies in the Structure and Psychology of Transcendence* (Baltimore: Johns Hopkins University Press, 1976), 82–106.

[3] Fukuyama, *The End of History*, 55.

* * *

Crucial to Hugo's endeavour to stir the reader's imagination about what lies beyond the text is his technique, dating back to *Bug-Jargal* (1820; expanded version, 1826) and *Notre-Dame de Paris*, of combining both tragic and comic conventions to provide especially rich closures to his historical fiction. At the 'end of history', a happy-ever-after union counterbalances the self-sacrificial death of the hero. The self-effacing disappearance of Jean Valjean in *Les Misérables* is offset by the life-affirming alliance of his adopted daughter, Cosette, with the revolutionary-turned-baron, Marius Pontmercy. In *Les Travailleurs de la mer*, Gilliatt crowns his solitary epic struggles against the elements by giving his beloved Déruchette in marriage to another, then drowning himself in the rising sea as their boat vanishes over the horizon. Gwynplaine, the mutilated protagonist of *L'Homme qui rit* (1869), has a chance to expound his vision of the ideal social order before the House of Lords before drowning himself in order to join his beloved Dea in death. And *Quatrevingt-Treize* likewise has a complex finale, with the death of the two revolutionary heroes, Gauvain and Cimourdain, the first by execution and the second by suicide—a death that reunites them, since 'ces deux âmes, sœurs tragiques, s'envolèrent ensemble, l'ombre de l'une mêlée à la lumière de l'autre'.[4] In each case, the story appears to wrap up the loose ends occasioned by Hugo's audacious *mélange des genres* throughout while dispelling the comic illusion of individual existence. Of what *use*, the reader may wonder at first, have the heroes' struggles been, either to themselves or to others? Does their selfless valour really reflect Fukuyama's 'directional and coherent historical process', or does the insouciance or derision of others imply that the human race is doomed to repeat its failures in spite of such exemplary behaviour? At stake is whether this repeating narrative schema involves more than the simple dichotomous division of history into happy 'winners' and tragic 'losers'.

A closer look shows that the futuristic bias of Hugo's historical novels—which engage with the political present through the lens of past events—shapes their conclusions in surprisingly open-ended ways. Rather than serving simply as vehicles for displaying his encyclopaedic knowledge of France's past, Hugo's works also allude to current social issues and offer a vision of a better, republican future. *Les Misérables*, which is set during the

[4] Victor Hugo, *Œuvres complètes*, ed. Jean Massin, 18 vols (Paris: Club français du livre, 1967–70), xv. 509; hereafter *OC*. All citations from Hugo are from the Massin edition of the *OC*, unless otherwise noted. More general references to *Notre-Dame de Paris* (hereafter *NDP*) are to book and chapter; and to *Les Misérables* (hereafter *MIS*), *Les Travailleurs de la mer* (hereafter *TM*), *L'Homme qui rit* (hereafter *HQR*), and *Quatrevingt-Treize* (hereafter *QVT*), to part, book, and chapter.

Restoration (1814–30), contains an occulted history of Louis-Napoléon Bonaparte's treachery, coup d'état, and illegitimate reign under the Second Empire (1852–70). The malevolent Thénardier is thus invested with the physical and moral traits of Hugo's arch-enemy. In *Les Travailleurs de la mer*, Gilliatt's single-handed battle to salvage the engine from a shipwrecked steamboat turns a tale of life in the Channel Islands during the 1820s into an allegory of the poet's one-man stand as the 'last republican outlaw' against Napoléon's III's 'hypocrisy'. The overlapping time frames of *L'Homme qui rit* can be clearly seen in Gwynplaine's first and only sitting in the House of Lords, where his ambition to serve as 'le Verbe du peuple' (xiv. 364) echoes Hugo's own aspirations as an elected representative during the Second Republic (1848–51). Finally, *Quatrevingt-Treize* not only considers retrospectively the violent birthing of the First Republic (1792–1804) during the Terror (1793–4); through the personage of Gauvain, it also offers France lessons on the nature of the ideal republic in the aftermath of the bloody Commune (March–May 1871).

Given their tangled temporal dimensions, it is little wonder that the extent of genuine closure in the novels has been open to debate. Alexander Welsh, for instance, sees the double dénouement of *Les Misérables*—the death of the 'active hero' and the marriage of the 'inactive hero'—as expressing contradictory desires regarding the rapid evolution of History in the nineteenth century. By ceding his place to Marius, his 'passive' contrary, Jean Valjean is able to figure the reassuring end of history itself through his death.[5] The notion that Hugo's dying protagonists point to the cessation of historical evolution has, however, more recently given way to the view that such a pattern is, in fact, illusory. What Dominique Peyrache-Leborgne calls 'la fin ouverte' of *Les Travailleurs de la mer*, *L'Homme qui rit*, and *Quatrevingt-Treize*—where death constitutes a sublime moment that leads to 'l'union définitive avec le divin'[6]—suggests that, in the later Hugo, death may be read as nothing short of a new beginning, a sort of 'post-historical' existence. The simultaneous knotting and unknotting of the various narrative strands in his dénouements would thus open on a 'future anterior posited outside itself',[7] a future that beckons to dead and living characters alike, to Hugo's bourgeois reader—and perhaps to those who seek a better world today. In some miraculous way, the 'happy ending' would apply to all who actively challenge the status quo.

[5] See Alexander Welsh, 'Opening and Closing *Les Misérables*', *Nineteenth-Century Fiction*, 33 (June 1978), 17–18, 20–1.

[6] Dominique Peyrache-Leborgne, 'Victor Hugo et le sublime: Entre tragique et utopie', *Romantisme*, 82 (1993), 26, 27.

[7] J. Hillis Miller, 'The Problematic of Ending a Narrative', *Nineteenth-Century Fiction*, 33 (June 1978), 4.

* * *

The poet himself was no stranger to audacious devotion in the name of the common good. In December 1851, at the height of his artistic and political career, he flung aside everything to defy Louis-Napoléon's treacherous *coup d'état* by going from street to street in an attempt to get the people to mount the barricades and the soldiers to put down their arms. A price was soon put on his head. Fulfilling the outlaw destiny that he had forecast as early as *Bug-Jargal* and *Han d'Islande* (1823), Hugo fled into exile, first to Brussels, then with his family to the Channel Islands, where he remained defiantly, refusing the general amnesty of 1859, until the fall of Napoléon III's Second Empire. The dazzling shower of poetic, fictive, historical, and metaphysical works produced during this period both infuriated his enemies and guaranteed his enduring fame. His mastery of satirical invective in *Napoléon le Petit* (1852) and *Châtiments* (1853), of lyricism and visionary poetry in *Les Contemplations* (1856), of epic verse in *La Légende des siècles* (1859), and of the philosophical essay in *William Shakespeare* (1864), and the peerless integration all these genres (along with drama) into three prose narratives—*Les Misérables*, *Les Travailleurs de la mer*, and *L'Homme qui rit*—greatly heightened his reputation at home and abroad. That the lessons in principle, resolution, and self-sacrifice embodied by the heroes of his novels—Jean Vajean, Gilliatt, and Gwynplaine, respectively—were practised by the writer himself was also not lost on the reading public. Hugo's fervent republican idealism found a huge audience, while the self-styled emperor met his Waterloo in the aftermath of the ill-fated Franco-Prussian War (1870–1). To read Hugo, then, is to explore our own moral, political, and aesthetic challenges and to put them in a wider perspective. As we shall see, the fiction published both during and after the poet's exile provides a treasury of rhetorical strategies for imagining history and envisioning the future, thereby illuminating the role of the metaphorical imagination in defining the political ideal.

Despite his global reputation, the millions who paid tribute as he lay in state under the Arc de Triomphe after his death in 1885, and the media extravaganza that accompanied his funeral and burial in the Panthéon, Hugo's star was largely eclipsed by the realist, naturalist, and modernist schools in the first half of the twentieth century. Naomi Schor's analysis in *George Sand and Idealism* of the long-standing critical disregard for Sand and her ideological position explains the poet's fate as well. Allied with what were considered to be the negative connotations of 'femininity', both Romantic literature and idealist philosophy fell out of fashion. It took the revival of Hugo scholarship in France in the 1960s and the centenary of his death in 1985 to succeed at last in reversing this powerful anti-Hugolian tradition. Indeed, the bicentennial celebration in 2002 of the poet's birth ensured worldwide interest in his work in the new millennium.[8] The 150th anniversary in 2012 of the publication of *Les Misérables* will doubtless focus further attention on his fiction. The foremost French Romantic poet and playwright and the first French historical novelist, Hugo continues to attract scholarly attention in such areas as genre studies, poetics, feminist criticism, Marxist criticism, Kantian studies, psychoanalytic theory, post-colonialism, and semiotics. Yet, despite the remarkable diffusion of his fiction—*Les Misérables* has been one of the most widely read novels in the world since its publication in 1862—most criticism remains focused on his poetry and drama.

Notwithstanding the 2002 bicentenary of Hugo's birth, only four major books on the novels besides my own have appeared in either the English- or the French-speaking world since the 1960s—Richard B. Grant's *The Perilous Quest: Image, Myth, and Prophecy in the Narratives of Victor Hugo*, Victor Brombert's *Victor Hugo and the Visionary Novel*, Myriam Roman's *Victor Hugo et le roman philosophique*, and Isabel Roche's *Character and Meaning in the Novels of Victor Hugo.*[9] My work fills this lacuna by tracing the repeating motifs and tropes through *all* of the novels. I analyse these verbal patterns in the light of Hugo's aesthetic theories; of his political activism not only as a representative and a senator in the French Parliament but also as a republican exile for nineteen years; and of studies on metaphor, narrative, and the Romantic sublime.[10] As a result, I demonstrate the congruities between the poet's imaginative universe and his evolving sociopolitical outlook.

In *The Early Novels of Victor Hugo: Towards a Poetics of Harmony*, I examine Hugo's initial conception and elaboration of the genre in the fiction of his youth—*Han d'Islande, Bug-Jargal, Le Dernier Jour d'un*

[8] For a magisterial account of the rebirth and development of Hugo studies from the 1950s, see Bradley Stephens, 'Victor Hugo: *État présent*', *French Studies*, 63/1 (2009), esp. 68–72.

[9] Richard B. Grant, *The Perilous Quest: Image, Myth, and Prophecy in the Narratives of Victor Hugo* (Durham, NC: Duke University Press, 1968); Victor Brombert, *Victor Hugo and the Visionary Novel* (Cambridge, MA: Harvard University Press, 1984); Myriam Roman, *Victor Hugo et le roman philosophique: Du 'drame dans les faits' au 'drame dans les idées'* (Paris: Honoré Champion, 1999); and Isabel Roche, *Character and Meaning in the Novels of Victor Hugo* (West Lafayette, IN: Purdue University Press, 2007). By way of contrast, the *MLA Bibliography* lists over 400 volumes on Charles Dickens, over 500 on John Milton, and over 2,400 on William Shakespeare—comparable literary figures—during the same time frame.

[10] I am also keenly aware that the many transpositions of Hugo's fiction into other forms of popular art (plays, movies, ballets, operas, and rock musicals) present both opportunities for and impediments to bringing his *written* work to a larger audience.

condamné (1829), and *Notre-Dame de Paris*.[11] His attempts to found a French Romantic aesthetic based on what Pierre Albouy has termed a '*poétique de l'harmonie*'[12] gives rise to a poetics of unity in diversity, of resemblance through difference. Throughout these works, repeating patterns of discord and transcendence structure a remarkably coherent universe, one in which familial, ethical, and political concerns correspond to a hierarchy of aesthetic values. In defining both his own originality and his continuity with the neoclassical past, the young writer explores new dimensions of the Romantic sublime.

In a second volume, *Figuring Transcendence in* Les Misérables*: Hugo's Romantic Sublime*, I focus on the evolution of Hugo's aesthetic into a '*poétique de la transcendance*',[13] considering Hugo's prose masterpiece as a completely integrated metaphorical system.[14] The radical disjunctions in Hugo's poetic voice and ethical vision that appear after the death of his beloved daughter, Léopoldine, in 1843, and his exile in the Channel Islands under the Second Empire figure the 'distance' that separates the self and others, vehicle and tenor, past, present, and future. By the same token, the intricate interweaving of characters, plot, subplots, themes, imagery, topography, and digressions in the text reveals a vision of transcendent harmony beyond apparent discontinuities. Superficial chaos is deeply ordered by self-repeating, fractal-like designs. As such chaos theorists as Edward Lorenz, Benoit Mandelbrot, and Mitchell Feigenbaum have demonstrated, many natural phenomena that may be initially perceived as random or chaotic reveal underlying motifs of order and unity after closer scrutiny. According to James Gleich, these non-linear 'fractals' are defined by their self-similarity, that is, by their 'symmetry across scale. [They imply] recursion, pattern inside of pattern.'[15] They contain the infinite within the finite. The verbal patterns in the later Hugo likewise participate in self-similar, recursive configurations. In contrast with the earlier novels, religious motifs identify the sublime not just with utopian ideals (and, now, the overthrow of Napoléon III's grotesque Second Empire) but with artistic death and resurrection. Through this compatibility of political and spiritual impulses, Hugo reconciles the voices of *engagement* and disinterest, of the living and the dead, that dominate in his two major poetic works of the period—*Châtiments* and *Les Contemplations*, respectively.

[11] Kathryn M. Grossman, *The Early Novels of Victor Hugo: Towards a Poetics of Harmony* (Geneva: Librairie Droz, 1986); hereafter *EN*.

[12] Pierre Albouy, 'Hugo, ou le Je éclaté', *Romantisme*, 1–2 (1971), 54.

[13] Albouy, 'Hugo, ou le Je éclaté', 54.

[14] Kathryn M. Grossman, *Figuring Transcendence in* Les Misérables*: Hugo's Romantic Sublime* (Carbondale: Southern Illinois University Press, 1994); hereafter *FT*.

[15] James Gleick, *Chaos: Making a New Science* (New York: Viking, 1987), 103.

In this book, I place the last three novels of Hugo's maturity—*Les Travailleurs de la mer*, *L'Homme qui rit*, and *Quatrevingt-Treize*—within the same imaginative matrix. Situating the three texts in relation to each other, to the previous fiction, and to various poetic and critical works published in exile and in the initial years of the Third Republic (1870–1940), after Hugo's triumphant return, I consider the *terminus* of the structural and thematic shifts in the writer from harmony to transcendence. As in *Les Misérables*, the disharmony associated with social tumult, apocalyptic vision, and oxymoronic tensions provides an essential component of the later Hugo's Romantic sublime. Still, rather than merely capitalize on the runaway success of *Les Misérables* by recycling its prominent features, each work makes an original contribution to the political and aesthetic trajectory inscribed by the entire *œuvre*. While none has touched the popular acclaim of *Les Misérables*, each testifies to Hugo's narrative daring and to the wizardry of his own 'special effects'. I argue that such effects, most notably the dizzying spatial optics and manipulation of temporal dimensions, function not as mere playful gimmicks or novelistic flourishes but as important means of figuring and communicating his notion of transcendence.

My analysis demonstrates and summarizes the unity of vision that underlies the poet's work through more than fifty years and 50,000 pages of printed text. From this perspective, the *Œuvres complètes* appear as a vast, unbounded, multi-layered verbal network that extends onwards and outwards, from book to book, from poetry to theatre to essay to narrative and back again, an infinitely expanding universe. The result of this architecture is to reconfigure our disordered experience of the world into something far more coherent—a construction of meaning that strives to change perceptions and to promote social action. Through the seduction of the sublime, Hugo's later narratives both satisfy his readers' yearning for a *different* mode of being and stimulate their imagination of alternative futures.

* * *

Methodologically, my research draws on Thomas Weiskel's discussion of *The Romantic Sublime: Studies in the Psychology and Structure of Transcendence* and, especially, on Paul Ricoeur's reflections on analogical paradigms in *The Rule of Metaphor* and on historical discourse in *Time and Narrative*.[16]

[16] Paul Ricoeur, *The Rule of Metaphor: Multi-Disciplinary Studies of the Creation of Meaning In Language*, trans. Robert Czerny (London: Routledge & Kegan Paul, 1978; hereafter *RM*); and *Time and Narrative*, trans. Kathleen McLaughlin Blamey and David Pellauer, 3 vols (Chicago: University of Chicago Press, 1984–8; hereafter *TN*). In addition, Ricoeur's thinking on the relationship between the self and other moral agents in *Oneself as Another*, trans. Kathleen Blamey (Chicago: University of Chicago Press, 1992; hereafter *OA*), and on the dynamics of historical memory in *Memory, History, Forgetting*, trans.

In considering what Albouy's 'poetics of transcendence' might entail in both narrative form and content, I apply Weiskel's insights regarding English Romantic poetry to illuminating Hugo's poetic novels—works that combine the linking features of narrative in spinning epic tales with the categorical breaks and leaps associated with metaphoric imagination. On the one hand, motifs of contiguity in Hugo correspond to what Weiskel calls the *negative sublime*—that is, 'the mode of the sublime in which the absence of determinate meaning becomes significant... since it resolves the breakdown of discourse by substitution'. Like an unobstructed metonymy that continues on and on in undifferentiated sameness, the negative sublime operates spatially as a 'featureless... horizontality or extension: the wasteland'. One need only recall the little boy struggling in a blizzard through a vast expanse of deserted whiteness at the opening of *L'Homme qui rit* to grasp the concept, which Hugo fully exploits in all his works. On the other hand, motifs of substitution constitute, for Weiskel, the contrapuntal *positive sublime*, in which the mind is overwhelmed by a sense of absolute, apocalyptic metaphoricity: 'Verticality is the appropriate dimension, and the image is inevitably some variant of the abyss.'[17] Whereas the unbroken monotony of the negative sublime elicits horror, terror accompanies the revelation in the positive sublime of universal identity. When, for example, Javert suddenly perceives Jean Valjean's moral superiority in *Les Misérables*, he finds himself thrust into an upside-down universe from which suicide is the only conceivable exit. As with *Les Misérables*, Hugo figures transcendence in his last three novels by developing intricate verbal constructs. Here, metaphorical patterns of resemblance, recursiveness, and paratactic leaps intersect with metonymical patterns of extension, linearity, and hypotactic continuity. In my overview of Hugo's first five novels in Chapter 1, I provide more concrete illustrations of these syntagmic and paradigmatic structures that undergird his lifelong exploration of ethical, political, and aesthetic issues.

Ricoeur's far-ranging philosophical enquiry into the foundations of both moral consciousness and literary creativity offers additional overarching strategies from which to investigate Hugo's texts. Through the twentieth-century lenses of hermeutics and phenomenology, Ricoeur pursues many age-old questions—why we are capable of great evil, what the nature is of historical knowledge, how we represent our personal experience of the world (past, present, and future) through language, what the relations and obligations are between ourselves and others. In so doing, he provides a rigorous theoretical structure for understanding Hugo's literary enterprise.

Kathleen Blamey and David Pellauer (Chicago: University of Chicago Press, 2004; hereafter *MHF*), shapes my analysis of the ethical and sociopolitical aspects of Hugo's work.

[17] Weiskel, *The Romantic Sublime*, 28, 26, 27.

The Holocaust in Ricoeur recalls and elucidates the Terror of the French Revolution—and the catastrophic destruction of the Second Republic—in Hugo. For both writers, the impulses of poetry and history are not mutually exclusive but strive towards common ends. In short, Ricoeur's analysis provides the tools for examining lyrical historical fiction, in this case that of Victor Hugo, but potentially of other novelists as well.

At first glance, the philosopher's treatment of metaphorical redescription in *The Rule of Metaphor* appears as a 'lyrical' prelude to the more 'realist' study in *Time and Narrative* of historical emplotment—a form of mimēsis. But when one considers Ricoeur's insistence that our experience of time, whether lived in the present or extrapolated from past events, is refigured in historical discourse, the congruity of the two works grows clearer. That he designates metaphor as a kind of *description* and emplotment as a kind of *figuration* suggests that the realms of mimēsis and poiēsis are intimately related. Thus, in his treatise on metaphor, Ricoeur argues that, rather than simply constituting a static function that substitutes one term for another, metaphor in fact sets in motion a dynamic, predicative, semantic operation. Because metaphor involves a 'transposition of terms' (*RM* 17)—a displacement *elsewhere* that is structurally related, in my reading, to the sense of transport in the sublime moment—it represents a 'categorical transgression . . . a deviation in relation to a pre-existing logical order' (*RM* 22), that produces a new way of seeing the world. In other words, the metaphorical statement 'is a kind of syntagma' (*RM* 76) that incorporates, rather than opposes, aspects of the metonymic process. In breaking old categorizations 'to establish new logical frontiers' (*RM* 197), metaphor comprises fiction and redescription, invention and discovery, creation and revelation alike. As Ricoeur puts it, 'the creative dimension [of poetry] is inseparable from [a] referential movement. *Mimêsis* is *poiêsis*, and *poiêsis* is *mimêsis*' (*RM* 39). Both conjoin in the 'new semantic pertinence[s]' (*RM* 214) generated by metaphorical meaning.

The unitive process of metaphorical language finds its counterpart, in Ricoeur, in the ways in which we represent ourselves in time. In *Time and Narrative*, the philosopher develops a theory of historical discourse that sheds further light on Hugo's historical novels. The mimetic function of historical representation turns out to be highly imaginative. If 'emplotment is the operation that draws a configuration out of a simple succession' (*TN* i. 65), then bringing order out of the chaos of passing moments through narrative, whether fictive or historical, entails considerable invention. Moreover, since literary plots by definition bind together beginnings and endings, they 'propos[e] to the imagination the triumph of concordance over discordance' (*TN* ii. 23)—not unlike the dialectical tension and reconciliation of tenor and vehicle in metaphor. The 'discordant concordances' that Ricoeur underscores throughout his thinking on historical narrative and that are implied in the logical 'clashes' resolved by metaphor (see *RM* 190, 195) are closely related, in my view, to Hugo's 'poetics of transcendence'.

At the heart of the osmosis in Ricoeur between metaphor and mimēsis is that both are modes of 'standing for', of making the distant near. The notion, for instance, of a heritage that is 'handed down and assumed... enables us to see how every turning backwards comes from a resoluteness that is, in its essence, turned toward the future' (*TN* iii. 74). It is the solidity of being at the centre of the plotted movements that assures that we traverse past, present, and future with a sense of meaningful, coherent identity. But the coincidence of different time frames in the human psyche is a strictly fabricated perception. The 'relations between the construction of history and... a past that is abolished yet preserved in its traces' assume, for Ricoeur, 'the name "standing-for" (or "taking the place of")' (*TN* iii. 100)—a concept that gestures as much towards metaphorical substitution as towards the existence of a 'real' past. Indeed, Ricoeur connects the two realms explicitly when he remarks that 'the refiguration of time by narrative... is the heir of... metaphorical redescription' with regard to 'the relationship of "taking the place of" or "standing-for"' (*TN* iii. 155). In concluding his reflections on history, Ricoeur again stresses this symbiotic relationship: 'The redescription referred to in *The Rule of Metaphor* and the refiguration of *Time and Narrative* thus change their roles, when, under the aegis of "Time, the artist," are conjoined the power of redescription unfolded by lyrical discourse and the mimetic power imparted by narrative discourse' (*TN* iii. 273). Far from representing opposing impulses, poetry and historical narrative share the capacity to reshape our perceptions, and hence our understanding, of the world around us. Because the narrative function of history aims 'to refigure our historical condition and thereby raise it to the level of historical consciousness' (*TN* iii. 102), it applies as much to epic, to fiction, as to critical history.

At the same time, Ricoeur's earlier discussion of the 'interplay of [semantic] distance and proximity' (*RM* 205) in metaphorical statements resembles the combination in historical reconstructions of 'the force of reenactment and of taking a distance, to the extent that being-as is both to be and not to be' (*TN* iii. 155). After all, in metaphor something 'both "is not" and "is like"' (*RM* 7) something else. The ability to 'see' one entity 'as' another is fundamental to historical as well as to metaphorical reference. The 'assimilation that occurs [in metaphor] between alien ideas, ideas distant from one another' (*RM* 195), is thus the poetic equivalent of projecting oneself imaginatively into past eras and creating analogies that make sense of them today. In historical re-enactments, 'it is always through some transfer from Same to Other, in empathy and imagination, that the Other that is foreign to me is brought closer' (*TN* iii. 184). While metaphorical leaps are in general conceptualized spatially, historical gaps evoke temporal bridging. Still, the two operations are essential to understanding the conjunction in Hugo's later novels of poetic and historical discourse. Each work is both a historical novel *and* a poetic narrative, the two modes enriching each other in substantial and often surprising ways.

Hugo's frequent allusions to himself as a historian in *Les Misérables*[18] return in the last three novels as he battles to assure his own place in history—both literary and sociopolitical. As he nears the end of his life, how will he say goodbye? Will he ever be able to escape the narrow confines of his island and return to France from exile? The ageing poet increasingly embraces what Ricoeur categorizes as the 'constitution of historical time through the reinscription of phenomenological time on cosmic time' (*TN* iii. 127). That is, he re-creates the past by projecting his own lived, discontinuous experience onto the continuous time of the universe. In so doing, Hugo anticipates future time as well, developing a hopeful vision that opposes the ills of past and present alike. The utopian overtones and open-ended closures of the later novels noted above thus become part of a larger reflection by Hugo on the heritage he himself will leave to future generations.

So, when Ricoeur contends that, while 'it is certainly true that the great novelists of the nineteenth century can be read as auxiliary historians . . . True mimesis of action is to be found in the works of art least concerned with reflecting their epoch' (*TN* iii. 191), he invites us to look at Hugo afresh. The question is: by commenting indirectly on the present through representations of past and future history—representations that marry masterful plotting developments with unusually figurative language—does the poet's mimetic art equal, if not surpass, that of his realist rivals? At the very least, the conjunction in Hugo's historical novels of lyrical and narrative discourse, of the 'power of redescription' and 'mimetic power', provides a model for the ways in which 'history . . . makes use of fiction to refigure time and . . . fiction makes use of history for the same ends' (*TN* iii. 181). Hugo the historian sequences time through emplotment in order to demonstrate, for example, the idea of progress, while Hugo the poet sets his tales in times past in order to recollect and highlight some of the unique, discreet moments of human existence.

* * *

The relation between metaphoric redescription and historical refiguration in *Les Travailleurs de la mer*, *L'Homme qui rit*, and *Quatrevingt-Treize*

18 See esp. *FT* 201–14.

raises a number of issues and questions that will help to frame my overall argument. First, how do story and history intersect and interact in these texts? In returning to the historical novel after a thirty-year hiatus, the exiled poet signals renewed interest in the genre. One might surmise that, following the failure of the Second Republic, history had become for him an urgent and tragic matter, one divorced from the spirit of intense playfulness of, for instance, *Han d'Islande* or *Notre-Dame de Paris*. In the case of all three novels published in the wake of *Les Misérables*, Hugo relays his reader not just to earlier times but also to exotic places—the British Crown-dependent Channel Islands, aristocratic England, and royalist Bretagne, respectively. These temporal–spatial configurations are, in turn, occasions for both mimetic reconstructions and metaphorical statements, where notions of the same, the other, and the analogous, as analysed by Ricoeur, assume key roles. An examination of these features reveals Hugo's ambivalence about the future—an ambivalence suggested by the commingling of tragedy and comedy, dystopia and utopia, in his double endings.

Second, in the light of the double displacement in space and time in each text, what is the connection between their recursive, nesting patterns and their historical discourse, the synchronic and the diachronic? Does Hugo use his intensely visual imagination to structure time as well as space? Certainly, Weiskel's account of the positive and negative sublime casts the experience of transcendence in spatial terms through the image of a vertical axis, on the one hand, and a horizontal axis, on the other. If, in Hugo, various *mises en abyme* correspond to the vertical–positive sublime, might the overlap between past, present, and future in the novels constitute the temporal equivalent? In this study, I look at the ways in which Hugo attempts to figure both temporal and spatial depth in his later fiction.

Devoting a chapter to each of the three later novels, I follow an equally diachronic and synchronic approach. While the poet's predilection for sweeping vistas of past, present, and future history presents special challenges to interpreting his works, the basic patterns repeat themselves in remarkably similar ways. In Chapter 1, I illustrate my critical methodology by summarizing my research on Hugo's previous fiction. This discussion thus lays the foundation for my fundamental argument that, like *Les Misérables*, the last three novels of Hugo's maturity use 'discordant concordances' to explore and communicate a vision of the world at once poetic and historical. The passage from the 'poetics of harmony' of the narratives of his youth to the 'poetics of transcendence' of the 1860s and 1870s nevertheless constitutes not so much a break with his creative past as its recuperation in new, more complex forms.

Chapter 2 examines the poetico-political universe of *Les Travailleurs de la mer* in the light of such relatively contemporaneous works as *La Légende des siècles*, *Les Misérables*, and *William Shakespeare*. Through such comparisons, we see that the upsurge of epic and philosophical writing during this period spills over into *Les Travailleurs de la mer* as well. Instead of partitioning his thinking into well-defined subjects and genres, Hugo creates a monumental system where works bleed into each other. Thus, when François-Victor Hugo (1828–73) began publishing in 1859 his translation of William Shakespeare's complete works, he requested a preface from his famous father. The resulting essay not only circled back to the establishment of Hugo's aesthetics in the *Préface de Cromwell* (1827). It also projected the *usefulness* of his artistic labours for present and future generations. Following the spectacular success of *Les Misérables*, *Les Travailleurs de la mer* at first seems to head off in an entirely different direction by depicting the mighty battles against nature of a lone hero on one of the Anglo-Norman reefs. What *use* are his triumphs, one might ask, if there is no one to notice them—and if they yield no reward in their aftermath? Hugo suggests, I argue, that the means is also the end, that creative activity can be a goal unto itself because, as a mode of transport, it transforms everything it touches. Monsters and metaphoricity, the grotesque and the sublime, serve to *move* the reader into new realms of being. That *Les Travailleurs de la mer* was considered, after *Les Misérables* and *Notre-Dame de Paris*, 'le troisième dans l'ordre des succès de Victor Hugo (treize éditions entre 1885 et 1915)'[19] underscores its potential to interest readers today.

Chapter 3 looks at *L'Homme qui rit*, a work set in late-seventeenth- and early-eighteenth-century England. Like *Les Travailleurs de la mer*, it reveals Hugo's extraordinary rhetorical and visionary powers. The heightened, almost hallucinogenic atmosphere of *L'Homme qui rit* presents an image at once dystopian and utopian of human potential. Once again, the protagonist fails in his mission. Can the same be said of Hugo? As we shall see, this novel complicates, enriches, and extends the almost coded language and historical concerns of the earlier narratives. When the text is viewed in this prism, we discover an all-encompassing verbal web that testifies not only to the poet's globalizing vision but also to his extraordinarily ambitious literary and social agenda. Though their unusual length has left both *Les Travailleurs de la mer* and *L'Homme qui rit* largely untaught in the Anglophone world, consideration of their artistic parity with *Les Misérables*—an even longer novel whose readership presently extends

[19] Jean-Bertrand Barrère, *Victor Hugo à l'œuvre: Le Poète en exil et en voyage* (Paris: Klincksieck, 1970), 83.

into many secondary schools—should attract new audiences. Hugo's concern with his literary and political legacy, manifested as in *William Shakespeare* in his later novels, indicates an abiding fear that he might well die while still in exile. Through its reminiscences of John Milton's *Paradise Lost* (1667), I show that *L'Homme qui rit* offers a singular strategy for perpetuating his fame in the literary afterlife.

In Chapter 4, I turn to Hugo's final novel, *Quatrevingt-Treize*, conceived as early as 1862[20] and composed in the wake of the Commune, Hugo's defeat in the 1872 national legislative elections, and the death the next year of François-Victor. Set in both Paris and Brittany during the Reign of Terror, the text explores the question of violence in the service of revolutionary ideals, thereby completing Hugo's lifelong reflections on the sublime and the grotesque. The exoticism of the Channel Islands in *Les Travailleurs de la mer* gives way here to that of the unchartered terrain of north-west France and of the 'uncivilized' royalist Breton peasants who inhabit it. This play on space and time contains not just a political but also a personal element. Hugo's rivalry with François-René de Chateaubriand (1768–1848) and Sir Walter Scott (1771–1832) at the outset of his career—a rivalry that had expanded, in *Les Misérables*, to such celebrated epic poets as Homer, Vergil, and Dante, in *Les Travailleurs de la mer*, to Shakespeare (1564–1616) and the English Romantics, and, in *L'Homme qui rit*, to Milton (1608–74)—now includes his Victorian contemporary Charles Dickens (1812–70), as well. Hugo's aspiration to rank among the literary greats of all time highlights his literary genealogy by paying homage to fellow spirits from the English sixteenth, seventeenth, and nineteenth centuries who had embraced and modelled an aesthetic combining grotesque and sublime elements. The complex patterns that ordered the textual elements of *Les Misérables* thus continue to accrue in the last three novels. Beneath the poet's probing contemplation of French patriotism and republican idealism, they offer a stunning tribute, both social and artistic, to Great Britain, which had granted him nineteen years of asylum—and a lifetime of literary inspiration.

Some might contend that the unity of vision that runs through Hugo's fictional, poetical, and theatrical works simply reflects his obsession with a handful of themes and issues. I argue instead that, given his enduring capacity for harnessing rhetorical mastery to sociopolitical aims, Hugo's unusually lengthy career in a variety of genres offers a unique field of study to literary scholars, historians, and aestheticians. How does his *œuvre* develop and change? What strategies does he deploy to infuse his

[20] Bernard Leuilliot, 'Introduction', in Victor Hugo, *Quatrevingt-Treize* (Paris: Livre de Poche, 2001), 22–3.

narratives with dramatic and poetic elements? In what ways is exile in the Anglophone Channel Islands reflected in his writing? What, in particular, can we learn by looking at the last three novels? Though neither *Les Travailleurs de la mer* nor *L'Homme qui rit* nor *Quatrevingt-Treize* has achieved the monumental stature, critical and popular alike, of *Les Misérables* or *Notre-Dame de Paris*, each text extends Hugo's utopian vision in new and distinctive ways. Most important to this evolution is the elaboration of his notion of metaphorical parity through the construction of multi-level symmetries that reveal, not the complacency of a well-established sexagenarian novelist, but the ambitious programme of social reform that drove his political and literary efforts.

While the early Hugo—the brash Romantic composer of *Han d'Islande*, *Bug-Jargal*, *Le Dernier Jour d'un condamné*, and *Notre-Dame de Paris*—took increasingly anti-establishment, democratic positions, and while the middle Hugo—who began drafting *Les Misérables* in 1845—embedded a scathing satire of Napoléon III's Second Empire within a celebration of the ethical and aesthetic sublime, the late Hugo intensifies and consolidates many motifs from these earlier works by incorporating them into intricate verbal designs with distinctive temporal dimensions. Apparent chaos is structured by both metaphorical redescription and historical refiguration into a myriad of intra- and intertextual links. In discussing the final novels of a very mature author, then, I will focus both on what is unique in each one and on what connects it to his previous fiction—that is, on what makes each work Hugolian in an ever-growing sense of that term. Despite the astonishingly different plots and characters of *Les Travailleurs de la mer*, *L'Homme qui rit*, and *Quatrevingt-Treize*, the conjunction of politics and poetics in this trio offers a stunning model of Romantic *engagement*, long after French Romanticism had become officially passé. At the end of his career, Hugo does not aspire to be remembered either as a literary *enfant terrible* or as the occupant, between Népomucène Lemercier and Charles Leconte de Lisle, of seat fourteen at the Académie Française, but as someone who would be read 500 years hence—the Vergil, the Dante, and, above all, the Shakespeare of France.

1

From *Han d'Islande* to *Les Misérables* and Beyond

It has been more than thirty years since I spent a summer in the Jardin du Luxembourg reading *Les Misérables* for the first time. That season saw my idea for writing an article on Hugo's masterwork turn into a project for a book on all of the novels. Several tomes later, I can say that it was plainly a taller order than I expected. But during that period, I have benefited from the shower of scholarship—mostly French—surrounding the bicentenary of Hugo's birth and the centenary of his death, as well as the development of Ricoeur's philosophical system from the mid-1970s till the beginning of the twenty-first century.

Since Hugo's later novels frequently refer to his earlier works, some of which may be unfamiliar to a general audience, my aim in this chapter is to summarize my overarching argument regarding Hugo's passage from a 'poetics of harmony' in the narratives published from 1823 to 1831 to a 'poetics of transcendence' in the ones published from 1862 to 1874. I also provide illustrations for the critical frame and methodology that guide the chapters that follow. In this way, I elucidate the distinctive features that separate *Han d'Islande*, *Bug-Jargal*, *Le Dernier Jour d'un condamné*, and *Notre-Dame de Paris* from *Les Misérables*, *Les Travailleurs de la mer*, *L'Homme qui rit*, and *Quatrevingt-Treize*, along with the recurring elements that connect the two series. Beginning with the novels of Hugo's youth, I look first at their narrative displacements in time and space; next at their exuberant embrace of a *mélange des genres*; then at the intergenerational, ethical, and political tensions that mark the plots; and finally at the development of Hugo's Romantic aesthetics. I conclude by outlining the ways in which *Les Misérables* is linked to and deviates from the earlier texts.

OTHER TIMES, OTHER PLACES

Hugo's purported claim in a diary entry, at the age of fourteen, that he wanted to be 'Chateaubriand ou rien' (i. 966) has been widely cited as evidence of the boy's ambition and prescience of his own genius—as well as the sign of his nascent egotism.[1] This objective notwithstanding, Hugo soon fixed on an even more ambitious goal—to compete with Sir Walter Scott, who had created a new popular genre, the historical novel, at the outset of the nineteenth century. Feeding throughout his adolescence on Scott's works, which were translated into French beginning in 1816, Hugo displayed his deep familiarity with them in his review for *Le Conservateur littéraire* of *A Legend of Montrose* (1819) and *The Bride of Lammermoor* (1819), dated 25 December 1819, where he also managed to comment on the preceding six novels. It is therefore little wonder that his first efforts at writing fiction focused on the same genre. On a dare from his older brothers Abel (1798–1855) and Eugène (1800–37), he drafted in 1818 a short novel, *Bug-Jargal*, about the slave rebellion in Santo Domingo in 1791, which was subsequently expanded into its final version after Haiti was granted its independence from France in 1825. In between, he produced *Han d'Islande*, his first full-length novel (and the first French historical novel), which contains an equally exotic setting, this time in late-seventeenth-century Norway. Despite his attempts at local colour in each text, the writer's lack of specific knowledge about or lived experience in either place results in something more like the creation of general 'atmosphere' than in the luminous evocations of an *Atala*. Still, the predilection for imaginative travel in both time and space was plainly established early on in Hugo's career.

His third novel, *Le Dernier Jour d'un condamné*, interrupts this pattern with a first-person narrative situated in contemporary France that indicts capital punishment. But Hugo was already thinking about *Notre-Dame de Paris: 1482*, a companion piece on social injustice that appeared two years later in the wake of the 1830 July Revolution. Once again, the story in *Notre-Dame de Paris* takes place in France, this time, however, in late medieval Paris—an era so 'alien' to Hugo's nineteenth-century reader that the setting required extensive description. Based on considerable archival research, the work at last established Hugo as a true heir of Scott.[2] In fact, according to Richard Maxwell, it is one of the most important novels of

[1] Adèle Hugo claims that Hugo had inscribed the note in his *journal intime* on 10 July 1816 (*Victor Hugo raconté par un témoin de sa vie: 1802–juin 1821*, in *OC* i. 966). But without the diary itself there has never been any independent verification of the entry.

[2] The novel has been frequently compared to *Quentin Durward* (1823), which Hugo reviewed in 1823 for *La Muse française* and which likewise takes place during the reign of Louis XI. See, e.g., Jean Gaudon, *Le Temps de la contemplation: L'Œuvre poétique de Victor Hugo des* Misères *au* Seuil du gouffre *(1845–1856)* (Paris: Flammarion, 1969), 17; Laurence M. Porter, *Victor Hugo* (New York: Twayne, 1999); and Roman, *Victor Hugo et le roman philosophique*, 148–53.

the nineteenth century, one that hugely influenced a raft of British artists and writers, most notably Charles Dickens.[3]

What occurred during the 1820s to turn Hugo into such a literary star? For one thing, he had developed a repertoire of authorial voices in his role as co-editor, with his two brothers, of *Le Conservateur littéraire* from December 1819 to March 1821. In this role, he reviewed dozens of books by his contemporaries, thereby increasing his store not just of models to emulate (or to avoid) but also his knowledge of what kinds of works appealed to a wide readership. Raised almost exclusively by his mother, he was eager to please—and to achieve glory, if not fortune, by his own wits. At the same time, the 1820s saw his talents burgeon, beyond the three novels already mentioned, into four volumes of poetry—*Odes et Poésies diverses* (1822), *Nouvelles Odes* (1824), *Odes et Ballades* (1826), and *Les Orientales* (1829)—and three plays—*Cromwell* (1827), *Amy Robsart* (1828), and *Marion de Lorme* (1829). In other words, by the age of twenty-eight, he had already launched his career as an important lyric poet (with several royal pensions from Louis XVIII); a popular, skilful, and controversial playwright (*Marion de Lorme* was banned by Charles X for political reasons); and a crusading novelist (given the anti-establishment message of *Le Dernier Jour d'un condamné*). The riotous battle between literary liberals and conservatives in the opening days of his 1830 play *Hernani* only burnished his reputation as the leader of the new French Romantic school. With the publication of *Notre-Dame de Paris* the next year, that reputation spread well beyond France.

As the foundational modern 'urban mystery',[4] *Notre-Dame de Paris* transports the reader to the year 1482—at the dawn of radical discoveries and disjunctions. Amid the vivid cast of characters and the twists and turns of a captivating plot, we learn, for instance, about religious architectural history, the superstitious medieval mindset, the geographic layout of Paris, and the oppressive system of justice. But change is on the way. Thanks to the imminent boom in exploratory voyages that begins with Columbus's journey to the New World ten years later and, as the narrator explains in detail, the recent invention of the printing press, a revolution in learning, perceptions, and aspirations is inevitable. The 'historical refiguration'—to use Ricoeur's concept—performed by the text inscribes the French fifteenth century in a continuum that extends from the theocracy and monumental architecture of the Egyptians to the storming of the Bastille in 1789: the significance of the moment becomes clear in the light of what preceded and of what was yet to come. The omniscient narrator who, in 'Paris à vol d'oiseau' (III. 2), surveys

[3] Richard Maxwell, *The Mysteries of Paris and London* (Charlottesville, VA: University Press of Virginia, 1992).

[4] See Maxwell, *The Mysteries of Paris and London*, 25–57.

the city from atop Notre Dame Cathedral and imposes order on its chaotic jumble of streets and buildings likewise stands astride history, reorganizing disparate events into a narrative of human progress.

This attempt to familiarize the exotic, though most in evidence in *Notre-Dame de Paris*, dates back to *Han d'Islande* and *Bug-Jargal*. Inventing in the former text customs and scenery that were doubtless aimed at passing for Nordic, Hugo produced fairly comic early efforts. The monstrous, cannibalistic dwarf Han living in a cave with his pet polar bear Friend; the evil courtiers d'Ahlefeld and Musdoemon conniving to keep their old enemy Count Schumacker locked away in an ancient prison; the executioner Orugix preparing to wield his blade at every turn—all partake of a fictive world bearing little resemblance to the original. The reader has only to suspend disbelief to enter into the story. While a similar lack of genuine local colour weakens the initial version of *Bug-Jargal*, published in 1820 in *Le Conservateur littéraire*, a great deal more research informs the second version. Much of the expansion, in fact, offers more details about the insurgent slaves, including the names of their leaders—some historically accurate—and their superstitious customs imported from Africa. The dance of the *griottes*, for example, before the white prisoners in the rebel camp both adds to the threatening atmosphere and helps to root the action in a faraway place. The characters' eccentricities signal their off-centre status—morally, culturally, and geographically.

Along with the historical discourse that provides the reader of *Notre-Dame de Paris* with a change of scenery, one finds strange characters whose behaviour is relatively unpredictable. The beggars, or *truands*, that inhabit the darkest recesses of Paris are not so much genuine gypsies as members of a society that mirrors the one that surrounds them. Their 'king', Clopin Trouillefou, can be as vicious and unjust as Louis XI, just as the handicapped who plea for alms throughout the city are as able-bodied as their wealthier targets. The most exotic personage, though, is the young gypsy dancer Esmeralda, a creature so ethereal and otherworldly that she all but casts a spell on those who hear her sing and watch her dance in the city streets. Hugo's poetic discourse is abundantly apparent in his descriptions of the girl, whose beauty defies ordinary language. At this point, the reader is displaced not only in time and space but also in language in a move from the mimetic realm to the lyrical.

MÉLANGE DES GENRES

The mixture of historical and poetic elements, it turns out, is just one dimension of Hugo's famous *mélange des genres*. For he explicitly characterizes *Han d'Islande* as 'un long drame dont les scènes étaient des tableaux, dans lesquels les descriptions suppléaient aux décorations et aux costumes. C'était une idée que les compositions de Walter Scott m'avaient inspirée et que je voulais tenter, dans l'intérêt de notre littérature' (Lettre à Adèle Foucher, datée du 16 février 1822; ii. 1168). According to Hugo, the marriage of fiction with the conventions of theatre, a genre in which he excelled and in which he counted on obtaining glory, represented an original approach to renewing French fiction. Along with *Han d'Islande*, *Bug-Jargal*, *Le Dernier Jour d'un condamné*, and *Notre-Dame de Paris* reflect his endeavour to vie with the example of Scott in the modern literary arena through the use of dramatic components.[5] The generic combination, however, had an additional root in Hugo's adolescence. Besides his voracious appetite for Scott, the budding writer haunted *le théâtre des boulevards* as a teenager, taking in the popular melodramas of his day. As Peter Brooks has demonstrated, melodramatic conventions permeated much of Balzac's narrative literature published from the early 1830s on.[6] But Hugo appears to have employed them even earlier in his novels, judging by the multitude of components derived from melodrama that inform both *Han d'Islande* and *Bug-Jargal*. Examples include the tribunals, ethical evidence, and recognition scenes that shape both texts. In *Han d'Islande*, young Ordener seeks proof that will exculpate Count Schumaker, his beloved Ethel's father, of new charges of treason. The trial is nothing short of a madcap adventure that ends with the dull-witted giant impersonating the minuscule Han being unmasked by the fiend himself and the presiding judges exposed as the true traitors. In *Bug-Jargal*, the villainous rebel leader Biassou holds rigged trials for captive colonial slave owners and tricks them into condemning themselves—a justice no less perverted than the white masters' previous treatment of their slaves.

This shift from comedy to irony in dealing with questions of law and justice continues in *Le Dernier Jour d'un condamné* and *Notre-Dame de Paris*. The satirical first preface to *Le Dernier Jour*, entitled 'Une Comédie au sujet d'une tragédie', implies that the magistrates are not impartial at all but follow their vested interests in the courtroom; and the narrative

[5] Jean-Bertrand Barrère notes that Scott allowed the young writer to 'prendre conscience de ses aspirations en matière de création romanesque' ('Victor Hugo et la Grande-Bretagne', *Revue de littérature comparée*, 28 (1954), 142). See Harry E. Shaw's comparison of Hugo and Scott in *The Forms of Historical Fiction: Sir Walter Scott and his Successors* (Ithaca, NY: Cornell University Press, 1983), 110, as well as my discussion of the literary relation between Hugo and Scott in *EN* 20–1, 45–6, 60, 161–4.

[6] Peter Brooks, *The Melodramatic Imagination: Balzac, Henry James, Melodrama, and the Mode of Excess* (New Haven, CT: Yale University Press, 1976), 110–52.

further impugns the legal system as vengeful and those who participate in it as mechanical and unfeeling. Since the execution of the condemned man lies outside the text itself, almost all the drama (and melodrama) takes place in his head as he anticipates losing it on the guillotine. We do not obtain equal insights into the inner lives of the two victims of justice in *Notre-Dame de Paris*, the beautiful Esmeralda and the deaf hunchback bell-ringer Quasimodo who loves her, but their suffering is no less apparent. Indeed, Quasimodo's mutism is, for Brooks, a standard convention of melodrama, where one character is unable to articulate his own defence.[7] The deaf magistrate who 'hears' Quasimodo's case can no more understand his answers than the hunchback the questions posed. Their conversational tag game in the mode of the classic routine of 'Who's on first?' would be comical were it not such a clear indictment of the nonsensical way the law is meted out. Satire also dominates Esmeralda's trial scene, where her virtue fails to be recognized—a twist in the standard melodramatic convention[8]—and she is tortured until she confesses to a murder she has not committed. In fact, the 'deceased' victim Phœbus, who had tried to seduce the innocent girl, is alive and well and preparing to marry someone else. The terrifying confrontations between Esmeralda and Claude Frollo, the lustful but rigidly dogmatic archdeacon who contributes in major ways to the perversion of justice in the novel, are juxtaposed to a number of other highly melodramatic moments. In two memorable twinned scenes, the outsiders, Esmeralda and Quasimodo, come to each other's aid, she by giving him water after he is beaten and exposed on the pillory, and he by literally sweeping her off her feet as she is about to be hanged and swinging with her up into the heights of the sanctuary–cathedral.

Hugo's mastery of dramatic conflict and resolution, honed by his experience writing for the stage, contributed to his ability to construct exciting plots, while his talent in epic, lyrical, and satirical poetry alike multiplied their generic resonances. We have already observed the satirical barbs aimed at the criminal justice system in the early novels. Hugo's epic inspiration can be viewed most plainly in the political dimensions of his works, where various characters dramatize conflicting tendencies that vie for control of the nation (see the next section). But Hugo's interweaving of lyricism and drama is his hallmark. *Bug-Jargal*, for example, contains a love song by the black hero for Marie, the narrator's white fiancée—the potential miscegenation symbolizing another *mélange des genres*; and the condemned man in *Le Dernier Jour d'un condamné* recalls shining

[7] See Brooks, *The Melodramatic Imagination*, 56–62.
[8] Brooks, *The Melodramatic Imagination*, 31–2.

moments from his childhood playing with his brothers and sharing his first kiss with a Spanish girl named Pepita (ch. 33). In *Notre-Dame de Paris*, Quasimodo leaves a mute parable for Esmeralda in the form of two vases, one handsome but cracked, and the other ugly but intact: he hopes to persuade her to look beyond (Phœbus') appearance to the ugliness beneath and to seek the beauty inside (his own and other) unsightly physical envelopes. Lyricism also characterizes passages devoted to female beauty, such as Esmeralda's enchanting vision of gracefulness, to innocent love, to the harmonies heard from atop Notre Dame Cathedral, and to the equally monumental construction of 'la seconde tour de Babel' (iv. 144), composed of all written human works. Above all, Hugo's metaphorical language forges new and often surprising connections between diverse aspects of a given novel—and even between different works—creating a kind of verbal web that entices the reader into a remarkably rich universe.

In addition to finding drama, poetry, and narrative combined in an original *mélange des genres*, one can identify in all four novels elements of the four core literary *mythoi*—tragedy, comedy, romance (quest), and irony—analysed by Northrop Frye in *The Anatomy of Criticism*. According to Frye, conjunctions of these four 'myths' are extremely rare: his main example is James Joyce's *Ulysses*,[9] but Hugo's fiction fully qualifies as well. The generic grab bag represented by his narratives was so shocking to the neoclassical tastes of the period that Hugo himself was viewed as some kind of literary monster by contemporary critics. Yet his readers and audiences loved him for the soaring rhetoric, unparalleled drama, and unconventional viewpoints that stimulated both the mind and the senses. The quest motif is evident from the outset, when Ordener must scour the wilds of Norway to find both the murdering Han and evidence to exonerate and liberate the falsely imprisoned Schumacker. In *Bug-Jargal*, the white narrator Léopold d'Auverney strives to rescue his fiancée, Marie, after she is apparently kidnapped by one of her father's slaves, the novel's eponymous hero. And in *Notre-Dame de Paris*, four men—the poet-philosopher Gringoire, along with Claude Frollo, Quasimodo, and Phœbus—all pursue Esmeralda. Irony and romance are, in Hugo, hardly mutually exclusive. But it was the co-presence of tragedy and comedy that especially shocked neoclassical sensitivities, which considered the two modes to be incompatible.

Hugo had attracted the attention of the Académie Française at the tender age of fifteen in its annual poetry contest and then won two awards, including first prize, from the Académie des Jeux Floraux de Toulouse in

[9] Northrop Frye, *The Anatomy of Criticism* (Princeton, NJ: Princeton University Press, 1957), 313–14.

the 1819 competition.[10] But these early laurels and increasing literary glory in the public sphere in the 1820s and 1830s did not translate into acceptance into the realm of the 'Immortals' of the Académie itself for many years. So, although French Romanticism is sometimes dated from the publication of Lamartine's *Méditations poétiques* in 1820 (if not from the appearance of François-René de Chateaubriand's *Atala* and *René* in 1801 and 1802, respectively), Hugo was the first of his generation to be appointed to the reactionary Académie Française—but not until 1843. In any event, the double ending in *Notre-Dame de Paris* that brings out the tragic–comic resonances running throughout the text testifies to Hugo's ease by the early 1830s with this rather Shakespearean mix of generic tones and establishes the pattern for the dénouements of all four later novels.[11]

Finally, Hugo's willingness to draw on popular literary conventions, as in the melodramatic scenes in his narratives, also extends to elements from Gothic fiction. The unsettling staples of the English Gothic novel—mystery and suspense, Gothic architecture or ruins, persecuted maidens, powerful and menacing male figures, monsters, madmen, and demons, an atmosphere of doom and terror—appear in one form or another in each of the early works. One need think only of the cannibalistic Han drinking his victims' blood from the skull of his deceased son to grasp the mock-ghoulish tone of *Han d'Islande*. In *Bug-Jargal* Biassou's captives are similarly threatened with death and dismemberment, albeit in a much more tragic vein, not unlike the prisoner on death row in *Le Dernier Jour d'un condamné*, who is haunted by horrific thoughts and dreams. In each case, the sublime notes of tragedy are counterbalanced by grotesque images, characters, or scenes that belong more to the comic domain, a mélange explicitly propounded by Hugo in his Romantic manifesto, the *Préface de Cromwell*, but first put into practice in his earlier novels. According to this aesthetic doctrine extolling 'la féconde union du type grotesque au type sublime' (III. 1. 51), pairing the lofty sublime with the disordered, 'unnatural' grotesque serves to create higher, more transcendent harmonies than the single-modal neoclassical sublime. Thus, according to the narrator of *Notre-Dame de Paris*, the use of monstrous gargoyles on the exterior of Notre Dame adds to the overall awe-inspiring effect of the Gothic cathedral. The same holds true of the opposition in Hugo of sublime and grotesque characters, whereby the deformed slave/witch doctor Habibrah in *Bug-Jargal* is played off against the selfless outlaw

[10] See Graham Robb, *Victor Hugo: A Biography* (New York: W. W. Norton, 1997), 61–2, 71.

[11] One might say the same of *BJ*, given the double framing, though there each ending concludes in tragedy.

hero Bug-Jargal, or the deaf, one-eyed hunchback Quasimodo renders all the more resplendent Esmeralda's grace, beauty, and mercy. As we shall see, these multiple approaches to mixing genres are quintessentially Hugolian, marking the novels of the poet's maturity as well those of his youth.

ETHICS, POLITICS, AND GENERATIONAL GAPS

Along with the exotic settings and generic mélange that characterize Hugo's early fiction, the reader discovers a world where parents and children are consistently in conflict, a comic staple that sometimes results in tragedy. In *Han d'Islande*, the sins of the older generation are visited upon the children, who struggle to find their own voices—and to prove their virtue. D'Auverney rejects the model offered by his vicious slave-owner uncle in *Bug-Jargal* and ends his life as a captain in the Revolutionary Army, which has carried the conflict between old and new ways onto another plane. While the plot of *Le Dernier Jour d'un condamné* at first seems devoid of intergenerational tensions, critics have noted that the condemned man's crime is very possibly parricide. Equally important, his allusions to the king, Charles X (1824–30), who might save him from the guillotine, recall the death of the national father figure, Louis XVI, some years before. And the Oedipal plot of *Notre-Dame de Paris* pits the twenty-year-old Quasimodo against his adoptive father Claude Frollo (also a father-archdeacon of the Church), who lusts after the fifteen-year-old Esmeralda. When the hunchback hero throws the villainous Frollo to his death from atop the cathedral, he symbolically slays the forces of order aligned against him and his beloved gypsy dancer.

As one might surmise, the tensions in the novels between parents and children have numerous ethical and political resonances. Most obviously, they enter into Hugo's thematics of social justice, a feature of his work from the outset. The evil schemer d'Ahlefeld, against whom Ordener and Ethel are pitted in *Han d'Islande* (and who loses his own son Frédéric to the insatiable Han), is not just responsible for falsely imprisoning Count Schumaker. He is also one of the judges who presides at Ordener's trial on trumped-up charges of treason. The triumph of youth in this case also leads to the liberation of Norway from the grip of a sinister cabal. The setting of *Bug-Jargal* amid the 1793 slave revolt in Saint-Domingue likewise points to another level of significance beyond the basic storyline of love, friendship, and paradise lost. As a member of the island militia, d'Auverney is allied with the colonialists who abuse their slaves while profiting from their labor—and who are as vigorously satirized in the text as the manipulative black rebel leader Biassou and his *obi* henchman Habibrah. D'Auverney's relatively conventional mindset prevents him, first from discerning in his friend, the slave Pierrot, the African prince and titular slave ruler, Bug-Jargal, and second from realizing that all Bug-Jargal's actions are aimed at preventing bloodshed, even at the cost of his own life. Only after the black hero has sacrificed himself to save d'Auverney does the latter recognize the other's moral superiority. (In many ways, *Bug-Jargal* serves as the prototype of *Les Misérables*, where the ex-convict Jean Valjean proves ethically superior to the representative of law and order, the policeman Javert, who must in the end recognize the sublimity of his outlaw nemesis.) The utopian rhetoric in Bug-Jargal's entreaties to both d'Auverney and Biassou suggests, at the very least, some reflection on the young author's part about the question of achieving social harmony.

As we discussed above, Hugo's satirical treatment of corrupt authority extends to *Le Dernier Jour d'un condamné* and *Notre-Dame de Paris*, the twinned texts conceived at roughly the same time but published before and after the 1830 July Revolution, respectively. The ethical actions of the condemned man, who is uncontestedly a murderer, are not the subject of the first-person narrative, but rather his intense psychological suffering in the face of his capital sentence. That society can impose such an extreme form of revenge through the judicial system brings it down to the level of the criminals it seeks to punish. The theme of revenge, also highlighted by the far-off villains in *Han d'Islande* and *Bug-Jargal*, now impugns the French powers that be in their exercise of 'justice'. At the same time, the implication of the king at several points in the narrator's sufferings, as well as in his fantasies of beheading, indicates that, already in 1829, the supposedly monarchist Hugo—who was receiving pensions for his early royalist odes—was developing republican sympathies. The physical decrepitude and moribund policies of the Bourbon kings Louis XVIII and Charles X, following the fall of Napoléon in 1815, certainly appealed less and less to Hugo's generation, and the poet's reconciliation in 1827 with his father Léopold, a general in Napoléon's army, had accelerated his evolution in the 1820s from ultraconservative to more liberal political principles.

By the time Hugo began to write *Notre-Dame de Paris* in the wake of *les Trois Glorieuses,* France was governed under a constitutional monarchy by a new king from a different branch of the royal family, Louis-Philippe d'Orléans. But the ethical and political concerns of *Le Dernier Jour d'un condamné* continued to reverberate in his new work. Gringoire's 'trial' and near-death experience at the beginning of the novel with the bandits who inhabit the back alleys of Paris no more represents genuine justice than the incompetent magistrates, false charges, and flimsy evidence that lead Quasimodo to be whipped and exposed on the pillory and Esmeralda to be incarcerated, tortured, and finally executed. While Gringoire's misadventures are the stuff of comedy, the gypsy dancer's hanging tragically fulfils the fate that pursues both of them throughout the text. When, against all odds (not to mention realist standards), Esmeralda quenches the thirst of her would-be kidnapper on the pillory, or when Quasimodo sweeps down from the cathedral façade to rescue the hapless gypsy from the gallows, they enact moments of transcendence whereby individuals triumph over social institutions. From a wider perspective, one might see in Hugo's depiction of medieval justice a further gloss on the current and equally inhumane legal system exposed in *Le Dernier Jour d'un condamné.* To be sure, the veiled reference by Louis XI's henchman to the storming of the Bastille 300 years later recaptures the menace of an ugly end to Charles X's reign in the companion novel. But the enormous potential of such lowly, dispossessed creatures as Quasimodo and Esmeralda moves the political dial even further to the left. The vast symphony for a thousand voices comprised of all the church bells in Paris—and that can be heard from atop Notre Dame Cathedral—gestures towards the superior harmony for which society should strive by valuing each of its citizens.

Despite the political overtones of the early novels, the reader finds very little utopian or visionary discourse—a lacuna that remains unfilled in Hugo's fiction until the publication of *Les Misérables* some thirty years after the appearance of *Notre-Dame de Paris.* (I outline the reasons for this shift in the later works from a 'poetics of harmony' to a 'poetics of transcendence' in my discussion of *Les Misérables* below.) Instead, in the initial years of his career Hugo's attempts at historical refiguration centred on casting himself as the French heir of Sir Walter Scott, who used the British past to reflect more upon its present than its future. The temporal play in *Han d'Islande*, *Bug-Jargal*, and *Notre-Dame de Paris*, then, is only loosely and implicitly future directed. The past may comment on the present, but the utopianism associated with the later Hugo is not yet in evidence in the sociopolitical discourse of the first four narratives. Still, the visionary qualities of a poem like 'La Pente de la rêverie' (*Feuilles d'automne*, 1831), also appear, for example, in the condemned man's vivid nightmares and waking delusions, as well as in Gringoire's encounter with the creeping, crawling scum of Parisian nightlife and in Claude Frollo's mad hallucinations about Esmeralda when he mistakenly believes she has been hanged. Though space precludes delving into the intensely humorous aspects, both verbal and conceptual, of *Han d'Islande*, *Bug-Jargal*, and *Notre-Dame de Paris*,[12] playfulness and prophetic gravitas are difficult to

[12] See, e.g., *EN* 24–5, 173–5, 187–8.

mix. In any case, Hugo's use of an array of characters—from unprincipled (e.g., d'Ahlefeld, Biassou) to conventional (e.g., d'Auverney, Frollo) to humanitarian (e.g., Bug-Jargal, Esmeralda)—to illustrate various ethical stances turns out to have important aesthetic implications that also help to shape the later novels.

AESTHETIC HARMONIES

Given the tensions in Hugo's childhood between feuding parents and his early struggles with the reigning literary powers, one might posit a certain anxiety of influence, in Harold Bloom's terminology, behind the intergenerational motifs in his texts. Like his characters, the aspiring novelist–poet–playwright is both conscious of his lineage(s) and eager to impose his own stamp on the world. From Chateaubriand and Scott to such contemporaries as Alphonse de Lamartine, Alfred de Vigny, Théophile Gautier, and Charles-Augustin Sainte-Beuve, rivalries abounded. Hugo's rise to fame—which coincided with founding his own family—did not take long. Married to his childhood friend Adèle Foucher in 1822 at the age of twenty and the father of four within the next eight years, he became the acknowledged head of the new Romantic school by the late 1820s. But what, exactly, did Romanticism mean to him? What specifically characterizes Hugo's understanding of and agenda for the first literary movement in almost 200 years to challenge the ascendency of neoclassicism?

In *The Early Novels*, I argue that the young writer's plots concerning familial strife reflect his own struggles to define himself in relation to his literary predecessors. On one level, the villainous masters and/or fathers (Count d'Ahlefeld, d'Auverney's uncle, Claude Frollo) are simply overthrown by the next generation. But some fathers, like Schumaker, are revered and preserved, whether in person or in memory, through their children's efforts. And some of the heroes' contemporaries, like the vacuous Frédéric d'Ahlefeld or the womanizing Phœbus, also meet their own form of 'fin tragique' (iv. 341). From this perspective, Hugo's works represent both breaks from and a certain continuity with the past. Neither Ordener nor Bug-Jargal seeks to dispense entirely with the past, but rather to identify and embrace the best in old and new generations alike. The literary parallel is that, for Hugo, some aspects of neoclassicism are worth saving. To be Romantic is to reconcile past and present, to create a higher harmony between apparently conflicting aesthetic ideals.

Several examples will suffice. Although the conventional d'Auverney can discern no difference between Biassou and Bug-Jargal, who are linked equally in his mind with death and destruction, the reader clearly interprets the first character as unprincipled and the second as principled. From the colonialists' standpoint, both are outlaws and so completely reprehensible. But, whereas Biassou merely wants to grab power, exact revenge on his former masters, and exploit the ex-slaves on the island to his own advantage, Bug-Jargal's rebellion is a selfless stance against oppression and for a more egalitarian society. In other words, Hugo's black hero incorporates his friend d'Auverney's orderliness and rationality in his dream of a world that confers universal liberty, equality, and fraternity. Only after Bug-Jargal has sacrificed his life for him does the 'neoclassical' d'Auverney recognize the sublimity of his 'Romantic' *frère*. Similar structures pervade *Notre-Dame de Paris*, where the cathedral itself models the successful integration of the symmetrical, formal, Romanesque elements at its very core with the more fanciful, organic, Gothic elements that adorn it and make it soar. The resulting architectural 'hybrid', accreted over time, figures the *mélange des genres* that characterizes all Hugo's fiction. Likewise, the monstrous but kind-hearted and self-abnegating Quasimodo 'dethrones' his inflexible master–father Frollo in a dramatic gesture that suggests the dawn of a new moral, political, and artistic order. Once again, Hugo elaborates an aesthetic vision closely allied to a progressive sociopolitical stance. In his system, the Romantic movement is the literary equivalent of the French Revolution—without the Terror. One cannot create progress *ex nihilo*, but only by diligently studying the past, acknowledging one's origins, and building on the best of what has come before.

Perhaps because he had already experienced in his young life so many political peripeteias—Napoléon's loss at Trafalgar and return to power in 1814 and his fall again the year later at Waterloo; the rapid switch at the same time from empire to monarchy to empire and back again; the July Revolution and deposal of the Bourbons—Hugo became increasingly immersed in historical sources in preparation for composing his historical narratives. The background to *Han d'Islande* and *Bug-Jargal* is largely invented, and the narrators spend little time showing off their knowledge. In contrast, the writer's archival research is widely displayed in *Notre-Dame de Paris* through a multitude of digressions that, under a different pen, would stand as sparkling displays of erudition functioning as *hors d'œuvres* to the work itself. Beginning with *Notre-Dame de Paris*, however, the lengthy digressions in Hugo turn out to be integral parts of his argument. The use of vertical and horizontal axes to represent what Weiskel labels as the positive and negative sublime, respectively, dates as far back as *Han d'Islande*. For instance, the description of Ordener's wanderings through the desolate Norwegian landscape expresses the feeling of going 'on and on' in an undifferentiated wasteland—a staple of the Hugolian imagination—but it is not yet attached to any overarching significance. In *Notre-Dame de Paris*, on the other hand, spatial axes connect to the larger conceptual frame of the novel. Thus, the spectacular height of the cathedral, which later morphs into an abyss that swallows Claude Frollo, accentuates the familial and ethical relations between the archdeacon, Quasimodo, and Esmeralda through apocalyptic images of spiritual transcendence and divine retribution. By the same token, the great description of 'Paris à vol d'oiseau', as seen from the cathedral heights, places Notre Dame at the centre of the narrative activity while bringing the medieval city back to life and orienting the reader to the location of many of the places named in the text. The 'discordant concordances' produced by a multitude of voices, angles, and seemingly irrelevant, if not conflicting, information come together in the text to re-create a verbal form of the symphony of bells heard from atop the cathedral itself.

As noted in the Introduction, horizontal and vertical axes in Hugo suggest, respectively, metonymical/syntagmic and metaphorical/paradigmatic relations—those most closely associated with narrative structures, on the one hand, and with poetic structures, on the other. Each set of motifs is repeated throughout Hugo's work, and, from *Notre-Dame de Paris* on, the patterns become systematically balanced and interwoven to fashion the whole textual fabric. Far from constituting pure abstractions, the metaphorical and metonymical structures in the novels correspond to a wide range of easily recognizable themes and images. The notion of proximity that characterizes metonymical motifs of contiguity or extension can be found, for instance, in bodily extremities (legs, hands, tails); in forms of dependency and bondage (chains, ties, slavery, parasites); in social continuity (through children, tradition, legacies); in forms of imitation (repetition, tracing, reproduction, copying); in linear processes (logic, progression, hypotaxis); and in physical or ocular pursuit (watching, stalking, trailing, reading). By the same token, the notion of filling or bridging a gap that characterizes metaphorical motifs of resemblance and substitution embraces originality over continuity; empathetic identification over slavish imitation; and the irregular, recursive processes of poetic, creative imagination over the linear, the symmetrical, and the prosaic.

The key role played in Hugo's works by spatial configurations partially explains one element of the writer's enduring appeal—his extraordinary visual imagination. In narratives, poetry, and drama, Hugo creates astonishingly detailed vistas, panoramas, and tableaux that can then take on symbolic or metaphorical dimensions. The movement from vivid representation to symbolic schema is a persistent rhetorical tactic. Such metaphorical constructs, already prominently displayed in *Notre-Dame de Paris*, become considerably more complex in his later novels. The overarching image of the spider's web that permeates *Notre-Dame de Paris*—ensnaring Frollo, Esmeralda, Quasimodo, and the reader alike—develops multilevel proportions in *Les Misérables, Les Travailleurs de la mer, L'Homme qui rit,* and *Quatrevingt-Treize*. My study of *Les Misérables*, summarized in the next section, has shown that Hugo's elaborate congruities in the earlier novels between the rhetorical structures of metonymy and metaphor and the experience of transcendence—ethical, political, and aesthetic—develop during his exile into intricate patterns that reveal their self-similarity at every level of the text. In *Notre-Dame de Paris*, we have observed, Hugo highlights the union in the cathedral (and hence, in the work that bears its name) of 'une loi de géométrie' and 'une loi de poésie' (iv. 137), of Romanesque order and Gothic inventiveness.[13] Beginning with *Les Misérables*, the 'geometric' qualities reside in multilayered symmetries—that is, in the recursive designs traced by verbal patterns. Here, different places and times are superimposed and interconnected through Ricoeur's metaphorical redescriptions and historical refigurations that forge analogies between disparate entities and experiences. For the mature Hugo, this intensely visual geometry of chaos informs not only natural phenomena, but also his artistic *œuvre* and his depiction of history.

LES MISÉRABLES AND HUGO'S POETICS OF TRANSCENDANCE

In the three decades that separate *Les Misérables* from the four earlier novels, Hugo had fallen in love with the beautiful actress Juliette Drouet, who remained his devoted companion for fifty years; been elected to the Académie Française; become a peer of France in 1845 under Louis-Philippe's rule; won a seat in 1848 as a representative to the French parliament of the newly formed Second Republic; and vigorously supported Louis-Napoléon Bonaparte's successful candidacy for president. Yet his life was far from charmed. His wife Adèle had ceased to sleep with him in the early 1830s; his beloved daughter Léopoldine died in September 1843 in a boating accident, at the age of nineteen and eight months pregnant, while he was traveling with Juliette in Spain; and Louis Bonaparte had seized power in an 1851 *coup d'état*, declared himself emperor, and forced Hugo into an exile that would, along with the Second Empire, last nineteen years.

[13] See *EN* 166–9, 196–206.

According to Albouy, Léopoldine's death represented a deep and irreparable rupture in Hugo's life that took the form of radical disruptions and discontinuities in the poetic works, beginning with *Châtiments* and *Les Contemplations*. Certainly, the break with his homeland because of Louis-Napoléon's treachery would have magnified the sense of loss and bereavement. Such gaps and fissions, along with their resolution, are also reflected in the visionary, prophetic poetry written during exile, including *La Légende des siècles*, *La Fin de Satan* (1886), and *Dieu* (1891). In any event, it is essential to note that Hugo began composing *Les Misérables*, under the title *Jean Tréjean* (and later, *Les Misères*) in 1845 and that he concluded his novel on the battlefield of Waterloo in 1861. The book, published in *feuilletons* the following year, was an instant smash hit—indeed, a global phenomenon—that remained undiminished by time. (As required reading in the Soviet bloc, it was the most widely read work of fiction in the world until the end of the twentieth century.) In my exploration of the novel, which attempts to account for this enduring mass appeal, the notion of transcendence plays a primary role. What, in short, is transcended in the text, and how is this accomplished?

As with the historical novels of his youth, Hugo displaces the reader into another time, ostensibly the period between Napoléon's 1815 defeat at Waterloo and the hero Jean Valjean's death in 1833. But the timeline is not so straightforward. Valjean's prison sentence begins with the theft of a loaf of bread in 1795, and the lives of Bishop Myriel, the *conventionnel* G., and the young protagonist Marius's grandfather M. Gillenormand extend even further back, into the first half of the eighteenth century. Moreover, by casting the villainous innkeeper Thénardier as a surrogate for the scheming Napoléon III, Hugo links the dramatic developments in the text with contemporary events. Finally, the visionary discourse of Marius's revolutionary friends, who seek to bring forth the Republic in 1832, points both backward to the Revolutions of 1789 and 1830 and forward to the social upheaval that will end the current imperial regime, as well as to the better world beyond in the twentieth century. Such a totalizing view of history—one that takes in and imposes sense on what saint Augustine calls the 'present past', 'present present', and 'future present' (*TN* i, p. xx)—is but one way in which Hugo structures his work to elicit resonances between different temporal and spatial layers.

To this end, spatial *dépaysement* is much less important than in *Han d'Islande* or *Bug-Jargal*. Rather, in the mode of *Le Dernier Jour d'un condamné* and *Notre-Dame de Paris*, the action remains confined to France. Even the scenes staged outside of Paris—whether at Myriel's home in Digne in the south-east or at the Thénardiers' inn in Montfermeil on the outskirts of the capital or in Montreuil-sur-mer in the industrial north, where the escaped convict Valjean re-creates himself as the wealthy philanthropist M. Madeleine—contain very little local colour. It is *time* that needs to be refigured, and an enormous amount of digressive space is devoted to evoking *Zeitgeist*: the engineering feats of Brunesceau in the eighteenth century as he strove to construct and sanitize the sewers of Paris, using underground rivers as the basis of the conduits; the *conventionnel*'s faith in the old Revolutionary ideals and his thoughtful defence of regicide; a chapter devoted to the year 1817; several chapters aimed at explaining the halfway Revolution of 1830 and Louis-Philippe's subsequent rule; the revolutionary ferment in the student *quartiers* in 1832 and the eventual pitched battles with government forces. The plethora of details can at times seem overwhelming—they just go on and on, not unlike the metonymical sublime.

At the same time, the accounts of some historical developments are clearly meant to be savoured, such as the description of Napoléon's defeat at Waterloo. As in the sweeping, organizing view of the streets of Paris from the top of the cathedral in *Notre-Dame de Paris*, the narrator helps his reader to grasp the entire set-up for the conflict between opposing armies, from the geographical layout of the terrain to Napoléon's beliefs and strategies to the machinations of destiny. While fascinating in itself, the episode achieves additional significance when we realize that Napoléon's fall from grace into a sunken road that he had failed to perceive mirrors various gaps—the recess in which Jean Valjean hides from Javert outside the convent, the grave where he is voluntarily buried in order to be 'resurrected' under a new identity, the open-air passageway between two of his houses in Paris, his trek with a wounded Marius on his back through the sewers of Paris, the torn piece from Marius's coat stolen by Thénardier—by which the ex-convict triumphs in the novel. In this way, historical time and narrative time reflect each other through repeating, often spatial, imagery. Let us also recall that the notion of filling gaps marks the positive, metaphorical sublime, and that, in its extreme form, the metaphorical sublime figures the apocalyptic imagery of universal identity. Given this power to structure a coherent universe by bridging apparent differences and discontinuities, the pervasiveness of the vertical/metaphorical sublime in the text contributes to its transcendent qualities.

Hugo achieves another order of transcendence by drawing on the enormous generic mixture featured in the earlier novels. Lyrical and comic moments, epic confrontations, melodramatic trial scenes and revelations, Romantic quests, biting satire, prophetic visions, personal and social tragedies, Gothic atmosphere—all are present in *Les Misérables*. Consider these examples:

- Myriel unexpectedly forgives Jean Valjean, who has repaid the bishop's hospitality by stealing his silver, and 'buys' the ex-convict's soul for good (melodrama).
- Fantine, a young woman with a child out of wedlock, must turn to prostitution, loses her job, and ends up selling parts of her body in order to support her little girl (tragedy; social satire).
- The mayor of Montreuil-sur-mer stuns a packed courtroom by unmasking himself as Valjean in order to save the accused, a poor man who simply resembles him (melodrama).
- Javert spends his life pursuing Jean Valjean, who himself pursues redemption (romance).
- The outlaw hero rescues the child Cosette from her 'slaver', Thénardier, and later engineers their thrilling escape from Javert by fleeing through the dark, labyrinthine streets of Paris, into a cul-de-sac, and over an 'impenetrable' wall (Gothic novel).
- Marius leaves expressive 'fragments' declaring his adoration for the adolescent Cosette under a rock in her garden (lyricism).
- The Thénardiers abandon their young son, Gavroche, and pimp out their teenage daughters (tragedy).
- A fat bourgeois boy throws away his half-eaten biscuit as homeless children starve nearby (social satire; tragedy).
- Young revolutionaries make puns and share utopian visions of a better, republican future before dying on the barricades (comedy; prophecy; epic).
- Javert has a quasi-religious conversion that leads to his suicide when he recognizes Valjean's virtue and measures his own obsession with rules against the other's lifetime of self-sacrifice (melodrama; tragedy).
- Thénardier sinks from living in the sewers (where, for Hugo, one finds the rotting corpses of emperors—an implicit swipe at Napoléon III) to trafficking in slaves in the Americas (social and political satire).

The examples multiply by the hundreds, perhaps even the thousands, as the reader considers narrative details large and small—and that is my point. When one seeks illustrations of Hugo's *mélange des genres*, the text proves nearly inexhaustible. We shall return to this observation later in the present chapter.

As for the familial, ethical, and political aspects of the novel, they hold both important similarities and differences with the earlier narratives. The motif of intergenerational strife is mainly centred on Marius. First, his royalist grandfather Gillenormand rejects his father, M. Pontmercy, a brave veteran of Napoléon's wars, who remains self-exiled from them both. Next, the young man 'discovers' both his father and republican ideals through written legacies—a revelation that leads him, too late, to Pontmercy's deathbed and to a serious rift with his grandfather. Then, Gillenormand and Marius are reconciled after the latter, severely wounded, is rescued from the barricades by Jean Valjean. After marrying his beloved Cosette (and failing to recognize his 'father-in-law's' salvific gesture while taking him for Javert's murderer, until Thénardier inadvertently unravels both mysteries), he systematically detaches Cosette from her adopted father. And finally, the young couple, who rush to Valjean's side mere moments before he dies to request his forgiveness, receive the saintly outlaw's blessing. Critics have pointed out the resemblance between Marius's relationship with Pontmercy and Hugo's discovery of his own father, along with Napoleonic glory and republican ideology, soon before Léopold's death. Perhaps more interesting, however, is that Marius ends up saving Pontmercy's legacy, just as Ordener saves Schumaker's in *Han d'Islande*; or that he both rejects and recuperates three paternal figures; or that he receives from Valjean a benediction passed down by Myriel, a father of the Church, who had earlier received it from the dying *conventionnel*.

For, unlike the early novels, *Les Misérables* features an equally kindly and *powerful* father in the personage of Jean Valjean. Schumaker was imprisoned and ineffective; d'Ahlefeld was forceful but evil; d'Auverney's uncle was a wicked slave-owner; and Frollo devolved from devoted Catholic *père* and adoptive father to Quasimodo to depraved authoritarian. But Valjean is only tangentially associated with evil because of his time in prison—for trying to feed his widowed sister's children—and a brief relapse after his release when he steals a child's coin. If Marius appears in the end to be capable of internalizing Valjean's extraordinary social conscience,[14] it must be remembered that the real action hero in the text, the character who physically rescues others, is the vigorous but ageing ex-convict. A stand-in for the mature Hugo, the protagonist likewise spends much of his adult life in exile—on a prison galley, in hiding from Javert, unwelcome in Marius's home after the wedding—even as he quests for self-respect by rigorously obeying his inner voice. By the same token, one might argue that, in receiving his moral awakening from Myriel, Valjean also plays the part of the bishop's spiritual son. So, when the outlaw hero

[14] See Kathryn M. Grossman, 'Nouer, dénouer, ouvrir: la fin des misérables', in Pierre Laforgue (ed.), *Pratiques d'écriture: Hommage à Jean Gaudon* (Paris: Klincksieck, 1996), 228–35.

fails to recognize and obey Javert's authority as an agent of law and order, he structurally repeats the Oedipal revolt of one generation against the other. By countering the devious Thénardier-Napoléon III as well, he assumes the symbolic function of the French nation seeking to regain its self-regulated, republican way in the face of an unprincipled foe.

The true complexity of the text becomes apparent, though, when we realize that Jean Valjean's character is not merely opposed to Thénardier's and Javert's but also exhibits some of their qualities. For, like the dishonest innkeeper, the ex-convict knows all the tricks of deceiving others and escaping from impossible situations—so much so that he cannot himself be trapped or duped. That both are associated with twisting, winding space in the text confirms their affiliation at one level. At the same time, Valjean's adherence to the stringent dictates of his own conscience makes him even more 'law-abiding' than the rectilinear, legalistic policeman. Politically, one might say that he represents the ideal citizen of a republic, one who thinks for himself and who devotes himself to the common good. For Hugo's depiction of Paris under post-Napoleonic monarchic rule and of its self-centred bourgeoisie, then, read Haussmann's neoclassical city and the complacent citizens of the Second Empire. The aesthetic implications of these motifs become clear in the light of our earlier reading of *Notre-Dame de Paris*, where the generous ethos of the social outcasts, Esmeralda and Quasimodo, triumphs morally over Claude Frollo's unyielding dogmatism, just as the young Romantic movement is fated to unseat rule-bound neoclassicism. From this perspective, Javert reiterates the stance of the neoclassical father, while Jean Valjean proves himself the worthy Romantic son by displaying a higher form of self-discipline. In this schema, Javert functions in the text as a metonymical construct, that is, as a character who worships logic, believes in tradition, and stalks and spies on others. Jean Valjean, on the contrary, functions as a metaphorical construct, that is, as a character who bridges gaps, exercises creative imagination, and identifies empathetically others—a role that further allies the hero with an essentially *poetic* world view.

What then can be made aesthetically of Thénardier, a character whose closest counterpart is more Biassou in *Bug-Jargal* than, say, the ultimately likeable bandit leader, Clopin Trouillefou, in *Notre-Dame de Paris*? In the late 1820s and early 1830s, Hugo was eager to defend the new school against the old fogeys still running the literary arena. In the 1860s, the text indicates that he is now thinking of his own legacy to the nineteenth century. Romanticism has long been deemed dead and gone, whether one measures its demise from the ascendency of Balzacian realism in the 1830s or the failure of Hugo's last play, *Les Burgraves*, in 1843. In Thénardier, the reader can identify the traits of what the poet would deem false

Romanticism—unskilful plots, lackadaisical writing, superficial sentimentality—an art form well destined to the trash bin of history. Jean Valjean embodies, on the other hand, the traits of true Romanticism—exceptionally well-structured stories, rhetorical mastery, uplifting models with collective social ramifications—that some might consider passé, but that should stand the test of time alongside great classical and neoclassical literature. Rather than repudiate his artistic past or attempt to appeal to modern, realist sensibilities, Hugo champions the cause of French Romanticism. In other words, *Les Misérables* expresses the writer's faith in the enduring attraction of his work long into the future. The novel's continuing success to this day certainly suggests that Hugo's confidence was, in this case, well placed. One might venture that *Les Misérables* surpasses its own historical limitations in part by acknowledging and drawing on so many different artistic traditions and rhetorical registers, from the very low to the very high—to put it another way, by being such an aesthetically *inclusive* work.

The secret to creating such a captivating text lies perhaps in stimulating the reader on a variety of levels that turn out to be intimately interrelated. My research in *Figuring Transcendence* has shown that many facets of the text—themes, images, plot, characters, spatial configurations, historical and philosophical digressions—correspond to other aspects on the same and/or different levels. Whether guided consciously or unconsciously by the writer, the deeply organizing principles that bring order, or 'geometry', out of apparent verbal chaos produce multidimensional associations that reflect and repeat each other at every scale. In a way, the reader is ambushed by the 'discordant concordances' of these textual resonances, which continue to play off and enrich each other as one proceeds through the narrative. The textual web becomes a tender trap, one that rewards the reader with new echoes, insights, and harmonies with each rereading. In this respect, the sheer *inexhaustibility* of *Les Misérables* contributes to the reader's sense of transcendence. As the nexus of the metonymical and the metaphorical sublime, the text both moves forwards, syntagmically, through a wealth of fascinating episodic and descriptive details, while superimposing those same details one upon the other, paradigmatically, in seemingly infinite depth. The (horizontal, metonymical) time of the narrative intersects with the (vertical, metaphorical) space of recursive patterns to create a unified work of art. The refiguration of both story and history—past, present, and future—to forge links between scattered moments and episodes is matched by metaphorical redescriptions that draw connections between disparate phenomena. In both cases, the distant is made near, as Ricoeur would say, in one globalizing vision that enables the reader to travel in space and time—right between the pages of the novel.

In many respects, *Les Misérables* could have been the culmination of Hugo's career as a novelist, the crowning achievement that drew threads from the earlier narratives into an intricate textual fabric. Indeed, it was acclaimed worldwide at the time as his masterpiece. He could easily have rested on his glory, given the demands of his poetic and political agendas while in exile and then afterwards, when he returned to France as a venerated artist and republican hero and was soon elected to the Senate. Yet, three long and substantive historical novels followed *Les Misérables*, works that exhibit similar poetic and narrative qualities. All were well received but have remained in the shadow of their sensational predecessor. In the chapters that follow, I examine *Les Travailleurs de la mer*, *L'Homme qui rit*, and *Quatrevingt-Treize* in order to demonstrate Hugo's continued mastery of the genre and to tease out their distinctive contributions to his *poétique de la transcendance*. Above all, we shall see whether Hugo merely repeats the winning formula of *Les Misérables* or if he reinvents his art in new and exciting ways.

2

Monsters, Marvels, and Transport in *Les Travailleurs de la mer*

As we have seen in Chapter 1, both the processes and the constants of the Hugolian imaginary are astonishing. Through prose, poetry, theatre, and essays, a rich panoply of images, themes, and motifs is continually re-worked and recycled in new permutations that reflect Hugo's concerns of the moment as well. Following Léopoldine's death in 1843, the complex harmonies of the earlier novels shifted into a higher key, the later works integrating the disjunctions of death and resurrection into even more intricate patterns. After fleeing to Brussels in late 1851 to escape Louis Bonaparte's wrath for defying his *coup d'état*, Hugo moved first to the Channel Island of Jersey; was expelled two years later, along with his two sons and thirty-two other republican outlaws; and ended up in Guernsey, likewise in the Channel Islands, in 1855. By 1859, the exiled poet was putting the finishing touches on the first series of *La Légende des siècles*, which would appear before the end of the year; preparing to take up and complete his prose masterwork, *Les Misérables*, after a break of more than ten years; incubating a second novel, which would become *Les Travailleurs de la mer*; and collaborating with a network of republicans aligned like him against the despotic regime of Napoléon III. He was also proudly watching as his son, François-Victor, began publishing his translation of Shakespeare's *Œuvres complètes*, a project undertaken in 1853 while sharing his father's exile. Finally, having been asked by François-Victor to write a preface to the edition, Hugo was jotting down ideas for what would become *William Shakespeare*, a monumental essay on the nature of genius. The genesis of *Les Travailleurs de la mer* in tandem with various stages of *La Légende des siècles*, *Les Misérables*, and *William Shakespeare* suggests that it is closely related to the other three works.

On the surface, nothing would seem less likely. The epic poems in *La Légende*, taken together, depict the evolution of history—past, present, and future—from darkness into light. The emphasis on historical refiguration, which includes lyrical and satirical interpretations of human experience, seems far removed from the events depicted in *Les Travailleurs de la mer*. In *Les Misérables*, the ex-convict Jean Valjean sacrifices himself for friend, foe, and stranger alike, offering a vision of transcendent justice—that is, of grace—to Javert, the legalistic police inspector who pursues him. In contrast, there is no outlaw hero in *Les Travailleurs de la mer*, and no clear-cut figure of law and order. *William Shakespeare* is a philosophical text with a polemical intent. This voice and mode of discourse appear within some digressions in *Les Misérables* but seem foreign to *Les Travailleurs de la mer*, which relates the exploits of a single man pitted against the forces of nature. Prefaced by a long dissertation on the Channel Islands, where the action takes place, the novel presents itself as a voyage into the exotic world inhabited by Hugo himself. The peculiarities of this Anglo-Norman space would seem to trump connections with the literary or political history of the outside world.

Yet, although generic distinctions always blur in Hugo's works, the analogical associations generated within and among them create overdetermined texts that offer much more coherence than initially meets the eye. Thus, *Les Misérables* draws on a set of master tropes, repeated at multiple levels, to figure the unrepresentable, from the most abject moral, political, and artistic chaos to the ethical, utopian, and aesthetic sublime.[1] Published only four years after the phenomenal success of *Les Misérables*, *Les Travailleurs de la mer* constitutes an equally macrometaphorical, poetic narrative. Set in the exiled poet's own 'marginal' home on the outskirts of France, the text elaborates a vision of human creative potential. After initiating the reader into the strange, 'alien', Anglo-Norman culture, Hugo probes the many dimensions of exploration itself. Science, dreams, meditation, natural forces, physical prowess, selfless devotion, even death—all serve, in his metaphorical system, as vehicles for expanding and moving the boundaries of our universe, both internal and external.[2] If the role of genius, for Hugo, is to 'faire advenir le possible à l'existence et de multiplier les potentialités humaines jusqu'au point sublime où le possible et l'impossible se rejoignent',[3] metaphorical language is the preeminent means by which *poetic* genius fulfils its responsibility. The result of using poetic discourse in *Les Travailleurs de la mer* to communicate this

[1] See, e.g., *FT* 99, 184–5, 190–1, 313–16.

[2] This violation of boundaries typifies Romanticism in general, whether through space (exoticism), time (the historical novel), mental functions (dreams, drugs, trances), or spiritual transcendence (prayer, visions, prophecy). From Blake, Byron, and Coleridge to Hugo, Baudelaire, and Rimbaud, the drive to go *beyond* physical human limits informs Romantic literature.

[3] Peyrache-Leborgne, 'Victor Hugo et le sublime', 22.

'point sublime' is, in Victor Brombert's words, 'some of the most astonishing prose Hugo ever wrote'—a work that itself seems at times to cross 'a line of demarcation, penetrating into a world that is drenched in the strange light of visionary poetry'.[4] Given the poetic nature of the novel, I argue that the work is allied to the artistic aims and metaphorical language not only of *Les Misérables* but also of *La Légende des siècles* and *William Shakespeare.*

At the same time, the political dimensions of *Les Misérables*, which develops a shadow history and indictment of the Second Empire, leads the reader to look for references to contemporary events in Hugo's other works during this period as well. The cunning but dull-witted treachery of Louis-Napoléon Bonaparte as portrayed by Thénardier, the model of republican citizenship embodied by the self-legislating Jean Valjean,[5] the urgent call to revolution—these features of his 1862 text might certainly be recycled elsewhere in ways that would likewise avoid the imperial censors. For example, in 'Vingtième siècle', the penultimate section of *La Légende des siècles*, Hugo presents a double perspective on history, looking back at the foundering 'ancien monde' (x. 644) and forward to a lofty vision of future progress in the twin poems 'Pleine mer' and 'Plein ciel', respectively. To the reader of *Châtiments*—the poet's earlier excoriation of emperor and empire alike—his evocation of both the nineteenth and twentieth centuries from a futurist perspective affirms that politics is still very much on his mind. After all, the hideous wreck of the former pride of the oceans, *Léviathan*, carries the name of Thomas Hobbes's famous seventeenth-century treatise on the modern state (1651). Representing 'le Progrès dans sa conception industrialiste: chaudière, charbon, mécaniciens',[6] *Léviathan* is destined for an equally material end. Its inglorious fate, which resembles that of Mess Lethierry's technological wonder, the steamboat *La Durande*, in *Les Travailleurs de la mer*, establishes an initial affiliation between Hugo's poetic reading of history and his seemingly apolitical tale of life in the Channel Islands in the 1820s.

Though critics have noted the parallels between *Léviathan* in 'Pleine mer' and the *Durande* in *Les Travailleurs de la mer*, none has commented

[4] Brombert, *Victor Hugo and the Visionary Novel*, 145. Grant, too, considers *TM* to be an 'extraordinary work, one of Hugo's greatest' (*The Perilous Quest*, 180), while Porter qualifies the narrative as 'a great regional novel' (*Victor Hugo*, 77). Just one film has ever been made of *TM*, in 1914. However, a French–Soviet adaptation, directed by Edmond Séchan, was televised as a mini-series in 1986 and shown in Paris in Feb. 2010 as a single movie during the Festival Victor Hugo et Égaux.

[5] See, respectively, *FT* 50–3, 97–9, 224–5, 252–3, and 197–9, 249–52.

[6] Pierre Laforgue, *Victor Hugo et La Légende des siècles: De la publication des* Contemplations *à l'abandon de* La Fin de Satan *(avril 1856–avril 1860)* (Orléans: Paradigme, 1997), 291.

on the inverse relation of the two vessels, the first embodying humanity's struggle with the elements, the second its triumph over nature. At the same time, the apparent metamorphosis of the anti-imperial stance in 'Vingtième siècle' into a more 'poetic' meditation on human ingenuity and creative potential in *Les Travailleurs de la mer* has remained largely unquestioned. Indeed, one might argue that the exiled writer's extensive reflections on genius in *William Shakespeare* had turned his interest from the sociopolitical arena to the realm of 'more elevated', aesthetic concerns alone.[7] Was venting his spleen in *Les Misérables* about Napoléon III's Second Empire sufficiently cathartic for Hugo? Or was he just getting started?

To untangle the connections between historical refiguration and metaphorical redescription in the novel, I consider *Les Travailleurs de la mer* in the light not only of contemporary French politics but also of its multiple 'prefaces'. According to the author's half-page preface to the novel itself, a triple fate weighs on us all: 'l'anankè des dogmes, l'anankè des lois, l'anankè des choses . . . A ces trois fatalités . . . se mêle la fatalité intérieure, l'anankè suprême, le cœur humain' (xii. 551). The first form of fatality, he declares, is featured in *Notre-Dame de Paris,* the second, in *Les Misérables,* the third, in *Les Travailleurs de la mer*, and the fourth, in each. If the 'fatality of the heart' inspires the lyrical aspects of his book, I maintain that the 'fatality of things' points beyond the weight on humanity of the natural world to the human construct of oppressive sociopolitical dogmas. To support this claim, I look first at the novel's liminal discussion of the exotic 'Archipel de la Manche'—a discussion suppressed in the first edition of the novel—for possible references to current events. Next, I unravel the metaphorical universe of *Les Travailleurs de la mer* to determine if it suggests reference points outside itself. This reading reveals that the political and artistic motifs from 'Vingtième siècle' transform the 'dénouement' of *La Légende des siècles* into a second, poetic 'preface' to the novel. I conclude with a study of the work's *other* preface, Hugo's essay on William Shakespeare. My analysis demonstrates that, rather than represent a radical departure from Hugo's literary *engagement* as a republican outlaw, *Les Travailleurs de la mer* offers an occulted image of present

[7] For Tony James, *TM* 'belongs . . . with the magma of texts on creativity and metaphysical problems which make up Hugo's book entitled *William Shakespeare* . . . and the contemporary unpublished texts surrounding that work' (*Dream, Creativity, and Madness in Nineteenth-Century France* (Oxford: Clarendon Press, 1995), 199). Pierre Laforgue groups the novel with other works of what he terms Hugo's 'période anglaise'—*William Shakespeare* (hereafter *WS*), *Mangeront-ils?* (a play), and *HQR*—all composed between 1863 and 1868 ('La Révolution française vue d'Angleterre', in A. R. W. James (ed.), *Victor Hugo et la Grande-Bretagne* (Liverpool: Francis Cairns Publications, 1986), 121).

and future French history. The novelist's textual weaving thus both resembles and extends the macrometaphorical structure of *Les Misérables*.

A GUIDEBOOK TO *LES TRAVAILLEURS DE LA MER*: 'L'ARCHIPEL DE LA MANCHE'

Hugo's emphasis not only on other times but also on other places in the three early historical novels returns in the setting of *Les Travailleurs de la mer*. From the outset, it is evident that the reader will be entering a *different* world, given the extended 'guide' to the Channel Islands that serves as the novel's preface.[8] Or, at least, that was the original plan. On the eve of publishing his monumental prose epic, Hugo received a letter from his friend and confidant Paul Meurice lamenting the fact that the original 'chapitre préliminaire'—a twenty-two-chapter guide to the Channel Islands—had been inexplicably suppressed in the proofs. As Meurice diplomatically put it, 'Le lecteur n'est pas *introduit*. Il se fait tout de suite assurément à ce milieu que vous rendez si réel, mais il est d'abord un peu dépaysé' (dated before 11 February 1866; xiii. 758). Without a proper initiation, the poor French reader feels quite out of his element in this strange fictive land.

While the exiled poet responded by acknowledging the reader's odd impression of being thrust into a 'brusque nouveauté locale', he outlined the powerful reasons that prevented him from using 'L'Archipel de la Manche' to preface his novel: 'Ce chapitre préliminaire est tout un livre... Quand je l'ai écrit, je me croyais *poeta integri status*, j'ignorais le bizarre guet-apens organisé contre moi par les bonapartistes, les classiques, les dévots, et ces *républicains agréables à la police*; aujourd'hui je suis renseigné et averti. Il faut ôter à ces violences les prétextes' (dated 11 February 1866; xiii. 759). Against the charms of Hugo's multifaceted guide to his home away from home was aligned a veritable cabal of reactionary forces. But what 'violences', one might wonder, could possibly be aroused by this orientation to the exotic flora, geology, geography, and Anglo-Norman mores of Guernsey, Jersey, Aurigny, and Sark? Can the edenic–utopian cast of Hugo's descriptions be read in more than one way? And does his primer on the Channel Islands, with its aesthetic of the 'grotesque céleste'

[8] According to Myriam Roman, 'L'Archipel de la Manche' 'entre en résonance avec les guides et les ouvrages utilisés par Hugo, tout comme les œuvres écrites sur le sujet par son entourage' ('Les Îles anglo-normandes: Insularité et communauté dans *Les Travailleurs de la mer*', in Lumilla Charles-Wurtz (ed.), *Victor Hugo 6: L'Écriture poétique* (Caen: Minard, 2006), 225).

(xii. 520), also serve as a guide to the spectacular voyage of the imagination that awaits the reader of *Les Travailleurs de la mer*? Perhaps, as Roland Barthes suggests, one of the delights of the novel is that 'il parvient à se faire écouter indirectement',[9] in and through its apparently extraneous preface. In this section, I explore these critically neglected issues, so crucial to unravelling the peculiar pleasures of the novel.[10]

As one peruses the correspondence surrounding the publication of *Les Travailleurs de la mer*, two themes emerge. On the one hand, Hugo is almost paranoid about the conspiracies of various ideologues back in France and so about the need to maintain utmost secrecy in all matters pertaining to the book's appearance. He thus enjoins his wife and children not even to communicate with the editors: 'J'ai plus d'ennemis que jamais, rien ne doit transpirer de ce livre... La haine est plus aux aguets que jamais; il faut la déjouer' (dated 5 December 1865; xiii. 738). The less information circulating about his new work, the better. On the other hand, Hugo invests the preliminary chapter with enormous psychic energy, declaring to his editors that it is truly 'une préface... pleine de faits curieux et très développée' (dated 26 November 1865; xii. 735). When they appear not to understand its import, he replies, 'ce *chapitre préliminaire*... tient au cœur même du livre. Il n'en sera d'ailleurs que mieux accueilli comme préface de la seconde édition' (dated 12 December 1865; xiii. 739). 'L'Archipel de la Manche' is, he insists, intimately related to the exposition of the novel.

The two themes converge in a letter to his wife, Adèle, where he expresses optimism in the face of adversity: 'J'ignore quel sera le succès des *Travailleurs de la mer*; j'ai à compter avec tous ces acharnements

[9] Roland Barthes, *Le Plaisir du texte* (Paris: Seuil, 1973), 41.

[10] Most critics who discuss 'L'Archipel de la Manche' focus primarily on its realist and/or didactic functions. Thus, Grant associates Hugo's 'emphasis on the reality of the islands' with the opening scenes of *TM*, where the reader is 'still located in a reasonable world that is recognizable as our own' (*The Perilous Quest*, 182), while David Charles declares the twenty-four prefatory chapters to be 'un ensemble cohérent, puisqu'il décrivent le cadre de l'intrigue romanesque' (*La Pensée technique dans l'œuvre de Victor Hugo: Le Bricolage de l'infini* (Paris: Presses Universitaires de France, 1997), 77). Grant further connects the sort of 'maddened pedantry' that one finds in the preface to the encyclopaedism of the entire novel, which aspires towards the totalizing synthesis of epic ('Victor Hugo's *Les Travailleurs de la mer*: Towards an Epic Synthesis', *L'Esprit créateur*, 16/3 (Fall 1976), 242; see also 231, 245). Cf. Porter, who sees in 'L'Archipel' Hugo's expression of 'gratitude to the land that has sheltered him in exile, by lovingly describing its landscape, flora, people, and customs' (*Victor Hugo*, 77); cf. also Henri Meschonnic, *Pour la poétique IV: Ecrire Hugo* (Paris: Gallimard, 1977), 143. More recently, Frank Lestringant has examined the text in the light of the tradition of maps of and fiction about islands, including works by Jules Verne, in 'L'"Archipel de la Manche", ou l'Insulaire de Hugo', *Studi francesi*, 47/2 (2003), 267–74; and Myriam Roman ('Les Îles anglo-normandes') has looked at the discourse surrounding the Archipelago in both the preface and the novel itself.

coalisés. Mais je me sens cuirassé ... Je suis content de cette œuvre' (dated 27 December 1865; xii. 744). Hugo's pleasure in the text reveals a profound identification with the subject of his story: the reference to 'acharnements coalisés' and the association of 'cuirassé' with battleships recall the epic struggles of his solitary hero Gilliatt, who must combat the forces of wind and tide to rescue a precious vessel shipwrecked on a tiny Channel reef. The conflation is confirmed by Hugo's remark, in a letter to his editor, that to publish the preliminary chapter in the second edition would constitute 'une sorte de rescousse' (dated 26 November 1865; xii. 735). If need be, the preface would save the novel, rallying the interest of the public in what lay beyond. In short, the correspondence indicates that including the pre-text in the first edition might have served as a 'pretext' for either suppression or harsh critical reception, whereas adding it subsequently would illuminate the 'heart' of his work. The liminal 'Archipelago' would perhaps steer Hugo's reader not just *through* the exotic Anglo-Norman world on the fringes of France but also *towards* a fresh perception of the homeland.[11]

A Stranger in a Strange Land

At first glance, the poet's detailed evocation of his Channel refuge offers little more than a Romantic set piece, combining vivid local colour with more philosophical musings on history, geography, and nature. The meandering organization of the twenty-two chapters is at once disarming and baffling. After touching on 'Les Anciens Cataclysmes' that ripped away whole sections of France to produce the archipelago, the preface describes the layout, fertility, natural hazards, rock formations, farms, and capital of Guernsey, followed by assorted facts and figures on the other islands (chs 2–9). Next we learn about the history, legends, religious sects, geography, and Anglo-French dialect of the region, along with some of the peculiar distinctions between Guernsey and Jersey (chs 10–16). Reflecting Hugo's Rabelaisian love of words, lists, and oddities, his travelogue is, at least up to this point, quite a hodgepodge. The closing chapters raise a tribute to the spirit of freedom and industriousness that informs the islands, which, the writer reminds us, have sheltered more than one French refugee (chs 17–22): 'Où prospérait le banditisme, le commerce règne ... Là où ce peuple a été pirate, il est pilote. Et il est plus entreprenant et plus hardi que jamais. Ce

[11] In this way, the preface would join the novel in combining the two kinds of realism identified by Barthes—'le premier déchiffre le "réel" (ce qui se démontre mais ne se voit pas); le second dit la "réalité" (ce qui se voit mais ne se démontre pas)'—thereby adding 'à l'intelligible du "réel" la queue fantasmatique de la "réalité"' (*Le Plaisir du texte*, 73–4).

pays est resté le pays de l'aventure en devenant le pays de la probité' (xii. 539). Demonstrating a remarkable aptitude for progress, the 'pilot'–archipelago is both a moral pioneer and a model for other nations. Hugo's guidebook thus appears to end rather cleverly, even generously, by pointing to the real Channel Archipelago as the true guide.

Or does it? For readers of *Notre-Dame de Paris*, where cathedral and book are continually affiliated, it is difficult not to view the passage, and so perhaps the entire preface, as self-referential. Rather than the rambling of a Hugo in his dotage, as his enemies and the imperial censors might imagine, the 'preliminary chapter' of *Les Travailleurs de la mer* is a palimpsest that bares the state of mind of France's last republican outlaw. His account of the Channel Islands not only shows where his hero Gilliatt comes *from*; it reveals where Hugo has come *to*. Behind the disarming façade lies the fully armed warrior. Having refused Napoléon III's general amnesty in 1859, Hugo is eager to broadcast his ideological, as well as his geographical, position to anyone willing to read between the lines. Just as *Les Misérables* stands as a shadow history of the Second Empire, his 'Archipel de la Manche' is intensely political because it highlights and extols the antithesis of present-day France. Here, as elsewhere, the pleasure of the text 'consiste à . . . politiser ce qui apparemment [n'est pas politique]'.[12] Like Jonathan Swift's *Gulliver's Travels* (1726), the preface to *Les Travailleurs de la mer* purports to be a travelogue, complete with natural history, but in fact comments extensively on the contemporary political scene.

Looking again at Hugo's closing tribute, for example, we can see that the edenic, utopian discourse used to characterize the islands and their inhabitants presents a reverse image of his absent homeland. On one side we find a 'pilot' productively engaged in 'commerce'; on the other, an unevolved 'pirate' living off 'banditry'. From this perspective, other passages depicting the idyllic qualities of the archipelago—what Pierre Laforgue calls 'l'ailleurs presque utopique de l'archipel anglo-normand'[13]—begin to assume distinctly sociopolitical resonances. Thus, the useful activities of its denizens mirror the fertility of the islands themselves. If France were cultivated like Jersey, 'au calcul [d'un] excellent agronome pratique . . . [elle] pourrait nourrir deux cent soixante-dix millions d'hommes, toute l'Europe' (xii. 524). Natural resources and human industry combine to create genuine wealth, sufficient to share with others. The importance of agriculture to social progress, previously treated in *Les Misérables*, is a theme with which Hugo deeply identifies, sometimes in surprising ways:[14] 'Terre fertile, grasse, forte. Nul

12 Barthes, *Le Plaisir du texte*, 44.
13 Laforgue, 'La Révolution française', 125.
14 See *FT* 233–4.

pâturage meilleur,' he declares elsewhere in the preface. 'Le froment est célèbre, les vaches sont illustres. Les génisses des herbages de Saint-Pierre-du-Bois sont les égales des moutons lauréats du plateau de Confolens. Les comices agricoles de France et d'Angleterre couronnent les chefs-d'œuvre que font les sillons et les prairies de Guernesey' (xii. 516). Under the guise of local colour, the poet surreptitiously places himself (*célèbre, illustres, lauréats, chefs-d'œuvre*) at the centre of a nurturing setting that rivals anything Europe can offer. *Terroir* matters.

The enlightened, civilized attitude that undergirds the society of the archipelago extends beyond agriculture to other domains as well. Everywhere one looks, one finds 'le même fait à l'état d'utopie en Europe et de progrès accompli dans les Channel Islands' (xii. 528). France need only turn to its tiny neighbours to discover guides or models for its lost revolutionary goals of liberty, equality, and fraternity. Here, for instance, 'on fraternise' (xii. 529) from one island to another, much as the sea befriends the creatures on the tiniest keys: 'Ces grandes fraternités, c'est toute la nature' (xii. 517), Hugo claims, and those who live close to nature participate in the same tendencies. Indeed, the French republican ideal of universal brotherhood is alive and well in the Channel: 'A dater du dix-septième siècle, ces îles ont été fraternelles au monde entier; l'hospitalité est leur gloire. Elles ont l'impartialité de l'asile. Royalistes, elles accueillent la république vaincue; huguenotes, elles admettent le catholicisme émigré' (xii. 535). The related ideal of social equality likewise emerges in the islanders' attitude towards refugees, who are treated impartially regardless of their origins or creeds. We might note in passing that Hugo again refers to himself here, both overtly as one of the vanquished republicans and more allusively (in a typical bit of wordplay) as a Hugue(o)not. What better way to signal his status as a (political) protestant? Finally, he elaborates extensively on the state of the islands as one of 'pleine liberté' (xii. 533), where people are free to assemble, to declaim publicly against the government, to publish whatever they wish: 'Pensez, parlez, écrivez, imprimez, haranguez, c'est votre affaire. Tout entendre et tout lire, d'un côté, cela implique, de l'autre, tout dire et tout écrire. Donc franchise absolue de parole et de presse' (xii. 534). For the poet, who risks having his words gagged and muzzled at home, speaking and writing openly is clearly one of life's greatest pleasures.[15]

Through his 'Archipel de la Manche', then, Hugo holds up to France a portrait of its ideal self, a reminder of who his nation was and where it was

[15] Both Barrère (*Victor Hugo à l'œuvre*, 98) and Grant ('Victor Hugo's *Les Travailleurs de la mer*', 237) have previously remarked on Hugo's celebration of freedom under English law in this part of the preface.

headed before it was derailed by the 1851 *coup d'état* of Louis-Napoléon. At the same time, he indicates that he has more or less abandoned the notion of an earthly Eden: 'Des rêveurs, quelques-uns illustres, ont rêvé la restitution du printemps perpétuel à la terre... Cherchons ailleurs l'éden. Le printemps est bon; la liberté et la justice valent mieux. L'éden est moral, et non matériel. Etre libres et justes, cela dépend de nous. La sérénité est intérieure. C'est au-dedans de nous qu'est notre printemps perpétuel' (xii. 538). The islands may not be paradisal in the usual sense of the word; still, their moral pre-eminence is the outward reflection of the exile's own sense of self, a world consonant with his aspirations to social freedom and justice—a world, in short, where harmony overcomes discord.

Sublime Fanaticism

This correspondence of inner and outer universes in the preface to *Les Travailleurs de la mer*, a poetic motif intricately developed in *Les Misérables*,[16] leads the reader towards a startling realization. The guide that Hugo offers his reader does not merely oscillate between the preface and the archipelago; it also includes a third, more occulted term—the writer himself. As one who keeps the republican flame alive, achieving true serenity by living the republican moral life, Hugo proposes himself as an exemplar to his fellow countrymen. The free and confraternal place to which he has come is as much his mature self as the Channel Islands. As with many of Hugo's metaphorical analogies, the identification between self and location is communicated through the use of self-similar structures.[17] We therefore learn in the first chapter of the preface about the 'Anciens Cataclysmes' that broke off parts of France and flung them into the ocean; later, Hugo alludes to his own situation as a castaway: 'Ces îles... étaient écueils, elles sont refuges. Ces lieux de détresse sont devenus des points de sauvetage. Qui sort du désastre, émerge là. Tous les naufragés y viennent, celui-ci des tempêtes, celui-là des révolutions' (xii. 535). A piece of France tossed into the sea, he has emerged intact, as firm and unyielding in his convictions as the rocks on which he stands.[18] When he provides a fanciful litany of place names and other words that are common to 'cette vieille Gaule' (xii. 524) and that derive from the prefix *hou*, he suggests a profound identity, an interpenetration, between himself and the archipelago. He also looks forward to the plot of his novel, which centres

[16] See *FT* 265–77.
[17] See *FT* 256–65.
[18] Cf. Roman, 'Les Îles anglo-normandes', 226.

on a devastating shipwreck, while alluding to Gilliatt, who single-handedly combats a mighty tempest, as a kind of alter ego.

Similarly, when Hugo underscores the 'dislocation énorme mêlée à l'harmonie' (xii. 520) that defines the rocks along the wild coastline, he inscribes the Channel Islands within a *mélange des genres* that resembles his own Romantic aesthetic. Again, inner and outer worlds coincide in Ricoeur's notion of 'discordant concordances'. The expatriate poet has found an environment in which he feels perfectly in his element. For him, the far—the place he knows as home—has become the near. Immersed in a 'grotesque céleste', where chaos and creation intersect in constantly decomposing forms that evoke 'l'idée de grandeur, non de beauté' (xii. 519), he can dream of artistic creations as vast, excessive, and monstrous as nature itself. As he declares in a subsequent reflection in the preface on human creativity: 'Tout borne l'homme mais rien ne l'arrête. Il réplique à la limite par l'enjambée. L'impossible est une frontière toujours reculante' (xii. 537). Rather than being disheartened by boundaries, humanity enjoys the challenge of transgressing them. The same is also true of the writer. Though he may be limited by the narrow confines of his island home, imagination carries him into other realms altogether. After finishing the novel, the reader rediscovers in these observations explicit parallels to the superhuman efforts of Gilliatt himself.

By the same token, Hugo's linkage of the grotesque harmonies of the archipelago to his own—and thus Gilliatt's—immoderate works contains a political parallel. If Hugo often strains towards overdetermination, his aim here is not simply to project an illusion of textual coherence, a basically aesthetic objective, but to steer the reader towards the social dimensions of his fictive enterprise. In an apparently digressive musing on fanaticism, which he describes as 'hideux quand il persécute, auguste et touchant quand il est persécuté' (xii. 536), he both denounces the zealous right-wing cabal that seeks to silence him and aggrandizes his own intransigent republican stance. Though no less an extremist than his enemies, his martyrdom sets a noble example. Holding firm to his cause—the 'Eden' that lies within—he adheres without wavering to a 'grand et sombre hymne intérieur' (xii. 536), all the lyrics of which he faithfully sings in his soul. As one might suspect, this 'hymn' has strong affinities with Hugo's Romantic art:

> Il pénètre du sublime même le grotesque, et, quelles que soient la poésie et la prose de ses prêtres, il transfigure cette prose et cette poésie par l'immense harmonie latente de sa foi. Il corrige la difformité des formules par la grandeur des épreuves acceptées et des supplices subis. Où la poésie manque,

> il met la conscience. Le libretto du martyre peut être plat, qu'importe, si le martyre est magnanime. (xii. 536)

The mixture of sublime and grotesque, the overarching sense of harmony, the subsumption of deformity by grandeur—all recall Hugo's lifelong attempt to reconcile disparate entities in a universal artistic form. They also recall his description of the island coastline, which thus becomes the outer figuration of his inner anthem to the republic. Once again, Hugo's guidebook to 'L'Archipel de la Manche' directs the reader towards more ideological concerns. The poet–protagonist's martyrdom (*épreuves, martyre*) provides the model for self-sacrifice to the reader. One need not be a poet, or a literary hero, he implies, to follow in their steps; conscience alone suffices. Those living the most 'flat', ordinary lives are equally capable of generous devotion to the ideal. Fanaticism, however distorted and extreme, gives rise to the sublime moral beauty of self-abnegation.

The imposition of order on apparent chaos, of law on ethical or artistic excess, corresponds to the geometry that underlies the jumble of islands forming the Archipelago. Because 'l'archipel de la Manche dessine le triangle' (xii. 526), according to Hugo, the triangular form of the largest island, Guernsey, repeats and condenses the larger figure.[19] In other words, the self-similar patterns within and among the islands correspond geographically to Hugo's verbal symmetries. Just as 'la vocation de l'archipel est de se reproduire, par mise en abymes et miniaturisation, creusé en chacune de ses unités par une sorte de dynamisme fractal',[20] Hugo uses this creative principle to forge his own infinite regressions and metaphorical mirrorings. But the phenomenon is not limited to geography. From a sociological viewpoint, the islands represent a miniature version of the future: 'Ces microcosmes reflètent en petit, dans toutes ses phases, la grande formation humaine. Jersey, Guernesey, Aurigny, anciens repaires, ateliers à présent. Anciens écueils, ports maintenant' (xii. 539–41). The evolution of these locales from bandit hideouts to breeding grounds for production and commerce provides a paradigm for social progress and announces 'le destin de la France moderne, celui de l'Europe unie que Hugo appelle de ses vœux'.[21] In the end, the Channel Islands present several orders of *mises en abyme* that operate not only in space but also in time—a pattern that, we shall see, recurs in *L'Homme qui rit* and *Quatrevingt-Treize* as well.

[19] See Lestringant, 'L'"Archipel de la Manche"', 270.
[20] Lestringant, 'L'"Archipel de la Manche"', 272.
[21] Lestringant, 'L'"Archipel de la Manche"', 273.

As our scrutiny of Hugo's preface to *Les Travailleurs de la mer* has shown, his 'Archipelago' is as much a moral as a travel guide, one that takes both the islands' confraternal culture and the exile's self-sacrifice as its models. Little wonder, then, that Hugo thought it wise to remove this 'pretext' for any 'violences' that his enemies might be planning on the eve of the novel's appearance. Given its sociopolitical overtones, his orientation to the universe inhabited by Gilliatt might have aroused suspicions about the text itself. At the same time, the preface points insistently towards the aesthetic dimensions of such *engagement*. Social and artistic *audacities* are intricately interrelated in the novel, just as they were in *Les Misérables*.[22] The mingling of both realms likewise recalls 'Vingtième siècle', with its two-pronged look at the past and the future. In exploring the occulted 'heart' of the novel towards which its suppressed preface gestures, I begin by showing that the metaphorical network in the text fully reflects its poetic antecedent in *La Légende des siècles*.

FROM POETIC TO POLITICAL DISPLACEMENTS

The image of piloting, of course, is intimately related to that of transportation, most obviously Mess Lethierry's marvellous steamboat. At the same time, the idea of conveyance or transferral recalls Ricoeur's definition of metaphor as a 'transposition of terms' or 'displacement' that involves the substitution of a strange, unconnected, 'alien' name (*RM* 17, 18). Through this trope, what was distant and different suddenly seems near and analogous. Metaphor thus constitutes a sort of *transport*, whereby it comes to resemble the sublime moment itself. The 'affective aggrandizement'[23] that accompanies the experience of transcendence entails a sense of being transported out of normal space and time; similarly, the movement inherent in the metaphorical process represents a 'deviation' (*RM* 22) from a given order. Far from being mere self-inflation, then, poetic claims to pushing back the boundaries of the known world, to charting new territories, may be wholly justified. Indeed, for Ricoeur, poetic discourse obscures the distinction 'between discovering and creating and between finding and projecting' through the workings of imaginative 'redescription' (*RM* 306). By combining fiction and redescription, invention and discovery, creation and revelation, metaphorical language in effect resituates our logical frontiers and perceptual boundaries.

[22] See *FN* 188–201.
[23] Weiskel, *The Romantic Sublime*, 4.

Gilliatt, the reclusive protagonist of *Les Travailleurs de la mer*, uses multiple modes of transport, including dreams, meditation, science, agility, love, self-sacrifice, and death itself, to challenge our notion of the humanly—and inhumanly—possible. From Lethierry's steamboat to metaphorical transpositions to the rapture of the sublime to political displacements, being 'transported' involves an encounter with otherness. Single-handedly salvaging the *Durande* at what is literally the farthest reach of his world, this suffering but triumphant 'Job Prométhée' (xii. 704) transcends the apparent limits of his own knowledge and strength to conquer a range of natural and psychological 'monsters'. But, while the numerous variations on the motifs of movement and displacement in *Les Travailleurs de la mer* point insistently towards the transpositions of metaphor, the sublime, and political exile, their connections to both Hugo's republicanism and his totalizing '*poétique de la transcendance*' have not been explored. On the contrary, following the author's apparent disclaimer in a letter to Paul Meurice, 'Ce n'est pas un livre de combat; il est écrit, non pour la minute, mais pour la postérité' (23 January 1866; xiii. 755), critics have concluded that the work serves no 'immediate political purpose'.[24] Our reading of the prefatory 'Archipel' makes us question this interpretation. In this section, I connect the motifs of movement in *Les Travailleurs de la mer* with Hugo's larger aesthetic, epistemological, and political project. As I show, these motifs not only become figures for metaphorical language and poetic vision per se; they also counter the oppressive post-Republican order of the Second Empire. I look first at the kinds of dynamism involved in Gilliatt's venture, then at the various transpositions that structure the key scenes or 'movements' of his ordeal, and finally at the powerful intertwining of politics and poetics in the text.

The notion of displacement, transposition, or transferral is, from the outset, essential to Gilliatt's ordeal. Consider his mission: to rescue intact both the engine and other mechanical parts of the *Durande*, the first steamboat in service in the Channel Islands. In a daring gamble, the industrious, honorable old seaman Mess Lethierry had invested all his available capital in 'cette machine... unique et impossible à remplacer' (xii. 584), turning an innovative idea into reality. An emblem of travel, mass movement, and technological progress, the *Durande* had secured the man's fortune and reputation by providing a relatively reliable means of transportation to and from the French mainland:

[24] Grant, *The Perilous Quest*, 181. Although, in Brombert's opinion as well, 'Poetic vision clearly takes precedence over immediate political efficacy' (*Victor Hugo and the Visionary Novel*, 164), for the author of *Châtiments* (hereafter *CHAT*) and *MIS*, the first in no way precludes the second.

> Le navire à vapeur, c'est la boussole complétée; la boussole indique le droit chemin, la vapeur le suit. L'une propose, l'autre exécute... Ah! comme c'était beau sur les vagues cette cheminée altière, ce prodigieux cylindre, ce pilier au chapiteau de fumée, cette colonne plus grande que la colonne Vendôme, car sur l'une il n'y a qu'un homme et sur l'autre il y a le progrès! (xii. 764)

Besides the references to both a compass and Napoléon's victory at Austerlitz, the passage bristles with phallic imagery that underscores the venture capitalist's deep identification with his creation.[25] The straight lines of transit miraculously traced by 'cette machine où l'homme met sa volonté, cette chaudière toute-puissante' (xii. 764), express the triumph of human will over natural forces, of geometry over chaos. In contrast with the shiny machinery of warfare, which chiefly serves the interests of those in power, his monstrous, fire-breathing Hydra contributes to collective progress.

But when Lethierry's trusted captain, Clubin, deliberately runs the boat aground as part of an elaborate scheme to defraud him and to cover up the theft, the ageing entrepreneur finds himself on the verge of emotional and economic bankruptcy. Depression sets in, his state of mind mimicking the paralysed ship itself: 'Mess Lethierry était réduit à la fonction machinale de vivre. Les plus vaillants hommes, privés de leur idée réalisable, en arrivent là. C'est l'effet des existences vidées. La vie est le voyage, l'idée est l'itinéraire. Plus d'itinéraire, on s'arrête. Le but est perdu, la force est morte' (xii. 758–9).[26] Having lost the *Durande*, he has lost his compass, his purpose in life, as well. He has, in short, become 'impuissant' (xii. 759). In desperation, he offers the hand of his niece and heir, Déruchette, to whoever might save the vessel's irreplaceable engine. Gilliatt, a versatile loner who has loved Déruchette from afar, secretly takes up the challenge.

The task is, to all appearances, impossible. Before he can disassemble and transport the motor back to Guernesey, Gilliatt must dislodge it from

[25] The allusion here to artistic creation is obvious. As James has shown with regard to the texts surrounding *WS*, Hugo's great meditation on the nature of genius, the work of art holds a paradoxical position: 'Although the work has come to birth in the world outside the poet, it continues in some sense to belong to his internal world' (*Dream, Creativity, and Madness*, 210). The steamboat is thus to Lethierry what the novel is to the writer himself. Cf. William R. Paulson's remarks on Lethierry's 'irremplaçable bien d'équipement industriel' as belonging to two opposing values systems ('L'*Anankè* des choses: Capitalisme et sacrifice dans *Les Travailleurs de la mer*', in David Ellison and Ralph Heyndels (eds), *Les Modernités de Victor Hugo* (Paris: Presses de l'Université de Paris-Sorbonne, 2004), 28).

[26] The mechanical motif is recycled throughout the novel. For example, Lethierry places, 'machinalement... sur la table' (xii. 760), a letter from Rantaine—his former associate who had stolen half his fortune ten years before. What he now realizes is that 'Rantaine était le Dieu dans la machine' (xii. 762), the transfer of the man's ill-gotten gains to an even more villainous Clubin supplying the motive for the latter's deliberate wrecking of the *Durande*.

the wrecked hull, now wedged between two giant rocks and suspended some twenty feet above sea level on the remote, inhospitable reef known as *les Douvres*. He must set the immobilized means of conveyance in motion through 'le sauvetage, le glissement et le transbordement de la machine' (xii. 724). To accomplish such a feat of engineering requires two long months of exhausting, methodical effort during which he must secure his own craft; find food, fresh water, and shelter where there is none; salvage every available scrap from the wreck; construct a working forge; transform bits and pieces of rope, chain, and wood into tools and instruments; and, lastly, free the huge engine and paddle wheels from the ship's carcass and lower them into his own sloop. Just as the poet's art lies in tapping the full potential of the words with which he works, Gilliatt 's'avise de la plurivalence virtuelle [des outils] dont il dispose'[27] in order to mould a host of latent possibilities into realities. He must also protect the hard-won fruit of his labours against wind, tide, and tempest. In essence, Gilliatt is called upon to accomplish alone—by sheer force of body, will, and intellect—what a team of skilled workers could never achieve in such a hostile environment. He must, in other words, transcend human boundaries. Metaphorically, he must reconstitute the useless and the incongruous into a new, harmonious, beneficial creation, beginning with the instruments of salvage themselves.

In this alien, desolate place, the One thus becomes the Many, filling the void with purposeful activity.[28] Though but an atom in the face of the infinite, Gilliatt displays the dynamism of a small army: 'cet héroïsme inouï . . . ce formidable combat accepté, cette lutte de Rien contre Tout, cette Iliade à un' (xii. 752) is an unsung epic worthy of the highest admiration. He is a true action hero, a human whirlwind who effects multiple constructive changes, an even more prodigious source of movement than Lethierry's steam engine. Sexual energy—the dream of being joined to Déruchette—stokes the furnace. As her uncle ironically declares, when Gilliatt later tries to renounce his claim so she can marry the man she loves, 'C'est en faisant la bouche en cœur du côté de ma vieille caboche que tu as taillé, coupé, tourné, viré, traîné, limé, charpenté, inventé, écrabouillé, et fait plus de miracles à toi tout seul que tous les saints du paradis' (xii. 773). The old seaman not only demonstrates a clear

[27] Claudie Bernard, '"Les Travailleurs de la mer" et le travail du texte', *Letteratura francese contemporanea le correnti d'avanguardia*, 7/17 (1986), 34; see also Myriel Moutet, 'Concentration et dissolution du moi dans *Moby Dick* et *Les Travailleurs de la mer*', in Dominique Peyrache-Leborgne and Yann Jumelais (eds), *Victor Hugo ou les frontières effacées* (Nantes: Pleins Feux, 2002), 371.

[28] Cf. Bernard's account of Gilliatt's absolute control of this process, based on a 'plan unitaire' ('"Les Travailleurs de la mer"', 35).

understanding of Gilliatt's motivation; he also recapitulates the other's exploits as a *homo faber*, the explosion of verbs capturing both his ceaseless motion and his multifaceted talents.[29] But will Gilliatt, like Lethierry's engine of progress, run out of energy? As we shall see, each phase of the hero's struggle is centred on the defence and/or transfer of vital forces. The significance of these *movements*, however, must be gauged in the light of the novel's other pre-text, 'Vingtième siècle', before we can glean their full political and aesthetic dimensions.

Filling the Void

As with the task itself of salvaging the *Durande*, imagery of displacement and transference is central to the scenes where Gilliatt prevails over a hurricane by internalizing its power, prevents an octopus from evacuating his insides into its own, saves his leaky craft from sinking, and trades his happiness for Déruchette's through self-abnegation. The storm's approach, at the vulnerable moment just before Gilliatt can set sail for home, embodies a sinister contradiction: 'Pas une ondulation, pas un plissement, pas une saillie qui se déformât ou se déplaçât. Cette immobilité en mouvement était lugubre... On eût dit l'effrayant talus de l'abîme' (xii. 725). As in *Les Misérables*, where the policeman Javert encounters a terrifying 'gouffre en haut' (xi. 915) in his dealings with the saintly outlaw Jean Valjean,[30] Gilliatt experiences the sublime as a looming, apocalyptic force that threatens to turn everything topsy-turvy. The 'montagne mouvante de vapeurs' (xii. 725) sweeping towards the reef threatens not to elevate but to crush him by destroying his entire enterprise.

Caught between the winds that converge from the four corners of the globe and the waves that can slither, crash, bite, hold fast, and shred like packs of marauding hydras, Gilliatt confronts all the legions of natural chaos combined. The grotesque, like the sublime, is in Hugo always a *dynamic* force, a force that *moves*.[31] Thus provoked, Gilliatt rises Titan-like to the occasion, using his ingenuity to harness the mighty storm in defending the barricaded reef. He may be no more than a single cog in the

[29] While some scholars have cast Lethierry in the role of active hero and Gilliatt in that of a more passive, inwardly turned dreamer (see esp. Grant, 'Victor Hugo's *Les Travailleurs de la mer*', 237–9, and Maxwell, *The Mysteries of Paris and London*, 294–6, 303), I concur with Brombert's assessment of this 'new Crusoe' as 'the archetypal *faber*, the maker and shaper of forms' (*Victor Hugo and the Visionary Novel*, 152). Cf. also Bernard, who sees in the machinating Clubin, on the other hand, a fallen *homo faber*, an 'anti-travailleur... [qui] retombe dans la loi de la faune (la série des mangeurs et des mangés) et même dans le domaine des artefacts' ('"Les Travailleurs de la mer"', 33; see also 34–6).

[30] See *FT* 90–5.

[31] Cf. Brombert, *Victor Hugo and the Visionary Novel*, 155.

universal 'engrenage', that 'déplacement incessant et démesuré ... ce mouvement de translation' (xii. 707) through time and space in which our existence is inscribed. As we have seen, however, his own immense and incessant 'displacements' confer on him an equally powerful, demiurgical status. Though the storm system now bears down with tremendous pressure, Gilliatt succeeds in dominating and redirecting 'l'immense machine des nuages' (xii. 735) by dint of superior intelligence, purpose, and tenacity. In effect, he internalizes its might, making it his own. For Hugo, this is the experience of the sublime. The 'traumatic disequilibrium of the sublime moment' is resolved through the 'metaphorical substitution of a "power within" for the external power'.[32] By introjecting the force of nature, Gilliatt counteracts the anxiety of engulfment. As in other classically sublime moments, the position of the subject undergoes a radical reversal: 'le spectateur, d'abord passif et réceptif, se sent devenir actif et tout-puissant.' But, whereas traditional representations of the sublime draw primarily on images of the vast and the limitless, Hugo adds the baroque notions 'de dynamisme et de métamorphose incessante',[33] thereby connecting the thematics of movement in the text not only to the psychological structure of the sublime but also to the rhetorical structure of metaphor.

In a vivid variation on the threat of being swallowed up, the demented fury of the tempest is soon replaced by an even greater horror: the blood-sucking monster of the deep. After staring down the eye of the hurricane, the lone warrior finds himself in the stranglehold of this 'viscosité ronde et plate' (xii. 739) that has long had its eye on *him*. The text links the watchful beast—'Au milieu de cette viscosité il y avait deux yeux qui regardaient. Ces yeux voyaient Gilliatt' (xii. 493)—not only with the storm—'Cet œil lugubre [de la tempête] était sur Gilliatt' (xii. 484)—but also with Gilliatt, that proud 'cyclope' (xii. 688) who masters the elements, and so with the demiurgic–visionary poet himself.[34]

The ensuing scene contains one of the most gripping examples of Hugo's visual imagination in the novel. As it swims, the octopus resembles 'une manche cousue avec un poing dedans' (xii. 741), not exactly harmless,

[32] Weiskel, *The Romantic Sublime*, 95; see also 105–6. For the relation between the psychological structure of the sublime, the role of conscience, and the literary oedipal complex in *MIS*, see *FT* 123, 145, 185, 234 n. 43.

[33] Peyrache-Leborgne, 'Victor Hugo et le sublime', 20.

[34] Hugo's use of the word 'cyclope' to describe the hero suggests that he may have been aware of, and responding to, the invectives privately employed by Sainte-Beuve to describe him. A grotesque 'Polyphème', the exiled Hugo seems doomed, under the pen of his former colleague, to impotent rage: 'Sur les brûlots que lance Hugo de l'île de Jersey, Hugo est dans son île du Cyclope: il nous lance des quartiers de rocher qui ne nous atteignent pas' (Charles-Augustin Sainte-Beuve, *Mes Poisons* (Paris: José Corti, 1988), 46, 61–2).

as the fist image suggests, but far from fearsome. Suddenly, the fist opens and the creature becomes nightmarish.[35] Its finger–tentacles transform it into an 'appareil de succion' (xii. 741), a hideous mechanical masterpiece that can suffocate and kill by displacement:

> La griffe, c'est la bête qui entre dans votre chair; la ventouse, c'est vous-même qui entrez dans la bête. Vos muscles s'enflent, vos fibres se tordent, votre peau éclate sous une pesée immonde, votre sang jaillit et se mêle affreusement à la lymphe du mollusque. La bête se superpose à vous par mille bouches infâmes; l'hydre s'incorpore à l'homme; l'homme s'amalgame à l'hydre. Vous ne faites qu'un . . . le poulpe . . . vous tire à lui et en lui, et, lié, englué, impuissant, vous vous sentez lentement vidé dans cet épouvantable sac, qui est un monstre. (xii. 742)

Hugo's sexually charged description makes it clear that the octopus seeks to penetrate and violate the virginal protagonist by transferring his succulent insides into its own empty interior.[36] It is one thing to become one with the universe; it is quite another to be horrifically ingested. Yet, while implosion is not explosion, they are metaphorically of the same order—two different ways to disappear. This episode also carries a symbolic value, since it further extends Gilliatt's exploration of the confines of the possible. The monsters that 'touchent la frontière humaine et peuplent la limite

[35] Many critics have noted, after Charles Baudouin (*Psychanalyse de Victor Hugo* (Paris: Armand Colin, 1972), 177), the relation of the octopus to the spider imagery in *NDP*. See, e.g., Joan C. Kessler, 'Babelic Ruin, Babelic "Ebauche": An Introduction to a Hugolian Problematic', *Stanford French Review*, 7/3 (Winter 1983), 288, and Grant, *The Perilous Quest*, 194. Spider and web imagery play an important role as well in *MIS* (see Grant, *The Perilous Quest*, 167, and *FT* 158, 237). Cf. also Jacques Seebacher, who rightly connects other aspects of *TM* with the social concerns of *NDP*. For the critic, the text is multivalent: 'abîme de l'Océan et abîme du cœur, sorte de confession autobiographique, mais aussi méditation technologique, historique, politique. Allégorie visionnaire du roman social, reprise évidente du coup de force de *Notre-Dame de Paris*' ('Introduction', in Victor Hugo, *Châtiments. La Conscience. La Vision de Dante* (Paris: Garnier-Flammarion, 1970), 18).

[36] Grant (*The Perilous Quest*, 194–5), Brombert (*Victor Hugo and the Visionary Novel*, 156), Bernard ('"Les Travailleurs de la mer"', 39), and Lise Revol-Marzouk (*Le Sphinx et l'Abîme: Sphinx maritimes et énigmes romanesques dans* Moby Dick *et* Les Travailleurs de la mer (Grenoble: ELLUG/Éditions littéraires et linguistiques de l'Université de Grenoble, 2008), 165–6) have previously commented on the psychosexual aspects of this scene. Claude Millet convincingly argues that, through such sexually loaded imagery, 'l'objet d'amour se dédouble, Déruchette et la pieuvre, la vierge et la putain' ('*Les Travailleurs de la mer* de Victor Hugo: Un roman d'amour', *Romantisme*, 115 (2002), 20; see also 21–3). I would add that the identity of these apparent antitheses as stars (Millet, '*Les Travailleurs de la mer* de Victor Hugo', 22) forecasts the use of similar imagery to connect Dea and Josiane, the opposing love interests in *HQR*. See also Jean Richer, 'Grands transparents dans *Les Travailleurs de la Mer*', in Anne Marie Amiot (ed.), *Idéologies hugoliennes*, Actes du Colloque Interdisciplinaire, 23–5 May 1985 (Nice: Serre, 1985), 111, and Roche, *Character and Meaning*, 99.

chimérique' (xii. 743) point to all the mysteries of creation, both good and evil, that beckon to those who dream and those who contemplate.[37]

Gilliatt survives this attack, only to discover that his boat has developed a leak and is in danger of submerging. The proliferation of forces allied against him in the tempest is doubled, one might say, by an almost endless series of ordeals: 'Après le dénuement, l'élément; après la marée, la tourmente; après la tempête, la pieuvre; après le monstre, le spectre' (xii. 751). The epic confrontation between the One and the Many is revealed as a self-renewing process.[38] In an instant replay of the struggle with the octopus, itself an inversion of the tempest scene, the ocean invades the inside of Gilliatt's vessel and threatens to draw it down into itself. In other words, the text reformulates the problem of inside and outside pressures with yet another instance of displaced fluids.

Once again, Gilliatt is moved to act. With much effort, he locates the hole and covers it from outside with an old dropcloth. When the ocean stretches the fabric and begins pushing it back through the fracture into the boat, the imagery is familiar: 'Cela ressemblait à un poing sous cette toile, s'efforçant de la crever' (xii. 749). The fist raised against him—an echo not only of the octopus but, more broadly, of the 'mille menaces [du vent et de la mer qui] lui avaient montré le poing' (xii. 751) since his arrival on the reef—constitutes a further transgression of interiority. Exhausted, Gilliatt throws all the material at his disposition, including his own clothing, into the breach, stopping the leak with a kind of compress before leaving events to take their course:

> il devenait passif... Ce tampon était son unique point d'appui. Gilliatt s'était épuisé et dépouillé à le composer et à le compléter... Comment se porterait cet obstacle inerte?... Plus ou moins de pression; toute la question était là.

[37] As 'une réflexion sur les limites de l'Être', Hugo's chimerical *pieuvre* is, for Pierre Laforgue, 'un ectoplasme poétique et philosophique' that 'conjugue la réalité et le possible' ('Réalité, possible et chimère dans *Les Travailleurs de la mer*', in Michel Viegnes (ed.), *Hugo et la chimère* (Grenoble: ELLUG/Éditions littéraires et linguistiques de l'Université de Grenoble, 2003), 54, 55, 56).

[38] Cf. Grant, *The Perilous Quest*, 195–6, who interprets this scene in the context of the mythic quest. Since 'the hero set[s] off on his journey without any assistance from a divine messenger' and, hence, protector, his '*hubris*, even if unintentional, does not go unpunished'. Cf. also Brombert's treatment of the 'dynamics of creation' (*Victor Hugo and the Visionary Novel*, 156) in the text as a process by which unity emerges from diversity, as well as Kessler's discussion of Babelic imagery—'the fragmentation of divine unity into the realm of proliferating materiality' ('Babelic Ruin, Babelic "Ebauche"', 294)—in *TM* and in Hugo's work in general.

> Tout allait se dénouer par une lutte machinale entre deux quantités mécaniques... Ce Gilliatt, qui avait été une providence, était, à la minute suprême, remplacé par une résistance inconsciente. (xii. 751)

All activity now resides, paradoxically, in passive resistance, as one pressure counteracts another. Here, as elsewhere, the use of scientific vocabulary points to Gilliatt's ability to tap into elemental forces. He may seem 'passive' and depleted; but, like the dreamer or the poet, he is productive even when motionless. In a climactic set of reversals, Gilliatt the 'lifesaver' (*providence*) gives up all control, entrusting his enterprise to a higher providence and allowing an unconscious, mechanical force to replace brilliant improvisation. Feeling himself 'se dissoudre' (xii. 752) in fatigue, impotence, and prayer, he abandons himself to sleep and awakes to find both his boat—and himself—intact. Like Jean Valjean in *Les Misérables*, who becomes stronger even as he pours himself into everyone else,[39] Gilliatt relies on a higher power to transcend his physical limitations. The human spirit goes where reason and science have not yet ventured.

One might also find a subtle connection between this sequence and Hugo's argument in *Notre-Dame de Paris* and *Les Misérables* about Romantic aesthetics. The roles previously played by Claude Frollo and Javert, who, we observed in Chapter 1, embody neoclassical order, would thereby pass in *Les Travailleurs de la mer* to the notion of the mechanical, rather than to another character. And, just as in the earlier works such order is more subsumed than opposed by Hugo's sublime Romantic outlaws—Quasimodo and Esmeralda on the one hand and Jean Valjean on the other[40]—Gilliatt's bold ingenuity does not reject science, reason, and mechanics. It simply applies them in novel ways. Whereas the mechanical and the organic denote mutually exclusive metaphors for the universe, they are intertwined in Hugo's conception of Romantic creativity, where nothing is wasted.

Having saved the engine of the *Durande*, Gilliatt goes on to save its namesake, Déruchette, who bears the diminutive of the same eponym.[41] Resourceful as ever, he knows what to do when he learns that the woman of his dreams loves another. 'Pas de déroute possible pour cette âme' (xii. 732), the narrator declares, as the hero instinctively follows his inner compass in battling the hurricane. Now he must conquer an even greater force, his own desire. The battle moves from outer to inner, from physical

[39] See *FT* 159–69.

[40] See *EN* 177, 185, 191, and *FT* 152–4, 174, 184–5.

[41] Cf. Grant, 'Victor Hugo's *Les Travailleurs de la mer*', 239: 'Hugo makes it clear that Déruchette and Durande are varieties of the same name and that the ship *is* (metaphorically) the girl.'

to spiritual.[42] While Lethierry extols him to Déruchette as a fellow 'qui en vaut cent, qui sauve les inventions des autres, qui est une providence' (xii. 775), Gilliatt appears to her as a wild man, red-eyed and covered with hair, rags, lacerations, and blisters raised by the octopus. Like Quasimodo or Gwynplaine, the heroes of *Notre-Dame de Paris* and *L'Homme qui rit*, respectively, he is nothing less than 'hideux' (xii. 775), and Déruchette lodges the only form of protest possible under the circumstances: she faints.[43] Gilliatt, in turn, refuses to play the role of life-sucking monster, preferring instead to empty *himself* out in order to ensure her happiness. If 'la conscience est la ligne droite, la vie est le tourbillon' (xii. 781), then he need only continue to move under his own steam, as it were, in order to reach safe harbour.

He therefore effects yet another metamorphosis, this time on himself. 'Lui, l'obstacle, il se changeait en providence' (xii. 784) for the two lovers, enabling them to marry through a series of personal interventions and foresightful manœuvres on their behalf. Isabel Roche calls attention to 'Gilliatt's highly *paternal* role in organizing and effectuating the young couple's marriage, which is reminiscent of Jean Valjean's role in arranging the marriage of Cosette and Marius [in *Les Misérables*]'.[44] By removing the only impediment to their union, Gilliatt for ever alters their trajectory. But, as with his boat, to shift the 'obstacle' is to invite death by submersion—a glorious version of Clubin's ignominious fate. Immobile on his rock and facing towards France, much as Hugo had been photographed on 'le rocher des Proscrits' on Jersey, the dynamic Gilliatt seems doomed to a pathetically *static* end. While Gilliatt's struggles on *les Douvres* are also auto-referential—'could Hugo on his island ever forget that he was the Defiant Poet?'[45]—this death scene on yet another rock shifts the focus from the power of defiance to that of self-sacrifice.[46] His selfless effacement by drowning, that is, by asphyxiation, fulfils his destiny of being crushed or suffocated. Death in this manner would represent a

[42] Much of Gilliatt's earlier heroism, we might note, likewise represented a victory over himself: 'Il avait vaincu l'isolement, vaincu la faim, vaincu la soif, vaincu le froid, vaincu la fièvre, vaincu le travail, vaincu le sommeil' (xii. 517). Hugo also uses the compass as a metaphor for conscience in *MIS* (see *FT* 149–52, 241).

[43] As the characterization of Gilliatt suggests, he has transcended the normal social and human order: 'Transformed into a mythic figure by his experience, he is too great for any accommodation to this world' (Grant, *The Perilous Quest*, 197).

[44] Roche, *Character and Meaning*, 164; see also 100, 210 n. 44, and Paulson, 'L'*Anankè* des choses', 36.

[45] Brombert, *Victor Hugo and the Visionary Novel*, 151.

[46] For an extraordinary analysis of the last page of the text, see Jean-Pierre Montier, 'Le "Finale" des *Travailleurs de la mer*: Horizon et limite du texte romanesque', *Littérature*, 135 (2004), 3–23.

parody of the sublime moment, in which he would fill himself with the Other, in this case, water. However, the text indicates that, as his eye follows the movement of the boat carrying away the young couple, Gilliatt somehow re-enters the cosmic order on yet a higher plane. Like him, 'Tout ce bleu, en bas comme en haut, était immobile' (xii. 791). Even as he ceases to breathe, his eye—the hallmark of inner life and poetic vision—remains active. As Ricoeur observes, 'the self attests to itself [in abnegation] by the very movement with which it removes itself' (*OA* 340). Self-sacrifice is self-affirming.

Death may lead to nothingness; 'l'immense tranquilité de l'ombre [qui] montait dans l'œil profond de Gilliatt' (xii. 793) may merely signal the final stop in the voyage of existence. Or, it may imply the unspeakable, breathless transport into the sublime, that 'accablement du ravissement' (xii. 767) with which Gilliatt the lover—and Hugo the Romantic visionary—are already familiar. If, as Victor Brombert finds, 'immersion and submersion—with their connotation of plunging and sinking—become [in the novel] the metaphor of metaphorical inversion',[47] Gilliatt's death is not only a most fitting end to this hypertropic text; it may also be taken as a merely *figurative* passing. My reading supports Dominique Peyrache-Leborgne's argument that the 'fin ouverte' of *Les Travailleurs de la mer* participates in a wider Hugolian sublime that systematically inhabits 'cette frontière indécidable, entre tragique et utopie': 'la mort est toujours ambivalente chez Hugo; fin tragique, elle conduit cependant à la transfiguration et à la connaissance. Ultime étape avant l'union définitive avec le divin, elle oppose aux apories du réel un optimisme métaphysique.'[48] Gilliatt's physical disappearance heralds his apotheosis. Conveyed by metaphorical language, the sublime is the sign 'de la réversibilité des contraires, de l'impulsion dialectique vers le spirituel, et c'est à travers la notion de sacrifice que se réalise essentiellement ce retournement'.[49] Gilliatt's last leap into the unknown marks, so Hugo suggests, a new beginning.

For the poet still ensconced on his St Helena, defiance remains the order of the day. *His* stasis is movement. Ruined he may well be, not unlike Lethierry: 'Avoir été dans son pays l'homme idée, l'homme succès, l'homme révolution! y renoncer! abdiquer! N'être plus! faire rire! Etre un sac où il y a eu quelque chose! Etre le passé quand on a été l'avenir! . . . avoir été la lumière et subir l'éclipse!' (xii. 764) is nothing short of Hugo's living nightmare. To see despotism sweep away the glorious

[47] Brombert, *Victor Hugo and the Visionary Novel*, 144.

[48] Peyrache-Leborgne, 'Victor Hugo et le sublime', 27; see also Roche, *Character and Meaning*, 142, and Moutet, 'Concentration et dissolution', 380–2.

[49] Peyrache-Leborgne, 'Victor Hugo et le sublime', 23.

Second Republic, to risk reputation and fortune alike by fleeing abroad, is to share in Lethierry's existential angst. The image here of an empty sack is especially striking. 'Décroître... la diminution... [le] Rapetissement' (xii. 763)—such a fate awaits the victim not only of the octopus or of bankruptcy, but also of political exile. Along with Gilliatt, however, the self-styled 'last republican' outlaw refuses to capitulate to exhaustion or despair. As the narrator declares about Lethierry's despondency: 'Le désespoir, c'est presque la destitution de l'âme. Les très grands esprits seuls résistent. Et encore' (xii. 759). Through the allusion to genius, the text suggests that what the senescent Hugo may have lost 'en vigueur', he has, like the embattled protagonist on *les Douvres*, 'regagn[é] en ténacité' (xii. 704). His resistance, however circumscribed, is anything but passive.[50] The extent to which Hugo actively engages with the current political scene in the novel remains, though, to be seen. We now turn to the poet's account of his offensive and defensive operations in 'Vingtième siècle', which, I argue, further clarifies the allegorical aspects of *Les Travailleurs de la mer.*

Of Shipwrecks and Airships

Our analysis thus far has shown that the storyline of Hugo's novel serves as the vehicle for a well-honed, but occulted, political message regarding the ordeals—and possible triumphs—of the exile's resistance to the Second Empire. The identification of 'Vingtième siècle' as its poetic counterpart both supports such a reading and provides additional tools for interpretation. The precious steamboat that Gilliatt struggles to salvage is affiliated with the imagined wreck of another vessel, purportedly in neighbouring England, as well as with its soaring counterpart of the future. From its opening verses 'Pleine mer', the first poem of 'Vingtième siècle', paints a grim picture of the realities imposed by history on the pomp and glory of

[50] Cf. the closing lines of Alfred, Lord Tennyson's 'Ulysses' (1833; pub. 1842), in *Selected Poetry*, ed. Norman Page (London: Routledge, 1995), 70—a monologue by the ageing hero of the Trojan War:

> Tho' much is taken, much abides; and tho'
> We are not now that strength which in old days
> Moved earth and heaven, that which we are, we are;
> One equal temper of heroic hearts,
> Made weak by time and fate, but strong in will
> To strive, to seek, to find, and not to yield. (v. 65–70)

While it is impossible to know if Hugo (or François-Victor) had read the poem or been exposed to its last line, a well-known Victorian motto, the resemblance between Ulysses' attitude and that of the elderly poet is striking. We will examine further the issue of Hugo's—and Gilliatt's—will in the fourth section of this chapter.

bogus progress and illicit dominion.[51] Instead of the quasi-utopian realm of the Channel Islands, with its little fishing boats, we traverse a dystopic universe dominated by one enormous vessel. If 'Le dernier siècle a vu sur la Tamise | Croître un monstre à qui l'eau sans bornes fut promise' (x. 642), yesterday's dream of limitless power and domain is unveiled as but fruitless illusion. Marshalling a battery of grotesque terms to describe the sundry 'putréfactions' of this 'mystérieuse et difforme machine' (x. 642), Hugo indicts the waterlogged vessel and the world for which it stands:

> Léviathan; c'est là tout le vieux monde,
> Apre et démesuré dans sa fauve laideur;
> Léviathan, c'est là tout le passé: grandeur,
> Horreur. (x. 642)

While the mighty ship (of state), whose name alludes to Hobbes's celebrated treatise, roamed the seas at will, striking awe and terror in all who beheld it, it was nothing more than a *machine infernale* allied with the forces of evil:

> Sa vie intérieure était un incendie;
> . . . . .
> Et pour âme il avait dans sa cale un enfer. (x. 644)

Instead of liberating humanity from its material confines, technological advances had, in this case, led only to enslavement.

The machine–vessel thus sailed on unhampered, the creatures carried along with it existing as mere cogs in the wheels of false progress:

> L'esclavage, parquant les peuples pour la mort,
> Les enfermait au fond d'un cirque de frontières
> Où les gardaient la Guerre et la Nuit, bestiaires. (x. 645)

Isolated from the rest of the universe and trapped, like *les misérables*, by their own ignorance and servitude, those inscribed in this tiny universe were unable to expand their personal horizons:

> Nul moyen de franchir tant d'obstacles obscurs;
> Sitôt qu'on voulait croître, on rencontrait la barre
> D'une mode sauvage ou d'un dogme barbare;
> Et, quant à l'avenir, défense d'aller là. (x. 645)

The machine was, by all measures, free; its denizens were not. Even dreams of the future were banished, along with all hope for change. The nightmare of totalitarian rules offers no exit.

[51] In this respect, *La Légende des siècles* (hereafter *LS*) inherits substantially from the scathing satire of Napoléon III's corrupt (and decaying) empire in *CHAT*.

But, according to the poet, time can ease all distress: 'La mer a ses écueils cachés, le temps aussi' (x. 644). Hugo's historical 'retrospective' does not include details of *Léviathan*'s demise. It is simply carried away by forces larger than itself:

> Le vent de l'infini sur ce monde souffla.
> Il a sombré . . .
>
> . . . . .
>
> Qu'est-ce que le simoun a fait du grain de sable?
> Cela fut. C'est passé. Cela n'est plus ici. (x. 645)

Viewing the colossal smugness of the Second Empire from the perspective of future time—the realm of the infinite—Hugo indicates his faith that the current regime in France is destined to an ignominious end. Some reef somewhere has Napoléon III's name on it. The twentieth century will have nothing but disdain for this once majestic construct long since fallen into ruin.

The message is clear. As Pierre Laforgue argues, the humanist myth of Progress crumbles in 'Pleine mer': 'Le XIXe siècle avec en son milieu la plaie du Deux-Décembre n'a pas tenu les promesses du XVIe, mais les a ruinées.'[52] One must instead look to the future—to the glorious new world that now stands revealed to the poet—to find the promise fulfilled. Here the degenerate state of the Second Empire will give way to an authentically human way of being. In 'Plein ciel', which Jean Gaudon deems 'le poème le plus follement optimiste qu'ait écrit Hugo',[53] he goes on to elaborate his vision of humanity as a glorious 'navire en marche . . . Dans l'éther sublime' (x. 647), loosed from all earthly constraints and climbing inexorably into the infinite. Its name, *Délivrance*, indicates the limitless horizons that will open up to this 'marcheur de l'infini' (x. 652) that will escape the wilderness for the Promised Land. Contrary to the ponderous monster *Léviathan*, *Délivrance* escapes gravity by leaps and bounds: 'Oh! chacun de ses pas conquiert l'illimité!' (x. 657). In its ascension along the vertical axis of the sublime, it represents humanity's age-old dream of realizing all its possibilities, beyond the burdens of war, pestilence, and famine. As in *Notre-Dame de Paris*, the poet highlights his fascination with the synergistic relationship between science and art.[54] Combining 'le calcul de Newton' and 'l'ode de Pindare' (x. 648), 'le chiffre et le songe' (x. 650)—not unlike the union of 'une loi de géométrie' and 'une loi de poésie' (iv. 137) in the earlier novel, Hugo's audacious vessel is

[52] Laforgue, *Victor Hugo et La Légende des siècles*, 292.

[53] Jean Gaudon, *Le Temps de la contemplation*, 35. See also Bernard Leuilliot, 'La Loi des tempêtes', in Jacques Seebacher and Anne Ubersfeld (eds), *Hugo le fabuleux: Actes du Colloque de Cerisy, 30 juin–10 juillet 1985* (Paris: Seghers, 1985), 94.

[54] See *EN* 166–9, 196–206.

able to 'vaincre ce qui n'a ni fin, ni bord, ni fond' (x. 650) to found a free, enlightened, universal community.[55]

In this way, the mission of *Délivrance* is as much political as intellectual:

> Il civilise. O gloire ! Il ruine, il flétrit
> Tout l'affreux passé qui s'effare;
> Il abolit la loi de fer, la loi de sang,
> Les glaives, les carcans, l'esclavage...
>
> . . . . .
>
> Tous les spoliateurs et tous les corrupteurs
> S'en vont; et les faux jours sur les fausses hauteurs... (x. 655–6)

Once again, Hugo forecasts the inglorious end to Napoléon III's regime represented by the shipwreck of 'Pleine mer'. The vile usurper of the Second Republic will be replaced by the soaring 'usurpateur sacré, vainqueur béni' (x. 657) that transcends the frontiers of space and time.[56] The metaphorical redescription in 'Vingtième siècle' of past and future history transports the reader *elsewhere*, while offering a commentary on present-day France. The poem can thus be considered the temporal counterpart of the spatial defamiliarization in 'L'Archipel de la Manche'.[57]

In *Les Travailleurs de la mer*, Hugo returns patently to the imagery of 'Vingtième siècle' through the extended metaphor of the shipwrecked *Durande*. The divergent images associated with *Léviathan* and *Délivrance* coalesce in the narrator's descriptions of Lethierry's stranded steamboat. On the one hand, the marvellous 'chaudière toute-puissante' (xii. 764) that connects the Channel Islands with the French mainland in the 1820s stands with the twentieth-century airship of 'Plein ciel' as an unambiguous symbol of technological progress. Not only has the steamer brought prosperity to Lethierry; it is also 'la fortune du pays' (xii. 601), which has profited immensely from the ability to transport its cattle. On the other hand, the depiction of the *Durande* taps into the treasury of grotesque imagery that marks *Léviathan*. It appears in port, at least to the ignorant villagers, as 'on ne sait quel masse informe, une silhouette

[55] The political connection is all the more evident in the light of Hugo's declaration, in *WS*: 'De 89 est sortie la Délivrance, et de 93 la Victoire' (xii. 307).

[56] Cf. Porter, who likewise considers that the poem 'uses the image of a dirigible... to symbolize how material progress can lead to the conquest of the unknown' (*Victor Hugo*, 119), a journey at once moral, spiritual, epistemological, and poetic.

[57] A variation on multiple temporal perspectives can be found several years later in *MIS*, where the narrator's litany of ancient civilizations long since vanished—India, Chaldea, Persia, Assyria, Egypt, Babylon, Nineveh, Tarsus, Thebes, Rome (xi. 710)—adumbrates the fall of the Second Empire. By the same token, the revolutionary leader Enjolras's shining dream of France's future in 'Quel horizon on voit du haut de la barricade' (v. 1. 5) looks forward to the day when human potential will be unleashed (see *FT* 212–13, 233–5).

monstrueuse qui sifflait et crachait, une chose horrible qui râlait comme une bête et qui fumait come un volcan, une espèce d'hydre bavant dans l'écume et . . . se ruant vers la ville avec . . . une gueule d'où sortait de la flamme' (xii. 578). The resemblance of the *Durande* to the image of the 'ancien monde' in 'Pleine mer' is remarkable. The hideous, fire-breathing steamboat recalls, at least superficially, that construct

> Sur qui le mal, flot vil, crachait sa bave infâme,
> Plein de fumée, . . . mû par une hydre de flamme,
> La Haine . . . (x. 645)

As if the point might be lost on the reader, the narrator goes on to add that some islanders saw in Lethierry's *Bateau-Diable* an instrument of false progress: 'Cette bête de feu et de fer ne ressemblait-elle pas à Léviathan?' (xii. 579), they wonder. The answer impugns their puritanical insularity and backwardness: 'Ce n'est pas la première fois que l'ascension du progrès est qualifiée retour au chaos' (xii. 579). The steamer is Lethierry's labour of love, a means of commerce and communication rather than of 'Hate' and discord.[58]

Nevertheless, like *Léviathan*, the *Durande* founders on one of life's 'écueils cachés' (x. 644)—in this case a desolate Channel reef—thus setting in motion Gilliatt's heroic efforts to salvage the engine from the wrecked hull now jammed between the rocks above.[59] 'La Durande était tout le contraire d'un navire coulé à fond; c'était un navire accroché en l'air' (xii. 671): suspended between sea and sky where it is buffeted by wind and tide alike, the boat neither sinks nor flies but rather strikes a balance between the opposing destinies of the two vessels in 'Vingtième siècle'. Providing a 'trait d'union' between the two rocky pillars on *les Douvres*, the wrecked *Durande* spells out a giant 'H majuscule' (xii. 670)—an echo of the front view of Notre Dame Cathedral widely identified with the novelist—that points to Hugo himself.[60] Yet, within the context of this description, the clever self-reference seems little more than a typical Hugolian joke. Or does

[58] David Charles's assertion that '*Durande* ou *Léviathan*, c'est bien le même bateau' (*La Pensée technique*, 82) is, in my view, only partly correct, since Hugo invests Lethierry's invention with much more positive connotations as well.

[59] Others have pointed out the relationship between Hugo's own salvific efforts in *Les Contemplations* (hereafter *CONT*) with regard to the deceased Léopoldine and Gilliatt's striving to preserve the *Durande*/Déruchette (xii. 586; see, e.g., Bernard, '"Les Travailleurs de la mer"', 38). While the assonant coupling of *Durande* and **D**éruchette could well refer to the lost **D**idine as well, I believe that it might also allude to Hugo's more recent grief over his other daughter **D**éd**é** (Adèle II; 1830–1915), who by the early 1860s had irrevocably sunk (*sombré*) into madness.

[60] Cf. Jean Maurel's argument, based on Hugo's lifelong predilection for puns, that the self-signalling device can be found as early as *HI*, 'le livre de ce petit sauvage à la **hache** de pierre tournoyante' (*Victor Hugo philosophe* (Paris: Presses Universitaires de France, 1985), 30; emphasis added).

the teasing about authorship/authority (if not the risks of writing on water) camouflage more weighty matters?

While the *Durande* plainly combines features of *Délivrance* and *Léviathan*, its political implications are far less obvious. As we have seen, *Léviathan* and *Délivrance* represent alternative futures for the French nation, the former, a state that enslaves humanity, and the latter, one that liberates it. In contrast, the *Durande*'s narrative function appears much more mechanical, both literally and figuratively. A machine that requires human agents to harness its energy becomes a pawn in a complicated plot of betrayal (by Clubin) and redemption (by Gilliatt). In this way, the positive and negative roles played in 'Vingtième siècle' by *Délivrance* and *Léviathan*, respectively, are mapped in *Les Travailleurs de la mer* to Gilliatt and Clubin. The repeating pattern extends from poem to narrative and from objects to personages. Still, however great the differences between these two characters as *moral* agents, their adventures on a solitary atoll seem at first glance far removed from the *political* arena. Hugo's villain dies drowned in the 'arms' of an octopus well before the hero's arrival; and Gilliatt's epic struggle to transform his bleak surroundings into a salvage workshop while battling the elements—including the octopus and a hurricane—celebrates the triumph of creative genius over the material world. Perhaps the *Durande*'s resemblance to the vessels in 'Pleine mer' and 'Plein ciel' is, in the end, mere coincidence, given the lack of political references and the focus on the power of poetic vision in the rest of the novel.[61] From this perspective, the potential of the text for historical refiguration—aside from its rather charming portrayal of a remote section of the United Kingdom in the 1820s—would appear to be minimal.

Though the hypothesis is tempting, several clues lead the reader to look more closely at Hugo's text. In the first place, Clubin's unanticipated death by submersion curiously echoes the watery fate of *Léviathan*. Like the grand vessel, which 'pour âme . . . avait dans sa cale un enfer', Clubin's outward integrity masks an inner horror. Following Hugo's metaphorical filiation, the lifelong hypocrisy of this 'monstre en dessous[,] [qui] vivait dans une peau d'homme de bien avec un cœur de bandit' (xii. 648), recalls the pretensions to probity of Louis-Napoléon Bonaparte, similarly satirized in *Les Misérables*.[62] Thus, the one's lifelong knavery, which culminates in the 'savant naufrage' of the *Durande*, constitutes a reading of the other's 1851 *coup d'état*: 'Clubin, dès sa jeunesse, avait eu une idée . . .

[61] Thus, for Grant, when Gilliatt 'enters into the world of natural forces, where social considerations are stripped away, a nearly pure mythic adventure emerges' (*The Perilous Quest*, 189).

[62] See *FT* 85 n., 252.

passer pour homme probe et partir de là, attendre sa belle... deviner le moment; ne pas tâtonner, saisir; faire un coup et n'en faire qu'un, finir par une rafle, laisser derrière lui les imbéciles' (xii. 648). Clubin's financial chicanery gestures towards the devious president of the Second Republic, his duplicity, gamesmanship, and utter ruthlessness capturing, for Hugo, the essence of the French emperor. If the 'embrasement intérieur de cette âme' (xii. 648) corresponds to the hidden evil in *Léviathan*, Clubin's exultation in realizing a complex scheme of betrayal and theft paints a repulsive reflection of and on the proud, egomaniacal 'despote gêné', that 'traître' whose 'petitesse' is capable of 'énormité' (xii. 649), namely, 'Napoléon le Petit'. When Hugo continues, 'L'hypocrite est un titan, nain' (xii. 649), the connection to his arch-enemy is complete.[63]

But, if the ability to remove his mask at long last constitutes a 'délivrance' (xii. 649), Clubin's triumph is short-lived. The 'hidden reef' in *Les Travailleurs de la mer* is arguably not the wrong shoal on which he mistakenly rams the *Durande* but the octopus, that even greater con artist, lurking in the depths of the sea.[64] Like Clubin, the octopus is described as a sneaky master of the ambush: 'La pieuvre, c'est l'hypocrite. On n'y fait pas attention; brusquement, elle s'ouvre' (xii. 741; see also 744, 747). Another Thénardier, himself a figure for the tyrant–impostor in *Les Misérables*, the creature combines force and cunning to overwhelm its unsuspecting victims. Clubin's end is deeply ironic: 'Il y a des cavernes dans l'hypocrite, ou pour mieux dire, l'hypocrite entier est une caverne,' Hugo explains. 'Quand Clubin se trouva seul, son antre s'ouvrit. Il eut un instant de délices; il aéra son âme. Il respira son crime à pleine poitrine' (xii. 649). What the villainous captain does not anticipate is that a more treacherous creature awaits the opportunity to burst forth from its own (underwater) cavern, where 'aeration' swiftly turns to suffocation. Elaborating on the earlier message in 'Pleine mer', Hugo implies that the emperor is fated to outwit himself, falling when he least expects it.

Just as Clubin's character carries the negative sociopolitical connotations of the 'sinistre vaisseau' (x. 643) in 'Pleine mer', much of the positive imagery surrounding *Léviathan*'s counterpart in 'Plein ciel' recurs in relation to Gilliatt. Not that Hugo's hero can actually fly up into the heavens like

[63] Exploiting the opportunity to lambaste the emperor anew, Hugo develops at length this psychological portrait of Louis-Napoléon as supreme hypocrite, referring obliquely to his 'trône', his 'mauvais règne', and his Faustian pact—'l'hypocrisie est une avance; Satan le remboursa' (xii. 650)—as an indictment of the Second Empire. Cf. Roman, 'Les Îles anglo-normandes', 229, and Revol-Marzouk, *Le Sphinx et l'Abîme*, 279–80.

[64] Cf. Pierre Albouy, *La Création mythologique chez Victor Hugo* (Paris: José Corti, 1963), 275; Bernard, '"Les Travailleurs de la mer"', 33; Brombert, *Victor Hugo and the Visionary Novel*, 160–1; Charles, *La Pensée technique*, 101; and Revol-Marzouk, *Le Sphinx et l'abîme*, 279–81.

Délivrance: what soars is his boundless imagination, which enables him to transcend the limits of the humanly possible. His goal—'délivrer [la Durande]' (xii. 674) from its imprisonment by *les Douvres*—at first seems unattainable. Physically, mentally, and spiritually, he must go where no human has ever gone. When he manages to scale the higher Douvre in an attempt to find shelter before commencing his labours, we learn that 'jamais rien que d'ailé n'avait posé le pied là' (xii. 681). The seaman who defies gravity thus joins the winged *Délivrance* as a vehicle with a 'higher' mission.

Other motifs intersect to connect Gilliatt to the 'char merveilleux' (x. 648) envisioned in 'Vingtième siècle'. First, both demonstrate the triumph of creative activity that combines science and art, 'le chiffre et le songe' (x. 650). We learn early on that Gilliatt is 'l'homme du songe. De là ses audaces, de là aussi ses timidités. Il avait ses idées à lui' (xii. 569). A true 'original', he draws inspiration and solace from his rêveries, turning them into practical innovations. Thus, from the outset of his two-month ordeal on the reef, Gilliatt enters a dream state that enables him to use all his mental resources in solving the engineering problems posed by the shipwreck: 'Tant qu'il dormait, il croyait veiller et vivre; quand il se réveillait, il croyait dormir. En effet, il était désormais dans un songe' (xii. 684). Through the conjunction of imagination and technology, both hero and airship represent the power of purposeful, industrious labour in the service of selfless dreams. It is no accident that the burst of activity on the atoll by Hugo's *homo faber* mirrors that on the bridge of *Délivrance*:

> L'homme y fourmille, l'homme invincible y flamboie;
> Point d'armes; un fier bruit de puissance et de joie;
> Le cri vertigineux de l'exploration! (x. 650)

Steadfast effort in the name of an ideal, Hugo argues in both texts, is the most productive work of all. Equally important is his emphasis in 'Plein ciel' on the notion of exploration, which plays a crucial role in *Les Travailleurs de la mer* as well. In fiction as in poetry, the heuristic function of metaphor, which has the power 'to break... old categorization[s], in order to establish new logical frontiers', creates an 'experience of reality in which invention and discovery cease being opposed' (*RM* 197, 246). Dreams and action, poetry and politics, reflect each other as keys to the revealed universe.

To this end, Gilliatt echoes *Délivrance* by harnessing even the harshest conditions to further useful flights of fancy. The vessel makes use of every wind from gust to tempest to continue its upward climb:

> Qu'importe le moment! qu'importe la saison!
>
> . . . . .
>
> Qu'importe! Il va. Tout souffle est bon; simoun, mistral! (x. 651)

Gilliatt, too, channels the forces of nature to his own ends. Locating a cavern in the rock too windy for habitation, he decides to turn it into a forge: 'Se faire servir par l'obstacle est un grand pas vers le triomphe. Le vent était l'ennemi de Gilliatt, Gilliatt entreprit d'en faire son valet' (xii. 687). His conversion of the drafty niche from 'enemy' to 'servant' again draws on both art and science, a metaphorical imagination seconded by superior engineering skills.[65] To tame the excessive blasts of air, he diverts another inconvenience, a constant trickle of water into the cavern: 'Gilliatt songea à se servir de cette eau pour discipliner ce vent' (xii. 687). With the elements under his control, 'maître de l'air, de l'eau et du feu' (xii. 688), he becomes a kind of mythical alchemist, able to bid nature to fulfil his commands.[66]

As such, he is impervious to the notion of insuperable tasks. When it seems that 'Gilliatt fût au pied de ce mur: l'impossible' (xii. 698) because he risks breaking the machinery into pieces in attempting to dismantle it, he is no more perplexed than when he encounters the 'sombre *Non possumus*' (xii. 702) of cosmic forces that resist his efforts and sap his life energy. He endures—and triumphs over—every ordeal that comes his way, a modern 'Job Prométhée' (xii. 704) who counters the hostility that surrounds him with brilliant inventiveness and sheer perseverance: 'L'épuisement des forces n'épuise pas la volonté. Croire n'est que la deuxième puissance; vouloir est la première' (xii. 704). To be useful, ideas must be infused by the will to realize them. Reinventing through a kind of 'rêverie curieuse' (xii. 699) the mechanical device of a nameless sixteenth-century carpenter, Giliatt succeeds in lowering the *Durande*'s engine into his own boat by an ingenious combination of the resources at hand: 'C'était une étrange collaboration de toutes les forces naturelles, soumises. D'un côté, la gravitation, apportant la machine; de l'autre, la marée, apportant la barque... L'élément recevait un ordre et l'exécutait' (xii. 712).[67] His indomitable will

[65] According to Pierre-André Rieben, 'En rattachant explicitement la science à la *rêverie* [et] à l'*intuition*, Hugo rend également à la création humaine son unité, en refusant le partage schématique entre raison et sentiment qui domine la conception habituelle de la science, de l'art, et de leurs rapports respectifs... Ce rapprochement suggère, lui aussi, une contiguïté inhabituelle entre les deux univers traditionnellement considérés comme distincts de l'art et de la technique' (*Délires romantiques: Musset, Nodier, Gautier, Hugo* (Paris: José Corti, 1989) 147; see also 170).

[66] The point is reiterated several chapters later: 'Il avait pour combustible l'épave, l'eau pour moteur, le vent pour souffleur, une pierre pour enclume, pour art son instinct, pour puissance sa volonté' (xii. 697). Gilliatt again bends fire, water, and wind to his will with the help of an innate sense of creativity (much as Hugo weaves numerous metaphorical analogies in the text between the animal, vegetable, and mineral domains). The Shakespearean echoes of such prowess will become clearer below.

[67] Hugo elaborates on the genius of 'ordinary' people in *WS*, where he praises the nameless, voiceless, unknown inventors who have made huge contributions to human progress without being recognized by official versions of history: 'Dans cette histoire il y a

continually bends nature to his command—a subject to which we will return in the final section of this chapter. Tapping into cosmic powers that transcend his own, Gilliatt illustrates in human terms the soaring *Délivrance*.

Political Monsters

These gifts serve Gilliatt especially well during his twenty-hour battle with the wild hurricane that threatens to unravel his weeks of arduous toil and his subsequent encounter with the octopus, scenes that continue to reveal the thread of Hugo's political thought. Following the poet into voluntary exile, Gilliatt prevails, at least symbolically, over the usurper of the Second Republic, in the various forms assumed by perfidy and hypocrisy in the text: first, the hurricane, then, the octopus. All along, nature has stacked the cards against him in a 'duel louche dans lequel il y a un traître' (xii. 703)—an allusion to both Clubin and Louis-Napoléon that becomes increasingly explicit. Now he dares to defy the raging winds, those 'tyrans des lieux inconnus' that enforce 'la dictature du chaos' (xii. 720), as well as the madly dashing waves whose foam resembles 'la salive d'un léviathan' (xii. 730), further references to the Second Empire. The worse the storm gets, the more his strategy becomes to 'faire la part à la tempête', to use his tools not just to fight but to 'aider le vent' (xii. 733). For example, he barricades his loaded boat behind a section of the *Durande*'s detached bow, so that 'la lame, en frappant dessus, était comme le marteau qui enfonce le clou, et l'appuyait au rocher et le consolidait' (xii. 728). Once more, an 'enemy' is turned into a 'servant', thanks to the marriage of science and art.[68] As with *Délivrance*, the hero's association with cosmic forces carries a political message: 'Il semble que l'Océan, qui est un despote, puisse être, lui aussi, mis à la raison par des barricades' (xii. 727). When Gilliatt stands astride his improvised breakwater and dares the tempest to sweep both him and the fruit of his labours away, he defies on behalf of Hugo himself not just 'la légitimité d'un ancien régime des forces naturelles'[69] but the despotic powers that be.[70] Through extended

tout, excepté l'histoire . . . La civilisation date par règnes et non par progrès . . . derrière le lourd décor des hérédités royales, la mystérieuse dynastie des génies est à peine entrevue' (xii. 319).

[68] Cf. Rieben, *Délires romantiques*, 145.

[69] Paulson, 'L'*Anankè* des choses', 35; see also 37.

[70] Cf. Georges Piroué, who describes Gilliatt's duel with the storm as a struggle 'contre le mal absolu incarné, tantôt aveugle et stupide, tantôt au contraire astucieux et pervers' (*Lui, Hugo* (Paris: Denoël, 1985), 48)—an apt image for Hugo of Louis-Napoléon Bonaparte. If Clubin's brief triumph bursts forth as an 'orage joyeux' (xii. 648), then Gilliatt symbolically

metaphor, the novelist depicts his own courageous part in recent history—a part that he then refigures or reinscribes within universal time (see *TN* iii. 127).

Both protagonist and airborne vessel thus epitomize the spirit of human 'Audace', which, the poet claims in 'Plein ciel', requires only a sail in the wind or a board on the sea 'Pour vaincre ce qui n'a ni fin, ni bord, ni fond, | Pour dompter le vent, trombe, et l'écume, avalanche' (x. 648). The *Délivrance* slips its earthly mooring to reach the stars. Gilliatt must likewise dominate wind, waterspout, and watery avalanches to protect his salvaging project from the hurricane. If, in its multiplicity, wind alone represents 'le démon Légion', the combined forces of nature concentrated in the hurricane offer an almost unimaginable challenge: 'Avoir affaire à une tourmente, c'est avoir affaire à toute la mer et à tout le ciel' (xii. 722). The enemy's resources are apparently inexhaustible—a mark, here, of the metonymical sublime, since the trials just go on and on. But the hero's ingenuity, like the poet's, is more than equal to the call. In this way, Gilliatt's ability to escape through imaginative invention the severe material limits of recovering a shipwreck from a barren reef parallels Hugo's efforts to transcend his own constraints through literary creation. Pushing back the frontiers of 'the impossible', the sublimely monstrous hero redefines the boundaries of what is humanly possible. Though utterly alone, armed with little more than wits and sinew, Gilliatt is hardly helpless. Rather, he makes use of everything at hand, not unlike Robinson Crusoe—or the 'defenceless', disabled, disenfranchised poet. Just as Hugo turns 'worthless' fictive words into anti-imperial bombshells, his protagonist taps into every resource available to launch his assault on the wreck and to protect his labours from attack by outside forces.[71]

But Gilliatt never hesitates in his relentless striving to outmanœuvre a more powerful enemy: 'D'un côté l'intarissable, de l'autre l'infatigable' (xii. 734). As in the confrontation of David and Goliath, he engages in the struggle of 'Nothing against Everything' that ends in the triumph of superior wits. Indeed, the hurricane itself supplies the force necessary to defeat it. The gale may well be a 'génie' (xii. 733); Gilliatt uses its own 'ideas' to deliver the final blow. When the storm reaches its paroxysm, the

vanquishes the fictive villain in the tempest and, through him, the very real one on the throne.

[71] Cf. Piroué's insightful comparison of Gilliatt and Crusoe (*Victor Hugo romancier, ou les dessus de l'inconnu* (Paris: Denoël, 1964), 40). Yves Gohin notes the textual dialogue as well: 'L'épopée de Gilliatt est bien sûr, pour une part, la récréation du mythe de Robinson' ('Introduction [to *Les Travailleurs de la mer*]', in Victor Hugo, *Notre-Dame de Paris: 1482* et *Les Travailleurs de la mer*, ed. Jacques Seebacher and Yves Gohin (Paris: Pléïade-Gallimard, 1975), 1279). Cf. also Roman, 'Les Îles anglo-normandes', 236.

semi-destruction of the *Durande*'s wreck facilitates the construction of a fifth improvised barricade to protect the engine, one that proves impenetrable. 'L'ouragan, aveugle, avait travaillé à cette barricade dernière' (xii. 734), the 'toils' of the storm in the end assuring victory to its more adroit adversary. In his triumph, Gilliatt reveals himself to be even more cunning than 'le mal absolu incarné'.[72] Having cut the tempest down to size, he mocks the thunderhead as a 'cruche' (xii. 735)—both a 'pitcher' from which he can drink and a 'blockhead' that he can fool. And the narrator adds: 'C'est une joie ironique pour l'intelligence combattante de constater la vaste stupidité des forces furieuses aboutissant à des services rendus, et Gilliatt sentait cet immémorial besoin d'insulter son ennemi, qui remonte aux héros d'Homère' (xii. 735). The more pressure he exerts on the exiled poet, Hugo suggests, the more Napoléon III may *unwittingly* be doing him 'favours' by mobilizing the full range of his mental and verbal powers. Historians, by definition, refigure history by choosing and interpreting a certain range of subject matter; poets, it would appear, refigure history simply by resisting and rising above it.

Even when the hurricane, that 'bête, [qui] vient boire à l'océan; succion inouïe' (xii. 721), metamorphoses into the multi-pronged octopus, it meets more than its match in the intrepid seaman. Joining Clubin and the emperor as one of the 'sinistres patiences embusquées dans l'abîme' (xii. 744), the nightmarish creature endeavours to smother Gilliatt and to suck him dry but ends up decapitated instead: 'La pompe aspirante détruite, le vide se défit' (xii. 745). For all his treachery, Napoléon III is as fundamentally vacuous as the deflated storm—or as the dangerous but empty-headed airbag that patrols the seas. He may even be a big enough 'blockhead', so the text implies, to share the ignominious fate of Louis XVI. When Gilliatt looks up at the night sky after his labours and sees 'au lieu de César, Dieu' (xii. 752), the reader understands that through him Hugo symbolically vanquishes his own imperial nemesis, along with the other's 'legions' of unthinking supporters.

Monsters like the octopus or Napoléon III 'touchent à la frontière humaine et peuplent la limite chimérique' (xii. 743); moral and spiritual *audace* easily carries one beyond, into utopian realms. To dare to counter the freaks of nature and culture is to be transported into new realms of being. The 'skills of the toilers of the sea become emblematic of heroic revolutionary achievement'[73]—not just in relation to France's past, but also in relation to its future. 'Quelle révolution!' Lethierry exclaims when Gilliatt returns his machine. 'Avoir été cherché ma gueuse de machine! En

[72] Piroué, *Lui, Hugo*, 48.
[73] Brombert, *Victor Hugo and the Visionary Novel*, 148.

pleine mer! dans ce guet-apens d'écueil! . . . C'est pis que la Bastille!' (xii. 771). Beneath the comic portrait of the old seaman, the reminder of all the ambushes Gilliatt has endured and outmanœuvred, along with the allusions to French revolutionary action, challenges the reader to be equally clever and audacious. As Hugo demonstrates through his epic tale, only humans can make salvific gestures: nature and machines are incapable of self-sacrifice, of becoming Prometheus or Job (cf. *TN* ii. 80). And only humans can persevere to bring forth a new, *republican* regime—the social equivalent of Gilliatt's 'mise en liberté' (xii. 713) of the *Durande*.[74] 'By [enduring], initiative is clothed with an ethical signification that announces the more specifically political and cosmopolitan characterization of the historical present' (*TN* iii. 233): simply by carrying out the intention to act, one enters the moral and sociopolitical realms.

In sum, the correspondence surrounding the preface puts a political spin on Gilliatt's superhuman adventures by investing the multiple forces of nature that he confronts with the negative connotations of Hugo's enemies. So, when Gilliatt undertakes to defeat wind, tide, tempest, and octopus, each representing a manifold danger, he figures the poet's struggles with 'the Bonapartists, the neoclassicists, the sanctimonious, and those *republicans pleasing to the police*' (xiii. 759) in attempting to publish his novel: 'Une immense mauvaise volonté entourait Gilliatt . . . Il subissait l'oppression d'un ensemble épuisant . . . C'était presque quelqu'un . . . Il ne tenait qu'à lui de fuir, mais puisqu'il restait, il avait affaire à l'hostilité impénétrable . . . La coalition des forces obscures l'environnait' (xii. 702–3). The hero's battle against the assembled forces of darkness is plainly Hugo's own. In rescuing the *Durande*, he is as single-minded as the novelist in his devotion to a presumably hopeless mission. 'Fanaticism' breeds, in each case, daring deeds and acts of genius.

Opposing tyranny with every fibre of his being, Hugo unmasks the hypocrisy of Napoléon III through such treacherous villains as Clubin and the octopus, while providing a model of single-minded heroism. His

[74] As Gohin points out, it was not difficult for the readers of Hugo's pamphlet *Napoléon le Petit* or of *CHAT* to find 'dans le crime de Clubin (traîtrise, guet-apens) l'équivalent du coup du 2 décembre, et dans le sauvetage de la Durande l'histoire prochaine du rétablissement de la République' ('Introduction', 1268). Gilliatt's 'résurrection de la Durande' (xii. 776) thus joins an array of similar images in *MIS* that point towards the rebirth of the French Republic. That Hugo's hero also saves Ebenezer, Déruchette's future beloved, from drowning ('Je vous reconnais. C'est vous qui m'avez sauvé la vie' (xii. 783)); preserves the couple's happiness by selflessly enabling them to marry ('On se laisse faire à qui sauve' (xii. 783); 'ce Gilliatt, la catastrophe d'hier, le salut d'aujourd'hui' (ii. 787)); and 'resurrects' Lethierry by rescuing his engine ('J'étais par terre, aplati, mort. Il me remet debout sur mes quatre fers!' (xii. 772))—all these 'salvage' projects ally him with Jean Valjean as a model of the republican ideal (see *FT* 162–3, 173, 188–201).

disclaimer to Paul Meurice notwithstanding, Hugo gestures beyond the text to speak to the political 'moment' by systematically blurring the boundaries between reality and fiction.[75] According to Tony James, for example, the chapters on sleep (I. 1. 7; 'A Maison visionnée habitant visionnaire') and on Gilliatt's discovery of the subterranean cavern (II. 1. 13; 'Ce qu'on y voit et ce qu'on y entrevoit') represent 'poetic, fictional attempts to render mimetically the glimpsings of another world, the mystery of the process of "concretion", and the hybrid, phantasmagorical nature of the resulting "monsters"'. This transformational process that unites opposites and turns one thing into another is, of course, metaphor itself. At the same time, the poet's reflections on 'the creation of monsters and their relation to the real and the possible'[76] enable us to glimpse that improbable but all too real *political* monster, Napoléon III. Beneath all the fanfare regarding progress lies the message that history may well be moving in the wrong direction.[77]

To some, the nothingness of writing may seem a 'passive' mode of resistance. Writing is, after all, just a sequence of words, mere air, without substance. But the insistence throughout the novel on Gilliatt's ability to harness the wind—whether by playing the bagpipes or fabricating a bellows or capitalizing on the energy of the hurricane—points to Hugo's own gift for words and his belief in their unleashed power. Indeed, given his well-known predilection for puns, we might read Gilliatt's forceful *souffle* and well-engineered *soufflet* as emblems of poetic inspiration and outrage, a divine *afflatus* rife with political energy. Like the breath of God in the Creation, it moves the world into new being.[78] As Hugo puts it even more baldly in *Les Misérables*, regarding the fate of the most infamous tyrants and usurpers, 'les faiseurs d'exemples . . . soufflettent plus utilement, en présence du genre humain, [l']ignominie sans réplique'

[75] Sainte-Beuve himself recognized Hugo's tenaciously aggressive stance: 'M. Hugo n'est pas seulement un exilé, c'est un combattant. Il est dans son île, comme Éole, il y fait la guerre, comme Sentus Pompée' (*Mes Poisons*, 62).

[76] James, *Dream, Creativity, and Madness*, 206, 208.

[77] Cf. Brombert's observation that Lethierry's steam engine 'is saved not by modern means but by primitive skills . . . Progress is in fact repeatedly seen as moving in a problematic, if not a nefarious direction' (*Victor Hugo and the Visionary Novel*, 149). As the critic shows, the 'dissatisfaction with the order of reality . . . and the aspiration to brighter worlds' correspond to the view of creation as an ongoing 'project', one that echoes the 'divinely enacted antithesis of good and evil'. At the same time, I argue that what Brombert identifies as 'cosmic moral struggle' (p. 161), with its continual inversions and reversals, is the ethical counterpart of metaphorical process.

[78] Brombert, *Victor Hugo and the Visionary Novel*, 156, connects this motif of divine inspiration with passages in both Hugo's early poem 'La Pente de la rêverie' (*Feuilles d'automne*) and *QVT*. (One might also consider its affiliation with the image of the Aeolian harp in English Romantic literature.)

(xi. 745). The irrepressible satirical impulse of exile—running from the journalism of *Histoire d'un crime* (1851; pub. 1877) and *Napoléon le Petit* to the poetic vituperation of *Châtiments* to the hypertropic prose of *Les Misérables*—reappears in the macrometaphorical system of *Les Travailleurs de la mer* as well. His work represents nothing less than the republican labourer's fist—a literary *bras d'honneur* that counters the menacing 'poing' of both the octopus and the storm—raised against despotism. Through Gilliatt, that 'Job combattant et faisant front aux fléaux' (xii. 704), he issues a call to *le peuple* by offering an image of their *possible* heroic selves.

So long as the old windbag has breath in him, Hugo now implies, he will continue to pursue from his rock-barricade 'cette lutte de Rien contre Tout, cette Iliade à un' (xii. 752), in order to thwart the manœuvres of Louis-Napoléon and his partisans and, ultimately, to unseat 'le pirate douceureux' (xii. 648) at the helm of his nation.[79] The final transposition to be operated by this 'unique... [writing] machine' will not be metaphorical but political, when Napoléon III at last assumes the poet's place in exile. For Hugo, there could be no more glorious instance of trading places. As one of the prodigiously creative 'hommes océans' (xii. 159) extolled in *William Shakespeare,* his apparent defencelessness masks inexhaustible power. Along with the ocean—or the wind—he is both the One *and* the Many, diversity in unity, the voice of the multitude, the inexorable turning tide that will sweep away the phony Second Empire. Whatever the literary fate of his book, effecting this present displacement will be one of his most glorious *œuvres*. Counting himself, then, among *les travailleurs de la mer*, Hugo figures through Gilliatt's story his own dynamism, verbal ingenuity, and stubborn striving to salvage that other precious vehicle of progress, the republican ship of state, from the despotic powers that had usurped it.[80]

[79] Hugo's contemporaries had often described him in language related to the notions of *souffle* and *vent,* not always in the most laudatory terms. For example, the right-wing journalist Louis Veuillot evokes Hugo in his role as conservative representative to the Legislative Assembly in 1849 as 'en scène, avec une mémoire sûre et des poumons pleins de vent' (Victor-Marie Hugo, *Œuvres complètes*, ed. Paul Ollendorff and Albin Michel, 46 vols (Paris: Imprimerie nationale, 1904–52), xxxiii. 683). And Barbey d'Aurevilly asserts, in his review of *Chansons des rues et des bois* (1865): 'M. Victor Hugo, ce gigantesque trompette-major... a voulu être un Tircis littéraire et souffloter, et trembloter, et chevroter, dans la flûte en sureau de l'Idylle, avec ces lèvres et cette poitrine qui sont de force' (quoted in André Maurois, *Olympio, ou la vie de Victor Hugo* (Paris: Hachette, 1954), 464).

[80] The trope of the 'ship of state', introduced as early as 1513 in Machiavelli's *Il Principe*, was already a cliché in the oratory of the French Revolution. Cf., e.g., George Danton's declaration that 'le vaisseau de l'État est battu par la tempête' in his 27 Apr. 1793 speech, 'Sur un nouvel impôt et de nouvelles levées' (in *Discours civiques de Danton*, ed. Hector Fleishmann (Paris: Fasquelle-Charpentier, 1920), 135). As Grant points out, Hugo's vision

Gilliatt's skills as a literal and figurative 'pilot'—one who both guides ships and provides an example of purposeful self-sacrifice—thus stand in stark contrast to the treacherous activities of the 'pirate' Clubin, as forecast by the novel's preface. Using the latter figure for Napoléon III as a foil for Gilliatt's heroism, Hugo extends in *Les Travailleurs de la mer* the shadow history of the Second Empire laid out in *Les Misérables* as part of his expanding verbal construct. Yet again, he realizes Barthes's vision of the text as 'cette personne désinvolte qui montre son derrière au *Père Politique*'.[81] Jean Valjean, Gilliatt, Hugo: three outcasts with one agenda—the renewal of French republican aspirations and the expulsion of Thénardier/Clubin/Napoléon III from the homeland. The pleasure, Hugo suggests, would be as much the reader's as his. As we shall see, the role of poets in responding to this political imperative is an important subtext not only of *Les Travailleurs de la mer* but also of Hugo's earlier essay, *William Shakespeare*. The relation of the specifically aesthetic dimensions of the novel to both its social outlook and its *philosophical* preface constitutes the focus of the final section of this chapter, where we will consider the literary resonances of Gilliatt's extraordinary resolution and creativity.

THE SHAKESPEARE OF FRANCE?

The final piece of evidence supporting a twofold political and metaphorical reading of *Les Travailleurs de la mer* is the novel's affiliation with *William Shakespeare*. The ancestry of this remarkable text on the nature of genius goes back to the poet's teenage years as an avid reader of Sir Walter Scott's historical fiction. As noted in Chapter 1, Hugo's early works fulfilled his vision of marrying narrative with drama in the mode of Scott to produce the modern French novel. At the same time, we saw that he also cast a wider generic net—evidence of even larger aspirations. His ambition is, for example, very much in evidence in 'Sur Walter Scott: A propos de *Quentin Durward*', where he testifies to a significantly enlarged perspective since the beginning of his career: 'Après le roman pittoresque, mais prosaïque, de Walter Scott, il restera un autre roman à

of the steamship as a motor of social progress is related to his fundamental nationalism. France is, for the poet, 'destined to overcome the stifling and imprisoning institutions of church and monarchy and bring liberty and prosperity to the world' ('Victor Hugo's *Les Travailleurs de la mer*', 236; see also 239). A veritable *prisonnier d'État* under Napoléon III, the French nation must itself be freed if it is to fulfil its privileged role as the engine of worldwide progress. On Hugo as sea-man, see Brombert, *Victor Hugo and the Visionary Novel*, 165–6, and Maxwell, *The Mysteries of Paris and London*, 303.

[81] Barthes, *Le Plaisir du texte*, 84.

créer, plus beau et plus complet encore, selon nous. C'est le roman, à la fois drame et épopée, pittoresque, mais poétique, réel, mais idéal, vrai, mais grand, qui enchâssera Walter Scott dans Homère' (v. 131).[82] Pretending to have foreseen his own creative trajectory, the author of *Notre-Dame de Paris* insists not just on the dramatic side of his fiction but also on its poetic quality. Similarly, Hugo implies that his true rivals, the writers against whom he measures himself, are no longer just Scott and other contemporaries, such as Byron, Chateaubriand, Lamartine, and Vigny, for whom he had expressed his admiration in *Le Conservateur littéraire* and *La Muse française.* They henceforth include the greatest poetic figures of all time: Homer, Vergil, Dante, Shakespeare, Milton.

This idea recurs powerfully thirty years later with the publication of *William Shakespeare*, soon after the triumph of *Les Misérables* and two months before Hugo began drafting *Les Travailleurs de la mer*. While François-Victor pursued the monumental task of translating Shakespeare's works, Hugo took pleasure in developing the expected preface into a longer dissertation on genius.[83] The result is a far-reaching treatise. Although the name of Shakespeare is often evoked, the quantity of direct commentaries on the English playwright and poet makes up less than 20 per cent of the whole. As in the *Préface de Cromwell*, his earlier Romantic manifesto, Hugo offers a totalizing view of literary history, both secular and sacred: 'Homère, Job, Eschyle, Isaïe, Ézéchiel, Lucrèce, Juvénal, saint Jean, saint Paul, Tacite, Dante, Rabelais, Cervantes, Shakespeare'—along with others—forge 'l'avenue des immobiles géants de l'esprit humain' (xii. 189)—that is, his genealogy. As such, the text offers important messages, first about who is most obviously excluded from the list, and second about Hugo's imaginary relationship with Shakespeare in particular.

On the one hand, the almost complete absence of Scott in this essay implies that Shakespeare himself may not be central to its aims. When Hugo cites the visit of the Scottish novelist to the Hebrides, where he could sit on the 'chaise du Barde' (xii. 285), he suggests that someone has perhaps succeeded Scott, just as Scott had substituted himself, so to speak,

[82] The passage, which appeared in *Littérature et Philosophie mêlées* (1834), is an intercalation in Hugo's recycled essay 'Quentin Durward ou l'Écossais à la cour de Louis XI', originally published in *La Muse française* in June 1823 (ii. 431–8). See Roman, *Victor Hugo et le roman philosophique*, 160.

[83] Barrère affirms that: 'La collaboration du père et du fils a été intime, à ce moment-là . . . Plus d'une fois, Victor Hugo, nous le voyons dans ses lettres, s'est fait lire et expliquer par son fils des vers, non seulement de Shakespeare, mais de Wordsworth, de Swinburne, etc.' (*Victor Hugo à l'œuvre*, 73; see also 76–7). Laforgue further discerns a political dimension for Hugo in his son's literary labours: 'traduire Shakespeare, c'est le *faire passer* d'Angleterre en France; et dès lors la traduction du génie anglais par un exilé français prend un sens éminemement politique' ('La Révolution française', 123).

for Shakespeare. After all, is it not really an issue for the author of *William Shakespeare* to claim his place in 'la prodigieuse constellation' of artistic, philosophical, political, scientific, mathematical, and religious geniuses going back through the centuries, in the 'groupe sacré des vraies étoiles' that 'dans le profond ciel de l'avenir . . . se lève éblouissant' (xii. 323)? The list of visionaries guiding humanity with which *William Shakespeare* closes seems to diminish the stature of the eponymous subject not only by surrounding him with fifty other 'phares', but also by giving to understand that a much more contemporary name is missing—that of Victor Hugo.

On the other hand, the relationship of *William Shakespeare* to the *Préface de Cromwell*—where, we might recall, Hugo praises the 'féconde union du type grotesque au type sublime' (III. 1. 51),[84] and thus the *mélange des genres* of which Shakespeare was the most illustrious practitioner since the Baroque period—signals a long meditation on, if not a hidden rivalry with, the English playwright. Because Shakespeare was renowned at once for his plays and for his poetry, two areas that Hugo wished to dominate in his own century, it is possible that the conception of *Les Travailleurs de la mer* comprised an element of literary competition at its origin. Thus, Hugo writes on the proofs of the prospectus for *William Shakespeare*: 'le poète de l'Angleterre jugé par le poète de la France'.[85] His commanding attitude evinces a relatively recent evolution, since Jean Gaudon considers the satirical aim of *Châtiments* a decade before as testifying to 'une volonté plus ou moins consciente d'être le Dante d'un siècle dont il n'avait pas su être le Shakespeare'.[86] With the publication of *Les Contemplations*, *Les Misérables*, *William Shakespeare*, and, finally, *Les Travailleurs de la mer*, Hugo would have returned to his ambition to equal the English poet. According to Bernard Leuilliot, Hugo recognized himself in François-Victor's politically charged comments on Shakespeare's plays, seeing himself as the Bard's successor: 'Celui-ci a pris la place de Chateaubriand dans le pari tacite sur lequel il entend désormais fonder l'autorité de toute son œuvre: être Shakespeare, ou rien.'[87] To avoid the 'prosaïque', his novel, 'à la fois drame et épopée, pittoresque, mais poétique, réel, mais idéal, vrai, mais grand, qui

[84] For the young Hugo, 'Shakespeare, c'est le Drame; et le drame, qui fond sous un même souffle le grotesque et le sublime, le terrible et le bouffon, la tragédie et la comédie, le drame est le caractère propre . . . de la littérature actuelle' (III. 1. 57). See Barrère, *Victor Hugo à l'œuvre*, 79; Porter, *Victor Hugo*, 33; and Roman, *Victor Hugo et le roman philosophique*, 127.

[85] Quoted in Barrère, *Victor Hugo à l'œuvre*, 77.

[86] Jean Gaudon, *Le Temps de la contemplation*, 177.

[87] Bernard Leuilliot, 'L'Histoire réelle telle qu'en Shakespeare', in A. R. W. James (ed.), *Victor Hugo et la Grande-Bretagne* (Liverpool: Francis Cairns Publications, 1986), 155. See also Meschonnic for an excellent analysis of the poetic aspects of *TM* (*Pour la poétique IV*, 150–64).

enchâssera Walter Scott dans Homère', will be inspired to some extent by Shakespeare, while yet surpassing him. Such a rivalry can be seen in the Shakespearean presence in *Les Travailleurs de la mer* revealed, first by the resonances between Gilliatt, the Bard, and Hugo, and then by the intertexual links between the novel and *The Tempest* (*c.*1611), Shakespeare's last play.

To speak of a true *rivalité romanesque* similar to the one between Hugo and Scott, would, of course, be senseless, since the genre did not go back as far as the age of Shakespeare. The latter could not have threatened the reputation of Hugo in that particular arena. Already, with *Les Misérables*, Hugo had attained an international acclaim that eclipsed that of Scott, even at its apogee. But what of his own future? Would he die in exile? Would he be remembered in the twentieth century and beyond, in the light of the continual evolution of taste, which had already neglected Scott, at least in France, for a long time, and which currently preferred realism to Romanticism? Would someone wish to dedicate himself to translating his works 350 years after his death, as François-Victor had done for Shakespeare? At stake, in other words, was the artistic immortality that so few of his predecessors enjoyed—except for those whom he praises in *William Shakespeare.* The bitch goddess of fame is, after all, notoriously fickle.

Channelling Shakespeare

At first glance, the role of the English playwright in *Les Travailleurs de la mer* seems limited to the sole mention of his name in the chapter title, 'Comme quoi Shakespeare peut se rencontrer avec Eschyle' (II. 2. 2). This title, which recalls the book devoted to Æschylus, 'Shakespeare l'ancien', in *William Shakespeare* (I. 4), creates an obvious link between the two works and invites the reader to look for others. One must therefore wonder if the 'Chaise Gild-Holm-'Ur', which awaits Gilliatt throughout the novel and on which he dies drowned, does not refer to the 'chaise du Barde' (xii. 285) likewise carved into the rock along the sea coast.[88] Hugo's essay on the nature of genius is thus much more as well. The 'Shakspeare' who, in 'Plein ciel', would be dazzled by the vessel constructed by 'le chiffre et le songe' (x. 650) becomes, in the poet's musings on what he terms 'les hommes océans' (xii. 159), a model for Gilliatt's limitless, indomitable, and irreducible creative energy.[89] Like the ocean

[88] Cf. Laforgue, 'La Révolution française', 132 n. 27, and Roman, 'Les Iles anglo-normandes', 225.

[89] Note Hugo's use here of the 'metaphor maxima' or condensed metaphor, where one noun modifies another—a wilful violation of French grammar rules. He typically uses this figure to indicate something that transcends normal human experience (see Laurence M. Porter, *The Renaissance of the Lyric in French Romanticism: Elegy, 'Poëme' and Ode*

itself, the celebrated English poet and playwright—'ce Tout dans Un' (xii. 159), another manifestation of the One and the Many—answers to no law but his own. In imagery reminiscent of 'Plein ciel', as well as of *Les Travailleurs de la mer*, Hugo asserts that geniuses in general are 'outrés' because they are not 'circonscrits' (xii. 192) by what is already known, later elaborating: 'ce sont des êtres impérieux, tumultueux, violents, emportées, extrêmes, chevaucheurs des galops ailés, franchisseurs de limites, "passant les bornes", ayant un but à eux, lequel "dépasse le but", "exagérés", faisant des enjambées scandaleuses, volant brusquement d'une idée à l'autre . . . parcourant le ciel en trois pas' (xii. 259–60). In a word, the Bard and other geniuses bear a striking resemblance to *Délivrance*, as well as to the intrepid saviour of the *Durande*. When Hugo mentions that Voltaire, in introducing Shakespeare to France, 'prononça *Gilles*' (xii. 168) instead of Will, the connection to *Gill*iatt is complete.[90]

Aside, then, from its exotic function in the novel as an Anglophone name, *Gilliatt* serves as a coded word that marks the author's preoccupation with Shakespeare. Both join the long line of sublime Hugolian 'outlaws'—Ordener, Bug-Jargal, Esmeralda and Quasimodo, Jean Valjean—who follow their own lights, not society's dictates. The circle closes when one recalls that *Les Travailleurs de la mer* celebrates the mighty *will* (*volonté*) of Gilliatt, a will that allows him not only to escape from numerous dangers—destitution, the tempest, the octopus—but also completely to dominate inhuman circumstances to bring about the extraordinary salvation of the *Durande*'s motor. As we have already learned with regard to his improbable victory, 'croire n'est que la deuxième puissance; vouloir est la première' (xii. 704). The presence of Shakespeare, the literary giant, can be glimpsed behind the titanic, Promethean figure of the solitary hero.[91] By thus developing a relationship between *Will* and Gilliatt, the novelist refers

(Lexington, KY: French Forum, 1978), 85–6). Hugo refers to the interrelation between dreams and science several times in *WS*, noting, for example, at one point that 'Dante combine et calcule; Newton rêve' (xii. 222), and at another that 'l'art doit aider la science. Ces deux roues du progrès doivent tourner ensemble' (xii. 280).

[90] The reference to 'Gilles' is hardly accidental, since Hugo repeats it several more times (see xii. 256, 267). Cf. Alain-René Gélineau, who declares, regarding *WS*: 'et c'est ainsi qu'on s'en va dans les élargissements sans bords de la méditation infinie'; likewise, in *TM*, 'la conscience devient de plus en plus vaste, et même infinie, illimitée, sans bornes, au fur et à mesure de son exploration dans les couches profondes de la pensée' (*Victor Hugo et l'expérience de la transcendance* (Paris: Argel, 1984), 30). As we have seen, the theme is thoroughly explored in 'Plein ciel' as well. Cf. also Barrère's view that, for Hugo, 'la leçon de Shakespeare, c'est pour lui d'être soi-même sans aucune contrainte [esthétique]' (*Victor Hugo à l'œuvre*, 79).

[91] According to Barrère, Hugo appreciates in Shakespeare, among other things, 'd'avoir été mal jugé pendant près de deux siècles dans son pays, et plus encore en France; injustice dont il pensait être victime dans le sien' (*Victor Hugo à l'œuvre*, 80).

the alert reader to his recent meditation on genius, and thus, in some way, to himself.

The comparison extends, moreover, beyond the aesthetic arena. While *William Shakespeare* serves as a vehicle for Hugo's encyclopaedic knowledge of a whole host of geniuses, to whom he pays tribute,[92] the work plainly enters the political sphere in the chapter devoted to Æschylus: 'Tant qu'Eschyle vécut, il fut contesté. On le contesta, puis on le persécuta . . . il fut exilé' (xii. 207–8). This allusion to Hugo's own tenuous situation reverberates throughout the essay. Consider, for example, his self-constructed genealogy. Akin to such luminaries as 'Voltaire à Ferney . . . d'Aubigné à Genève . . . Dante à Vérone . . . Juvénal à Syène . . . Tacite à Méthymne . . . Eschyle à Géla . . . Jean à Pathmos' (xii. 272), the exiled poet bides his time in the Channel Islands, having assumed with other French leftists of his time 'une place de persécution' (xii. 274; see also 239, 294, 322). By evoking, through the fate of others, his self-sacrifice and suffering as a Republican outlaw, Hugo unleashes a shower of more or less veiled attacks on Napoléon III. From the 'despote' (xii. 219) who might try to curtail the freedom of the press unleashed by Gutenberg's invention to 'l'imposture et le parjure' (xii. 251–2) of Iago to the duty of the socially conscious poet to 'insulter les despotes' (xii. 281) to the diatribe against 'les octroyeurs de constitutions' (xii. 286), he points insistently towards the usurper of the Second Republic.[93] As he foretells, regarding 'les despotes' who have dominated history: 'Cette usurpation va cesser, [l'heure des penseurs] arrive enfin, leur prédominance éclate . . . l'avenir leur appartient' (xii. 315). The poet raises a prophetic voice, predicting that Napoléon III will be swept from power, from his seemingly impregnable throne, by the wave of the future. One order of beings who consider themselves above the law will be replaced by another, more benign, confraternity of 'outlaws'.

At the same time, the great geniuses of the ages, like the *Durande* or *Délivrance*, will defy gravity/the grave to take their rightful places in human history. The lesson is once more given by Æschylus, that 'naufragé insubmersible' (xii. 189) whose 'vaste nom . . . surnage' (xii. 208) despite the loss of most of his works. Though current tastes may judge the ancient

[92] Cf. Grant's view that the encyclopaedic scope of *TM* is related to its aspiration towards 'epic synthesis' ('Victor Hugo's *Les Travailleurs de la mer*', 233; see also 241–2).

[93] In further enjoining, 'Opposons . . . le rêve de l'avenir au rêve du passé, la liberté au despotisme' (xii. 286), Hugo consolidates the connection between *WS*, *TM*, and the message of 'Vingtième siècle'. The novelist's remarks, in effect, second François-Victor's 'dénonciation du despotisme moderne' (Leuilliot, 'L'Histoire réelle', 149; see also 148) in his preface to *Richard III*. Cf. Jean Gaudon, who rightly sees in a passage on death in Hugo's essay 'une méditation sur le sort de Bonaparte. Il n'y a pas, en littérature, de coïncidence' (*Temps de la contemplation*, 544). Cf. also Albouy's assertion that, in *WS*, Hugo associates his own outlaw status with the myth of Prometheus (*La Création mythologique*, 223, 255).

Greek playwright 'barbare, extravagant, emphatique, antithétique, boursouflé, absurde' (xii. 204)—in other words, much the same as Hugo himself—the message is plain: one cannot repress true genius. And, thanks to Gutenberg, despotism can no longer throttle the printed word: 'La pensée impossible à entraver, le progrès inarrêtable . . . le livre imperdable' (xii. 219–20), this is the legacy of the printing press. Recycling a theme previously developed in *Notre-Dame de Paris*, Hugo claims that 'l'exemplaire n'est plus épuisable . . . l'unité est grosse de l'innombrable' (xii. 220).[94] Along with the inexhaustible Gilliatt, who continuously multiplies his energies, books—and their writers and readers—can prevail over a multitude of forces set against them.

Far from conflicting with the 'higher' functions of poetry, political *engagement* completes them: 'L'utile, loin de circonscrire le sublime, le grandit' (xii. 280), the essayist maintains.[95] Indeed, being socially *useful* enhances poetic beauty: 'Non, l'utilité patriotique ou révolutionnaire n'ôte rien à la poésie' (xii. 290). It is therefore in the poet's deepest interest as an artist to put his genius in the service of humanity. He must not concentrate on formal beauty alone, but instead inspire others to share his dreams: 'L'art pour l'art peut être beau,' Hugo remarks, 'mais l'art pour le progrès est plus beau encore. Rêver la rêverie est bien, rêver l'utopie est mieux' (xii. 280). As the quintessential 'homme du songe', Gilliatt assumes the proportions of the ideal artist—one committed to creating a better world. Such complete commitment requires overstepping normal boundaries to seek what lies *beyond* the known world: 'Le rêveur doit être un pionnier; la strophe doit vouloir' (xii. 308). To refigure history in reality rather than in the mind alone, dreams and imagination must be harnessed to volition. In this perspective, Gilliatt's audacity and perseverance, his will power and persistent striving, embody not only the galactic airship of 'Plein ciel' but also the courageous spirit of poetic genius.

So, when Hugo declares in *William Shakespeare*, 'détrôner les usurpations au milieu des tonnerres; voilà l'œuvre' (xii. 308), he forges a link between Gilliatt's conquest of the tempest and his own verbal thunder directed at those in power. A modern-day Juvenal, he hurls blazing invective, 'effrayant incendie de poésie qui brûle Rome en présence des

[94] For the author of *NDP*, 'l'invention de l'imprimerie est le plus grand événement de l'histoire. C'est la révolution mère . . . Sous la forme imprimerie, la pensée est plus impérissable que jamais: elle est volatile, insaisissable, indestructible. Elle se mêle à l'air . . . comment extirper l'ubiquité?' (iv. 141). See *EN* 190–3, 205–6.

[95] Or, as he expresses it in another formulation, 'être utile et beau, c'est être sublime' (xii. 283).

siècles' (xii. 178), against the current empire.[96] Like the storm in *Les Travailleurs de la mer*, 'Shakespeare est légion' (xii. 297)—the figure of the irrepressible outlaw poet himself. Imploring, as do other geniuses, 'Viens me souffler dans les ailes, ouragan!' (xii. 288), he will use words as tools to unleash his fury on tyrants present and future. Hugo's threat is scarcely veiled. 'Le poëte est à la fois fait de menace et de promesse,' he declares. 'L'inquiétude qu'il inspire aux oppresseurs apaise et console les opprimés' (xii. 289). Fixing his gaze on the horizon of the future provokes a double effect, because the hopeful vision that he can offer the victims of oppression implies the dissolution of current reality.

Despotic reigns—those of 'Pleine mer' and France, for example—may be identified with 'la frontière, l'ornière, la routine, la cécité' (xii. 313): the poet transcends such boundaries with a single look forward. What he sees is that

> ces apparences qu'on prenait pour des réalités, ces princes, ces rois, se dissipent; il ne demeure que ce qui doit demeurer, l'esprit humain d'un côté, les esprits divins de l'autre, la vraie œuvre et les vrais ouvriers, la sociabilité à compléter et à féconder, la science cherchant le vrai, l'art créant le beau, la soif de pensée, tourment et bonheur de l'homme, la vie inférieure aspirant à la vie supérieure. (xii. 294)

Once again, *William Shakespeare* reveals its affinity with both 'Vingtième siècle' and *Les Travailleurs de la mer*, first by associating science and art; then by underscoring the evaporation of illusory realities (the 'all-conquering' *Léviathan* sinking into the depths; the veil of fog lifting for Clubin to reveal *les Douvres*, rather than a shoal nearer to shore, as he had planned); and finally by lauding true productivity and the workers who engage in it. Even in death, the writer's labours will continue to be fruitful: 'les poëtes sont morts, leur pensée règne. Ayant été, ils sont . . . Les autres trépassés se reposent, les morts de génie travaillent. Ils travaillent à quoi? A nos esprits. Ils font de la civilisation' (xii. 295).[97] Poetic *work* is never in vain. The chimerical horizon of *Léviathan*/Clubin/Napoléon III vanishes, fulfilling one destiny posited in 'Plein mer'—'Cela fut. C'est passé. Cela n'est plus ici' (x. 645); in contrast, the liberating energies of *Délivrance*/Gilliatt/Hugo leave permanent traces

[96] Similarly, Juvenal stands in *MIS* as a figure of the vengeful poet seeking retribution from a corrupt regime (see *FT* 50, 203, 235 n. 44).

[97] Hugo's faith in the future, evidenced from the beginning to the end of *WS*, provides a map for reading *TM* as well. 'Le temps présent travaille au temps futur, donc travaillez et espérez' (xii. 175), he urges early on. Likewise, the essay ends on a vision of the 'engloutissement' of the 'pléiade des hommes de force', while 'dans le profond ciel de l'avenir . . . se lève éblouissant le group sacré des vrais étoiles' (xii. 323)—the constellation of artists, scientists, and philosophers who have shaped humankind. Social misery gives way to 'cette parole: *Délivrance*' (xii. 309), Clubin to Gilliatt, Louis-Napoléon to Hugo: 'Départ des maîtres; les libérateurs arrivent' (xii. 323).

because they 'civilise[nt]' (x. 655). Through their indelibility, Ricoeur's 'constructions of history' (*TN* iii. 100) are turned as much towards the future as the past. Thanks to the printing press, the poet's unstoppable, inexhaustible thought will prevail (*règne*) over the powers that be, pouring itself into other minds and raising them to a higher level of self-awareness and civic virtue. In so doing, he believes, he will effect 'la transformation de la foule en peuple; profond travail' (xii. 274). His persuasive interpretation of the 'present past' will *move* others to rethink—and then transform—the 'present future' (see *TN* i. 7–22, ii. 94, iii. 260).

Key to this transfiguring process for Hugo is, we have seen, the notion of poetic breath, which like God's creative power infuses new life into humankind. The hurricane-force winds that lift him to the spheres of the ideal carry others along as well, giving rise to 'la vie inférieure aspirant à la vie supérieure'. Conversely, poets derive their force, mission, and legitimacy from their close contact with the 'populace' for whom they speak: instead of rejecting the tastes and experiences of 'ces exilés de la joie qu'on nomme les pauvres', Hugo considers it both useful and necessary that 'le souffle du peuple traverse ces toutes-puissantes âmes' (xii. 271).[98] His political exile enabling him to empathize more deeply than ever with *les misérables*, he is adamant that art and beauty must be accessible to everyone. We might therefore surmise that, when he exclaims 'Ce qu'il faut à la civilisation... c'est une littérature de peuple' (xii. 276), he is anticipating the *usefulness* of *Les Travailleurs de la mer* for present and future generations. The creative heritage passed down by Shakespeare is intimately related to the poet's sociopolitical 'resoluteness that is... turned toward the future' (*TN* iii. 74).

Inspiration, aspiration, respiration: the immense liberating storm that figures Shakespeare's work—'On sent, en abordant l'œuvre de cet homme, le vent énorme qui viendrait de l'ouverture d'un monde' (xii. 236)—blows not just through *William Shakespeare* but through Hugo's novel as well. His appeal in the essay, 'Ouvrons les intelligences toutes grandes. Aérons les âmes' (xii. 308), recalls Gilliatt's status as 'maître de l'air, de l'eau et du feu' (xii. 688), as he channels his energies productively, in ways that will be helpful to others. His efforts (and Hugo's) contrast with those of Clubin, who imagines a false future centred entirely on

[98] The writer sums up the Creator's omnipotence—a major conceptual model for the poet's view of creativity and creation—in similar terms: 'L'ouragan des miracles souffle perpétuellement. Jour et nuit les phénomènes en tumulte surgissent autour de nous de toutes parts... Ce tumulte, c'est l'harmonie. Les énormes ondes concentriques de la vie universelle sont sans bords' (xii. 227). The imagery of breath, storms, waves, and boundlessness again announces *TM*. Note also the self-similar spatial image of 'ondes concentriques' to signal transcendence.

himself, another kind of 'airiness' altogether. The villain is, like the octopus, a 'pompe aspirante' (xii. 504) that sucks others dry to satisfy his own needs. Once alone on the reef, we have observed, Clubin 'aéra son âme. Il respira son crime à pleine poitrine' (xii. 649), as he speculates about the risks he will take to expand his stolen capital. Even when he discovers his perilous situation on *les Douvres*, Clubin envisions being saved by a passing boat if he signals from a nearby rock.

Such idle dreams end in his losing his breath altogether, whereas Gilliatt's creative rêverie forges for the windy blast in the rocks 'une espèce de poumon' (xii. 391) that allows him to regulate its 'souffle' (xii. 390). Similarly, the hero's mastery of the sea, where 'chaque gonflement de la vague enflée [est] comme un poumon', constitutes a symbolic power over 'aspiration' and 'expiration' (xii. 402), over life and death.[99] Hugo reiterates the point further on, in his reflections on monsters and the terrible law of universal death: 'Vivons, soit. Mais tâchons que la mort nous soit progrès. Aspirons aux mondes moins ténébreux' (xii. 501). The yearning of 'la vie inférieure' towards 'la vie supérieure' extolled in *William Shakespeare* as the wave of the future is illustrated in *Les Travailleurs de la mer* by Gilliatt's pensive nature and by his salvific actions. If he is sometimes 'halluciné comme un prophète' (xii. 506), it is because his fertile insights point towards the poet's visionary function. Thus, in appearance, the writer employs 'empty' words to spin fictions for people's entertainment. But the fact that his hero 'faisait des choses qui semblaient inutiles, signe d'une préméditation attentive' (xii. 416), suggests a much higher ambition on Hugo's part. Like the sea, 'les hommes océans' may seem to generate a 'prodigieux travail inutile' (xii. 393); later generations, however, will recognize it as both profoundly prescient and necessary. Gilliatt's Promethean ordeal and triumph add up to far more than just Romantic myth-making: they also underscore the titanic task undertaken by the poet to enlighten and inflame the French people, to inspire them to embrace an alternative future.

Hugo's Mighty Tempest

The hidden associations in both *William Shakespeare* and *Les Travailleurs de la mer* of the 'Bard' with Gilliatt, along with the more obvious identification of Hugo with Shakespeare in his essay on genius, thus set

[99] Hugo's contention that 'l'océan entier est dans une bourrasque' unites the extremes of air and sea into one metaforce: 'Une vague, c'est le gouffre d'en bas; un souffle, c'est le gouffe d'en haut' (xii. 460). It is no accident, therefore, that the terms used to describe the two elements in the novel hold much in common. Consequently, the description of the monstrous storm that rages on *les Douvres*, where 'on sent que c'est le poumon de l'infini qui souffle' (xii. 472), combines both dimensions of the vertical sublime.

up a triangulation whereby Gilliatt yet again corresponds to Hugo. The example of Æschylus' renown, which 'surnage' (xii. 208) above the 'naufrage' of his writings, provides a clue to even wider associations here. Run aground in the Channel Islands, more or less like the *Durande*, Hugo sees himself as a castaway whose name might yet float above history. He notes, in regard to one of his drawings proposed as an illustration for *Les Travailleurs de la mer*: 'Au revers de ce carton, j'ai barbouillé ma destinée: un bateau battu de la tempête au beau milieu du monstrueux océan, à peu près désemparé, assailli par les ouragans et par toutes les écumes et n'ayant qu'un peu de fumée qu'on appelle la gloire, et que le vent arrache, et qui est sa force' (xviii, drawings 737–8 and catalogue note).[100] Far from trembling and sinking in the midst of the political storm that carries him far from familiar shores, Hugo imagines himself still upright on the crest of the waves, upheld by his creative powers. Like the poet–novelist's verbal virtuosity, Gilliatt's ingeniousness permits him to vanquish the forces of nature assembled in the tempest. After he succeeds in improvising a successful barricade to protect the *Durande*, his position 'debout sur l'autre moitié' (xii. 734) of the vessel suspended above the waves—a stance, we have seen, that signals his affiliation with Hugo—repeats this image of almost magical levitation. What strikes the reader in these metaphorical analogies, as well as in the identification between Hugo, Gilliatt, and Shakespeare, is that, from a certain angle, Gilliatt also resembles the protagonist of *The Tempest.*[101] For, the almost superhuman powers of the hero, 'maître de l'air, de l'eau et du feu' (xii. 688) on his reef, turn him into a kind of Prospero, the Duke of Milan and a magician who commands the storm to do his will when he makes his brother Antonio, who had dethroned him, wash up on his desert island. A closer look at Shakespeare's work will make the connection more evident.

The play begins by invoking a tempest out at sea and the fear of those whose ship is leaking.[102] The grounding of the *Durande* perhaps alludes to

[100] I am referring to the drawing tellingly known by the title *Ma Destinée*.

[101] Barrère verifies that in 1824 Hugo 'connaissait déjà, par la traduction Letourneur revue par Pichot et présentée par Guizot, *Hamlet, Macbeth, Timon d'Athènes, le Songe d'une nuit d'été, Roméo et Juliette, Othello, La Tempête*' (*Victor Hugo à l'œuvre*, 76). Moreover, the scene in one of the most celebrated chapters of *MIS*, 'Une Tempête sous un crâne' (i. 7. 3), where Jean Valjean's conscience fights against his instinct of self-preservation on 'le champ de bataille des passions' (xi. 201), forecasts Gilliatt's epic struggle against the hurricane. The evocation of Homère, Milton, and Dante in the third paragraph of the chapter (xi. 202) demonstrates the relationship between this episode and Hugo's literary ambitions communicated in *WS* and occulted in *TM*. Finally, we should note that *The Tempest* itself echoes Vergil's *Aeneid* (29–19 bc)—a resonance prolonged in and by Hugo's novel.

[102] As in *TM*, the tempest in the play is 'a storm to end all storms' (Noel Cobb, *Prospero's Island: The Secret Alchemy at the Heart of* The Tempest (London: Coventure, 1984), 28). In Elizabeth Fowler's view, the trope in *The Tempest* of the boat that cannot be steered refers

this scene: 'Le déchirement d'un flanc de navire sur un bas-fond en pleine mer est un des bruits les plus lugubres qu'on puisse rêver' (xii. 645), affirms the narrator of *Les Travailleurs de la mer*. Whereas the passengers entrusted to Clubin save themselves by using the lifeboat, the latter remains 'heroically' on the reef, which he believes to be much closer to shore than it is—a shore where he intends to swim with Lethierry's fortune. This deceitful gesture resembles Antonio's, as well as that of Louis-Napoléon Bonaparte, who had betrayed his republican partisans, including Hugo. According to Prospero, who reveals his past to his daughter Miranda, his brother had usurped the government of Milan from him while he was plunged in scholarship. Using François-Victor's translation, we read: 'Ma confiance,—cette bonne mère, enfanta de lui—une perfidie, aussi grande par contraste—que l'était ma foi en lui' (sc. ii).[103] The arrival of the two traitors on inhospitable islands permits the triumph of transcendent justice. Though Antonio remains unrepentant, Prospero ends up renouncing vengeance by freeing him and his travel companions. In the case of Clubin, his mistaken calculation leaves him exposed to the octopus, a predator even more terrible than himself.[104] The fact that the magician 'subverts' his own power[105] affiliates him with Gilliatt, who cedes Déruchette's hand to Ebenezer and then stages their wedding, where he plays the role of the father rather than of the groom.

Other textual details firmly link the two works: the personification of nature; the positive image of voluntary labour;[106] the primacy of

to the ship of state ('The Ship Adrift', in Peter Hulme and William H. Sherman (eds), The Tempest *and its Travels* (Philadelphia: University of Pennsylvania Press, 2000), 37)—a theme that we have already observed in Hugo's novel.

[103] William Shakespeare, *La Tempête*, trans. François-Victor Hugo, in *Œuvres complètes de W. Shakespeare*, 18 vols (Paris: Pagnerre, 1859–72), ii. 189. Further page references to François-Victor's translation of *The Tempest* will be provided after the scene number. Identifying in the play five instances of the motif of lost rights, Richard P. Wheeler remarks that: 'Usurpation . . . is everywhere in *The Tempest*' ('Fantasy and History in *The Tempest*', in Nigel Wood (ed.), *The Tempest* (Buckingham: Open University Press, 1995), 140).

[104] Concerning the way in which Prospero resolves his need for revenge, see Bernard J. Paris, '*The Tempest*: Shakespeare's Ideal Solution', in *Bargains with Fate: Psychological Crises and Conflicts in Shakespeare and his Plays* (New York: Plenum, 1991), 261–77. As for Caliban, he is 'captured by his dream of imminent but elusive riches' (Wheeler, 'Fantasy and History', 155), much like Clubin.

[105] See Donna B. Hamilton, *Virgil and* The Tempest*: The Politics of Imitation* (Columbus: Ohio State University Press, 1990), 86.

[106] The leitmotif of useful work, which produces human progress and of which Gilliatt and Lethierry are the instruments, undergirds all of *TM*. In Shakespeare, see especially the monologue of Ferdinand, for whom 'les plus pauvres moyens mènent à des fins magnifiques' (sc. v; 231).

dreams and reverie.[107] Gilliatt's minimal diet, moreover, recalls Prospero's menace that Ferdinand will drink 'l'eau de la mer' and eat 'les coquillages des ruisseaux, les racines sèches, et les cosses—où les glands ont été bercés' (sc. ii; 204). And the *coup de foudre* between Déruchette et Ebenezer repeats that between Miranda et Ferdinand—along with the sacrifices that this love entails for Gilliatt and Prospero, respectively.[108] Finally, the 'magic', or 'miracle' (xii. 771), of the restitution by Gilliatt of the *Durande*'s motor to Lethierry matches the restoration of the ship to the voyagers by '[des] événements [qui] ne sont pas naturels' (sc. ix; 329) at the end of Shakespeare's play. One can even distinguish, in the last image of Gilliatt disappearing beneath the rising tide, a reference not only to the drowning of Léopoldine Hugo in 1843, but also the despair of Alonso, king of Naples, who believes that his son Ferdinand has drowned.[109]

From this perspective, the octopus corresponds to Caliban, the wild and deformed creature who inhabits the island before the others get there. According to Prospero, Caliban is an 'être de ténèbres', who is 'monstrueux dans ses goûts—comme dans ses formes' (sc. ix; 272, 273).[110] Likewise, as we have seen, 'Le monstre' (II. 4. 2) who attacks Gilliatt from the bottom of a 'trou de ténèbres' (xii. 738) is merely another version of Clubin, whose hypocrisy makes him a 'monstre en dessous' (xii. 648).[111] Such a reading suggests that, for Hugo, the treachery of Antonio—who, far from being bothered by his conscience, encourages Sebastian, Alonso's brother, to carry out a *coup d'état* in order to become king of Naples (sc. iii)—renders him the moral equivalent of Caliban and the political equivalent of Napoléon III,

[107] James treats this subject in *TM* and *WS* in an apt way (*Dream, Creativity, and Madness*, 199–211). See also Meschonnic, *Pour la poétique IV*, 139–42; Jacques Neefs, 'Penser par la fiction (*Les Travailleurs de la mer*)', in Jacques Seebacher and Anne Ubersfeld (eds), *Hugo le fabuleux: Actes du Colloque de Cerisy, 30 juin–10 juillet 1985* (Paris: Seghers, 1985), 98–101; and Rieben, *Délires romantiques*, 170.

[108] And so, Gilliatt becomes a 'providence' (xii. 784) for the two lovers, just as Ferdinand receives 'une seconde vie' from Prospero, Miranda, and 'l'immortelle Providence' (sc. ix; 268). For a fascinating discussion of Déruchette's choice of Ebenezer/Jacob over Gilliatt/'[le] grotesque Esaü', see Millet, *Les Travailleurs de la mer* de Victor Hugo', 16–19.

[109] Let us note, moreover, that Prospero makes the ambiguous claim that he is afflicted in the same way as Alonso: 'J'ai perdu ma fille . . . Dans la dernière tempête' (sc. ix; 266–7). The intensity of the connection between Prospero and Miranda, along with what Wheeler calls 'the repressed sexual dimension of his longing for his daughter' ('Fantasy and History', 154; see also 139, 152, 157), recalls the complex relationship between Hugo and Léopoldine.

[110] Although Caliban's repulsive appearance seems to link him equally to Gilliatt, whose hideous exterior makes Déruchette faint, it is the figuration of the villain's soul that matters in Hugo. In the poet's system, Gilliatt would correspond to Quasimodo in *NDP*, the hero whose look is grotesque and whose actions are sublime, while Clubin's model would be Claude Frollo, the priest superficially allied with the divine but whose soul is damned.

[111] As for Caliban, he is 'captured by his dream of imminent but elusive riches' (Wheeler, 'Fantasy and History', 155), much like Clubin.

and hence a literary model for Clubin. (The affinities between the two characters extend to the phonetic similarity of their names.) The comic ending of *The Tempest*, in contrast with the tragic dénouement of *Les Travailleurs de la mer*, takes nothing away from this fundamental schema. On the contrary, the harmonious resolution of Shakespeare's play indicates that the ideal republic described by the blathering old counsellor Gonzalvo—a republic where the arts are forbidden and where no one works ('Nulle occupation: tous les hommes seraient fainéants, tous!' (sc. iii; 214))—constitutes a false utopian route (one that Shakespeare himself parodies), that nothing valuable can be done without effort or sacrifice or genius to point the way to a better world. Hugo's *Travailleurs* might thus be said both to emulate and to extend Shakespeare's *Tempest*.

Less well known in the Anglophone world than *Notre-Dame de Paris* or *Les Misérables*, *Les Travailleurs de la mer* invites a new reading through its Shakespearean reflections, as well as through its intrinsic epic, poetic, dramatic, and political values. Mixing drama and lyricism in his anti-'prosaic' story, Hugo aspires to outshine the Bard in a work superior to all that Shakespeare might have done.[112] But the status of *The Tempest* as Shakespeare's last work allies his play to Hugo's novel in yet another way. When Prospero declares in the final scene that, after seeing Miranda and Ferdinand marry, he intends to return to Milan, 'où je donnerai à ma tombe une pensée sur trois' (sc. ix; 274), he foresees the disappearance of the Bard himself several years later.[113] That *Les Travailleurs de la mer* ends similarly on a meditation on death in the chapter 'La grande tombe'

[112] The role of his 1866 novel in this long-standing rivalry appears all the more important when one considers that the exceptionally specialized vocabulary of the text permits Hugo to rise to the quasi-legendary level of Shakespeare in this regard. The facts are intriguing. Shakespeare had used 29,066 different words (including proper nouns) in his complete works (Marvin Spevack, *The Harvard Concordance to Shakespeare* (Cambridge, MA: Harvard University Press, 1973), p. v). The 8,824 terms introduced in *TM* elevate the total number of words used by Hugo up until then (including 8,881 proper nouns, but without counting either *HI* or *BJ*, with everything exotic that these two novels have to offer) to 29,483 (see Étienne Brunet, *Le Vocabulaire de Victor Hugo*, i (Paris: Champion-Slatkine, 1988), 16, 309, 311). The reputation of the poet as a master of the French language is not in the least exaggerated. Indeed, his vocabulary is more varied than that of Chateaubriand or Zola or Proust (see Brunet, *Le Vocabulaire*, 22), perhaps because, as Charles Baudelaire put it, 'Victor Hugo a mangé préalablement le dictionnarie de la langue qu'il était appelé à parler' ('Victor Hugo', in *L'Art romantique*, ed. Henri Lemaitre, in *Curiosités esthétiques et L'Art romantique* (Paris: Garnier, 1962), 735). Hugo's verbal ability to prevail over the greatest master of the English language—an ability realized once and for all with *TM*—cannot fail to dazzle. Regarding the maritime language and linguistic inventions in the novel, see Jean-Bertrand Barrère, 'Victor Hugo et le franglais', in A. R. W. James (ed.), *Victor Hugo et la Grande-Bretagne* (Liverpool: Francis Cairns Publications, 1986), 17, 19.

[113] My reading of the play agrees with Cobb's, which explains this remark as 'Shakespeare's farewell to the stage' (*Prospero's Island*, 194).

(III. 3. 5) is not a coincidence. Gilliatt, sitting like Hugo–Prometheus on his rocky perch, watches the boat carrying off Déruchette and Ebenezer move further away:

> L'œil de Gilliatt, attaché au loin sur le sloop, restait fixe.
>
> Cet œil ne ressemblait à rien de ce qu'on peut voir sur la terre. Dans cette prunelle tragique et calme il y avait de l'inexprimable. Ce regard contenait toute la quantité d'apaisement que laisse le rêve non réalisé; c'était l'acceptation lugubre d'un autre accomplissement. (xii. 793)

The 'accomplissement' of the solitary hero, who expires while assuring the happiness of the woman he loves after saving her homonym, the *Durande*,[114] echoes Prospero's preparations for death, now that he has regained his usurped title and given his daughter in a marriage of love. And Hugo, who risks dying in exile, doubtless projects, along with Shakespeare, his contemplation of death onto his own personage.[115]

Such reflections belong to broader preoccupations for Hugo. Following in the traces of the great writers since Vergil, he evokes and comments on the ways in which other artists—especially the early English Romantics—met their deaths. How do poets say goodbye? How does Hugo want to be remembered? The memory of Shakespeare conjured up by the 'Job Prométhée' of *Les Travailleurs de la mer* is joined, for example, by that of Percy Bysshe Shelley (1792–1822), the expatriate author of *Prometheus Unbound* (1819) who drowned in a storm off La Spezia (in his schooner the 'Ariel', named after the 'airy spirit' in *The Tempest*) and whose heart, according to the legend, did not burn in cremation. The watery fate, the imperishable heart, would suit the Hugolian myth as well. According to John Heywood Thomas, Hugo may have become acquainted with Shelley through François-Victor, who had included an abbreviated twenty-six-page translation of the English writer's lengthy 1813 philosophical poem *Queen Mab* in the volume of Shakespeare's *Œuvres complètes* devoted to *A Midsummer's Night Dream* and *The Tempest*.[116] For Albouy, 'il nous paraît vraisemblable que Hugo ait connu le *Prométhée délivré*, de Shelley . . . par

114 Though Gilliatt salvages the *Durande*'s engine, he never manages to find its figurehead, carved in the image of Déruchettte—a clear omen that he will never possess Déruchette herself.

115 It is in this sense that one can repeat Meschonnic's conclusion that: 'L'idylle, le drame, intégrés à l'épopée, et tout ce langage [dans *TM*], sont une interrogation à l'Inconnu' (*Pour la poétique IV*, 164). See also Montier's interpretation of Gilliatt's final *regard*: 'À la lettre, le texte ne dit rien d'autre que la progressive assimilation de l'œil de Gilliatt avec la forme planétaire. De fini et déterminé, son désir devient pressentiment d'éternité' ('Le "Finale"', 14).

116 John Heywood Thomas, *L'Angleterre dans l'œuvre de Victor Hugo* (Paris: A. Pedone, 1934), 151.

son fils, François-Victor...ou aussi par Pierre Leroux'.[117] The generic mélange, too, of Shelley's great lyrical drama—which, like *Les Travailleurs de la mer*, includes dreams, visions, prophecies, and dramatic dialogues—suggests that the French poet was familiar with, if not responding to, the work of his English counterpart.[118] And we would be remiss not to mention that *Frankenstein, or the Modern Prometheus* (1818), authored by Shelley's wife, Mary (1797–1851), anticipates *Les Travailleurs de la mer* to the extent that it involves machines, nature, and monsters. Finally, who could forget that another liberal expatriate, George Gordon, Lord Byron (1788–1824), had nearly drowned in his first attempt to swim the Dardanelles? Or that he had died instead at Missolonghi amid the Greek insurgents fighting the Turks for their independence?[119] Again, some degree of identification on Hugo's part with the irrepressible English Romantic seems probable.

An epic battle for freedom, a wild coast where one might drown, an inflexible attitude towards tyranny, the generous sacrifice of self—all these tropes are found as much in the image of himself that the exiled poet endeavours to put forward as in the plot of his novel. When Gilliatt delivers the *Durande* from its rocky prison, or when he battles indefatigably against the Ocean-'despote', against 'la dictature du chaos' of the winds, or against that 'sinistr[e] patienc[e] embusqué[e] dans l'abîme' (xii. 727, 720, 744) figured by the octopus, he duplicates the photos of Hugo at the time, installed on 'le rocher des Proscrits' opposite France or with his arms crossed and a penetrating look to signal the poet–avenger of the Second Republic.[120] Unlike Prospero, Hugo had no intention of pardoning 'l'usurpateur' who had cast him onto his island. When he died, these visual as well as textual representations would retain their full intensity—and their social effectiveness. We know what triumph he subsequently experienced, living still.

117 Albouy, *La Création mythologique*, 236.

118 Certainly, Shelley's Prometheus–Lucifer figure bears an uncanny resemblance to the redeemed protagonist of Hugo's *La Fin de Satan* (1886; intended, with *Dieu* (1891), as one of the two concluding sections of *La Légende des siècles*). See also Albouy's discussion of the links between Hugo–Prometheus and Napoléon III–Jupiter (*La Création mythologique*, 223–4).

119 See Hugo's article on Byron's death in *La Muse française* (July 1824), where he declares that: 'Le génie de notre époque peut être aussi beau que celui des époques les plus illustres, il ne peut être le même' (ii. 460)—a conception of Romanticism that will continue to evolve in the *Préface de Cromwell* and *WS*.

120 See Pierre Georgel, 'La "Figure" de Victor Hugo: Les Images', in Pierre Georgel (dir.), *La Gloire de Victor Hugo* (Paris: Éditions de la Réunion des musées nationaux, 1985), 106–7, 113–15.

To conclude, I argue that, given its sweeping epic vision, intricate metaphorical motifs, and timely political commentary, *Les Travailleurs de la mer* ranks with *Les Misérables* as one of Hugo's greatest works. In addition, it is evident that the exiled Hugo's poetic, fictive, and critical works—from *Châtiments* to 'Vingtième siècle' to *Les Misérables*, *William Shakespeare*, and *Les Travailleurs de la mer*—form a single, consistent, purposeful *œuvre* that *labours* to undermine Napoléon III's illegitimate regime. Taken together, these many texts use a public dictionary to reveal Hugo's private thesaurus, conjoining politics and aesthetics, poetry and polemic, in self-similar, nesting patterns. His metaphorical flights, whereby seemingly disparate entities are brought into relationships of equivalency, enable him to weave the strands binding *Léviathan*, Clubin–hurricane–octopus, Caliban, and France's emperor, on the one hand, and *Délivrance,* Gilliatt, Shakespeare, and the poet himself, on the other. Though virtually incarcerated on his island, both Prometheus on his rock and Job on his dunghill, Hugo celebrates the freedom of imagination allied with science, which together allow him to 'go boldly' into a happier, *foreseeable* future. The visionary poet–novelist is attuned to evolving realities. After all, just four and a half years after the publication of *Les Travailleurs de la mer*, Napoléon III was, quite literally, history.

From the exotic world of 'L'Archipel de la Manche' to Gilliatt's uncommon physical and moral valour, *Les Travailleurs de la mer* serves as a vehicle that transports Hugo's reader into realms far from the comforts of home. If, as Ricoeur contends, 'the practice of narrative lies in a thought experiment by means of which we try to inhabit worlds foreign to us' (*TN* iii. 249), the text serves as an excellent guide to the last two panels of the novelist's triptych—that is, to *L'Homme qui rit* and *Quatrevingt-Treize*. The first conveys us to England in the century of Shakespeare's death; the second, to the wilds of Brittany during the post-Revolutionary *Vendée*. In each case, we are called to contemplate the present through the analogical lenses of history and metaphor alike.

3

Dystopia and Poetic Vision in *L'Homme qui rit*

Although the work of metaphor in *Les Travailleurs de la mer* allows Hugo to refigure both the recent past on the Channel Islands and present-day France by aligning these two temporal frames, there is not a great deal of history per se in the novel. Much of the storyline depicts one man's struggle with nature outside the social and cultural realms, so the text exudes a sense of timelessness. History itself resides in the wings, off-stage as it were, in the prefatory 'Archipel de la Manche', which both counterbalances the tale that follows and guides the reader in apprehending its occulted political implications. With *L'Homme qui rit*, however, the scene shifts to late-seventeenth- and early-eighteenth-century England, thus heralding a more traditional form of historical narrative, one replete with local colour, detailed settings, and a large cast of characters—some based on real figures from Britain's past. Still, traditional need not mean conventional. After all, since *Notre-Dame de Paris* Hugo's novels had transcended 'le roman pittoresque, mais prosaïque' of Sir Walter Scott by inventing a mixed genre, 'à la fois drame et épopée, pittoresque, mais poétique, réel, mais idéal, vrai, mais grand' (v. 137). We might therefore anticipate that *L'Homme qui rit* would be as grandly epic and lyrically evocative as *Les Misérables* and *Les Travailleurs de la mer*. But would Hugo rely on similar strategies to achieve these ends in his new work, or would he attempt to refresh his 'signature' approach to narrative? To avoid the prosaic in *Les Travailleurs de la mer*, for example, he renewed the 'ideal' represented by Jean Valjean's superhuman heroism by investing Gilliatt with even greater physical prowess. Another innovation was to shift the vertical axis of the apocalyptic sublime that ran in *Les Misérables* from the abyss of the sewers to a transcendent Heaven to one ranging from the depths of the ocean to the looming, storm-filled heavens. How could the novelist continue invigorating the Hugo 'brand' in his current narrative? And would he still seek to settle political scores? We should recall that, when the novel was published in 1869, Hugo was still in exile in Guernsey, no closer to returning to his beloved nation than the day he had landed there fourteen years earlier.

To rework the relations between historical refiguration and metaphorical redescription in *L'Homme qui rit*, Hugo differentiates the role of the hero, Gwynplaine, from that of both Jean Valjean and Gilliatt. The latter remains solitary to the end, dying alone, just as he had prevailed alone over the tempest, the octopus, and physical deprivation. In other words, Gilliatt's existence is essentially asocial, as well as ahistorical—even if his acts are consistently benevolent and helpful towards his neighbours, and even if by salvaging the *Durande* he promotes the economic welfare of all the Channel Islands. Likewise, his refusal to claim Déruchette's hand in marriage against her will reveals not so much a social conscience as the ability to triumph over his own desire through the altruistic intensity of his love. In contrast, because the disfigured and socially exiled Gwynplaine inhabits a populous land during a well-defined historical period, Hugo finds far more opportunities for explicit political commentary than he did in writing *Les Travailleurs de la mer.*

At the same time, by setting the story in late- and post-Restoration England, Hugo distances it from his readers in time and space, allowing him more readily to elevate some of the ethical motifs already present in *Les Misérables* to transhistorical principles. Gwynplaine, too, is hardly a clone of Valjean, who qualifies as grotesque only because of his status as an ex-convict. Rather, the protagonist of *L'Homme qui rit* takes up where the 'hideux' (xii. 775) Gilliatt leaves off—genuinely repulsive on the outside. And, like *Les Misérables*, where the grotesque resides most squarely in imagery surrounding the Paris sewers, the wretched poor, the miscreant Thénardiers, the criminal underworld, and despotic government, *L'Homme qui rit* systematically allies the materially repulsive and the politically dystopian. Thus, Hugo demonstrates that human society can produce moral monsters and oppressive regimes as abhorrent as anything produced by nature.

Similarly, the utopian discourse that pervades the travelogue–preface to *Les Travailleurs de la mer* recurs in the narrative proper of *L'Homme qui rit*, just as one finds in *Les Misérables*. While Clubin and the octopus certainly fall into the category of Hugolian grotesques, the largely asocial aspects of *Les Travailleurs de la mer* preclude the development of a utopian vision in the body of the novel itself. Once again, though, Hugo varies his approach to this rhetorical register. Gone are the young revolutionaries of *Les Misérables* through whom the writer channelled not only political satire but also rousing speeches about a better world that he might well have dreamed of delivering as an elected representative to the Chambre des députés under the Second Republic. In *L'Homme qui rit*, the opposition—Cromwell and his republican colleagues—have *already* been defeated and a constitutional monarchy *already* installed, as of 1688.[1] Instead of a cohort of idealistic insurgents, there remains at the time of Hugo's narrative but one lone figure of integrity, Gywnplaine, to carry the banner of social equity to the seat of dystopia—namely, the halls of Parliament.

In this chapter, I explore how Hugo incorporates features of previous works while inventing new tactics to figure and communicate the sublime. Viewing the text in the light of the earlier novels—especially *Les Misérables* and *Les Travailleurs de la mer*—is essential to this effort, but we should also recognize that Hugo composed *L'Homme qui rit* with future narratives in mind. As he declares in the 1869 preface: 'Le vrai titre de ce livre serait *l'Aristocratie*. Un autre livre, qui suivra, pourra être intitulée *la Monarchie*. Et ces deux livres, s'il est donné à l'auteur d'achever ce travail, en précéderont et en amèneront un autre qui sera intitulé: *Quatrevingt-treize*' (xiv. 27). Conceived as the first of a three-part project,[2] the novel thus aims teleologically towards a republican 'dénouement'. In *Les Travailleurs de la mer*, Hugo brings order out of the chaos of nature; in *L'Homme qui rit*, he identifies and makes sense of historical patterns. As in his previous work, his powerful visual and metaphorical imagination plays a central role in constructing verbal networks.

Representations of history are evident from the outset of *L'Homme qui rit*, when the reader is plunged into the dark moral underside of late-seventeenth-century England. But we are far from Balzacian mimēsis here, because any semblance of verisimilitude soon gives way to the phantasmagoric. The monstrous appetites that dominate the text have inspired a number of twentieth- and twenty-first-century spin-offs, including the figure of the Joker in the Batman comic series and movies and in James Elroy's fictive account in *The Black Dahlia* (1987) of the mutilation and murder of an aspiring young Hollywood actress in the 1940s.[3] Both the menacing shadows of Gotham and the sleazy underside of modern 'culture' reflect the dark cravings that besiege protagonists and polity alike in Hugo's narrative.

[1] Not until the Second Reform Act of 1867 did all male householders in England win the right of universal male suffrage granted in France in 1848.

[2] See Albouy, *La Création mythologique*, 243, and Roman, *Victor Hugo et le roman philosophique*, 597.

[3] The Joker character first appeared in spring 1940, inspired in part by Conrad Veidt's indelible portrayal of Gwynplaine in the 1928 silent film version of *HQR*, directed by Paul Leni. More recently, Heath Ledger's portrayal of the Joker in *The Dark Knight* (2008) etches a vivid image of the physically and mentally twisted psychopath. Of course, the Joker mimes only Gwynplaine's disfigured exterior, since Hugo's hero remains a highly principled personage.

The reader is immediately plunged into the most extreme kind of tragedy, according to Northrop Frye's system, 'a world of shock and horror' dominated by 'what is technically known as *sparagmos* or the tearing apart of the sacrificial body'.[4] A little boy, abandoned in a raging blizzard by the bandits who had defaced him in order to prevent his rightful ascent to the peerage as Lord Clancharlie, stumbles first upon the carcass of a hanged man on a gibbet, and then on a baby girl buried in the snow on her dead mother's breast. This echo of the triad of social miseries involving man, woman, and child featured in the famous preface of *Les Misérables*—'les trois problèmes du siècle [sont] la dégradation de l'homme par le prolétariat, la déchéance de la femme par la faim, l'atrophie de l'enfant par la nuit' (xii. 49)—immediately signals an affiliation between the two texts. *L'Homme qui rit*, like *Les Misérables*, will focus on the most wretched members of society. Although causes of the miseries and the miseries themselves fluctuate from century to century, one can locate tantalizing analogies between the 'degraded' hanged man and the ex-convict Valjean, between the 'fallen' prostitute Fantine and the prone, half-dressed dead woman, and between such ignorant, exploited children as Cosette, Gavroche, and Eponine, and the blind baby orphan Dea and her disfigured ten-year-old saviour Gwynplaine.[5] Clearly, the world in which the children move is bleakly dystopian. Monsters reign.

That Dea and Gwynplaine are subsequently adopted by Ursus, a wandering philosopher–mountebank who scorns the aristocratic powers that be, plainly elevates Hugo's historical text to the level of political commentary. As a young man, Gwynplaine leads an itinerant but happy existence performing in a road show with his adopted family and dreaming of a blissful union with Dea, with whom he has fallen in love. He has no way of knowing that he is the legitimate heir of the exiled republican Lord Clancharlie, forced to flee England in 1660 with the return of Charles II and the Restoration of the British monarchy. Nor does Gwynplaine imagine the political conniving that takes place in London at the top of the social heap—all at the expense of the oppressed people. The victim of monarchic and social injustices alike, the deformed hero eventually gets to speak his (shockingly republican) mind in the House of Lords after his identity as the current Lord Clancharlie is revealed. By the same token, the narrator's exposure throughout the text of the gigantic fraud imposed on the English people by the hypocritical and self-absorbed ruling classes constitutes a secondary plot or story of *mis*-representation. Indeed, I argue

[4] Frye, *The Anatomy of Criticism*, 222, 148.

[5] The plight of Gwynplaine and Dea might well be considered even worse than that of the children in *MIS*—they are Hugo's ultimate victims of man and nature, respectively.

that, rather than amounting to 'an extremely bad piece of writing', as Richard Grant claims,[6] the text functions as an immensely concentrated system, where the parts recapitulate the whole.

Within this system, the novel poses important questions about the role of historical memory in imagining a better future. This issue has aesthetic as well as political dimensions, since, in weaving back and forth between different time frames, retro- and prospective thinking follows the recursive pathways associated with multi-level spatial figures. Though the plot focuses largely on Gwynplaine's attraction not only to Dea but also to the wicked temptress Duchess Josiane, the subsequent battle for his heart, soul, and body points to the continuing historical struggle between spiritual and material impulses. Situated between the lost utopian ideals of his unknown father and the dystopian realities that inhabit his country, Gwynplaine undergoes a radical metamorphosis as he attempts to bridge the gap between them. His shifts between classes and identities are precipitated by a series of ups and downs—the spatial equivalent of diverging temporal points. As he is elevated to the peerage, one wonders whether he will remember his lowly adopted family. Gwynplaine eventually finds himself, like his republican father, despised and rejected by the other lords, but not before he has a chance to plead the case of the nation's poor, that is, of his *other* self, to the aristocracy bent on preserving its own privileged status. In so doing, he defies the conventions of extreme tragedies, where 'the hero is in too great agony or humiliation to gain the privilege of a heroic pose',[7] clinging to hope rather than despair and challenging the powers that be on behalf of the voiceless, impoverished masses.

In this way, Gwynplaine's extraordinary social mobility becomes a metaphor for all who aspire to a *different* world—from utopian dreamers to self-absorbed social climbers. While Hugo's meek hardly end up inheriting the earth, their social mutability implies that such changes in fortune can also apply to their oppressors. The network of transpositions in the novel, or what Guy Rosa calls 'le motif de la réversibilité',[8] carry implications for imperial rule in nineteenth-century France as well. At the same time, the sociopolitical reversals and inversions in the text illuminate the connection in Hugo between historical refiguration and metaphorical redescription. By examining the mirroring effects in the novel at multiple levels, I show how Hugo creates a transhistorical narrative even more

[6] Grant, *The Perilous Quest*, 202.

[7] Frye, *The Anatomy of Criticism*, 222.

[8] Guy Rosa, 'Critique et autocritique dans *L'Homme qui rit*', in Guy Rosa (ed.), L'Homme qui rit *ou la parole-monstre de Victor Hugo* (Paris: SEDES, 1985), 9; see also Pierre Laforgue, 'Le Romanesque et l'écriture de l'histoire dans *L'Homme qui rit*', in Rosa (ed.), L'Homme qui rit *ou la parole-monstre de Victor Hugo*, 242).

ambitious in scope than *Les Misérables*. To this end, I look in the first part of this chapter at the grotesque aspects of the work, from physiques to attitudes to polity, then in the second part at the sublime end of the spectrum, which encompasses not only Gwynplaine's utopian vision but also the stunning geometry of chaos that powers Hugo's 'poetics of transcendence'. I conclude by examining the startling resonances between *L'Homme qui rit* and the most celebrated text of the period in which the novel is set—namely, John Milton's *Paradise Lost* (1667). As in his rivalry with Shakespeare, Hugo pays homage to his great epic predecessor by incorporating elements from the plot and characters of *Paradise Lost*, thereby reinforcing his own apocalyptic vision not just of eighteenth-century England but also of present-day France.

GROTESQUE BEINGS, DYSTOPIAN WORLDS

Hugo's novel opens with a scene of such intense horror and despair that it launches the entire text under the sign of the grotesque. After finding his solitary way in a blizzard up and down the treacherous cliffs of the English coastline, the boy Gwynplaine finally reaches a plain where the wasteland image dominates: 'Dans ce grand monde crépusculaire ouvert de toutes parts, qu'y avait-il pour cet enfant? Rien. Il marchait vers ce Rien' (xiv. 63). This image of an absolute substantive without substance is heightened by the rotting corpse of the hanged man, a sort of 'néant visible' (xiv. 64) towards which the boy makes his way.[9] As he draws near, he begins to distinguish the decomposing body of the man on the gallows—a man whose fate as an outcast echoes that of Gwynplaine's father, Lord Clancharlie, some years earlier. The rotting corpse appears as a series of disarticulations and gaps: everything is falling apart, from the body itself to the cloth that no longer conceals it. Covered by a 'masque' of tar, it is an apparition of nothingness: 'L'enfant voyait la bouche qui était un trou, le

[9] The image of 'Rien' also reappears after Gwynplaine flees the corpse: 'L'enfant marchait, la lande continuait, nue à perte de vue' (xiv. 70), the very image of the negative sublime. Sea and earth are white, a nothingness repeated by the absence of light indicating a human habitation. The wilderness of Norway through which Ordener roams in *HI* is no more oppressive. For a compelling study of the traces of this scene in Zola's *La Fortune des Rougon* (1871), see Marie-Sophie Armstrong, 'Hugo à l'aire Saint-Mittre: Zola et la problématique de la propriété littéraire', *French Review*, 76/2 (Dec. 2002), 350–2. See also Jean-Claude Morisot's discussion of the effect of Hugo's novel, which Zola had read in proof form in 1869 and 'admir[é] sans réserves' ('Le Frénétique et le quotidien: Hugo, Zola et le "rire de force"', *Nineteenth-Century French Studies*, 18/3–4 (Spring–Summer 1990), 478), on the younger writer's depiction of the *rire forcé* of Second Empire France in his journalistic essays.

nez qui était un trou, et les yeux qui étaient des trous... La toile s'était moisie et rompue... Le crâne, fêlé et fendu, avait l'hiatus d'un fruit pourri. Les dents étaient demeurées humaines, elles avaient conservé le rire' (xiv. 66). Forecasting and reflecting Gwynplaine's own perpetual rictus for the reader, the 'laughing man' is a true Gothic horror. The holes in its face, the fissure in the fabric, the cracked skull, the lacuna in the rotten fruit—all figure a powerful *vanitas*, as well as the intervals to be filled by poetic imagination. The textual links to this opening, primal scene, where, as Ricoeur explains, the 'metaphorization of... terror and pity' becomes 'the condition for all... ethical instruction' (*OA* 242), are abundant. The grotesque in *L'Homme qui rit* thus bristles, from the outset, with sociopolitical considerations. The hanged man's dreadful end will shape our reading both of Gwynplaine's plight and of his father's self-imposed exile from the same nightmarish world—a world where grotesque desires explode at every level of society.

Harsh Realities

The status of the man on the gallows as an 'hors la loi du cercueil' (xiv. 64)—exiled even from the grave—unmistakably alludes to Hugo's own situation:

> Etre un reste, ceci échappe à la langue humaine. Ne plus exister, et persister, être dans le gouffre et dehors, reparaître au-dessus de la mort, comme insubmersible, il y a une certaine quantité d'impossible mêlée à de telles réalités. De là l'indicible... ce témoin noir, était... un reste terrible... De la nature d'abord, de la société ensuite. Zéro et total. (xiv. 64)

Both have lost their existence, the one literally, the other figuratively. Both are witnesses to appalling horrors. Both represent 'zero and everything', what they were and what they are at present. The resonances with the motif of 'Tout et Rien' in *Les Travailleurs de la mer* suggest a link to Hugo himself. The narrator continues: 'Cet être expiré était dépouillé... Sa moelle n'était plus dans ses os, ses entrailles n'étaient plus dans son ventre, sa voix n'était plus dans son gosier. Un cadavre est une poche que la mort retourne et vide' (xiv. 64). He is completely alienated from himself, emptied out like the victims of the octopus in *Les Travailleurs de la mer*. As in the companion passage in *Les Travailleurs de la mer* describing Lethierry's sense of loss, the poet speaks indirectly here about his own situation through images of diminution and disappearance.

But the description of the corpse in *L'Homme qui rit* is not entirely negative. The notion of being 'unsinkable' (*insubmersible*) recalls Hugo's alternative view of himself in *Les Travailleurs de la mer* as riding on the wave crests of destiny. Though he, too, is the 'épave d'un destin inconnu' (xiv. 65), the poet has managed to survive.[10] Again stressing the *indicible* in the hanged man—'L'inexprimable, qui est dans le désert, se condensait en lui' (xiv. 65)—Hugo's shadow history calls attention to the poet's indescribable suffering as a prophet crying in the desert of exile. When the narrator speculates, regarding the whereabouts of the man's *moi*, that it was now perhaps 'quelque chose d'errant autour de quelque chose d'enchaîné' (xiv. 64–5), he refers indirectly to the wandering exile/Prometheus now 'chained' (metonymically) to his rock in the Channel. The crows arrive on the hanged man like 'la venue d'une légion' (xiv. 68). Along with the legions of winds and waves that assail Gilliatt in *Les Travailleurs de la mer*, the birds' horrible 'poursuite d'un enchaîné' figures the 'combat spectre' (xiv. 69) of the emperor's supporters on the writer–activist tethered to Guernsey. And it is impossible to say who will win.[11] Hugo can be counted, with the novel's protagonists, among the poor and disenfranchised who inhabit dystopia.

The prophetic overtones recur in the narrator's observation that, for Gwynplaine, the hanged man's gaze constitutes a 'fixité indicible' (xiv. 67), the unspeakable residing as much in the grotesque as in the sublime. That a death's head can look is frightful: 'Pas de prunelles, et l'on se sent vu' (xiv. 67). As in a good horror movie or Gothic novel, the dead can see—and pursue—the living. The boy's 'épouvante' (xiv. 69) at the mere thought tells us that we are in the realm of terror, on the verge of the sublime. The sightless eyes represent a version of the visionary poet's 'fixed' gaze, as he contemplates what lies beyond, in unknown worlds, thus opening new vistas to the imagination: 'Il existe des réalités ici-bas qui sont comme des issues sur l'inconnu, par où la sortie de la pensée semble possible' (xiv. 65). Though horrible, the decaying body forces one to reflect, to meditate, to breach the gaps into realms of thought as yet

[10] Likewise, when the bandit's boat, the *Matutina*, loses its rigging, 'elle ne voguait plus, elle surnageait' (xiv. 92), while its crew clings to hope, one of 'les insubmergibles mirages de l'âme' (xiv. 96), after escaping the islets known as the Casquets. So, when Ursus keeps alive the hope that Gwynplaine has not perished in Southwark prison—'Cette flamme surnageante flotte éternellement sur la douleur humaine' (xiv. 302)—the reiterated metaphor suggests that the absent and exiled poet is the hope of those who suffer in France.

[11] Again, indirectly, the poet has 'le vent pour lui et la chaîne contre lui' (xiv. 69), the strength of his lungs militating against the restriction of movement. But the other side has its numbers. One of the 'legions' aligned against Gwynplaine is the snowflake: 'Le flocon inexorable et doux fait son œuvre en silence... Il est pur comme l'hypocrite est candide. C'est par des blancheurs lentement superposées que le flocon arrive à l'avalanche et le fourbe au crime' (xiv. 109). The descriptors associated with Clubin, the octopus, and the tempest in *TM* are reprised in *HQR*, which likewise stands as an *œuvre* that exposes and counters the treacherous and hypocritical *œuvres* of others.

unexplored. It invites us to plumb *l'inconnu*, not unlike Gilliatt in *Les Travailleurs de la mer*.

Through the narrator's description, it becomes obvious that the hanged man, whatever his crimes, is a victim: 'Il avait eu du sang qu'on avait bu, de la peau qu'on avait mangée, de la chair qu'on avait volée' (xiv. 65). In short, he has been robbed and, quite obviously, cannibalized in a 'demonic parody [of the Eucharist]'.[12] The violent ritual of material *sparagmos* has replaced the weaving of spiritual bonds in the Lord's Supper, where the communicants are united in the body and blood of Christ. If the point of hanging on the gibbet was the moral edification of people passing by, it is evident that society requires a new educational system—one that does not steal or desecrate bodies. The man's 'cadavr[e] émiett[é]' will even make the grass under it greener, since 'la terre se nourrit de l'homme' (xiv. 67) as much as man lives off the earth. The law has allowed nature to feed off every last shred of the dead man's being. Such imagery is reminiscent of the monster's handiwork in *Han d'Islande*, the legalistic ogres in *Le Dernier Jour d'un condamné*, and the criminal justice system in *Les Misérables*, as well as of the 'omnivorously' eclectic Hugo.[13] Ironically, 'on n'avait pas tenu à le garder vivant, mais on tenait à le conserver mort... Les exemples veulent le plein air, et les exemples goudronnés se conservent mieux. Ce goudron était de l'humanité. On pouvait de cette manière renouveler les pendus moins souvent... L'ordre se compose de ces choses-là' (xiv. 67). Conservation, order, setting examples: these are hallmarks, for the author of *Les Misérables*, of the legalistic rationalizations of the Second Empire. As in the case of Javert and nineteenth-century France,[14] seventeenth-century English justice embodies frightening contradictions.

The implication is clear: composed of inhumane acts supported by twisted logic, the authority on which such legal systems rest is bound some day to collapse. What Hugo calls 'la momie du peuple', multiplied by the thousands, may prove 'utile' (xiv. 67) in ways not dreamed of by the powers that be. It may call the people to a resurrection of their identity and integrity through revolution. The victim thus gets his revenge: 'Le tremblement éternel le faisait terrible... Il y avait dans sa durée hors de la tombe, de la vengeance des hommes et de sa vengeance à lui. Il faisait, dans ce crépuscule et dans ce désert, une attestation... Il dénonçait la loi d'en bas à la loi d'en haut' (xiv. 65). By enduring the brunt of cosmic forces, he

[12] Frye, *The Anatomy of Criticism*, 148.

[13] For *HI*, see *EN* 29; for DJC, see *EN* 115, 119; for MIS, see *FT* 61–3, 68; for Hugo, see *EN* 49.

[14] See *FT* 41–3, 88–95, 110–11.

himself has become *terrible*, an agent of the sublime. And his vengeance on the avengers of the law is absolute, witnessing to the awful injustice done to him body and soul before the bar of a higher court. For Ricoeur, 'horror attaches to events that must never be forgotten. It constitutes the ultimate ethical motivation for the history of victims' (*TN* iii. 187). This history, in *L'Homme qui rit*, begins with a biting critique of capital punishment as (dis)embodied by one man's carcass, then sweeps both backwards and forwards through time, real as well as fictive.

So, while the spectacle of the mutilated boy contemplating the hanged man might suggest a composition in opposites, Gwynplaine—the victim of unnatural experiments enjoined by James II (1685–7) and performed by the bandit *comprachicos*—bears a curious resemblance to the corpse on the gallows. Both fulfil the definition of a monster (from *monstrāre*, to show), as creatures meant for display, of texts inscribed by social forces. Illustrating 'the theatrical representation of pain' in gruesome public spectacles that link 'the right to punish with the personal power of the sovereign',[15] Gwynplaine is fated to display his disfigurement by order of the king through performances in both the streets and the House of Lords. Of his grotesque mien, described in a latter chapter entitled 'Où l'on voit le visage de celui dont on n'a encore vu que les actions' (ii. 2. 1), the narrator remarks: 'il est certain que la nature ne produit pas toute seule de tels chefs-d'œuvre' (xiv. 181). So perfect is he in his ugliness that he betrays the hand of an artist. The result is a disarticulated and reconfigured visage:

> Selon toute apparence, d'industrieux manieurs d'enfants avaient travaillé à cette figure. Il semblait qu'une science mystérieuse . . . avait ciselé cette chair . . . et créé, avec préméditation, ce visage. Cette science . . . avait fendu la bouche, débridé les lèvres, dénudé les gencives, distendu les oreilles, décloisonné les cartilages, désordonné les sourcils et les joues, élargi le muscle zygomatique, estompé les coutures et les cicatrices, ramené la peau sur les lésions, tout en maintenant la face à l'état béant, et de cette sculpture puissante et profonde était sorti ce masque, Gwynplaine. (xiv. 181)

A living 'masque', Gwynplaine is defined by the appearance of his face, remodelled by a combination of art and science. He is the living clay that has been skilfully reworked to obliterate any expression of its own, not unlike the man on the gibbet. Here, too, gaps are introduced everywhere (*fendu*, *débridé*, *dénudé*, *décloisonné*, *béant*) and harmony is destroyed (*désordonné*). That he is in no other way 'difforme' further indicates that

[15] Michel Foucault, *Discipline and Punish: The Birth of the Prison*, trans. Alan Sheridan (New York: Pantheon Books, 1977), 14, 80.

he is 'plutôt une création de l'art qu'une œuvre de la nature' (xiv. 183; see also 188), not an accident but a willed artefact, a kind of Frankenstein's monster. 'On avait mis sur lui un faux lui-même' (xiv. 185) and sent his real self into oblivion. Like the protagonist of *Le Dernier Jour d'un condamné*, Gwynplaine 'vivait dans une sorte de décapitation, ayant un visage qui n'était pas à lui' (xiv. 187). He is completely *other*, a masker, a person in disguise. But beneath *this* monstrous person lies *that* heroic soul, which the reader has already observed in the boy's struggles through the storm.[16]

Still, in this initial scene, Gwynplaine appears poised to enter *l'inconnu* as a victim, to risk a fate similar to that of the man on the gallows: 'Encore un instant, et l'enfant et le trépassé, la vie en ébauche et la vie en ruine, allaient se confondre dans le même effacement' (xiv. 68). The mixture of dead and living in a single erasure renews the theme in *Les Misérables* of the poor and outcast as the living dead.[17] At first, the dangers of the blizzard seem purely natural. Along with Hugo and the man's corpse, Gwynplaine finds himself 'dans un désert' (xiv. 60)—the overwhelming emptiness of the plains. The scene before him 's'élargissait comme l'infini et se taisait comme la tombe' (xiv. 61). The underdetermined landscape of Weiskel's horizontal/negative sublime suggests that, with the hanged man and the exiled poet, Gwynplaine will disappear into nothingness.

But combating nature is just the prelude to his struggle for survival. Though the boy's terror turns to pity when he rescues the blind and motherless infant Dea, his own pleas for compassion are ignored when he encounters 'Une autre forme du désert' (I. 3. 4; xiv. 116) in the inhospitable inhabitants of Weymouth and Melcombe Regis.[18] Here, the double-locked doors and windows 'recouvertes de leurs volets comme les yeux de leurs paupières' (xiv. 117) attest to the egotism of those who turn a blind eye to two children in need. No one is interested in the plight of the destitute, neither the rich nor the poor, who display 'la même surdité aux misérables' (xiv. 116). Such indifference retells the plight in *Les Misérables* of both Jean Valjean turned away from door to door in Digne and of the young revolutionaries trapped on the barricades in Paris when the surrounding houses fail to offer a means of escape.[19] The callousness of the

[16] The hero's outer joviality has nothing to do with his feelings: 'Derrière ce rire il y avait une âme, faisant, comme nous, un songe' (xiv. 186). He is a beast without, a soulful dreamer within.

[17] See *FT* 35, 37, 105–6.

[18] Weymouth turns out to be one of the few sites in England ever visited by Hugo. See Thomas, *L'Angleterre dans l'œuvre de Victor Hugo*, 153.

[19] 'Rien ne fait le cœur de pierre comme d'être chaudement entre deux draps' (xiv. 117), the narrator notes. As in *MIS*, the bourgeois mentality of the townspeople indicts the

townspeople to Gwynplaine's peril is the human equivalent of the horizontal sublime: 'L'enfant sentit le froid des hommes plus terrible que le froid de la nuit. C'est un froid qui veut... Maintenant il était entré dans la vie de tous, et il restait seul... Le désert impitoyable, il l'avait compris; mais la ville inexorable, c'était trop' (xiv. 118). The 'terrible' chill emanating from the closed houses again signals the sublime aspect of his experience, in this case the sense of complete solitude and emptiness, not in nature, but in the very heart of 'civilization'. The blind and deaf bourgeois indicate that Dea and Gwynplaine are not the only 'handicapped' people in the text. From bandits to bourgeois to monarchs, society is morally crippled.

The children's rescue by the impoverished mountebank–philosopher Ursus erases these experiences temporarily, as the three bond into a new family. To Gwynplaine's complaint that he is hungry and cold, Ursus at first replies, 'Tout le monde ne peut pas être heureux comme un lord. Va-t'en' (xiv. 119), and we believe that he, too, will lend a deaf ear to the boy. The irony, of course, is that Gwynplaine really is a lord, and a miserable one at that.[20] But the nearly extinguished voice in the 'desert' has at last encountered someone willing to listen—and to act with compassion, to save him as he has saved Dea, in a twinned 'seconde naissance'.[21] Thus, while Ursus seems to reject the boy, his intention soon becomes clear: 'en même temps que la lucarne s'était fermée, la porte s'était ouverte' (xiv. 120). As in *Les Misérables*, a closure in one place leads to an opening somewhere else.[22] A comic figure introduced in the first chapter of the novel, along with his pet wolf Homo, Ursus injects the first note of levity in Gwynplaine's terrible saga. After he has fed the children, he bemoans having to care for passersby: 'Maintenant... je vais avoir chez moi en sevrage l'avenir de la gueuserie d'Angleterre. J'aurai pour emploi, office et fonction... de perfectionner la laideur des gibiers de potence en bas âge' (xiv. 124). Recalling in comic mode the tragic fate of the hanged man, Ursus sees himself producing well-polished victims for future gallows. His creation would be a ludicrous *mélange des genres*. However, in adopting Gwynplaine, he replaces not only the boy's real father but also his symbolic father, the king, thereby creating a new set of paternal legacies. From this perspective, the selfish reaction of the townspeople to the boy's

complacency of the citizens of the Second Empire as well (see *FT* 57–64). Cf. Roche, *Character and Meaning*, 172.

[20] Again, Ursus compares the boy's ravenous manners to the way a lord would sup (xiv. 121), never dreaming that the stranger he is entertaining is, in fact, a lord.

[21] Baudouin, *Psychanalyse de Victor Hugo*, 211.

[22] See *FN* 266–7.

desperate situation merely reflects the attitude of those on top of the social ladder. As we shall see, Gwynplaine's double inheritance from Ursus and Clancharlie establishes the grounds for a scathing satire of authoritarian government that runs throughout the text.

Paternal Legacies

Ursus' political leanings are revealed early on by the narrator, who notes the anti-monarchal 'exhibits' that decorate the walls of his hut. The listing for Lord Clancharlie is annotated in the margin: '*Rebelle; en exil; biens, châteaux et domaines sous le séquestre. C'est bien fait*' (xiv. 43). This approval of the confiscation of Clancharlie's estate operates ironically, as an apparent repudiation of the writer's own stature as an exiled rebel. For Clancharlie was one of the peers of the realm 'qui avaient accepté la république' (xiv. 133), not unlike Hugo himself.[23] Even after the end of the revolution and the fall of parliamentary government, he had stuck to his views: 'à l'instant où le passé devenait l'avenir et où l'avenir devenait le passé, ce lord était resté réfractaire . . . il s'était volontairement exilé . . . il avait vieilli dans cette fidélité à la république morte. Aussi s'était-il couvert du ridicule qui s'attache naturellement à cette sorte d'enfantillage' (xiv. 134). Pointing to the end of the Second Republic and the return of the past in the form of Napoléon III's empire, Hugo invests Clancharlie with his own resistance, voluntary expatriation, and loyalty to the lost republican cause. Like the exiled baron, Hugo has borne his share of ridicule for such 'childishness'. But, as the text has already made evident, children know more about right and wrong than most adults.

Clancharlie's alienation, it turns out, functions in more ways than one. In his self-imposed Swiss exile, he is 'hors de son pays, presque hors de son siècle' (xiv. 134). Like Hugo on his rock in Guernsey, he is out of step with his time—or perhaps far ahead of it. Others see him as merely wedded to a rigid stance: 'Lord Clancharlie . . . se satisfaisait avec des phrases creuses. Cet homme était ankylosé par l'orgueil. Les mots, conscience, dignité, etc., sont des mots après tout. Il faut voir le fond' (xiv. 138). He has clung to mere words, refusing to embrace the present reality of Restoration England. His unmoving position evokes Gwynplaine, who 's'ankylosait' (xiv. 67) before the hanged man, foreshadowing their kinship well before it is revealed by the plot. Society judges the absent peer severely: 'Sous prétexte qu'il avait prêté ce sermon monstrueux, lord Clancharlie vivait hors du royaume . . . Il avait la sombre estime de ce

[23] Cf. Meschonnic, *Pour la poétique IV*, 165.

qui n'était plus; attache bizarre à des choses évanouies' (xiv. 137). Not only is his promise to support the Republic in bad taste (*monstrueux*); he lives in another place (*hors du royaume*) and another time (*choses évanouies*). What no longer exists has more value for him than what is, his nostalgia meshing with the *ubi sunt* motif threaded throughout the narrative.

In addition, Clancharlie's critics attack his fundamental ethics, maintaining he has 'une conscience myope' (xiv. 138) that considers actions too closely: 'L'excès de conscience dégénère en infirmité... La fidélité déraisonnable se descend comme un escalier de cave. Une marche, puis une autre, puis une marche encore, et l'on se trouve dans le noir... Les principes finissent par être un gouffre' (xiv. 138). Examining one's motives and deeds can only send one on the slippery slope leading to the 'farouche', to the 'wildness'/'unsociability' of an Ursus, for example. The metonymical sequence, whereby one descends step by step into the unknown, parodies Hugo's earlier rendition of the dangers of daydreaming in 'La Pente de la rêverie'. All of a sudden, one falls into the abyss of conscience, an image developed in *Les Misérables* by Jean Valjean's sacrifice of self to an unyielding notion of right and wrong.[24] The man's fate is brought up again in the House of Lords, where an elderly peer advises a younger man that 'il n'y a pas d'honnête homme' (xiv. 341)—neither Cato nor Aristides nor Thomas More. Alluding to Hugo's situation, the latter declares: 'D'ailleurs un homme qui reste en exil, c'est ridicule' (xiv. 341). When his interlocutor protests, 'Il y est mort,' he responds, 'Un ambitieux déçu. Oh! si je l'ai connu!... J'étais son meilleur ami' (xiv. 341). The claims to intimacy, of course, have no one to refute them. With such great friends, one hardly needs enemies, and Hugo is bitterly ironic on this point.

In short, Clancharlie is deemed an 'idiot' by his contemporaries for his 'étrange persistance républicaine' (xiv. 137). Unlike his profiteering peers, Clancharlie goes around 'vêtu des mêmes habits que le peuple, pâle, distrait, courbé... à peine attentif à la tempête et à l'hiver, marchant comme au hasard, l'œil fixe, ses cheveux blancs secoués par le vent de l'ombre, silencieux, solitaire, pensif' (xiv. 134). The use of vocabulary similar to that in 'Demain, dès l'aube' (*CONT* IV. 14), one of Hugo's best-known poems, again draws attention to the lord's affiliation with the exiled republican writer.[25] Clancharlie's tenacity recalls both that of the hanged man (xiv. 64), another sort of *mort vivant*, and Gwynplaine's

[24] See *FT* 159, 238–9; see also 294.

[25] Cf. Jean Gaudon, '"L'Homme qui rit" ou la Parole impossible', *L'Information littéraire*, 35/5 (1984), 198.

perseverance through the snowstorm (xiv. 111, 165). But no one else in the narrative finds it admirable. Some smile, others 'riaient tout haut' (xiv. 135). Old Hugo is considered a fool, the text implies, for having likewise had the 'aberration' to 'bouder le bonheur de son pays' (xiv. 137) by persisting in his republican faith. The poet's inability to join with everyone else in the 'consentement universel'—a far cry from his ideal of the Universal Republic—would be 'odieux', they say, were it not 'bouffon' (xiv. 138). Clancharlie, Gwynplaine, Hugo: three clowns who embrace the cause of the people and suffer the penalty. The laughing theme makes those who support the new version of the old regime ironic counterparts (if not complicit parties) to Gwynplaine's implacable mask.

The self-serving rhetoric of those who profit from the return of the monarchy under Charles II is manifest in their supercilious questions, rationalizations, and platitudes: 'Pourquoi ces exagérations de solitude et d'exil? . . . La vraie vertu, c'est d'être raisonnable. Ce qui tombe a dû tomber, ce qui réussit a dû réussir . . . Il faut que quelqu'un se dévoue . . . Vous vous bannissez? quelle vanité! Est-ce un défi? quelle audace! . . . Nous ne désertons pas, nous' (xiv. 135). All the arguments marshalled against Hugo are rehearsed here, ostensibly about Clancharlie. Hypocrisy turns cowardice into a duty and greed into rectitude. Virtue, sacrifice, devotion, and fidelity—all find topsy-turvy meanings in this Orwellian landscape. Hugo is a deserter; those who remain to profit are on the side of history because, after all, whatever is, is right. (Or, as Ursus says to Gwynplaine in his ironic discourse on the magnificence of the lords, 'Vénérons ce qui est' (xiv. 208).) France in the mid-nineteenth century is a place without passion, indifferent to ideals, oscillating in the wind like the man on the gibbet.[26] Leuilliot rightly points out the inspiration that Hugo drew from François-Victor's translations of and comments on Shakespeare's plays: 'Le "despotisme moderne"—ou son archéologie—fait aussi le sujet d'un roman comme *L'Homme qui rit*.'[27] The ironic description of the English Restoration, which installed Charles II on the throne, indicts the self-interest of those supporting the Second Empire 200 years later: 'L'Angleterre était heureuse; une restauration est une réconciliation d'époux; prince et nation ont cessé de faire lit à part . . . les pairs démocrates . . . avaient eu le bon sens de se rendre à l'évidence, d'être de leur époque' (xiv. 134). They have fallen into bed with their ruler, the better to profit from his ventures. Though the 'prince' may have waged war for reasons known only to himself, like Napoléon III in Crimea,

[26] The image also recalls the hapless poet Gringoire, who likewise seems fated to hang in *NDP*, adapting to whatever life hands him in order to survive (see *EN* 177–8, 180–1).
[27] Leuilliot, 'Histoire réelle', 154.

China, Italy, Vietnam, and Mexico, a little allegiance went a long way towards furthering one's own career. Swayed by 'toutes ces réalités . . . ce beau règne . . . cet excellent roi . . . ces augustes princes rendus par la miséricorde divine à l'amour des peuples' (xiv. 134)—terms familiar to Hugo's reader in the discourse surrounding the Second Empire—men rallied to the throne in exchange for lucrative positions. In other words, they sold themselves.

The dystopian world shunned by Clancharlie and embodied by the man on the gallows is further linked to monarchic authority through imagery of knots and, by implication, hanging (cf. *MHF* 83). If the government of Charles II is a 'nœud large, devenu très vite nœud étroit', under James II, 'l'étranglement commença' (xiv. 139), both literally and figuratively. The latter's repressive regime is satirized as orderly and paternal, not cruel and barbaric. The zeal of his henchman, Kirke, who 'multipliait les exemples' (xiv. 139)—warnings of examples *not* to follow—is matched by Hugo's enumeration of such lessons in inhumanity. The scope of the king's repressive actions can be seen in his approach to Clancharlie: 'Les pairies héréditairement transmissibles contenant une certaine quantité d'avenir' (xiv. 140), James II conspires with the *comprachicos* to sever the knot holding the baron's lineage (and Gwynplaine's facial muscles) together in order to occlude the future.

The rewriting of history to mask selfish motives and violent realities even extends to the image of the scaffold, which reappears in a passage 'praising' Charles II: 'L'épanouissement des cœurs . . . était complet, les gibets des régicides s'ajoutant à la joie universelle. Une restauration est un sourire; mais un peu de potence ne messied pas, et il faut satisfaire la conscience publique' (xiv. 136). An ardent opponent of capital punishment since *Le Dernier Jour d'un condamné*, Hugo undercuts the latter-day jingle, 'a restoration is a smile', with what might be considered 'gallows humour'. To satisfy the public 'conscience' through such executions is to make a mockery of the idea. The satire continues: 'on raillait . . . ces temps singuliers où l'on avait toujours de grands mots à la bouche, *Droit*, *Liberté*, *Progrès*; on riait de ces emphases. Le retour au bon sens était admirable; l'Angleterre avait rêvé' (xiv. 136). The utopian delusion had passed. Everything that had been sacred—that is still sacred to Hugo—is now profane. The 'emphases' of revolutionary parlance recall the criticisms of the poet as 'grandiloquent', thus allying revolution and Romanticism in a joint, very possibly lost, venture. Before discussing Hugo's strategies for recovering and revitalizing his own past later in this chapter, we will explore the proliferation of perverse desires under England's 'sensible' political system. I argue that the system of voids and knots, gaps and links, established by the imagery of hanging points towards the workings of human repulsion and attraction—as well as towards both metaphorical redescription and historical refiguration.

Darkness Visible: Dea and Josiane

Given the oppressive rule in Hugo's post-Restoration England—one that strangles not only the lower classes but also all forms of dissent—it comes as no surprise that many characters would dream of a *different* world. Yet, in *L'Homme qui rit*, most dreams assume a singularly unsavoury form. Indeed, the storyline teems with grotesque desires, presenting a powerful vision of human yearning and corruption that encompasses nearly everyone. The villain, Barkilphedro, perversely seeks to avenge himself on Duchess Josiane (on whom James II had bestowed the Clancharlie estate and peerage) for her many kindnesses to him; the pleasure-seeking Josiane tries to escape boredom by seducing Gwynplaine, now a virile but virginal 25-year-old *saltimbanque*, for an erotic treat; Gwynplaine's temptation by Josiane's material charms threatens to obliterate his devotion to the higher ideals embodied by his beloved companion Dea; and the aristocracy feasts throughout on the very substance of the impoverished English people. All manner of pernicious cravings are on display.

The novel's sombre plot and tragic ending—Gwynplaine walks off a boat into the Thames when Dea dies in his arms only moments after their emotional reunion—recalls the claim in the preface of *Les Travailleurs de la mer* that a triple fate weighs on humanity, 'l'anankè des dogmes, l'anankè des lois, l'anankè des choses', alongside 'la fatalité intérieure, l'anankè suprême, le cœur humain' (xii. 551). While the author identifies the first three forms of fatality with *Notre-Dame de Paris*, *Les Misérables*, and *Les Travailleurs de la mer*, respectively, all four converge forcefully in *L'Homme qui rit*. Thus, religious bigotry shuts down the protagonists' nightly performances in their travelling theatre, the Green Box, after it reaches London. Legal and political fate appears in the abuse of the English people by the monarchy and aristocracy, as well as in the torture and terror wielded by the criminal justice system. Natural fate occurs when a snowstorm kills Dea's mother, blinds the baby girl, and causes the child-trafficking *comprachicos* who had mutilated Gwynplaine's face to drown in the English Channel—or when the hero experiences the sudden come-on of the 'inaccessible' duchess as being annihilated by a shooting star. Interior fate, that of the human heart, resides not only in the adoption of the errant children by Ursus, a self-styled misanthrope, or in the symbiotic relationship of the two lovers, who 'see' into each other's souls, or in Gwynplaine's star-struck attraction to Josiane. It also operates literally, as when Dea dies from what appears to be a coronary aneurism after being separated from and then reunited with Gwynplaine. All too often, human longings are crushed by forces that transcend them: suffocation dominates the text, whether by social hierarchies, watery catastrophes, bursting blood vessels, or crucifixions under the guise of judicial interrogations. The recurrent imagery of aspiration and asphyxiation—an important organizing feature of *Les Travailleurs de la mer* as well—thus ties the Romantic subplot, which focuses on the hero's divided affections between Josiane and Dea, the real and the ideal, to a much wider vortex of desires.[28] In this subsection and the next, we shall examine in detail the temptations that draw Gwynplaine first towards Dea, then towards Josiane, and finally towards the power and glory of the English peerage.

Dea is defined in the text by her diaphanous, imprecise, floating qualities. At 16, she radiates light: 'Ses yeux... avaient cela d'étrange qu'éteints pour elle, pour les autres brillaient... Du fond de son obscurité incurable... elle jetait un rayonnement... Elle était la nuit, et de cette ombre irrémédiable amalgamée à elle-même, elle sortait astre' (xiv. 184). A beacon for others, Dea does not herself see. Her optic nerve having been paralysed in the snowstorm, she is as frozen in her own way as Gwynplaine. Yet, her soul is visible to the world through her transparent eyes, whereas Gwynplaine's is hidden, like the scheming Barkilphedro's, behind an impenetrable mask. The contrast seems absolute: 'Autant il était terrible, autant Dea était suave. Il était l'horreur, elle était la grâce... Elle semblait un songe ayant un peu pris corps' (xiv. 187). He is Quasimodo to her Esmeralda, the grotesque to her sublime, the real to her ideal.[29] As in *Notre-Dame de Paris*, however, the text undercuts the antithesis.[30] If he is her 'soleil' (xiv. 186), she is his 'étoile' (xiv. 188)—but both are stars. They are bound as soulmates, two halves of one expression. When the young couple is reunited at the end, Gwynplaine stresses their identity. Dea is, for him, 'l'enfant, l'épouse, l'étoile, le souffle... l'éternité' (xiv. 379), his ward, partner, and guiding light, his breath of life itself, beyond all space and time. It is fitting, then, that he seek death by suffocation when she expires. The lyrical passages describing their relationship contrast starkly with the epic dimensions, historical discourse, and satiric implications that dominate the text.

Their lives composed of shadows, together the two protagonists sum up human misery: 'Ces ténèbres, Dea les avait en elle et Gwynplaine les avait

[28] Cf. the allegorical readings of Dea and Josiane in Albouy, *La Création mythologique*, 247, 249; Piroué, *Victor Hugo romancier*, 113–14; Grant, *The Perilous Quest*, 219–20; and Brombert, *Victor Hugo and the Visionary Novel*, 191–6.

[29] As Albouy notes, both novels constitute versions of *La Belle et la Bête* (*La Création mythologique*, 248). See also Piroué, *Victor Hugo romancier*, 103; Meschonnic, *Pour la poétique IV*, 176; and Peyrache-Leborgne, 'Victor Hugo et le sublime, 24.

[30] See *EN* 172–7.

sur lui' (xiv. 184). They are the same but different, two faces of the same wretchedness. Little wonder, then, that they find happiness in each other: 'ces deux fatalités incurables, le stigmate de Gwynplaine, la cécité de Dea, opéraient leur jonction dans le contentement... à force d'intuition réciproque, ils en étaient venus à l'unité de rêverie' (xiv. 189). They are the world to each other, sharing their thoughts and dreams in a timeless ecstasy that they believe will never end. Their utopian Eden is an osmosis, an interprenetration of being—'l'exceptionnel bonheur de n'être pour l'autre rien qu'eux-mêmes'[31]—that mingles identities and excludes everyone else. As such, they replay the romance of Marius and Cosette in the garden on the Rue Plumet in *Les Misérables*.[32] They know a plenitude of happiness equal to Duchess Josiane's overflowing wealth, a plenitude without desire: 'époux à distance comme les sphères[,] ils échangeaient dans le bleu l'éffluve profond qui dans l'infini est l'attraction et sur la terre le sexe' (xiv. 190). Reflecting, for William Paulson, a pre-Oedipal state, 'Gwynplaine's and Dea's love is stable, eternal, and forever locked in the form of an original symbiosis'.[33] The 'gravity' that creates balance between them figures the closeness–distance tension in metaphorical identity, where 'things that... were "far apart" suddenly appear as "closely related"' (*RM* 194; see also 195–8, 205). Although set up as opposites, they embody the operations of metaphor, whereby antinomies are resolved on another plane.

Both are also bound by their roles in Ursus' creative theatrical offspring *Chaos vaincu*—a key element of the novel—presented nightly by Gwynplaine and Dea. The scenario is, on the surface, quite simple. Three reptilian forms crawl around in the dark. Representing 'les forces féroces de la nature, les faims inconscientes, l'obscurité sauvage' (xiv. 198), Ursus, the bear, and Homo, the wolf, hurl themselves on the man (Gwynplaine). It is obvious that the latter is losing: 'une minute de plus, les fauves triomphaient et le chaos allait résorber l'homme' (xiv. 198). He seems fated to yield to the law of the jungle, to become a creature of appetites alone. Suddenly, a whiteness (Dea) looms: 'Cette blancheur était une lumière, cette lumière était une femme, cette femme était l'esprit' (xiv. 198–9). Metaphorically, consciousness is born, elevating humanity to a higher state. The dawning light awakens the man, who discovers joy in vanquishing the brutish forces of the material.[34] Gwynplaine and Dea's

[31] Piroué, *Lui, Hugo*, 120.

[32] See *FT* 305–6.

[33] William R. Paulson, *Enlightenment, Romanticism, and the Blind in France* (Princeton: Princeton University Press, 1987), 190.

[34] According to Anne Ubersfeld, *Chaos vaincu* represents 'le fantasme récurrent de Hugo: c'est Léopoldine morte qui permet à son père sa victoire sur les monstres et le triomphe de son génie' (*Paroles de Hugo* (Paris: Messidor, 1985), 69). Cf. also Paulson's

idyll, reflected in the idealism of their theatrical allegory, is soon challenged by various manifestations in their lives of these same forces.

Hugo's plot is set in motion in 1705 by the sociopathic Barkilphedro, Josiane's manipulative Svengali who resents her wealth, youth, beauty, and power. He refuses to be grateful, even when she finds him a sinecure in the government unsealing bottles with messages that wash ashore: 's'était-elle privée de quelque chose dans le débordement haïssable de son superflu?' (xiv. 168), he asks himself, as he repays her favour with treachery. In obtaining the ear of Queen Anne, he realizes his ambition, not to make his fortune, but to 'défaire celles des autres . . . Nuire, c'est jouir' (xiv. 161). His delight is the pain of others. Because of her goodness to him, Josiane is his victim of choice, becoming in his mind a Gwynplaine-like object of inexpressible atrocities: 'Faire subir à Josiane ce qu'on appelerait aujourd'hui une vivisection, l'avoir, toute convulsive, sur sa table d'anatomie, la disséquer, vivante, à loisir, dans une chirurgerie quelconque, la déchiqueter en amateur pendant qu'elle hurlerait, ce rêve charmait Barkilphedro' (xiv. 166–7). While comparing the *comprachicos*' surgery on children with Barkilphedro's dream of torturing Josiane (as well as with Ursus' life-giving science), the text also recalls Esmeralda's suffering in *Notre-Dame de Paris* at the hands of the Inquisition. Like Claude Frollo, who cuts himself with a knife when Esmeralda screams, Barkilphedro feels pain alongside his victim's agony—yet desires only the sacrifice rather than the person herself. He is hatred incarnate, an ogre–vampire who thrives at the expense of others: 'Ambition, appétit, tous ces mots signifient quelqu'un sacrifié à quelqu'un satisfait' (xiv. 167). The cannibals in Hugo's previous novels are reprised by Barkilphedro in *L'Homme qui rit.*[35] Desire, for him, is never reciprocal. At the same time, his fantasy about inflicting ritualized torment allows him to enjoy vicariously 'the exclusive power of the sovereign and his judges',[36] thereby usurping official prerogatives by doubling James II's responsibility for Gwynplaine's disfigurement. To nurture his resentment, Barkilphedro internalizes all social injustice as his own, an ironic version of Gwynplaine's willingness to take on the cause of *les misérables*.[37]

analysis of the play (*Enlightenment*, 192–3), and Lucien Dällenbach, *Le Récit spéculaire: Essai sur la mise en abyme* (Paris: Seuil, 1977), 79–80.

[35] See *EN* 29, 84–5, 139, and *FT* 18–19, 62–3.

[36] Foucault, *Discipline and Punish*, 35.

[37] Cf. Ricoeur, who defines moral duty as 'the demand that the suffering inflicted on humans by other human beings be abolished' (*OA* 290). For the philosopher, 'sharing the point of suffering is not symmetrically opposite to sharing pleasure' because it should lead us to 'feelings spontaneously directed toward others' in the form of solicitude, that is, of 'a search for equality in the midst of inequality' (*OA* 191, 192). Ironically, the totalitarian exercise of power prepares the way for the democratic state (see *OA* 256–7), a viewed shared by Hugo.

When Barkilphedro avenges himself on Josiane by engineering her encounter with Gwynplaine, the rightful heir to the fortune she enjoys, he sets up a re-enactment of *Chaos vaincu* within the story itself. First, Dea begins to lose her ethereality for the maturing young man: 'Si pur que soit le jeune homme qui rêve d'amour, un certain épaississement de chair finit... par s'interposer entre son rêve [d'amour] et lui... Gwynplaine éprouvait on ne sait quel appétit de cette matière où sont toutes les tentations' (xiv. 236). The gap in the dream of love opened by appetite is filled by intimations of flesh. His earthly paradise requires that the ideal come to life. He wishes to contemplate Dea, not from afar, but in physical intimacy. His logic takes an inevitable turn: 'Il fallait à Gwynplaine cette femme. Il lui fallait une femme. Pente dont on ne voit que le premier plan' (xiv. 237). He slips from wanting *this* woman to being willing to settle for *any* woman. Along the inner fault line between flesh and soul, conflict rages: 'Deux instincts, l'un l'idéal, l'autre le sexe, combattaient... au plus obscur de lui-même' (xiv. 232) after he sees the alluring Josiane at his performance. What is a conscious struggle in Jean Valjean between good and evil principles on the 'pont de l'abîme' (xi. 807), when he discovers Cosette's love for Marius, takes place almost automatically within Gwynplaine. In the depths of his being, he performs the essence of *Chaos vaincu*, with Josiane, the dark, material, angel, in the role of the savage beasts over which Dea/the spirit triumphs.

For, 'Josiane, c'était la chair' (xiv. 144), seduction incarnate. A virginal temptress, she is neither impure nor chaste, simply bored and jaded. Only someone *different* will assuage her pride, a king or a monster, for example. When she amuses herself by attending Gwynplaine's show, she stuns the audience: 'c'était une apparition rose et fraîche, bien portante... Les fantômes gras, qu'on nomme les vampires, existent. Telle belle reine... qui mange trente millions par an au peuple des pauvres, a cette santé-là' (xiv. 229). The vampire theme is linked here to the parasitic existence of royalty at the expense of the poor, a version of Barkilphedro's unreciprocated pleasure. 'Avant tout, mettre l'espèce humaine à distance, voilà ce qui importe' (xiv. 146), Josiane opines. Contrary to Ursus' willingness to adopt orphaned children as his own, she creates a gulf between herself and everyone else. The one creates links between disparate entities, a metaphorical function; the other dissolves human bonds wherever possible.

Both seen and seeing, Josiane appears in the crowd as a rival star to Dea: 'C'était comme l'arrivée d'une planète inconnue. Cela venait du monde des heureux. L'irradiation amplifiait cette figure... On sentait, en voyant cette créature astrale, l'approche momentanée et glaciale des régions de félicité' (xiv. 228–9). While the 'rays' emanating from Josiane make her seem larger than she is, her artificial, calculating nature contrasts with Dea's sunniness. Yet Gwynplaine considers the duchess to be unapproachable, as impossible to possess as Dea. And now the irony of his fate becomes clear: 'l'âme, cette chose céleste, il la tenait, il l'avait dans sa main, c'était Dea; le sexe, cette chose terrestre, il l'apercevait au plus profond du ciel, c'était cette femme' (xiv. 231). The far becomes the near and the near the far in his upside-down universe.[38] For Gwynplaine, the spiritual is tangible, and the material is idealized.

The young man's conjunction with Josiane has wide-ranging consequences, it turns out, because the reflections into which he is drawn after seeing the duchess for the first time counter his dreams not only of love but also of social justice: 'On peut s'empoisonner avec des rêveries comme avec des fleurs... Le suicide de l'âme, c'est de penser mal... La rêverie attire, enjôle, leurre, enlace, puis fait de vous son complice' (xiv. 231). His 'fall' from grace in the edenic bliss of shared love with Dea comes in the form of the dilating spirals of reverie. A variation on 'La Pente de la rêverie', the passage associates Josiane's seductiveness with the danger of seductive dreams. Gwynplaine's 'suicide' begins here, with the gradual death of his 'soul'—that is, of Dea herself, who starts to fade away from this moment on. Distracted by other thoughts, he no longer puts her or his social mission at the centre of his existence.

A wise person once said, be careful what you wish for. When the hero stumbles upon a sleeping Josiane at the ancestral Clancharlie home she now occupies, she seems a vision of innocent beauty—till she yawns like a tigress. This 'Olympian' adheres to the law of the jungle. Both 'Eve' (II. 7. 3; xiv. 308) and 'Satan' (II. 7. 4; xiv. 313), she lies barely veiled by a diaphanous fabric: 'Au centre de la toile, à l'endroit où est d'ordinaire l'araignée, Gwynplaine aperçut une chose formidable, une femme nue' (xiv. 309). Like Frollo and Esmeralda in each other's grip or Gilliatt in the lair of the octopus in *Les Travailleurs de la mer* (III. 4. 3), he is the fly in Josiane's fatal web: '[Il] subissait une sorte de résorption. Des forces obscures le garrottaient mystérieusement. Une gravitation l'enchaînait' (xiv. 311). He feels himself being swallowed up and strangled.[39] The

[38] Cf. James, *Dream, Creativity, and Madness*, 226, and Paulson, *Enlightenment*, 194.

[39] The vampire theme in *HQR*, in my view, alludes not only to Hugo's self-absorbed exile on Guernsey but also to the self-consuming narcissicism of those in power. An image of *la Mère terrible* in *NDP*, *TM*, and *HQR*, the spider represents for Baudouin a form of *anankè*, whereby 'la présence d'une puissance maléfique et fatale' (*Psychanalyse de Victor Hugo*, 172; see also 169, 177)—the all-consuming mother—can mask a more personal hunger: 'L'araignée menaçante au centre de sa toile est par ailleurs un excellent symbole de

scene recalls the bandits' *naufrage* at the beginning of the narrative, the gravitational pull that keeps him rooted to the spot replaying the sinking of their vessel under the force of gravity. Suddenly, Josiane is no longer transcendent but immanent. The corporeal ideal has become real and has him in its clutches.

It is, we learn, as if one had long admired a faraway star. One day, the star turns into a comet, growing ever larger in the sky: 'O terreur, il vient à vous! . . . Ce qui arrive sur vous, c'est le trop de lumière, qui est l'aveuglement; c'est l'excès de vie, qui est la mort . . . L'escarboucle du fond de l'infini, diamant de loin, de près est fournaise . . . Et vous sentez commencer votre combustion par une chaleur de paradis' (xiv. 312). The terror of the sublime, when God invades the individual conscience or a distant star becomes an all-consuming meteor or a temptress from the abyss holds you in her power, overwhelms Gwynplaine. The gap has been breached, the remote appears close by, in this figure for metaphorical transposition (see *RM* 17–20). Just as Gwynplaine views Josiane as coming towards him from across the infinite, she considers her love a formidable magnet: 'Amour tout-puissant, puisqu'il t'a fait venir. La distance impossible était entre nous. J'étais dans Sirius et tu étais dans Allioth. Tu as fait la traversée démesurée, et te voilà' (xiv. 315)—yet another model for the unitive process of metaphorical discourse. Regardless of who is flying across space towards whom, Gwynplaine is dazzled to the point of blindness. The more he is attracted to Josiane, the more he resembles his true soulmate, Dea. Unable to distinguish high and low, near and far, good and evil, he experiences the apocalyptic moment where one encounters either heaven or hell.

The temptation begins with a gaze, as they look at each other in mutual fascination, 'lui par la difformité, elle par la beauté, tous les deux par l'horreur' (xiv. 313). Gwynplaine's outer appearance reflects Josiane's inner corruption. After all, she says, they were made for one another: 'Le monstre que tu es dehors, je le suis dedans . . . Il y a entre nous une affinité sidérale; l'un et l'autre nous sommes la nuit, toi par la face, moi par l'intelligence . . . Ton visage, c'est mon âme' (xiv. 316). They are, in short,

l'introversion ou du narcisme, cette absorption de l'être par son propre centre' (*Psychanalyse de Victor Hugo*, 169). See also Grant, *The Perilous Quest*, 216; Albouy, 'Présentation', to Victor Hugo, *L'Homme qui rit*, in *OC* xiv. 13; Charles Mauron, 'Les Personnages de Victor Hugo: Étude psychocritique', in *OC* ii, pp. xxxvi–xxxviii; Brombert, *Victor Hugo and the Visionary Novel*, 192–3; Sylvie Ballestra-Puech, '"Car Dieu, de l'araignée, avait fait le soleil": Métamorphoses d'Arachné chez Victor Hugo', in Dominique Peyrache-Leborgne and Yann Jumelais (eds), *Victor Hugo ou les frontières effacées* (Nantes: Pleins Feux, 2002), 109–11, 116–18; Delphine Gleizes, 'Les Paradoxes de la cave pénale: De quelques représentations carcérales dans l'œuvre de Victor Hugo', *Romantisme*, 126/4 (2004), 22; and Roche, *Character and Meaning*, 89–91.

inversions of each other. In opening her eyes to her monstrous depravity, the hero has in effect 're-created' Josiane by giving her a new identity. Their symbiosis is a meeting of monstrous equals. Because 'le difforme est l'envers du sublime' (xiv. 316), the *bateleur* is as great in his own way as she is in hers. He sports a supremely grotesque face; she is a sublime example of the twisted soul. Together they will *épater les bourgeois* through their brilliant outrage to social and aesthetic values.[40] The theme of boldness—highlighted not only in Gwynplaine's struggles as a child in the snowstorm but also in *Les Misérables* and *Les Travailleurs de la mer*—finds its ironic echo in the wild ambitions of Hugo's duchess.

Representing the savage forces unleashed on humanity in *Chaos vaincu*, Josiane claims that her love for Gwynplaine is a snake she carries in her heart. By associating him with the serpent, she again inverts reality in an effort to charm him. What she ostensibly offers is absolute subjection: 'Oserai-je être ta maîtresse, ta concubine, ton esclave, ta chose? avec joie' (xiv. 315), she proclaims. Such degradation will be the source of untold pleasure. Her plea seems to hold universal truths: 'La femme, c'est de l'argile qui désire être fange . . . Méprise-moi, toi qu'on méprise. L'avilissement sous l'avilissement, quelle volupté!' (xiv. 315). Like the crushing of the lower classes in the social hierarchy, her debasement will place her lower than him, lending zest to her proud sense of difference. The seduction occurs through the notion of all women aspiring to be mire, a primary material to be moulded by their 'masters': 'Pétris un astre dans la boue, ce sera moi!' (xiv. 316). Her allegorical significance as the temptation of matter unformed by spirit in *Chaos vaincu*, a force for devolution aiming to send the world back to its disordered beginnings, is evident.[41] When an 'extase aveugle et bestiale' (xiv. 316) invades the hero, the reader comprehends that the beasts are about to triumph. Given Dea's genuine purity, however, one must read this scene as a rhetorical ploy aimed at undermining both Gwynplaine's moral bearings and his appreciation of Dea's distinctiveness.

But, just as Josiane turns out to be Gwynplaine's inverse rather than his opposite, she is far from the antithesis of Dea. Both are blonds and virgins, the one a 'déesse' (xiv. 230, 240, 242, 316), the other, a 'divinité' (xiv. 184). Both appeal to Gwynplaine as a kind of 'Eve' (xiv. 190, 308). And both are stars to which he is attracted, and vice versa. Ursus' encouragement to his adopted son regarding Dea—'garde ton astre, araignée!' (xiv.

[40] Thomas ventures that Hugo himself was not wholly 'innocent du désir d'étonner "la modestie anglaise actuelle" en peignant le dévergondage de la duchesse Josiane' (*L'Angleterre dans l'œuvre de Victor Hugo*, 218–19), given that he was so greatly annoyed by the prudery of the Channel Island inhabitants.

[41] Cf. Brombert, *Victor Hugo and the Visionary Novel*, 192–4.

204)—further affiliates the two women through the image of the spider, Josiane in the one case and Gwynplaine in the other.[42] Their similarities point to a common ground—namely, the complex human psyche that houses forces of evolution and devolution alike: 'Est-ce que l'homme a, comme le globe, deux pôles?' the narrator asks. 'Sommes-nous, sur notre axe inflexible, la sphère tournante, astre de loin, boue de près . . . Le cœur a-t-il deux côtés, l'un qui aime dans la lumière, l'autre qui aime dans les ténèbres? Ici la femme rayon; là la femme cloaque. L'ange est nécessaire. Est-ce qu'il serait possible que le démon, lui aussi, fût un besoin?' (xiv. 317–18). Humanity may wear a mask, its intractible dark aspect interwoven with a more radiant surface. We may all have a starry side and a side of mud, a *côté Dea* and a *côté Josiane*, a mixture of the sublime and the grotesque that undermines personal and historical progress. In recycling the system of multi-layered equivalencies developed in *Les Misérables*, Hugo's metaphorical equation of different entities in *L'Homme qui rit* adumbrates his republican ideal, whereby all citizens—high and low, rich and poor, lords and street people—enter into a relationship of political parity.[43] Metaphor becomes, in Hugo, a means for grasping and conveying eternal historical truths. But is progress *within* history possible, in the light of the forces of retrogression? A preliminary reading of Gwynplaine's efforts to effect social change suggests that the task is far from easy.

Grotesque Polity

According to our analysis, the use of similar *topoi* to depict polar opposites in *L'Homme qui rit* calls into question the antithetical relationships themselves, thus inscribing the struggle between good and evil within the more global social issue of egalitarianism. Whereas the representation of women through Dea and Josiane might at first appear to adhere to the virgin–whore dichotomy and so to reflect an anti-feminist stance, this dichotomy is deconstructed by Hugo's creation of metaphorical connections and multi-level symmetries to figure his own unspeakable (republican) desires. The poet's idealism, like that of George Sand, 'harness[es] erotic energy to the chariot of state'.[44] Given the 'programme idéologique

[42] The hero replays Quasimodo's *araignée* to Esmeralda's *astre*, his 'cave' serving as a cathedral-like sanctuary, this time to two people who love each other. As Ubersfeld shows, the spider is not just a negative figure in Hugo, that of Baudouin's *Mère terrible*, but a representation of the poet-weaver aiming for 'on ne sait quelle résurrection' (*Paroles de Hugo*, 97).

[43] See *FT* 212–13, 231–2, 286–7.

[44] Naomi Schor, *George Sand and Idealism* (New York: Columbia University Press, 1993), 99.

précis' of the text's republican teleology, noted above, the shower of false appearances in the novel is staged not just to 'démasquer l'usurpateur, pointer du doigt la tartufferie, dénoncer la séduction portée aux cimes de l'art' by the English aristocracy and its minions, as Élise Noetinger asserts;[45] they also gesture towards a more authentic and, hence, more alluring future. To tease out the presence of this *other* future in the text, we must first consider its attractive evil twin—the attainment of wealth and power for one's own exclusive use.

A close reading shows that the social overtones of the Dea–Josiane symbiosis play out in the novel's political discourse as well. Tempted by the peerage through Barkilphedro, who has learned his true identity as the current Lord Clancharlie in the message that the drowning *comprachicos* had tossed into the sea, Gwynplaine risks falling into a second 'material' trap:

> Il était sur la montagne d'où l'on voit les royaumes de la terre.
> Montagne d'autant plus terrible qu'elle n'existe pas. Ceux qui sont sur cette cime sont dans un rêve.
> La tentation y est gouffre, et si puissante, que l'enfer sur ce sommet espère corrompre le paradis, et que le diable y apporte Dieu. (xiv. 282)

Once more, Gwynplaine is the victim of an illusion that may cause his moral downfall. He may abandon his self-sacrificial role in order to profit from a pact with the devil. In so doing, he would lose his right to claim justice for *les misérables*, whose cause he will have denied by becoming one of the oppressors. As with the temptation of Jesus in the desert, earthly goods and power are heaped before him: 'Des palais, des châteaux, la puissance, l'opulence, toutes les félicités humaines à perte de vue autour de soi, une mappemonde des jouissances étalées à l'horizon, une sorte de géographie radieuse dont on est le centre; mirage périlleux' (xiv. 282). In a version of his encounter with the corporeal Josiane, Gwynplaine is lured by the bounties available to one who has sold his soul. He is, the narrator says, like a man who has fallen asleep in a mole hole and awakened on the steeple of Strasbourg Cathedral. Gripped by a double helix that intertwines opposites in a dizzying dance, he again intersects with Dea as an '"aveugle ébloui"' (xiv. 282)—though in this case he risks tumbling into permanent spiritual darkness. As in *Les Misérables* and *Les Travailleurs de la mer*, apparent antitheses are resolved in apocalyptic moments, when universal identity reigns.[46]

[45] Élise Noetinger, 'La Sinistre Beauté du masque: Étude de *L'Homme qui rit* de Victor Hugo', *French Studies*, 53/4 (Oct. 1999), 152, 144.

[46] Cf. Grant, for whom *MIS* and *HQR* share many features, with one major difference: 'Apocalyptic imagery is at the heart of *HQR*, whereas in *MIS* it was merely important' (*The Perilous Quest*, 200). Regarding apocalyptic resolutions in *MIS*, see, e.g., *FT* 42–3, 74–5, 90–1.

The narrator goes on to offer a parable that links the social and sexual inducements in the text: 'Il fait nuit; une main pose une chandelle, vil suif devenu étoile, au bord d'une ouverture dans les ténèbres. La phalène y va' (xiv. 283). The false metaphorical transformation of animal fat into a star acts as a snare, not unlike Gwynplaine's encounter with Josiane. Those who are attracted to glitter as moths to a candle may be no more responsible for their actions than creatures of instinct. The narrator wonders if one can resist temptation any more than a leaf can defy gravity: 'Questions matérielles, qui sont aussi des questions morales' (xiv. 284). Are humans different from animals or sinking ships? Are we, too, subject to the laws of nature—the survival of the fittest, self-preservation, fatal attractions—or can we control, and thus be responsible for, our choices and actions? The 'material' and the 'moral' meet through the notion of obeying or disobeying laws, those of nature in the one case and of conscience in the other.

A man of conscience, Gwynplaine has long dreamed of speaking out on behalf of the strangled lower classes. His sublimated suffering gives rise to positive energy 'mise au service de la force amoureuse, mais aussi de la force populaire appelée à conquérir son autonomie'.[47] As in Sand's fiction, 'idealist fervor is conterminous with revolutionary fervor'.[48] Yet Gwynplaine's vision of his glorious oratory in the House of Lords proves to be just another misguided desire: 'Et puis, disait-il, je serai éloquent' (xiv. 285). He plans to reveal the real world to his peers, giving them the benefit of his experience: 'J'ai été près de tout ce dont vous êtes loin!' he will tell them. His prospects for success seem boundless: 'A ces practiciens repus d'illusions, il leur jettera la réalité à la face . . . et ils trembleront, car il sera vrai, et ils applaudiront, car il sera grand' (xiv. 285). The hero's musings on his 'sublime' status shift from the past to the vision of an 'assured' future where *je* has given way to *il*, as if viewed from a omniscient perspective. Clearly, the text suggests, the other lords are not the only ones 'repus d'illusions'. Gwynplaine's use of the past tense (*j'ai été*) separates him from his wretched roots, bringing him closer to his self-centred colleagues than he suspects. His futuristic fantasy of being the avenging angel of truth and justice is but a megalomaniacal moment. As Suzanne Nash notes, he suffers from 'self-delusion'—the belief that he will be 'the epic spokesman for God and humanity'.[49] Just as Hugo's

[47] Peyrache-Leborgne, 'Victor Hugo et le sublime', 25.
[48] Schor, *George Sand and Idealism*, 99.
[49] Suzanne Nash, 'Transfiguring Disfiguration in *L'Homme qui rit*: A Study of Hugo's Use of the Grotesque', in Robert L. Mitchell (ed.), *Pre-Text, Text, Context: Essays on Nineteenth-Century French Literature* (Columbus: Ohio State University Press, 1980), 10.

eloquence as 'le Verbe du peuple' (xiv. 364) failed to move his fellow representatives in the National Assembly, so is Gwynplaine doomed to disappointment in his powers of rhetoric.[50] Unfortunately for him, the lords cannot see beyond his appearance: 'il partageait avec tous les opprimés, dont il était l'incarnation, cette fatalité abominable d'être une désolation pas pris au sérieux' (xiv. 365). He is disfigured both inside and out, the mutilated face reflecting the inexpressible thought within. Reduced to a statue of mirth, he bears the weight of the *misérables* whom he represents—but for whom, it turns out, he cannot speak.

A terrible injustice is, in fact, done when Gwynplaine's own physical evidence is used against him by the other lords: 'Ainsi . . . ce rictus stigmate, image du contentement supposé des nations sous les oppresseurs . . . c'était l'accusation contre le bourreau qui se tournait en sentence contre la victime! . . . La royauté, après avoir eu raison de son père, avait raison de lui. Le mal qu'on avait fait servait de prétexte et de motif au mal qui restait à faire' (xiv. 364). The perpetuity of his disfiguration is repeated in the perpetuation of crimes from generation to generation. Though the text of royalty's guilt is written all over his face, others choose to misread it, seeing only the superficial grimace rather than the suffering of those who have been wronged. Such 'justice' is absurd. The hopelessness of trying to effect social change seems to dominate this passage, suggesting Hugo's discouragement after years of pointing out Napoléon III's misdeeds to his fellow citizens.

When Gwynplaine flees the House of Lords and subsequently discovers that his loved ones have vanished, he realizes that, in consenting to be tempted by Barkilphedro, he has made a poor exchange. Trading Ursus' shack and Dea's smile for wealth and power was a grave mistake: 'Pour une immensité mouvante où l'on s'engloutit et où l'on naufrage, il avait donné le bonheur! Pour l'océan, il avait donné la perle' (xiv. 363), a substitution he cannot reverse. He must pay for his mistakes with the only asset that remains—his own life. The final 'tentation sinistre' (xiv. 369) is that of suicide, his drowning foreshadowed by the fate both of the *comprachicos* and of those who asphyxiate at the bottom of the social heap. Gilliatt's lonely end by suffocation in *Les Travailleurs de la mer* is, however, transformed in *L'Homme qui rit* into Gwynplaine's implied happy reunion with Dea in the hereafter.[51] His tragic passing, like that of Jean Valjean in

[50] See Jean Gaudon, '"L'Homme qui rit" ou la Parole impossible', 200–2; Porter, *Victor Hugo*, 80; and J. A. Hiddleston, 'Suicide in the Novels of Victor Hugo', in J. A. Hiddleston (ed.), *Victor Hugo,* Romancier de l'abîme*: New Studies on Hugo's Novels* (Oxford: European Humanities Research Centre, 2002), 205.

[51] The fact that Gwynplaine smiles as he goes to join Dea proves, for Albouy, that '[il] accède au salut' ('Présentation', 8; see also 9 n. 9) in the novel's dénouement. Cf. Jean

the dénouement of *Les Misérables*, merely underscores the value of his social vision of a world where *anankè* is replaced by human confraternity.

In sum, through the motifs of desire and temptation that bridge social, spatial, and conceptual gaps, Hugo's critique of the English aristocracy sheds light on his republican enterprise. But is that all? And does Gwynplaine's failure to move his fellow peers in the House of Lords represent a defeat of those aims? Is 'l'échec ... de la parole révolutionnaire ...', as Domique Peyrache-Leborgne argues, 'donc aussi l'échec, en termes esthétiques, du sublime face à cette forme négative qu'est le grotesque social (la monarchie et le pouvoir despotiques ...)'[52]—or does the artistic and political sublime prevail after all? A re-examination of recurring patterns of inversion and self-similarity in the text reveals that the project of *L'Homme qui rit* explodes the confines of its apparently dystopian world view, one of doomed love, impossible dreams, and heroic fiascos. Contrary to the view that 'le grotesque [constitue] à lui seul l'esthétique du roman, quand le sublime est relégué sur les planches, dans les limites du *Chaos vaincu*',[53] the text offers glimpses of another world altogether. As in photography, the unflattering image of post-Restoration England is merely the negative of a more radiant body politic, itself but a piece of a larger Hugolian puzzle. When we consider the novel's apocalyptic imagery and hypertropic designs, we see the full scope of Hugo's enterprise.

POLITICAL AND RECURSIVE SUBLIMITIES

We have already observed hints that, despite its bleak, dystopian landscape, *L'Homme qui rit* contains more optimistic elements as well. The universal identities forged in Hugo's metaphorical crucible, for example, gesture towards an as-yet-to-be-realized egalitarian ideal, while Ursus' little adoptive family can be viewed as an exemplary template for a conscientious, confraternal, self-governing republic. At the same time, Lord Clancharlie's devotion to the republican principles of Cromwell's Commonwealth (1649–60) reminds the reader not only of France's vanished Second Republic but also of the writer's own heroism in exile. That

Gaudon, who sees in Gwynplaine's decision to join Dea in death a duplication of 'le geste de Charles Vacquerie [Hugo's son-in-law] se laissant couler avec Léopoldine au fond des eaux, en faisant de ce geste un geste d'espérance' ('"L'Homme qui rit" ou la Parole impossible', 203).

52 Dominique Peyrache-Leborgne 'Le Héros sublime dans *Titan* et *L'Homme qui rit*: D'une mythologie des belle-âmes aux fantastiques chimères', in Patrick Marot (ed.), *La Littérature et le sublime* (Toulouse: Presses Universitaires du Mirail, 2007), 335.

53 Noetinger, 'La Sinistre beauté', 411.

Gwynplaine manages to triumph in the end over all the temptations of sensuality and human ambition so readily proffered by Josiane and Barkilphedro, respectively, also invests his character with the power to move—and to inspire. His ability to change classes, to become *other* while remaining true to himself, is, I maintain, more than just a message of hope for the future of the French nation. It is equally a figure for the self-similar motifs that order Hugo's narrative into a sublimely complex verbal fabric. Reversals, inversions, superpositions, mirror images—all share in structuring the novel's underlying geometry.

Mixes, Matches, and Transpositions

From the outset, the ups and downs of Gwynplaine's career are as much literal as figurative, the young boy being obliged to clamber over the rough terrain of the English coastline in a blizzard in order to reach safety. The imagery of inversions likewise infuses the hero's encounters with Josiane, as well as the apocalyptic aspects of his sudden elevation to the peerage. The rhetoric of dramatic reversals, of course, is inherent in Hugo's aesthetic of mixing genres. In *L'Homme qui rit*, the apparent contrast between the sublime and the grotesque, the high and the low, reveals itself to be illusory, as in the deep identification between Quasimodo and Esmeralda in *Notre-Dame de Paris*, or in Jean Valjean's status as a saintly ex-convict in *Les Misérables*.[54] Superficial contradictions mark the characters in *L'Homme qui rit* as well. Notwithstanding his extreme poverty, the misanthropic Ursus, for instance, is the only person to take pity on the lost and orphaned Gwynplaine and Dea while the rest of the town sleeps. The errant 'lone wolf'—who lives with the tame Homo—may be a kind of 'sauvage, accepté par la civilisation' (xiv. 44). He is also clearly less 'savage' than his 'civilized' counterparts.

The disfigured Gwynplaine, who is deeply loved by Dea, also combines intersecting tendencies: 'Deux destinées extrêmes composaient son sort étrange. Il y avait sur lui un anathème et une bénédiction. Il était le maudit élu' (xiv. 187). An oxymoron like the sublime outlaw Jean Valjean, he mixes the high and the low, the cursed and the blessed, into one fate. In him, 'extremes' touch. Just as he and Dea are united in love, so are his two opposing fates intertwined. This multivalent situation is embodied in his gymnastic capacities: 'ses articulations, utilement disloquées, et propres à des flexions en sens inverse, avaient reçu une éducation de clown et pouvaient, comme des gonds de porte, se mouvoir dans tout les sens'

[54] See *EN* 172–7, and *FT* 94, 147–8, 170–2, respectively.

(xiv. 183). A figure of the people, he demonstrates remarkable flexibility, moving both backwards and forwards with extraordinary agility, thanks to his rearranged members. His multidirectional displacements might well open a door to the future.

One reversal is already inscribed in his flesh. According to the narrator, in Restoration England bandits could be hired to kidnap and dismantle the faces of children.[55] According to Hugo, the reigning powers instituted a false art:

> On prenait un homme et l'on faisait un avorton; on prenait un visage et l'on faisait un mufle . . . Qu'on s'imagine une orthopédie en sens inverse . . . Là où Dieu a mis la perfection, on rétablissait l'ébauche . . . Le bouffon de cours n'était autre chose qu'un essai de ramener l'homme au singe. Progrès en arrière. Chef-d'œuvre à reculons. (xiv. 45)

Turning men into stunted freaks, faces into snouts, and gazes into cross-eyed vision is the opposite of Ursus' alchemical magic, whereby the lame walk and the sick are cured. The philosopher's adherence to nature is countered by a 'scientific' obsession with the artificial.[56] To revert from the end point (*perfection*) to the beginning (*ébauche*), from a man to a monkey, is to evolve backwards, in other words, to undo progress itself. Other spurious creations arise when monkeys are treated as humans. 'Ces singes montés en grade faisaient contrepoids aux hommes brutalisés et bestialisés' (xiv. 46). The play on the 'savage' and the 'civilized' in the portrayal of Ursus and Homo and of the exploitation of children recurs in this account of beasts elevated and of humans degraded for the amusement of others.[57] Although these horrific

[55] 'Le masque de fer est arrachable, le masque de chair ne l'est pas' (xiv. 48). Rather than being contiguous with the face, the mask becomes the face, the extension, the essence. Metonymy shades into metaphor.

[56] Behind the neoclassical aesthetic of symmetrical perfection looms the destructive 'creativity' of those who wish to improve on natural harmony. Little wonder that, as an adult, Gwynplaine remembers his early childhood only as a 'passage de démons sur son berceau' and his being trampled in the dark 'sous des pieds difformes' (xiv. 192). The true monsters are those who (re-)create others as beasts, an 'aliénation de l'homme par l'homme' (Albouy, 'Présentation', 16). As in *MIS*, then, it is the historian's duty to expose social evils, wherever he may find them. In his scathing critique of the seventeenth century, Hugo uncovers the barbarity beneath the show of culture: 'il eut la naïveté corrompue et la férocité délicate, variété curieuse de civilisation' (xiv. 45). This oxymoronic period (*naïveté corrompue, férocité délicate*) curiously resembles Homo, the civilized wolf, and Ursus, the wild philosopher.

[57] In another case of role inversion, or what Roman calls 'une création à l'envers' (*Victor Hugo et le roman philosophique*, 424), Hugo mentions the 'homme, promu coq' (xiv. 46) by means of an operation on the larynx when he was a child. Now humans are no longer diminished by resembling animals but 'promoted' by such surgeries to the higher status accorded animals made to seem more 'human'. At the same time, the man's slavish imitations of a rooster contrast with Ursus' ability to mimic 'toutes sortes de cris d'oiseau' (xiv. 34). In a comic touch, Ursus reproduces the sounds of wild birds, according to his

transformations participate in the dystopian portrait of the British monarchy, they also undergird the much wider structure of the narrative itself. 'The arbitrariness of monarchical power' may not, as Anny Sadrin claims, be 'unquestionably Hugo's first and foremost subject in this novel'.[58] Still, it plays a key role in *L'Homme qui rit* by advertising its own monstrosity in the disfigured bodies of its victims.

Gwynplaine himself is a study in contradictions, an 'homme horrible' (xiv. 182) who makes others laugh when they simply look at him. 'Cette apparition, l'éclat de rire foudroyant' (xiv. 182), gives people the thrill of the sublime (*foudroyant*) with the comic liberation of the grotesque (*horrible*). 'Il faisait tant peur qu'il faisait rire' (xiv. 187): he is the terrible and the horrible combined, a *mélange des genres* whose face delights others in much the same way as Quasimodo's 'grimace... sublime' (iv. 53).[59] The effect is riveting: 'C'était un rire automatique, et d'autant plus irrésistible qu'il était pétrifié. Personne ne se dérobait à ce rictus' (xiv. 182). He is laughter incarnate, the cure for melancholy. But if he wipes away sorrow as a latter-day prozac—'Il était le pôle opposé du chagrin. Spleen était à un bout, et Gwynplaine à l'autre' (xiv. 181–2)—his polar opposition to spleen is just an illusion. People stop at the façade, taking his ability to affect them as his own reality, when in fact he is as sad as they. Like the mask of Comedy in antiquity, his face combines 'toute la parodie, qui aboutit à la démence, toute l'ironie, qui aboutit à la sagesse', a side that evokes laughter and a side that is 'pensif' (xiv. 182), a glimpse of Barkilphedro's 'madness' mixed in with Ursus' 'wisdom'. Some tragedy is implicit in the comic mien of this 'tête infernale de l'hilarité implacable' (xiv. 182), since he is doomed to express but one attitude—which he himself does not share. His situation is dire, an eternal, inflexible damnation: 'Il était infernalement bouffon. C'était le naufrage de la figure humaine dans un mascaron bestial' (xiv. 187). His 'foundering', like that of the *comprachicos*, is a harrowing process with little relief, comic or otherwise. The point is emphasized in the changes that

(somewhat uncivilized) nature, while the king's time-keeper has been altered to simulate a domestic fowl. Ursus' talents as a ventriloquist plainly tie him to the author himself, who inhabits a multitude of roles and speaks in a variety of voices. Cf. Roche, *Character and Meaning*, 186.

[58] Anny Sadrin, '"In the Name of the King": From Dickens's *Great Expectations* to Hugo's *L'Homme qui rit*', *Dickens Quarterly*, 18/4 (Dec. 2001), 218.

[59] The resemblance with Quasimodo is further suggested by the fact that, 'quand on avait ri, on détournait la tête. Les femmes surtout avaient horreur' (xiv. 183)—the same reaction elicited by the hunchback in *NDP* (iv. 53). Cf. Noetinger's perceptive comment that, among other theatres in the novel, 'la Chambre des Lords est une salle de spectacle occupée par une claque cruelle' ('La Sinistre Beauté', 410), much like the ignorant crowd in Hugo's medieval Paris.

Gwynplaine is able to effect in his aspect from time to time. By dint of sheer will, an important motif in *Les Travailleurs de la mer* as well, he is able to 'suspendre l'éternel rictus de sa face et à y jeter une sorte de voile tragique, et alors on ne riait plus devant lui, on frissonnait' (xiv. 182). The comic flips into the tragic, the grotesque into the sublime (*frissonnait*), the instant he becomes himself.

Beautiful on the outside but ugly within, Josiane is, like Gwynplaine, a *mélange des genres* as well as his own inverse: 'Si la vertu consiste dans l'escarpement, Josiane était tout l'escarpement possible, sans aucune innocence . . . Sembler facile et être impossible, voilà le chef-d'œuvre. Josiane se sentait majesté et matière' (xiv. 144; see also 273), the narrator explains. Combining the high (*majesté*) and the low (*matière*), the abundance of 'virtue' and the lack of innocence, she orchestrates the appearance of accessibility while proving impossible to conquer (*escarpement*).[60] Attracted by Gwynplaine's monstrosity, she tests his aptitude for defying physical limits. Indeed, he first perceives her as an unattainable dream that resembles his ordeal in the blizzard: 'Quel escarpement! Le rêve lui-même reculerait devant une telle escalade' (xiv. 231). Even his acrobatic gifts are unequal to the challenge. In masterminding their encounter, Barkilphedro envisions Gwynplaine's eternal debt: 'De protégé, [il] allait devenir protecteur . . . d'un pair de d'Angleterre. Il aurait un lord à lui! un lord qui serait sa créature!' (xiv. 132). A new Doctor Frankenstein will enter the young man's life, after the *comprachico* surgeon, manœuvring him like a marionnette. Barkilphedro is catapulted in his own imagination from being Josiane's metonymical extension to governing the entire operation. The beast once again controls the human. In linking the devolutionary commodification of human beings to the yearning for a better world, the novel recasts Fredric Jameson's claim that 'it is easier to write a history of matter than of consciousness' by doing both at once.[61] As in Hugo's lyrical and epic poetry, the textual interplay of interiority and exteriority, self and other, figures the vertical tension between, and reversal of, the high and the low.[62] We will study the relationship between such superpositions and multi-level spatial patterns further on in this chapter.

[60] Her image of herself as an oxymoron—'je suis l'immaculée effrénée. Je suis la vestale bacchante' (xiv. 315)—repeats the impossible mingling represented by her association with Gwynplaine.

[61] Fredric Jameson, *Marxism and Form: Twentieth-Century Dialectical Theories of Literature* (Princeton, NJ: Princeton University Press, 1971), 297. Or, as Brombert affirms: 'The problem for Hugo . . . was how to articulate the political on the spiritual, how to relate the clown's grimace to his political discourse' (*Victor Hugo and the Visionary Novel*, 173).

[62] See Albouy, 'Hugo, ou le Je éclaté', 60, 63, and Laforgue, 'Le Romanesque et l'écriture', 242.

Class Acts and Recovered Memories

Given the attraction between Gywnplaine and Josiane, it is no surprise that their 'similar differences'—a metaphor of metaphor, according to Ricoeur (*RM* 23, 192)—draw them into a relationship of parity. The Duchess's haughtiness is marked by her arrogant attitude towards the people: 'L'utilité d'être précieuse, c'est que cela déclasse le genre humain. On ne lui fait plus l'honneur d'en être' (xiv. 146). The higher one places oneself, the further one lowers everyone else. As we have previously noted, when Gwynplaine first glimpses her at one of his shows, he feels the distance between them acutely. Like the *misérables* crushed under the social hierarchy, he is caught in a vortex:

> il se représentait ce monde auguste, la seigneurie, dont était cette femme, inexorablement superposé au monde infime, le peuple, dont il était. Et même . . . N'était-il pas, lui, bateleur, au-dessous de ce qui est au-dessous? . . . il apercevait dans un lointain suprême, au-dessus de sa tête, comme par l'ouverture d'un puits au fond duquel il serait, cet éblouissement pêle-mêle d'azur, de figures et de rayons qui est l'olympe. Au milieu de cette gloire resplendissait la duchesse. (xiv. 231–2)

The impossible reality represented by the duchess offers Gwynplaine a new, revolutionary view of the world. Identifying himself with the infinitely small (*infime*) and Josiane with the infinitely great (*auguste*, *olympe*, *gloire*), he sets up a seemingly absolute polarity. How to bring such diverse entities together is the task of story and metaphor alike.

Their collusion begins when Josiane sends a message of love after the performance, and Gwynplaine's awe gives way to the headiness of the sublime moment: 'On ne sait quel renversement du monde, le fourmillement d'insectes en haut, les constellations en bas, engloutissait Gwynplaine . . . et lui faisait un nimbe dans le cloaque. Une toute-puissante . . . se donnait au damné de la nuit . . . et de cette abdication de la déesse, sortait . . . la royauté du misérable' (xiv. 240). Once again, the hero is overwhelmed by something akin to Javert's topsy-turvy conversion experience before the revelation of Jean Valjean's towering virtue. Josiane's abasement elevates Gwynplaine to the apogee of power, the vertical axis signalling this apocalyptic vision. When the two at last meet, however, radical inversions give way to conjunction. Josiane explains: 'Il y a quelqu'un en haut, ou en bas, qui nous jette l'un à l'autre . . . Fiançailles effrénées hors de toutes les lois!' (xiv. 314). The two extremes meet in their 'engagement'. That their liaison exceeds the bounds of both human and cosmic law reveals Josiane's will to defy convention. To possess Gwynplaine is, for the duchess, to turn traditional order upside down:

'Un bateleur vaut un lord. D'ailleurs, qu'est-ce que les lords? des clowns' (xiv. 314), she declares. The apocalytic shift, whereby lords and clowns enter into a relationship of parity, ironically anticipates the revolutionary upheavals of 1789, 1830, and 1848. By offering herself as an 'esclave' (xiv. 315) to Gwynplaine, a man whom she idolizes because she looks down on him, Josiane introduces an element of disorder into the social construct. As she declares: 'Mêler le haut et le bas, c'est le chaos, et le chaos me plaît' (xiv. 316). Gwynplaine's dreams of social equity, inherited from both Ursus and Clancharlie, are perverted here into a nightmare of anarchy—the starting point of *Chaos vaincu*. He seeks the elevation of *les misérables* by eliminating the class system; Josiane wants to abase herself with a deformed plebian lover in order to flout convention by defying social norms. Their symbiosis is a meeting of monstrous equals.

Josiane's ability to find in Gwynplaine her equal repeats on the personal level what occurs in the political realm. Since the past has a way of returning in the form of 'buried possibilities' (*MHF* 382), Gwynplaine recovers his own history in a series of movements. First, in Southwark prison, the bandit surgeon Hardquanonne, who had transfigured Clancharlie's rightful heir into a freak, reveals Gwynplaine's origins under torture—thereby verifying the *comprachicos*' written confession discovered by Barkilphedro—and formally identifies his victim. Terrified by the revelation, Gwynplaine seeks to reverse this act of recognition and to distance himself from the other. He feels instinctively threatened by their *rapprochement*: 'l'inintelligible aveu de cet homme se fermait sur lui comme la charnière d'un carcan. Il se figura cet homme et lui attachés au même pilori à deux poteaux jumeaux' (xiv. 262). Being connected to the man implies suffering a similar fate, that of being chained together on the gallows. In a melodramatic *coup de théâtre*, the sheriff responds to Gwynplaine, who calls himself 'un pauvre saltimbanque', by declaring: 'J'ai devant moi . . . lord Fermain Clancharlie, baron Clancharlie et Hunkerville, marquis de Corleone en Sicile, pair d'Angleterre' (xiv. 263). As the sheriff offers Gwynplaine his chair, symbolically ceding his place, the metaphorical transformation of the hero from clown back to lord is accomplished.

Second, Barkilphedro tempts the hero with the knowledge that he is the heir of Lord Clancharlie, thereby 'awakening' the young man from his twenty-five-year slumber. 'Vous vous croyez du peuple, vous êtes de la seigneurie. Vous vous croyez au dernier rang, vous êtes au premier. Vous vous croyez histrion, vous êtes sénateur . . . Vous vous croyez petit, vous êtes grand. Réveillez-vous, mylord!' (xiv. 270), he tells an astonished Gwynplaine. As in a fairy tale, the dormant prince attains consciousness of who and what he is—the opposite of everything he believed. He is truly *other*, metaphorically transmuted from muck to gold. The poor street performer is equal to the highest in the land. From a slave, he has become a master, invested with enormous power over others. Gwynplaine responds by fainting 'sous cette transfiguration croulant sur lui à coups de tonnerre' (xiv. 270). Whereas the tempest at sea swallows up the bandits who had mutilated him, this storm metamorphoses Gwynplaine from Nothingness to All.

The reversal of fortunes takes him utterly by surprise: 'Il n'y avait point assez de place entre ce que Gwynplaine avait redouté et ce qui lui arrivait. . . Les deux contrastes étaient trop serrés . . . Gwynplaine faisait effort pour retirer son esprit de cet étau' (xiv. 279). The space between the two states of being has evaporated, leaving the hero potentially crushed in a kind of pincer or vice. He is no longer who he was, but cannot yet distinguish what he has become: 'Gwynplaine se tâta . . . pour s'assurer qu'[il existait]. C'était bien à lui qu'on parlait; mais lui-même était autre . . . De même qu'on l'avait transporté dans ce palais, on lui avait changé ses vêtements' (xiv. 279). The hero's 'transportation' (see also xiv. 280) into another state of being—here, the elevation to the peerage—represents the sublime moment itself. He exists, but *otherwise*, at least to all appearances, as signalled by the change in clothing. The revelation of his condition is accompanied by considerable movement, as with Gilliatt on the reef in *Les Travailleurs de la mer*: 'A travers cette agitation, dans cette impossibilité de se tenir en place, il méditait' (xiv. 282). Gwynplaine's place keeps changing, a metaphor for his shifting identity.

Equally important, when Barkilphedro details the Clancharlie holdings, Gwynplaine makes a textual connection:

> Pendant que Barkilphedro parlait, Gwynplaine . . . se souvenait . . . Tous ces noms prononcés par Barkilphedro étaient inscrits aux dernières lignes de ces deux placards qui tapissaient la cahute [d'Ursus] . . . En arrivant . . . dans la baraque roulante de Weymouth, il y avait trouvé son héritage inventorié qui l'attendait . . . Détail étrange . . . il avait voyagé avec sa fortune affichée sur sa misère. (xiv. 280)

As the recollection of this exposure to the catalogue of his birthright rises to the surface, Gwynplaine has a retrospective *scène de reconnaissance*. At the time, the significance of the texts unconsciously inscribed in his memory escaped him (see *MHF* 433). Now, he realizes, 'l'oubli n'est autre chose qu'un palimpseste. Qu'un accident survienne, et tous les effacements revivent dans les interlignes de la mémoire étonnée. Gwynplaine croyait avoir retiré cette figure de son esprit, et il l'y retrouvait, et elle y était empreinte, et elle avait fait son creux dans ce cerveau inconscient, coupable d'un songe' (xiv. 239–40). Memories are texts that are never fully effaced, whole worlds engraved in our being. Amid the poverty of his rambling existence, Gwynplaine's wealth was displayed for all the world to see—if only it could have been recognized as such. The failure of imagination to make the leap from *this* deformed boy to *that* staggering fortune extends to society's inability to see the potential of its most wretched members.

Ominously, Barkilphedro depicts the hero's apotheosis as a choice: 'Lord Fermain Clancharlie, ceci est l'instant décisif. Le destin n'ouvre point une porte sans en fermer une autre. Après de certains pas en avant, un pas en arrière n'est plus possible. Qui entre dans la transfiguration a derrière lui un évanouissement. Gwynplaine est mort' (xiv. 281). Whereas Ursus' hospitable gesture in closing his window and opening his caravan door to the lost children was a positive development, the villain believes that the transformational process is an *engrenage* that allows no about-face. One cannot be *both* oneself *and* another, a notion that reflects his own lack of empathy. Transfiguration entails an erasure, rather than an enhancement, of self.[63] Multiple layers are impossible. The idea of inexorable progress becomes, in Barkilphedro's system, a rather scary—if not altogether negative—prospect. We should note that, when the hero later discovers the disappearance of both Dea and Ursus from Tadcaster Inn, he recalls this scene with irony: 'Cet homme [Barkilphedro] lui avait écrit dans le cerveau quelque chose d'obscur qui à présent reparaissait, et cela avait été écrit d'une encre si horrible que c'était maintenant des lettres de feu, et Gwynplaine voyait flamboyer au fond de sa pensée ces paroles énigmatiques, aujourd'hui expliquées: *Le destin n'ouvre pas une porte sans en fermer une autre*' (xiv. 362). The burning letters, like those inscribed in the slave Habribrah's flesh in *Bug-Jargal* or appearing to Madeleine in *Les Misérables*, take on enormous power.[64] The 'évanouissement' foreseen by the villain turns out to be the 'écroulement'–'univers évanoui'–'anéantissement' of his adopted family: 'Tout évanoui. Tout en allé. Tout perdu. La nuit. Rien. C'était là son horizon' (xiv. 362). The negative sublime glimpsed in the nothingness that engulfed him as a boy in the blizzard

[63] Barkilphedro presents Gwynplaine with all the written evidence of his true status, such melodramatic textual *realia*, including the queen's signature, offering proof of the hero's existence as *another*. At the same time, he suggests the arbitrary nature of the laws thus enacted. 'Tout peut s'annuler et disparaître . . . ', Barkilphedro warns. 'Il est aisé de vous effacer' (xiv. 281). Gwynplaine's apotheosis is as tenuous as a written line, ready to be scratched out if he does not obey the dictates of his new position. One monarch's order has him disfigured; another has him reconfigured as a lord. Both participate in a reification of the other's subjectivity, denying first his inherited and then his constructed identity.

[64] See *EN* 72–3 and *FT* 176.

returns in the personal disaster triggered by yielding to Barkilphedro's material seduction.

The temptation sets up a double movement for Gwynplaine that stokes the engine of catastrophe: '[Il] avait été en même temps enlevé sur un sommet et précipité dans un abîme. Il avait le... vertige de l'ascension et le vertige de la chute. Mélange fatal' (xiv. 281). The *mélange* of sensations operating over the vertical axis resembles Javert's precipitation into the 'gouffre en haut' (xi. 915) of Jean Valjean's towering morality in *Les Misérables*. Both rising and falling at once, Gwynplaine has trouble distinguishing the apogee from the abyss, the glory from the mortal danger. In essence, this 'aveugle ébloui' has a new but deeply flawed view of reality: 'Il fut comme celui qui met sa tête hors de l'eau. Il lui sembla qu'il voyait tout, le passé, l'avenir, le présent, dans le saisissement d'une clarté subite' (xiv. 282). Like the visionary poet, Gwynplaine captures all temporal dimensions in a single point—or at least he thinks so. He has the eye of eternity, that of God himself. Unfortunately, he has not yet attained the maturity to see the whole picture, including Barkilphedro's evil intent and manipulation of the young man's emotions. The appeal to his egotism generates, in fact, a pseudo-sublime moment: 'Ah! tour de roue définitif! j'étais en bas, je suis en haut. En haut, à jamais! me voilà lord... j'existerai' (xiv. 283). The reversal from low to high makes him as inaccessible in his own way as Josiane in hers. Now, he thinks, he will really live (*j'existerai*), as if his existence with Ursus and Dea were but a bad dream. The crisis of being, of 'reality', requires him to put on a new self. But his belief that the wheel of fortune turns in just one direction, that *peripeteias* are not temporary, belies his own experience and sets up the tragic dénouement.

Thus reattached to his heritage, Gwynplaine is delighted to become *other*:

> Je sentais bien sous mes haillons palpiter autre chose qu'un misérable... Pasteurs des peuples, conducteurs d'hommes, guides et maîtres, c'est là qu'étaient mes pères; et ce qu'ils étaient je le suis!... Quand mon père a été mort, ils lui ont retiré de dessous la tête la pierre de l'exil qu'il avait pour oreiller, et ils me l'on mis au cou, et ils m'ont jeté dans l'égout. (xiv. 282)

Beneath his rags–chrysalis, the lord–butterfly endured a sordid fate while sensing that his life held a different dimension entirely. Once punished for being his father's son, he has been transfigured into the leader he was born to be. His musings about the change in his fortunes continue, recycling images seen earlier in the text:

> J'ai été le morceau de chair becqueté sur une tombe par une troupe de corbeaux... Ah! c'est donc là qu'on m'avait précipité... sous le trépignement de tous, au-dessous du dernier dessous du genre humain... à l'endroit

> où le chaos devient le cloaque, au fond de la disparition! Et c'est de là que... je remonte! c'est de là que je ressuscite! Et me voilà. Revanche!' (xiv. 282–3)

His profound identification with the hanged man encountered at the beginning of the novel invests the scene with new significance.[65] He, too, was a victim of unjust 'justice' but has been reborn to a powerful, avenging role. As low as he once was, so low on the social rung that he had barely any identity at all, he is now high. Like Jean Valjean emerging from the pit in the sewers, 'tout ruisselant de fange, l'âme pleine d'une étrange clarté' (xi. 898), he is covered in filth but sublimely triumphant.[66] The emblem of all the *misérables* for whom he has been an advocate, Gwynplaine figures the mighty urge to right wrongs that will accompany the future rise to power of society's outcasts.

When Gwynplaine realizes that he is in Windsor and Dea in Southwark, he reaffirms their identity across the distance that separates them: 'Ah! voici que je redeviens moi!... Je ne suis pas lord pour être esclave... Est-ce qu'on se figure m'avoir déchaîné pour rien? On m'a démuselé, voilà tout. Dea! Ursus! nous sommes ensemble. Ce que vous étiez, je l'étais. Ce que je suis, vous l'êtes' (xiv. 305–6). Recapturing his selfhood from the insinuating Barkilphedro, the hero rejects the other's attempt to turn him into a metonymical extension (*esclave*). He has been freed, unleashed (*déchaîné*) on the other lords in order to speak his mind (*démuselé*), an image that evokes Homo freed from his chain and baring his teeth, as well as Gwyplaine's own rictus. His identification now expands to include not only Dea but also Ursus, parent and mate, past, present, and future. Everything that he has, and in which he had begun to find himself, is theirs instead: 'J'ai une femme, qui est Dea. J'ai un père, qui est Ursus. Ma maison est un palais et je le donne à Ursus. Mon nom est un diadème et je le donne à Dea... Ah! j'aurai vite enjambé l'intervalle, va!' (xiv. 306). The gap will be filled by his resurgence of generosity, as he reaffirms his affiliation with his adopted family—and thereby with all humanity. The far will become the near.

Gwynplaine's self-confidence reaches its peak in the House of Lords, where he seeks justice for all who suffer under the system that defaced and disinherited him in the first place. When he declares himself the true,

[65] Cf. Suzanne Guerlac, *The Impersonal Sublime: Hugo, Baudelaire, Lautréamont* (Stanford, CA: Stanford University Press, 1990), 39.

[66] The image is prepared when Gwynplaine awakes in Corleone Lodge after his encounter with Barkilphedro and is slow to take everything in: 'Il faut du temps pour revenir à la surface. Gwynplaine avait été jeté au fond de la stupéfaction' (xiv. 278). In a happy version of the novel's tragic ending, he touches bottom and rises again, as in Jean Valjean's plunge into the sewer *fontis* (v. 3. 6).

republican son of his father to the other peers, his identification with the victims of the English monarchy is complete.[67] What Ricoeur calls 'the bond of filiation' thus involves both a 'carnal tie' to his sire and a 'social bond' to his wider adopted family—his fellow citizens. With the return of the repressed—that is, of the 'horrible, the extreme figure of the history of victims'—in the adult Gwynplaine, 'indebtedness to people of the past . . . is transformed into the duty never to forget' (*MHF* 395, 164; see also *TN* iii. 189). Identifying in the end with both the hanged man and his outlaw father, Hugo's protagonist speaks for all the inarticulate masses. He is a creature of the abyss, the voice *de profundis* that cries in the wilderness (Ps. 130). 'J'ai été jeté au gouffre . . . ', he declares, 'pour que je rapporte la perle, la vérité. Je parle parce que je sais . . . J'ai éprouvé. J'ai vu' (xiv. 349). As in 'La Pente de la rêverie', he has seen the bottom and risen, as a visionary, to the top. It is his duty to share his extraordinary experiences.

Significantly, Gwynplaine's peers can only gape at this 'face de Prométhée, ravagée par les coups de bec du vautour' (xiv. 348). A living version of the hanged man, who is, like Gilliatt, also compared to Prometheus, he stands as a figure of the outlawed poet—and of suffering humanity in general.[68] Gwynplaine outlines for the lords what he observed as a boy when he first entered society: 'La première chose que j'ai vue, c'est la loi, sous la forme d'un gibet; la deuxième, c'est la richesse, c'est votre richesse, sous la forme d'une femme morte de froid et de faim; la troisième, c'est l'avenir, sous la forme d'un enfant agonisant; la quatrième, c'est le bon, le vrai, le juste, sous la figure d'un vagabond n'ayant pour compagnon et pour ami qu'un loup' (xiv. 349). His experiences at the beginning of the narrative return as allegories of social justice and progress that he recalls, reads, and interprets for those who are too blind to see. For each negative encounter (the law or gibbet) and its embodiment (wealth or the dead woman), there is a counterbalancing positive (goodness, truth, and justice or Ursus) that gives him reason for hope. Against all odds, the boy in the blizzard 'avait continué d'avancer . . . étrange lutteur au milieu de tous ces risques' (xiv. 109). Progress was hard won, but the fight went

[67] As Paulson rightly observes: 'Like Marius in *Les Misérables*, like Hugo himself, Gwynplaine has a revolutionary vocation through his father's example' (*Enlightenment*, 188; see also 196). Guerlac reaches a similar conclusion: 'L'Homme qui Rit has thus returned to haunt the aristocracy, not only as a *revenant* (ghost) of his father but also as avenger, as a return of the ghost or phantom' (*The Impersonal Sublime*, 49–50; see also 44, 55).

[68] Cf. Sadrin, '"In the Name of the King"', 223. The narrator stresses that Gwynplaine was moulded into another creature altogether—'un misérable taillé dans l'étoffe des grands par un roi, dont ce fut le plaisir' (xiv. 349)—by the powers that be. Misery is a human construct, not a natural phenomenon.

on. Having succeeded in reviving the dying child, Dea, he became *resolutely* oriented towards the future.

This sense of mission now assumes the form of prophecy. Today, Gwynplaine warns, the lords may oppress the people: 'Mais l'avenir, c'est le dégel sombre . . . L'apparence solide se change en submersion . . . Il viendra une heure où une convulsion brisera votre oppression, où un rugissement répliquera à vos huées' (xiv. 354). The seemingly immutable 'masque de contentement' (xiv. 354) worn by the wretched will crack, revealing the seething depths below. Like the *Matutina* in the grip of the storm, the lords' very existence is imperilled by their political intransigence. If, as Ricoeur asserts, the 'duty of memory is the duty to do justice, through memories, to an other than the self' (*MHF* 89), then for Hugo the historical novel plays an essential role in this process by resurrecting the stories of social victims and offering a vision of what might have been—or of what might still be. In the next two subsections, we will explore Gwynplaine's perception of the future and the thematics of inversion.

Rich and Poor as Alter Egos

While dramatic turns of event structure the overall movement of Hugo's narrative, they also invite a deeper reflection on the relationship between wealth and poverty. The two states seem to be wholly antithetical, but they are locked in a symbiotic embrace. Their opposition was once symbolized by 'la barre, coupure transversale, sorte de frontière marquant l'endroit où finit le peuple et où commence la seigneurerie' (xiv. 335), a few feet from the door of the original House of Lords. The physical sign both expressed and reinforced the social distance between upper and lower classes. Having invaded, then, the lords' inviolable space, Gwynplaine denounces their happiness based on fooling the masses: 'Etant ignorant, le peuple est aveugle . . . L'ignorance est gardienne de la vertu . . . l'ignorant est dans une nuit utile, qui, supprimant le regard, supprime les convoitises' (xiv. 137). Through her 'aveuglement', Dea joins Gwynplaine in representing the French people under the current regime. Such blindness must be protected, the rationalization goes, because it guarantees virtue—not wanting back what those with wealth and power have taken from them. Happiness for the 'haves' is a lack of desire in the 'have nots'. Identifying with the poor and outcast, Gwynplaine warns the lords by denouncing their vampirism: 'Vous avez tout,' he tells his peers, 'et ce tout se compose du rien des autres' (xiv. 349).[69] The lords live parasitically off the people,

[69] His argument echoes Ursus' earlier ironic claim that the poor exist to help the rich, that '[les] indigents . . . étoffent le bonheur des opulents' (xiv. 207). It is better to avoid the

their good fortune derived from the privation of others. They owe their existence to the poor. As a result, their everything is really nothingness—for both themselves and their victims. In this way, the two classes are at once themselves *and* the other; the poor and outcast are the alter egos, the inversions, of the rich and powerful, who cannot exist without them.

In his speech, Gywnplaine recycles the novel's vertical imagery into a vision of horizontal equality: 'Mylords, vous êtes en haut... Mais il y a au-dessous de vous quelque chose. Au-dessus peut-être. Mylords, je viens vous apprendre une nouvelle. Le genre humain existe' (xiv. 348). Shifting the relationship between superior and inferior, he implies that the 'Olympians' in all their complacent glory might be superseded by those beneath them. Though Gwynplaine himself was last night 'presque petit' in his vanity, today he feels in himself 'un grandissement étrange' (xiv. 348) as he assumes his responsibilities. This triple reversal (low to high to low to high) provides the authority for his speech to his 'peers'. However rich and great they may be, he announces, 'L'aube... arrive... Le soleil, c'est le droit. Vous, vous êtes le privilège. Ayez peur' (xiv. 348–9). Allying the dawn with revolution, that ultimate inversion,[70] he warns the other lords that their ascendency will inevitably end. The fact is that their world is 'si haut, vous êtes dehors' (xiv. 349). In their own way, the lords are as exiled from real life as those who cannot live it fully. The hero can show them the way: 'J'arrive de dessous la pression. Je puis vous dire ce que vous pesez' (xiv. 349). He can serve as the advocate of those crushed beneath the social hierarchy. 'O grands,' he urges, 'il y a des petits! ayez pitié. Oui! pitié de vous! car les multitudes agonisent, et le bas en mourant fait mourir le haut... Etes-vous égoïstes? sauvez les autres. La perdition du navire n'est indifférente à aucun passager... Oh! sachez-le, l'abîme est pour tous' (xiv. 351). The humble and the mighty are as intimately interwined as he and Dea. Because the abyss is the great equalizer, the wealthy should, out of self-interest, preserve those who voyage through life along with them. If some sink, all will sink, a lesson already observed in the case of the

weighty lords, Ursus asserts, than to be crushed by them: 'J'ai vu un jour un hippopotame marcher sur une taupinière... Mon cher, des taupes qu'on écrase, c'est le genre humain. L'écrasement est une loi' (xiv. 206). The mole is the 'mastodonte' of the flea, and the flea, the 'mastodonte' (xiv. 206) of the minuscule flagellate. While making a comic observation, Ursus suggests that the 'seigneurie' is as prehistoric as the 'mastodonte', and therefore doomed to extinction. The use of the mole, a nearly blind animal, to figure the people again points to Dea as a symbol of the dispossessed. Cf. Jean Gaudon's highly pertinent analysis of Ursus' 'bouffonerie du savoir' ('Les Vicissitudes du savoir', in Guy Rosa (ed.), L'Homme qui rit *ou la parole-monstre de Victor Hugo* (Paris: SEDES, 1985), 33) by what Albouy has termed 'un procédé de dérèglement du language' ('Présentation', 17).

[70] See Rosa, 'Critique et autocritique', 16.

comprachicos.[71] Saving others can only benefit the self. Ricoeur's thesis that 'the *autonomy* of the self [is] tightly bound up with *solicitude* for one's neighbor and with *justice* for each individual' (*OA* 17) is illustrated in Hugo's text.

But the destitute may become the equals of the privileged in the present life as well. The potential parity of both classes is apparent when Gwynplaine warns the other peers: 'Mylords, je suis l'avocat désespéré, et je plaide la cause perdue. Cette cause, Dieu la regagnera. Moi, je ne suis rien, qu'une voix. Le genre humain est une bouche, et j'en suis le cri. Je viens ouvrir devant vous... les grandes assises du peuple, ce souverain, qui est le patient, ce condamné, qui est le juge' (xiv. 349). Though the hero (like Clancharlie before him and Hugo afterwards) may be a voice crying in the wilderness, justice will prevail because one day the low who suffer (*patient, condamné*) will recognize and reclaim their other, elevated identity (*souverain, juge*). The world's *misérables* are really its masters, if only they realized their power.[72] The hero himself is a prime example of this dual nature, a *both/and* proposition: 'Je suis lord Clancharlie, mais je reste Gwynplaine. Je tiens aux grands, mais j'appartiens aux petits. Je suis parmi ceux qui jouissent et avec ceux qui souffrent' (xiv. 352). Like the oxymoronic Jean Valjean, Gwynplaine functions metaphorically (cf. *RM* 248). Aristocratic and lower-class identities merge in this social *mélange des genres* that, as Rosa puts it, 'incarne à la fois les deux classes antagonistes'.[73] He may be 'among' the great; his allegiance is 'with' their victims. He has been called to witness about his life of deprivation before those capable of eliminating such inequities—an act that gives meaning to his existence. His testimony thus joins that of the condemned man in *Le Dernier Jour d'un condamné* as both an indictment of the current system and a vehicle for suggesting an alternative reality.

Unfortunately for Gwynplaine, his inability to connect with the other lords signals a new turn of the wheel—and so a tragic dénouement (see *TN* i. 43). The narrator compares his experience to that of climbing 'une

[71] According to Rosa, the image of a perverse aristocracy is completely logical: 'L'unité même de la nature humaine veut que tout comportement inhumain entraîne la déshumanisation de celui qui s'y livre et que l'ordre social qui ne laisse subsister que des bourreaux et des victimes fasse, à la fin, du bourreau lui-même la dernière de ses victimes' ('Critique et autocritique', 15). To survive, the well-off must, for Hugo, not dehumanize anyone else.

[72] Cf. Gayla Gerstman's contention that Gywnplaine is empowered to speak for the voiceless people by the 'revelation that he is not one of the masses but is actually a member of the fortunate elite' ('The Mastery of Language and Language of Mastery in Victor Hugo's *L'Homme qui rit*', in Carrol F. Coates (ed.), *Repression and Expression: Literary and Social Coding in Nineteenth-Cenury France* (New York: Peter Lang, 1996), 82; see also 85).

[73] Rosa, 'Critique et autocritique', 13. Roman remarks that the British aristocracy displays a startling 'encanaillement [qui] montre que les classes commencent à se mêler par les bords' (*Victor Hugo et le roman philosophique*, 429).

pente à pic friable au-dessus d'une profondeur vertigineuse' (xiv. 353)—one of his ordeals as a boy in the snowstorm. The hero 'sentait son ascension crouler sous lui, et son auditoire était un précipice' (xiv. 353). Again, the high and the low are interchangeable and subject to reversal. Gwynplaine's life among the people undercuts his ability to deal with his peers: 'en s'imprégnant de l'immense âme humaine, il avait perdu, dans le sens commun de tout le monde, le sens spécial des classes reines' (xiv. 366). The general has eclipsed the specific, and he has no way of communicating with those chasing special interests. In yet another replay of Jean Valjean's emergence from the sewers, '[Gwynplaine] arrivait tout mouillé de l'eau du puits Vérité . . . Il répugnait à ces princes, parfumés de mensonges. A qui vit de fiction, la vérité est infecte' (xiv. 366). The Word from the abyss, that cold dose of reality that those living on fiction would prefer to ignore, goes unheeded. He is nothing but an interloper, an eruption in the calm of their Olympian existence: 'Les pôles extrêmes se repoussent. Nul amalgame possible' (xiv. 366). If extremes can meet in story and metaphor, society still lags behind.[74] There can be no true *mélange des genres* in early eighteenth-century England. This time, the fall from grace is permanent. Having played the Promethean role of 'un révolté . . . l'Apporte-lumière, trouble-fête effrayant . . . Lucifer [qui] arrivait sinistre, un flambeau à la main' (xiv. 365), he is rejected by the other peers and ejected from their earthly paradise of power and riches.[75]

On the verge of suicide at the end of the novel, Gwynplaine contemplates 'les embûches' (xiv. 366) he has encountered along the way. The embrace of a woman had 'l'effet de nœuds de couleuvre' (xiv. 367)—another reference to knots. And the temptation of changing classes opened 'au-dessus de sa tête, comme une trappe dans le ciel, le plafond social, et l'avait lancé par cette ouverture, et l'avait fait surgir . . . au milieu des princes et des maîtres' (xiv. 367). He fell upwards, through a second kind of 'gouffre en haut' (xi. 915), into the laps of the surprised peerage. This unexpected performance was a flop. To rise was to lose all. What the hero failed to take into account was the hatred of the other peers. With the narrator's comment that 'le sort a des coups de trahison . . . la destinée est

[74] The notion in *MIS* that 'toutes les extrémités se touchent' (xi. 504) still operates in many of the relationships between the characters in *HQR*, but here Hugo is more pessimistic about the tensions between social classes.

[75] While Sadrin points out that Gwynplaine is 'compared like Shelley's monster to Lucifer' ('"In the Name of the King"', 223), we will see later in this chapter that the reference also pertains to Milton's fallen angel in *Paradise Lost*. Cf. Joë Friedemann's observation that, 'au plan pragmatique, c'est Ursus qui a eu raison [que l'écrasement est une loi]' (xiv. 206). Gwynplaine a été écrasé par les lords' ('*L'Homme qui rit* ou les voix du silence', in Dominique Peyrache-Leborgne and Yann Jumelais (eds), *Victor Hugo ou les frontières effacées* (Nantes: Pleins Feux, 2002), 209).

piège et l'homme tombe dans des chausse-trapes' (xiv. 355), the ambush theme associated with Barkilphedro returns in the form of Gwynplaine's fall from grace. With the disappearance of Ursus and Dea from Tadcaster Inn, his shipwreck is complete: 'il était venu s'échouer à ce colossal écueil, la frivolité des heureux. Il se croyait un vengeur, il était un clown. Il croyait foudroyer, il avait chatouillé... Il avait sangloté, on était entré en joie. Sous cette joie, il avait sombré. Engloutissement funèbre' (xiv. 364). Like the bandits in the *Matutina*, he has been deluded about his ability to remain in control before incalculable dangers, and his disaster has been equally complete. Does his personal catastrophe imply, then, that the aristocrats' arrogance will go unpunished? Does Hugo's narrative leave no hope for social justice? In that event, one must one concur with Meschonnic's view that in *L'Homme qui rit* 'le bonheur n'existe qu'au passé', that 'le désespoir est la logique poétique du livre'.[76] Or one can instead interpret Gwynplaine's sacrifice as somehow *useful*.

Utopia Past and Future

An utterly grim world view would emerge from the text were the final reversal for Gwynplaine not matched by an implied turn in the fortunes of his hecklers. In shifting from the past to the future, the narrator's gaze implicates the reader as well. Divine justice awaits the privileged few who cannot see other selves in the poor, since 'toute action commise est une traite tirée sur le grand payeur ignoré' (xiv. 272). All misdeeds have consequences—a message that carries implications for present-day France as well. So, whereas Pierre Laforgue considers that Hugo's 'saut transhistorique entre l'Angleterre et la France... résiste à toute analyse rationnelle de l'Histoire',[77] the novelist is in fact seeking to discern and communicate universal truths that are not calendar dependent. After all, justice may extend over time, even when kings commit crimes. Thanks to 'les audaces du terrorisme monarchique', James II had many of his victims 'fleurdelysé[s]', replacing 'la marque de Dieu' with 'la marque du roi' (xiv. 49). Such lower-order substitutions strike at Creation itself. False metaphoricity impugns the art and the science of the period alike. The king's monstrous complicity with the bandits who mutilate children and inscribe his insignia into their flesh implicates French monarchists (*fleurdelysé*)—and imperialists—in similar acts of 'terrorism' and social devolution.[78]

[76] Meschonnic, *Pour la poétique IV*, 169.
[77] Laforgue, 'La Révolution française', 127.
[78] Gwynplaine finds himself in a situation both similar to and different from the Green Box: he would be better off as a true clown than as a serious person not taken seriously.

This is how absolute power works, Hugo suggests: it corrupts absolutely. Yet human legalities have their limits. Because the dispossessed are, on occasion, restored to their proper place in the social order, one must conclude that 'c'est Dieu qui retouche l'action du roi' (xiv. 272). In Hugo's system, such great sovereign 'masterworks' as turning children into freaks—or peers of France into outlaws—cry out for future 'retouching' by the supreme Creator.

Indeed, Gwynplaine argues, the lords are in danger of divine retribution: 'Est-ce que vous ne voyez pas que vous êtes dans une balance et qu'il y a dans un plateau votre puissance et dans l'autre votre responsabilité?' (xiv. 350). Vertical imagery again gives way to that of equality. Just as these 'judges' have the power of life and death over the destitute, so does their own fate hang in the balance. God may weigh on them just as they weigh on the poor. Already, they have received a foretaste of the future in Cromwell's Republic: 'Tremblez . . . les paradis bâtis sur les enfers chancelent . . . et ce qui est en haut penche, et ce qui est en bas s'entr'ouvre . . . c'est le peuple qui vient, c'est l'homme qui monte, c'est la fin qui commence' (xiv. 354). The voice of the abyss heard earlier in the narrative by the bandits here becomes that of the poor and starving. Top and bottom will reverse places as the meek finally inherit the earth. Even a chapter title regarding Gwynplaine's fate—'C'est à travers l'excès de grandeur qu'on arrive à l'excès de misère' (II. 9. 1; xiv. 359)—can be read as referring to the other lords as well. The high will become low; the sublime, grotesque; the mighty, *les misérables*. The message applies to contemporary England as well. In the chapter entitled 'Lex, rex, fex' (II. 4. 3; xiv. 247), the narrator remarks that although England in 1705 was not 'ce qu'elle est de nos jours', the nation is still sometimes 'très oppressif' (xiv. 248).[79] The old practice of executing people secretly in prisons, for example, is a nasty expedient to which England has returned, giving the world 'le singulier spectacle d'un grand peuple qui . . . ayant devant lui, d'un côté le passé, de l'autre le progrès, se trompe de visage, et prend la nuit pour le jour' (xiv. 248). The grotesque national laws expose

When one lord accuses, 'Nous revoici au temps où les animaux péroraient. Au milieu des bouches humaines, une mâchoire bestiale a la parole' (xiv. 352), we know that the inverse is true, that it is the lords who are the real beasts. The 'chaos de ricanements' (xiv. 353) that surrounds Gwynplaine resembles the demonic scenes of prisoners in both *DJC* (xiii) and *MIS* (iv. 3. 8). 'Toutes les exécutions ne se font pas sur les échafauds . . . Pas de supplice comparable à celui du misérable risible' (xiv. 354). The hero, like the writer, is associated with all condemned men as a victim of sarcasm—the mark of Christ's own suffering on the cross. Moreover, his 'execution' anticipates that of Gauvain at the end of *QVT* (iii. 7. 6).

[79] The chapter title recalls the expression in *MIS*, '*Fex urbis, lex mundi*' (xi. 822), a prediction that the poor will rise up to rule the world (see also the reference to Cicero, xiv. 292).

England to universal horror (*spectacle*). An illusion of progress is possible when one is incapable of distinguishing the past from the future—a reading error related to interpreting the masks worn by Gwynplaine, Josiane, and Barkilphedro. And what of the failure of France to see in the hypocritical Barkilphedro–Napoléon III the visage of 'night' rather than the harbinger of a new 'day'?

Gwynplaine reveals his own vision of a better world when he declares:

> Ah! cette société est fausse. Un jour viendra la société vraie. Alors il n'y aura plus de seigneurs, il y aura des vivants libres. Il n'y aura plus de maîtres, il y aura des pères. Ceci est l'avenir. Plus de prosternement, plus de bassesse, plus d'ignorance, plus d'hommes bêtes de somme, plus de courtisanes, plus de valets, plus de rois, la lumière. (xiv. 352)

In a passage that forecasts Gauvain's utopian vision at the end of *Quatrevingt-Treize*, the novelist elevates the fallen while symbolically ejecting Napoléon III and his toadies from the new Eden. In history, as in Gwnplaine's story, 'l'ascension est chute et la chute est ascension'.[80] Hugo's republican ideal becomes Gwynplaine's future, where the current social hierarchy of high and low will be reconfigured into something more equitable. 'Masters' will become 'fathers' (see xiv. 350), responsible for educating the masses and for giving them exemplary models to follow. So when Gwynplaine claims, 'Cette heure est déjà venue,—tu en étais, ô mon père!—cette heure est venue, et s'est appelée République, on l'a chassée, elle reviendra' (xiv. 354), his reference to Cromwell's Commonwealth several years earlier evokes the lost French Republic as well. In other words, Gwynplaine's hope for eighteenth-century England looks *back* to Hugo's past and *forwards* to his aim for the future. From this perspective, Gwynplaine's warning—'En attendant, souvenez-vous que la série des rois armés de l'épée est interrompue par Cromwell armé de la hache' (xiv. 354)—seems aimed at Napoléon III.[81] Powerful heads are doomed, perhaps by the agency of that seemingly far-off 'H'/*hache* on Guernsey. In any case, those who look backwards—to monarchies or empires—scheme in vain. The all-seeing eye of the future underscores the *vanitas* in the current glory of the few, condemned to individual and collective death. Hence, the 'pairie sans avenir' of one elegant young peer 'devait s'éteindre en 1709'; and Lord Halifax carries a title 'sous lequel s'était éteint le nom de Saville et devait s'éteindre le nom de Mountague' (xiv. 347). The caution to those currently in power is manifest. History abounds in

[80] Albouy, 'Présentation', 25.

[81] Yet, while some gaps appear in history (and in the truncated royal body), others are closed—here the one between Clancharlie and Gwynplaine, father and son.

subjects and citizens who believe, to borrow a recent expression, that 'regime change begins at home'.

From this analysis, it is evident that Hugo, too, maintains hope for the future. With Gwynplaine, he draws inspiration from those who have gone before, and whom he strives to keep France from forgetting. He seeks what Ricoeur terms 'a rebound-effect of the future on the past', whereby the recollection of 'the horizon of expectation of people of the past' (*MHF* 381) opens up new vistas in the present. Thus, the *ubi sunt* motif—the lost surgical art of the *comprachicos* (xiv. 48), the transformation of the Portland isthmus (xiv. 109–10), old Weymouth (xiv. 116–17), the building that originally housed the British Parliament (xiv. 334)—signals a gap in present experience that the text seeks to fill.[82] The novelist–historian's job is to fill such *lacunae* through imaginative re-enactments that bring people and places back to life. As the book title, 'Eternelle présence du passé; les hommes reflètent l'homme' (II. 1; xiv. 133), indicates, the historical novel combines past *and* present, the one integrated in the other. Conversely, examining one's own situation involves interrogating one's personal and collective origins, since 'the historical present is, in each era, the final term of a completed history, which itself completes and ends history' (*TN* iii. 239). By bridging temporal discontinuities through a 'poetics of transcendence', the text can also guide towards the future. Although God has 'des intermittences' (xiv. 182), most notably in the gaps in historical progress, the writer can span them by reminding his reader of where they have come from and where they should be headed.

One guidepost is the parallel between the English Restoration and the Second Empire. According to the narrator, the lords view 'l'interruption républicaine' (xiv. 343) after the Restoration as disrupting monarchy rather than the Restoration interrupting the Republic.[83] To counter this view, Hugo evokes a long list of the glories of the English Republic under Cromwell, then glosses them from the Restoration perspective: 'il n'y avait rien de sacré; la parole était libre, la presse était libre; on disait en pleine rue ce qu'on voulait; on imprimait sans contrôle ni censure ce qu'on voulait . . . tout l'ordre monarchique européen . . . avait été bouleversé. Enfin, on était sorti de cet odieux régime, et l'Angleterre avait son pardon' (xiv. 136). After making the Republic—that of 1848 as well as of 1649—sound like heaven on earth, Hugo seems to deflate it as an 'odious regime'.

[82] The *autrefois/aujourd'hui* dichotomy dates back to *DJC* (see *EN* 126–8).

[83] The parallels with nineteenth-century French history are, of course, multiple. Hugo rehearses this notion of God's 'discontinuities'—and of the historian's role in explaining them—in *MIS* (see *FT* 297–8).

However, this rhetorical tactic only serves to burnish the republican ideal by ironically casting its opponents as history's true 'idiots'.

For, despite the conservative drive of the English aristocracy, nothing lasts for ever—a lesson to the Second Empire. Linked to the 'work of mourning' the vanished Republic, the 'work of remembering' in Hugo's text thus attempts to counter the 'devious form of forgetting' imposed by Napoléon III's 'canonical narrative' (*MHF* 446, 448). Though Gwynplaine's failure to be heard would appear to deconstruct the poet's gap-spanning, metaphorical system, his recuperation of the national 'history of victims' transmits to the reader an ethical injunction for the utopian future. If Hugo is, like the hanged man's corpse, at once 'palpable et évanoui' (xiv. 65), it is because he may be gone but, thanks to works like *L'Homme qui rit*, not forgotten. Just a year and a half after publishing his novel, Hugo would enact his own 'return of the repressed' with a triumphant arrival back in Paris a day after the Third Republic was proclaimed.

We might end our discussion of the novel here, if its sole interest were the commentary on contemporary French events contained in Gwynplaine's initial destitution, rise to power, vision of an egalitarian society, and apocalyptic warning to the eighteenth-century English ruling class. Yet the carefully crafted correspondences between the two nations and the two centuries points to other sets of congruencies in the text, some more and some less obvious, that suggest an equally compelling aesthetic agenda. Stepping back, we can discern in the spatial motif of inversion and its temporal counterpart—the oscillation between different time frames—various iterations of recursive patterns. We therefore turn in the final subsections of this chapter to Hugo's elaboration of multi-level symmetries in and through his narrative.

Symmetrical Destinies

The symmetries not just of mirroring but of 'likeness at different scales'[84] are everywhere apparent in *L'Homme qui rit*. As we have already observed, for example, the main characters are constructed as reflections of and on each other. Ursus takes in and nurtures Gwynplaine, his labours in goodness matching the evils committed by the bandit surgeon Hardquanonne: 'Des inconnus lui avait travaillé le visage. Il avait, lui, travaillé l'intelligence' (xiv. 195). The bandit worked from the outside in, Ursus

[84] William J. Jackson, *Heaven's Fractal Net: Retrieving Lost Visions in the Humanities* (Bloomington: Indiana University Press, 2004), 65; see also Gleick, *Chaos*, 103, 308, and A. B. Çambel, *Applied Chaos Theory: A Paradigm for Complexity* (San Diego, CA: Academic Press, 1993), 186.

from the inside out.[85] Gwynplaine, too, has a malevolent twin in Barkilphedro, whose misdeeds as a self-appointed improvisational artist contrast with Gwynplaine's artistic genius in his performances on the road. Similarly, the disfigured protagonist is loved by the beautiful but blind Dea—who is able to peer into his beautiful soul. Through their mutual devotion, she becomes 'la cécité voyante' and he, 'la difformité aimée' (xiv. 209), two oxymora that reveal a little of each in the other. The narrator's statement that 'ils vivaient de plus en plus l'un par l'autre, l'un en l'autre, extatiquement' (xiv. 235) underscores their metaphorical interchangeability, including a capacity for empathetic identity. Gwynplaine is also an inversion of Josiane, who, we will recall, tempts him by declaring that he is the embodiment of her own grotesque soul: 'Vois comme je te ressemble. Regarde dans moi comme dans un miroir. Ton visage, c'est mon âme. Moi aussi je suis donc un monstre!' (xiv. 316). To see himself through the eyes of others, Gwynplaine need only look more deeply into her soul. The more he gets to know her inside out, she implies, the more he will understand how truly repulsive he is.[86] Finally, the text links Hardquannone and his victim in the recognition scene in Southwark prison. When the bandit 'terrible . . . éclata de rire' (xiv. 262), he imitates Gwynplaine's mutilation as a child that leaves him displaying a perpetual rictus. When he laughs again in a kind of 'sanglot' (xiv. 268), he mirrors the two sides of Gwynplaine's facial mask that grins on the outside and cries on the inside.[87]

This catalogue of reverse and inverse characters is complicated by their frequent triangulation. Hardquannone versus both Ursus and Gwynplaine, Gwynplaine versus both Dea and Josiane, Barkilphedro versus both Josiane and Gwynplaine—all play out an intricate pattern of differences and affinities reiterated in sibling rivalry.[88] Thus, Queen Anne's

[85] According to Sadrin, the 'Promethean character of the monster-maker', Hardquanonne, reveals Hugo's familiarity with Mary Shelley's *Frankenstein*, 'a text whose influence is much too obvious to go unnoticed: the choice of Switzerland as the hero's birthplace and of the North sea [*sic*] for his death by drowning, reflections on political exile and revolutionary ideals, and above all, Gwynplaine's monstrous looks are so many unmistakable signs that the novel has been deliberately written within the Shelleyan tradition' ('"In the Name of the King"', 221, 220–1). See also Roman, *Victor Hugo et le roman philosophique*, 243. We have already posited a connection between *Frankenstein* and *TM* in Ch. 2.

[86] See also Paulson's reading of the 'dreamlike fusion of opposites' in Gwynplaine and Dea and of the 'specular relation' between the protagonist and Josiane (*Enlightenment*, 191, 195).

[87] The hero, in turn, denies any link to the other man. Being connected to him—'attachés au même pilori à deux poteaux jumeaux' (xiv. 262)—implies suffering a similar fate: he sees his possible end mirrored in the other's torture and suffering. When Hardquanonne dies, the court doctor claims, 'Il a ri, cela l'a tué' (xiv. 269), an ironic ending that encapsulates Gwynplaine's destiny.

[88] Cf. the variant lists of double pairings supplied by Roman (*Victor Hugo et le roman philosophique*, 564) and Michel Granet ('La mise en abyme de l'aventure et de l'écriture

jealousy of her half-sister Josiane's great beauty casts them as *des sœurs ennemies*: 'Pour une reine laide une jolie duchesse n'est pas une sœur agréable' (xiv. 156).[89] The physical contrast between the sisters opens up a gap in their feelings towards each other. Moreover, Josiane's illegitimacy draws attention to the low rank of Anne's own mother: 'La fille de la mésalliance voyait sans plaisir, pas très loin d'elle, la fille de la bâtardise. Il y avait là une ressemblance désobligeante' (xiv. 157). Unflattering resemblances drive them even further apart. On a more comic note, one might say that Ursus' 'mésalliance' (xiv. 43) with Homo is repeated in the Queen's less than stellar parentage—a more poetic way of equating people with animals than the brutal experiments of the era.

The *sœurs ennemies* theme is recast and elaborated in the *frères ennemis* represented by Gwynplaine and his half-brother Lord David, who both share characteristics and oppose each other in their claims to the Clancharlie peerage. Clancharlie had been the 'amant sauvage' of Lord David's mother, who then moves on to one who was 'incontestablement apprivoisé, et même royaliste, car c'était le roi' (xiv. 140)—a variation on the wild–tame dichotomy in the text. According to the narrator, James II schemes to have Lord David assume the Clancharlie seat in Parliament 'par la porte d'une pairie substituée' (xiv. 141), since the rightful heir, Gwynplaine, has long since vanished. No one else becomes jealous, because it is just 'un nom qui continue' (xiv. 141) by means of a metaphorical substitution. Someone takes another's place, not by sacrificing himself heroically, like Jean Valjean at the court in Arras (*MIS* I. 7. 11),[90] but through the 'sacrifice' of the other. When the old republican father dies, 'le roi substituait lord David Dirry-Moir aux titres, droits et prérogatives dudit défunt lord Linnæus Clancharlie' (xiv. 142), on the condition that he eventually marry Duchess Josiane, as yet an infant. Lord David thus becomes both the 'fils légitime et l'héritier légal' of Clancharlie in the absence of '*toute autre filiation et descendance*' (xiv. 142) and the unwitting usurper of Gwynplaine's birthright. His false metonymical relation to Clancharlie is doubled by the false metaphorical relation to Gwynplaine. But, instead of following (metonymically) in his father's footsteps, the *fils naturel* born at the end of the Republic as Lord Clancharlie was fleeing England becomes an ardent royalist. While his father's hair turns white in exile, 'lord David prospéra sous Charles II. Après quoi il prospéra sous Jacques II' (xiv. 140). His lack of principle is already

dans *L'Homme qui rit*', in Guy Rosa (ed.), L'Homme qui rit *ou la parole-monstre de Victor Hugo* (Paris: SEDES, 1985), 50).

[89] See Albouy, 'Présentation', 6.

[90] See *FT* 143–7.

assured: 'un père renié ne nuit point à une fortune de cour qui commence' (xiv. 141). Rejecting his republican heritage will be good for his future. Little surprise, then, that Lord David easily switches allegiances when necessary: 'Après avoir prospéré sous Charles et Jacques, lord David prospéra sous Guillaume. Son jacobisme n'alla point jusqu'à suivre Jacques II en exil. Tout en continuant d'aimer son roi légitime, il eut le bon sens de servir l'usurpateur' (xiv. 143). He is as much an opportunist as the republicans who change sides under the Restoration. That he serves the 'usurper' is especially ironic, since he is one as well—and since the term also fits Napoléon III.

When Lord David and Gwynplaine at last encounter each other in Corleone Lodge in a 'scène de vaudeville',[91] their repartees play out their complicated relationship through a chiastic tit-for-tat:

> — Gwynplaine, je ne m'appelle pas Tom-Jim-Jack.
> — Tom-Jim-Jack, je ne m'appelle pas Gwynplaine.
> — Gwynplaine, je suis ici chez moi.
> — Je suis ici chez moi, Tom-Jim-Jack. (xiv. 320)

The embracing pattern (a–b–b–a–a–b) reveals as much the poet as the dramatist in this tense scene between the long-lost brothers. Neither, it turns out, is known by his correct name; each believes himself to be in his rightful, ancestral home. Naturally, Lord David perceives mockery in the hero's assertions: 'Je te défends de me faire écho . . . Trêve à tes parodies, misérable drôle' (xiv. 320). He views the other's repartee as simply parodic or imitative, rather than as genuine information from a co-equal.[92] At the same time, Lord David's repeated laughter at Gwynplaine's 'ridiculous' allegations invests him with the grotesque, in this case the ugly, self-satisfied side of the English aristocracy. The two are also equal, not as 'les deux amants [de Josiane]', as Lord David believes, but as 'les deux maris' (xiv. 320–1)—a point of view supplied by Barkilphedro, who thereby reminds the two men that they have both been rejected in the role of husband. As in Hugo's earliest novels, *Han d'Islande* and *Bug-Jargal*, even the most mismatched protagonists reveal striking dimensions of parity.[93]

The equation of the two rivals for both Josiane and the Clancharlie peerage recurs when Lord David confronts the other peers after Gwynplaine's speech, declaring that his half-brother is 'un monstre, soit. Mais

[91] Jean Gaudon, '"L'Homme qui rit" ou la Parole impossible', 200.

[92] The scene also resembles Quasimodo's examination before the deaf magistrate in *NDP* (iii. 1). See *EN* 187–8.

[93] See *EN* 25–9, 64–71, 95.

livré aux bêtes. J'aimerais mieux être lui que vous' (xiv. 357). His identification with the 'monster' rather than the 'beasts' suggests that he might one day ally himself with Gwynlaine's ideals, thereby replaying Marius' role in *Les Misérables* with regard to Jean Valjean. As Lord David scolds the young lords: 'Mylords, Fermain Clancharlie a été le lord, et vous avez été les saltimbanques' (xiv. 357); the clown is a prince and the princes clowns, in Hugo's topsy-turvy system. The metonymical transference and double metaphorical reversal signal the possible alliance of the hero's half-brother with both paternal and fraternal republicans, a hint of future developments. Lord David's remark, 'J'assistais à la séance, à ma place, comme héritier possible de pairie' (xiv. 357), forges further metaphorical links between him and Gwynplaine, whose place he will ostensibly take in the House of Lords after the close of the novel.

Later, as Gwynplaine prepares to commit suicide, he pens a brief testament: 'Je m'en vais. Que mon frère David me remplace et soit heureux' (xiv. 369), a final metaphorical substitution of one brother for the other. In the novel's 'future anterior',[94] he will occupy Clancharlie's seat in Parliament—hopefully for better rather than for ill. Lord David also underscores Gwynplaine's status as a *both/and* figure by maintaining that, despite the other peers' ridicule, the 'monstre' is better than they: 'Comme Clancharlie, il a la noblesse que vous avez, et comme Gwynplaine, il a l'esprit, que vous n'avez pas. Je fais de sa cause ma cause, de son injure mon injure, et de vos ricanements ma colère' (xiv. 358). Again, he identifies with the hero, whose cause he plans to embrace. In yet another reversal, though, Lord David ends by challenging Gwynplaine to a duel for a perceived insult to his mother. The sibling who, up to then, had identified with him once more becomes his *frère ennemi*. Lord David avers: 'Nous sommes frères... Ce qui fait que nous pouvons nous battre. On ne se bat qu'entre égaux. Qui est plus notre égal que notre frère?... Demain, nous nous couperons la gorge' (xiv. 358). The mutual throat-cutting underscores their equality as brothers within the fratricidal motif.

In a passage that recycles this imagery, Gwynplaine appears divided against himself when he discovers his aristocratic origins. Yesterday, he muses, he was a wandering performer; today, a prince: 'Confrontation... de la misère et de la puissance... devenant tout à coup les deux moitiés d'une conscience... Partage pathétique d'une intelligence, d'une volonté, d'un cerveau, entre ces deux frères ennemis, le fantôme pauvre et le fantôme riche. Abel et Caïn dans le même homme' (xiv. 340). Metaphorically linking adversity and prosperity through 'fantôme', Hugo shows them as but two

[94] See Miller, 'The Problematic of Ending a Narrative', 4.

sides of the same coin. Gwynplaine's 'conscience'—both conscience and consciousness in French—is not only split between the two; it also unites them. One mind, one will, one brain, one destiny: neither of the warring 'brothers' can win without destroying himself in the process.

The relationship between Lord David and Gwynplaine or Gwynplaine and himself also illuminates the minor episode involving the confrontation between two boxers from Scotland and Ireland, who had slept in the same bed and drunk the same amount of port from the same glass the previous night (xiv. 176).[95] The rivalry between the two 'brothers' thus rehearses in miniature the hostile siblings *topos* highlighted in the central plot. Restaging the David-and-Goliath-style battle between the big and little 'Han' in *Han d'Islande*, they look unequally matched but demonstrate that size is not all: 'D'un côté le coup de poing primitif... de l'autre le coup de poing de la civilisation... C'était l'art contre la nature. C'était le féroce contre le barbare' (xiv. 177). The tension between fraternal antagonists, as well as between the savage and the domesticated, ignorance and civilization, nature and art, constitutes a *mise en abyme* of the entire novel.

This study of resonant situations and characters in *L'Homme qui rit* casts new light on several familiar scenes, where similar reversals and double identities involve spatial dimensions. Here, as elsewhere in Hugo, the high and the low are not *either/or* but *both/and* propositions: 'En ce monde tout est pendule. Graviter, c'est osciller. Un pôle veut l'autre... Il existe une affinité profonde entre cette extrême hauteur et cet extrême abaissement' (xiv. 163). Instead of being purely dichotomous, extremes revolve around each other and, in their mutual attraction, even touch and intermingle. While the metaphor originally applies in the text to the rapport between Gwynplaine and Josiane, it extends to the sociopolitical arena as well. So, when Gwynplaine is tempted by Barkilphedro with the peerage, he is at one and the same time 'enlevé sur un sommet et précipité dans un abîme' (xiv. 281). His change of fortune turns out to be just one of a series of moral tests that parallel the trajectory of the bandits' doomed boat from reef to reef at the beginning of the novel: 'Charybde est la misère, mais Scylla est la richesse. Ceux qui se dressaient sous la foudre sont terrassés par l'éblouissement... L'ascension t'élèvera et t'amoindrira. L'apothéose a une sinistre puissance d'abattre' (xiv. 283). Poverty and wealth are to be equally avoided as dangers to the soul. While the former

[95] Thomas argues that, in his denunciation of the aristocracy's taste for the brutal pastime of boxing, Hugo creates an anachronism, one that in fact 'peint hardiment l'Angleterre du XIXe siècle'. Ursus' 'intermèdes shakespeariens' in the Green Box that demonstrate, on the contrary, 'les goûts éclairés du peuple' likewise depict 'un trait de l'Angleterre contemporaine' (*L'Angleterre dans l'œuvre de Victor Hugo*, 219, 220). Hugo's references to the contemporary sociopolitical scene are treated further on in this chapter.

may bring out the best in people, the latter kindles dreams of still greater heights that represent a spiritual downfall.

Likewise, after failing to inspire his peers in the House of Lords, the hero discovers himself 'sur le revers de son élévation, et il voyait l'autre côté de son éblouissement . . . Cette seigneurie était difforme, cette couronne était hideuse . . . ces palais étaient vénéneux' (xiv. 368). The flip side of his ascension, like his facial mask, is grotesque, the reflection of a deformed social system. Once again, being on top of the social hierarchy is no better than being at the bottom; the two fates are analogous. Though the rejection of Gwynplaine's calls for reform in the House of Lords reflects Hugo's own failures as an elected representative during the Second Republic, the spiritually impoverished rich are, the text predicts, destined to be overturned by the richly spiritual poor. As we shall see, such self-similar structures can be found beyond issues of character or spatial dimensions at multiple levels of the text.

Chaos Vaincu Revisited

Taken collectively, the multiplication of inverse and reverse mirrorings at different scales points beyond these visual effects per se towards other phenomena. For instance, as Victor Brombert affirms, Hugo was familiar with 'the recently invented technique of photography'.[96] He would have therefore known about photographic negatives and the functioning of the camera lens, both of which involve such symmetries. He would have also noted the relationship between the infinite regressions captured in convex mirrors—as in van Eyck's *Betrothal of the Arnolfini* (1434)—and the literary *mises en abyme* practised, for instance, by Shakespeare and Corneille in their plays within plays (see, for example, *Hamlet* (composed between 1599 and 1602) and *L'Illusion comique* (1635 or 1636), respectively).[97] Indeed, we have already noted, the novel contains such a drama in *Chaos vaincu.* The allegory of human striving to transcend baser instincts alludes to the actors' own situation—another *mise en abyme* of the novel itself. The dramatic confrontation of the sublime and the grotesque creates an aesthetic response that neither alone can evoke, not unlike the scene on the pillory in *Notre-Dame de Paris* (vi. 4).[98] The result is a rich multiplication of outlooks: 'Toute cette nuit et tout ce jour mêlés

[96] Brombert, *Victor Hugo and the Visionary Novel*, 200.

[97] For a fascinating overview of literary, rhetorical, mythical, historical, and critical treatments of mirrorings, see Joyce O. Lowrie, *Sightings: Mirrors in Texts—Texts in Mirrors* (Amsterdam: Rodopi, 2007), 1–39.

[98] See *EN* 172–7.

se résolvaient dans l'esprit du spectateur en un clair-obscur où apparaissaient des perspectives infinies' (xiv. 200). The complex interplay of opposites, which both contrast with and reflect each other, opens the hidden door to a universe of infinite possibilities.[99]

The notion of conquering chaos also serves as a template for *L'Homme qui rit*. We have already seen that Gwynplaine's 'partage pathétique' (xiv. 261) operates when he finds himself torn not just between two classes but between two women. As a result, the scenario of *Chaos vaincu* expands to include his own life. But that is only the beginning of Hugo's house of mirrors. Both the play and the storm at sea that engulfs the bandits' boat are re-enacted when Gwynplaine receives Josiane's letter and spends a 'tempestuous' night trying to sort out his thoughts and feelings. This time, though, the blizzard is contained in Gwynplaine's head. The dilemma that assails him in an 'orage d'émotions' (xiv. 242)—an echo of 'Une tempête sous un crâne' (I. 7. 3) in *Les Misérables* that also foreshadows Gauvain's moral tempest in *Quatrevingt-Treize* (III. 6. 2)—creates inner chaos: 'Flux, reflux, secousses, tournoiements, hésitations du flot devant l'écueil... apparition du naufrage de toutes parts... tout cela, qui est dans l'abîme, est dans l'homme' (xiv. 242). Gwynplaine is as much at sea as the *Matutina*.

The abyss within, an important motif of *Les Misérables*, reappears in much the same function. For the bandits, the saving exit from the abyss is death itself. For Gwynplaine (or Jean Valjean in the sewers), it appears in the light of infallible conscience/consciousness. Thus, in Corleone Lodge, the material temptations of Gwynplaine's new social status give rise to the 'monologue d'une tempête' (xiv. 283), where he unleashes both his anger at victimization and his lust for power. He is 'en pleine tempête intérieure', the narrator repeats, asking, 'Au moment où le flamboiement noir de l'éruption se dégorge à travers son puits pleins de tourbillons, le cratère a-t-il conscience des troupeaux qui paissent l'herbe au pied de sa montagne?' (xiv. 285). The use of the word 'conscience' (as consciousness) here is key, since it ties this passage to the awakening of Gwynplaine's conscience with the coming of dawn two lines later (see also xiv. 305).

The correspondence between microcosm and macrocosm continues when, just as the bandits lose their ability to steer, Gwynplaine feels himself out of control: 'De la boussole, il n'en avait plus... On ne sait quel irrémédiable bonheur s'entr'ouvrait, ressemblant à un naufrage... L'écueil... c'est la sirène... Un homme peut être désemparé comme un

[99] See Judith Wulf for a perceptive study of 'le discours chimérique' in *HQR* as a mode of suggesting 'des éventualités multiples' ('Chimère et référence dans *L'Homme qui rit*', in Michel Viegnes (ed.), *Hugo et la chimère* (Grenoble: ELLUG/Éditions littéraires et linguistiques de l'Université de Grenoble, 2003), 66).

navire. L'ancre, c'est la conscience. Chose lugubre, la conscience peut casser' (xiv. 312). Dragging Gwynplaine into the depths in a replay of the force of gravity pulling the *Matutina* into the abyss, Josiane threatens him with moral *naufrage*. The loss of his 'compass', the menace of the 'reef', the broken 'anchor'—all superimpose his plight on that of the bandits in a fractal-like pattern.[100] When Dea looks in on him in the morning, the storm suddenly dissipates: 'il sentit au plus profond de son être l'indéfinissable évanouissement de la tempête et la sublime descente du bien sur le mal' (xiv. 242–3). As light floods Gwynplaine's conscience, the reader knows that he has triumphed over material temptations in this scenario of *Chaos vaincu*.

The nesting configurations compound when Gwynplaine penetrates Josiane's web at Corleone Lodge, drawn to her inner sanctum: 'Par moments il croyait voir quelqu'un venir à lui... C'était lui, dans une glace, en habit de seigneur... Il se reconnaissait, mais pas tout de suite' (xiv. 307). In this 'recognition scene' where the hero meets himself both coming and going, he has, quite literally, become *other*. Gwynplaine's alter ego is further refracted in a *mise en abyme* created by all the sparkling surfaces that surround him: 'Les biseaux des cristaux taillés ajoutaient des effets de prismes à des effets de reflets... On ne savait si toutes ces facettes lumineuses... étaient des miroirs microscopiques ou des aigues-marines démesurées' (xiv. 307). The infinitely great and the infinitely small become indistinguishable in this metaphorical landscape that disorients Gwynplaine through the infinite regressions that send back images of himself. At last, he perceives Josiane through a gauzy cloth on her bed, in a kind of 'grotte de miroirs': the cloth becomes a 'toile', in the middle of which the naked woman serves as an 'araignée' (xiv. 309). Recalling the image of small vessels that are 'des mouches dans la toile d'araignée de la mer' (xiv. 81), Gwynplaine is entangled in Josiane's web. He is caught in an ambush by 'la boîte à surprises du sort' (xiv. 311), much like destiny's 'embuscade' (xi. 913) of Javert by means of Jean Valjean's virtue or Gilliatt's encounter with the octopus.[101] The object of a 'vertige arrangé exprès' (xiv. 311)—the recurring surprises doubling the *mise en abyme* of

[100] The tempest/shipwreck theme has political implications as well. Along the walls of the House of Lords, the huge tapestries given by Elizabeth I depict the enterprise of the Armada, 'depuis son départ d'Espagne jusqu'à son naufrage devant l'Angleterre' (xiv. 335). While the lords may take inspiration in these symbols of the nation's collective power, one can read the tapestries as the threat of divine retribution for their own misdeeds hanging over them as well. Cf. Roman, *Victor Hugo et le roman philosophique*, 712–13.

[101] The material temptation offered by Josiane in Corleone Lodge is associated with the one earlier presented by wealth and power through the image of the ambush. Thus, in contemplating his new social status, Gwynplaine meets 'l'embuscade du mieux, ennemi du bien' (xiv. 283), a pun on the notion of good(s).

the mirrors—Gwynplaine undergoes the experience of the sublime in a topsy-turvy universe.

This disruption reiterates that of the bandits in the tempest, a natural chaos where everything merges into a single, undifferentiated phenomenon. Even the dangers repeat themselves, as the boat moves from reef to reef: 'Le même phénomène d'envahissment de l'horizon par l'écueil se reproduisait avec la monotonie grandiose du gouffre. Les batailles de l'océan ont, comme les combats d'Homère, ce rabâchage sublime' (xiv. 99). In recycling itself, nature is, like Homer and recursive designs and Hugo himself, each time somewhat the same and somewhat different.[102] For instance, when the *comprachicos* at first evade death, they do so in a well-orchestrated way—'Ils s'étaient dégagés eux-mêmes des Casquets; mais devant Ortach la houle avait fait la péripétie; devant Aurigny, ce fut la bise' (xiv. 100)—via three variations on one peril. And, when the end comes, the scene forecasts future developments. Just as Gwynplaine risks being consumed by Josiane, the bandits' boat is slowly swallowed up by the sea: 'le fatal centre du globe les attirait . . . Ce n'était plus la gueule béante du flot, la double mâchoire du coup de vent et du coup de mer . . . le rictus de la trombe, l'appétit écumant de la houle; c'était sous ces misérables on ne sait quel bâillement noir de l'infini' (xiv. 103). The bandits are absorbed into the infinite, losing their lives and identities. Summing up their 'monstrous' adventures in the storm (*gueule béante, double mâchoire, appétit écumant*), the narrator reprises the notion of the rictus, suggesting that their fate is a form of poetic justice for their crimes against children, in other words, that they are responsible for their own deaths: 'C'était tout le contraire de la submersion par la marée montante. L'eau ne montait pas vers eux, ils descendaient vers elle . . . Leur poids était le fossoyeur' (xiv. 103). Unlike Gilliatt, who drowns in the rising tide as he watches his beloved Déruchette sail away with another man at the end of *Les Travailleurs de la mer* (III. 3. 5), the crew members sink under their own weight.

Their final minutes open up a visionary horizon: 'L'agonie est une échéance . . . Le passé revient et rentre dans l'avenir. Le connu devient abîme aussi bien que l'inconnu, et ces deux précipices . . . mêlent leur réverbération' (xiv. 105). A liminal experience between two gulfs, the one containing regrets and the other hopes, death mixes past, present,

[102] See Judith Wulf, '"Rabâchage" et formation du sens romanesque chez Victor Hugo', in Nigel Harkness et al. (eds), *Visions/Revisions: Essays on Nineteenth-Century French Culture* (Oxford: Peter Lang, 2003), 239, regarding Hugo's use of repetition in *MIS*, *TM*, and *HQR* as 'un moyen de déborder la signification sans céder à la tentation de l'illusion d'une déconstruction radicale'.

and future in one apocalyptic moment. The novel likewise merges history and utopian vision, the known and the unknown, in an eternal, narrative present—a 'confusion' or 'disorder' that may seem terrifying. But, as with the 'bird's-eye view' from atop the cathedral in *Notre-Dame de Paris* (III. 2) or the barricades in *Les Misérables* (V. 1. 5), this panoptic perspective leads from chaotic particulars to sweeping panoramas. Along with history, Hugo's historical novel 'lead(s) us back to those moments in the past where the future was not yet decided, where the past was itself a space of experience open to a horizon of expectation' (*TN* iii. 227). The meditation on the past in *L'Homme qui rit* enables the reader to see the present through new eyes, to dream of *other* possibilities in the open future of the past, which is the here and now.

Historical Visions

The mixture of temporal vistas in these and other passages suggests, then, that Hugo's superposition of self-similar patterns has a historical referent. On the stage of Hugo's novel, the chaos engendered by ignorance and obscurity is temporarily vanquished. Temporal dimensions overlap, as in spatial recursions, by mimicking each other: 'Qu'est l'histoire? Un écho du passé dans l'avenir. Un reflet de l'avenir sur le passé' (xiv. 336). The resemblances between different time frames create synchronic analogies within an essentially diachronic structure. 'Faire ressemblant, c'est là tout le devoir de l'historien' (xiv. 326), the narrator declares. In rendering a good likeness of his subject, another allusion to mirroring, the historian fulfils his obligations to present and future society. The mimetic quality of his work need not reside in exactitude but rather in capturing a true depiction of historical processes—a notion previously developed in *Les Misérables* and in 'L'Archipel de la Manche'.

Much of the text is grist for this effort. Consider, for example, the relation of the Green Box to the bandits' vessel: 'Cela ressemblait à une coque de navire qu'on aurait renversée, la quille pour toit, le pont pour plancher, et mise sur quatre roues' (xiv. 195). The Green Box is the mirror image of the *Matutina*, a point the narrator repeats when he describes the interior: 'Un aménagement de navire n'est pas plus concis et plus précis . . . Tout y était casé, rangé, prévu, voulu' (xiv. 196). Its inner neoclassical order, reminiscent of terms applied to the hyper-orderly Javert in *Les Misérables*, belies the 'Chaos' enacted without by Gwynplaine.[103] In fact, Gwynplaine's

[103] See *FT* 80–9, 114–16. The relation between social order and literature, developed at length in *MIS*, reappears in Hugo's satire on Restoration society. In contrast with Victor and François-Victor, who have been immersed in Shakespeare, 'on revenait à la belle

'claustration' (xiv. 209) in the Green Box after his performances is a happy exile: 'la Green-Box redressait son panneau comme une forteresse son pont-levis, et la communication avec le genre humain était coupé. D'un côté, l'univers et de l'autre cette baraque; et dans cette baraque il y avait la liberté, le bonheur, la bonne conscience, le courage, le dévouement, l'innocence, le bonheur, l'amour, toutes les constellations' (xiv. 209). This (Gothic) version of the lords' (neoclassical) chateaux described by Ursus is a miniature utopia, an Ark-like safe haven, a heaven on earth for Gwynplaine and Dea.[104] Perhaps it, too, is susceptible to a shipwreck, the text suggests, and, indeed, Ursus' little utopia is disrupted and disbanded by forces beyond its control. The boat metaphor resurfaces in the House of Lords, when Gwynplaine is surrounded by the 'tempête gaie et féroce' of the mocking lords: 'Une assemblée en gaîté, c'est la boussole perdue. On ne savait plus où l'on allait, ni ce qu'on faisait' (xiv. 355). Like the *Matutina* or the hero without a compass, the ship of state/House of Lords loses its bearing, having silenced the voice of its own conscience in the form of Gwynplaine's warning. Ursus' *Chaos vaincu* thus re-presents all the basic dramatic conflicts in the text itself, including those that take place on the historical plane. Microcosm and macrocosm are completely consonant.

Viewed from Hugo's multifaceted perspective, the relations between England and France in the novel are but variations on the *frères ennemis* theme. Like Josiane's unexpected conjunction with Gwynplaine, through a 'transfer from Same to Other, in empathy and imagination . . . the Other that is foreign to me is brought closer' (*TN* iii. 184; see also 228). For instance, the physical layout of the House of Lords is, according to the narrator, that of the ancient French parliament: 'Hincmar . . . décrit en 853 la chambre des lords en séance à Westminster au dix-huitième siècle. Sorte de bizarre procès-verbal fait neuf cents ans d'avance' (xiv. 336). France and England, past and future, meet in this unexpected spatial congruency. The lingering traces of William the Conquerer in the English monarchy, along with the use of the French language in English law, create lasting bonds between the two nations. Besides sharing both a

littérature. On dédaignait Shakespeare et l'on admirait Dryden' (xiv. 137). The baroque is out, neoclassicism is in, in a return to a purer style. 'C'est un grand bonheur pour les nations d'être ramenées par la monarchie au bon ordre dans l'état et au bon goût dans les lettres' (xiv. 137), the narrator—speaking for the mentality of the era (like the multi-voiced, soliloquizing Ursus)—opines. The return to neoclassical 'good taste' as a component of more 'orderly' behaviour allies these reflections with the politico-aesthetic considerations of the Second Empire. By contrast, Lord Clancharlie had in his youth 'ses incorrections et ses irregularities' (xiv. 140), terms that ally him with Hugo's mode of Romanticism.

[104] Cf. Piroué, *Lui, Hugo*, 124; Roman, *Victor Hugo et le roman philosophique*, 289–91; and Peyrache-Leborgne, 'Le Héros sublime', 327, 330–1.

historical and a linguistic heritage, England and France have related peerage systems: 'La création d'une égalité avec le roi, dite pairie, fut aux époques barbares une fiction utile. En France, le pair fut un faux roi; en Angleterre, ce fut un vrai prince... L'histoire n'est pas plus sûre de ce qu'elle dit que la légende (xiv. 330). Originating in France, the peerage split into two systems when it passed to England after the Norman Conquest in 1066. In each case, the notion of an equality with the king is, the narrator claims, simply a 'fiction' (xiv. 330) in barbarous times—much as myths and legends may in fact be 'truer' than history. As in Hugo's previous historical novels, history and story, fact and legend, are intimately intertwined, each revealing part of a larger verity.

In England, the power struggle between monarchists and reformers reached its apogee under Charles I: 'De cette acceptation du peuple par les lords sort le *bill des droits*, ébauche de nos *droits de l'homme*, vague ombre projetée du fond de l'avenir par la révolution de France sur la révolution d'Angleterre' (xiv. 332). Rather than find in the French Revolution an English precedent, the historian–author considers France's future (now his own past) to have projected itself retrospectively on Britain. England and France—past, present, and future—are inextricably linked in Hugo's transhistorical perspective. His narrative voice allows us to 'consider anticipations about the future as anticipated retrospections', because 'it can place itself at any point of time which becomes for it a quasi-present, and, from this observation point, it can apprehend as a quasi-past the future of our present' (*TN* iii. 260). So, while the French and English may seem to be rivals, if not enemies, their relations—like those between Dea and Josiane or Gwynplaine and Lord David—are far more complicated: 'Bien qu'à cette époque l'Angleterre querelle et batte la France,' the narrator remarks, 'elle l'imite et elle s'en éclaire' (xiv. 156). The two countries are more similar than different, sharing as they do in monarchic 'glory' and self-interest.[105] In this way, one country's history becomes, either implicitly or explicitly, a commentary on the other's. The reign of Queen Anne is thus 'une réverbération du règne de Louis XIV', and her court 'une réduction en petit de tous les grands hommes de Versailles, déjà pas très grands. Le trompe l'œil y est' (xiv. 155).[106] The *trompe l'œil* inherent in the French court—which appears larger than it is—operates in

[105] In his speeches during exile in Jersey and Guernsey (1852–70), Hugo frequently touches on the fraternal connections between the two nations. See esp. Barrère, 'Victor Hugo et la Grande-Bretagne', 164–6.

[106] Just as the destinies of Napoléon Bonaparte and Jean Valjean cross in *MIS* (see *FT* 189–96), so 'Anne apparaît en 1702, quand Louis XIV décline' (xiv. 156). The sense here, however, is that, while the names change, the succession of tyrants goes on.

England as well. Even the characters on this stage remain the same: 'Christopher Wren est un Mansart fort passable... Anne a un Racine qui est Dryden, un Boileau qui est Pope, un Colbert qui est Godolphin... et un Turenne qui est Marlborough' (xiv. 156). The repetition of the verb 'to be' sets up a metaphorical relationship of equivalency, where the English replace the French.[107] In their self-absorbed egotism, the two countries are more similar than different, the shift in scale notwithstanding. Monarchy in any time or place is, for Hugo, 'une réduction en petit' of republicanism.

The shining façade of England, as of France, is only that: the people suffer within. Hugo's post-Restoration England can be read as the metaphorical vehicle of which present-day France is the tenor. The 'struggle between flesh and spirit' is enacted not just in the Green Box and on 'the stage of England', as Grant observes.[108] It is also ongoing in nineteenth-century France. From this perspective, Barkilphedro's capacity for hypocrisy and self-deceit makes a political point: according to the narrator, 'nous vivons entourés de glissements sinistres... convenablement vêtu en empereur, [il] eût un peu ressemblé à Domitien' (xiv. 162–3). Though there is little textual reason to invoke *imperial* life, the image recurs when Barkilphedro considers all he has lost because others have kept him from realizing his potential, 'lui qui était fait pour être empereur' (xiv. 170). The novel's sociopolitical discourse is aimed directly at the Second Empire, the villain's likeness extending as much to Napoléon III—that supreme *usurpateur* and model of *tartufferie*—as to Domitian.[109]

Through this notion of history not simply as a cause-and-effect chain of events, but as a braid of self-repeating structures, the text provides many analogies to the present. The 'roman de l'évasion impossible' discerned by Miriam Roman points its readers towards their own era.[110] A keen

[107] Hugo adds a punchline, however: 'Grandissez les perruques pourtant, et diminuez les fronts' (xiv. 156). In other words, the English 'equivalents' are 'not equal' to their French counterparts. They are dwarfs in disguise, not unlike the eponymous fiend of *HI.*

[108] Grant, *The Perilous Quest,* 210.

[109] Even Barkilphedro's 'virtues' as a man of great 'patience, tempérance, continence, réserves, retinue, aménité, déférence, douceur, politesse, sobriété, chasteté' (xiv. 163)—a more subtle and less self-deluded version of Thénardier—are all qualities that associate him, too, with Louis-Napoléon. Whereas Albouy considers that Gwynplaine, 'le peuple difforme, mais qui pressent sa libération, est le Job-Prométhée de l'Ancien Régime' (*La Création mythologique*, 246), Brombert rightly perceives that the hero's vision of social equality 'leads to a political consciousness... that reaches into the nineteenth century, as topical allusions set up parallels, first with the Restoration under Charles X, then with the "corrupt" Second Empire and the rule of Napoléon III' (*Victor Hugo and the Visionary Novel,* 173). See also Rosa, 'Critique et autocritique', 10–11.

[110] Roman, *Victor Hugo et le roman philosophique*, 432. Cf. Rosa, 'Critique et autocritique', 10–11.

observer of History as well as a maker of *histoires*, Hugo considers that one of his roles is to use his unique ear to detect the sources of power in his century: 'Ceux qui dans un règne savent distinguer cette voix basse [de la souveraineté] et entendre ce qu'elle souffle à la voix haute [du souverain], sont les vrais historiens' (xiv. 164), the narrator says, regarding the relations between Barkilphedro and Queen Anne. Even though Barkilphedro's name 'n'est pas arrivé jusqu'à l'histoire' (xiv. 165), the reverse is true of Hugo's historical novel, which persistently gestures towards a contemporary example of the type.

The implication of the villain's relations of 'sovereignty' with Queen Anne is, of course, that Barkilphedro's treacherous double, Napoléon III, is manipulating the current Queen of England, Victoria. The stakes of such cooperation for Hugo himself are high, since cooperation between English and French royalty in legal matters can dissolve normal political borders: 'Louis XV faisait enlever dans Piccadilly les écrivains qui lui déplaisaient... George III empoignait en France le prétendant au beau milieu de la salle de l'Opéra. C'étaient deux bras très longs' (xiv. 248). By reaching across countries to annihilate the notion of safe haven, the 'brotherhood' of those purportedly 'hostile siblings', France and England, has enhanced the power of their rulers while undermining the liberties of their citizens in a grotesque form of Europeanism. The question posed is, what is happening in 1869? Are Victoria and Louis-Napoléon collaborating? Will Hugo lose his protection by traveling to London or even by remaining on Guernsey? Can Victoria rise above the tendency of the English to exhibit what the narrrator calls 'enthousiasme pour le despote d'à côté' (xiv. 156)? Victoria's warm relations with Napoléon III must have been particularly galling to Hugo, who would find no help for France from that quarter.[111]

[111] Thomas maintains that Hugo's unflattering portraits of Queen Elizabeth and Queen Anne in *HQR* reflect his having been 'témoin du royalisme excessif des Anglais contemporains, et surtout de leur "culte spécial" pour la reine Victoria' (*L'Angleterre dans l'œuvre de Victor Hugo*, 214). According to Sheila Gaudon, Hugo's distrust of the English government in general was justified by its acceptance of the 1851 *coup d'état*, Louis-Napoléon Bonaparte 'a[yant] gardé, de ses années d'Angleterre [1838–9, 1846–8], des relations personnelles qui devaient mettre du liant entre l'aristocratie anglaise et lui' ('Anglophobie?', in A. R. W. James (ed.), *Victor Hugo et la Grande-Bretagne* (Liverpool: Francis Cairns Publications, 1986), 59). The alliance of the two countries was further consolidated by their joint naval action against Russia in the 1853 Crimean War. In this way, 'les rivaux traditionnels se mettaient à l'unisson précisément au moment où la démocratie était expulsée de France. L'Angleterre victorienne soutenait la France de Napoléon le petit' ('Anglophobie?', 60). As we shall see in our study of *QVT*, Hugo projects his animosity towards such anti-republican Anglo-French pacts on the relations between the two countries at the end of the previous century.

Despite this potentially bleak outlook, Hugo's recognition of intricate historical patterns—patterns that he seeks to enable others to 'read' as well—suggests a sense of optimism regarding the larger picture. Hugo's 'intime méfiance . . . à l'égard de la linéarité de l'histoire,' whereby 'la linéarité de l'intrigue et les thèmes mélioristes sont constamment contredits et minés par le symbolisme d'une descente en spirale et les récurrences cycliques',[112] is contravened by the visionary's overarching perspective. Though the spread of light now seems as suspended in Britain as in France, progress is, for him, an inevitable process, moving from individual to collective independence. As in his 'Archipel to la Manche', Hugo deploys *mises en abyme* in time, as well as in space, to signal the emergence of a new world order. The use of spatial symmetries in *L'Homme qui rit* is matched by the temporal repetitions that emerge from overlapping, self-similar time frames, as history recycles itself in an upward spiral. Hugo's fictive 'exploration of the nonlinear features of phenomenological time that historical time conceals' (*TN* iii.132) proposes fresh ways to consider the idea of progress. Thus, through his role as an historian, Hugo reveals some of the oldest, and perhaps most surprising, sources of liberty in the modern age: 'Les deux puissances aveugles, monarchie et oligarchie, ne s'apercevaient pas qu'elles travaillaient pour un tiers, la démocratie' (xiv. 333) when they invented the peerage. Dea's blindness (*aveugle*), passing figuratively into the rival camps (*monarchie*, *oligarchie*) as lack of discernment and foresight, gives birth to the Enlightenment (*démocratie*).

History's recursive, nonlinear dynamics need not, therefore, be a source of despair. For Ricoeur, 'the present is wholly a crisis when expectation takes refuge in utopia and when tradition becomes only a dead deposit of the past' (*TN* iii. 235). Hugo's narrative, in contrast, revives the English past and reattaches it to the immediate French present through their shared dystopian features, which are then countered by Gwynplaine's vision of a happier future.[113] If the brief Second Republic and restoration of the French Empire are 'réverbération[s]' of Cromwell's Commonwealth and the English Restoration, the cycle may yet produce another happy reversal. After all, in creating the privileged peerage so long ago, the House of Lords ended up producing citizens' rights: 'L'aristocratie, ce vautour, a couvé cet œuf d'aigle, la liberté' (xiv. 334). Negative causes can create

[112] Victor Brombert, 'Ma destinée: "L'ordre, c'est le délire"', in Jacques Seebacher and Anne Ubersfeld (eds), *Hugo le fabuleux: Actes du Colloque de Cerisy, 30 juin–10 juillet 1985* (Paris: Seghers, 1985), 230.

[113] Albouy considers both *HQR* and *QVT* to be novels that 's'achèvent par l'ouverture—l'utopie étant précisément une ouverture' ('Présentation', 25). Cf. Nash's Bakhtinian reading of the disfigured Gwynplaine as a 'prophetic and transfiguring agent, opening the way to a more promising future' ('Transfiguring Disfiguration', 12).

positive effects; progress continues unimpeded, using everything to its own ends. When the lower classes reclaim their identity as the high, they will gain a new sense of self, one with new desires, as Gwynplaine does through Dea's love, or as Josiane does in seeing in her own soul his grotesque counterpart. Indeed, the empowering mirror held up to the people is nothing less than the novel itself, a reflection of their loving, aspiring, *worthy* selves. If, as Ricoeur maintains, 'history has always been a critique of social narratives and, in this sense, a rectification of our common memory' (*TN* iii. 119), then the same can be said of Hugo's historical narrative, which strives to reshape the way the French nation perceives its own evolution. The 1848 *représentant du peuple* continues in 1869 to plead his case before the bar of history.

Chaos vaincu? As we have seen, Ursus' masterpiece about humanity's ability to elevate itself over bestiality is replayed in Hugo's panoramic, transnational history in *L'Homme qui rit*. Mixing comedy, tragedy, satire, epic, drama, essay, and lyricism, along with a complex array of time frames, the novel traces a hidden geometry that orders its apparent lapses and discontinuities into a 'poetics of transcendence'.[114] Allying the refiguration of history with metaphorical redescription, it makes what is distant in both time and space 'stand for' both Second Empire France and its republican outlaws. By teasing out the overarching emplotment of history from its various meanderings and retrogressions, the novelist is able to defend the notion of progress and to suggest a hopeful vision of the future. The narrative's seemingly unending reversals gesture beyond mere oxymora towards the sublimities of social and aesthetic harmony. The constant personal and political reversals of fortune are part of a larger scheme—a notion, we shall see, that receives its full expression in *Quatrevingt-Treize*.

Hugo's mastery of his complicated plot line and unwieldy historical material is, in itself, most impressive. At the same time, his narrative not only constitutes an internally consistent macrometaphorical construct; its myriad recursions also encompass all the preceding novels. Certainly, the integration of 'l'anankè des dogmes, l'anankè des lois, l'anankè des choses, [et] la fatalité intérieure, l'anankè suprême, le cœur humain' (xii. 551), within this one text affiliates *L'Homme qui rit* with several preceding works, while underscoring its tragic focus. By the same token, the allusions to *Han d'Islande*, *Le Dernier Jour d'un condamné*, *Notre-Dame de Paris*, *Les Misérables*, and *Les Travailleurs de la mer*, among other works, demonstrate a way of dominating the writer's own artistic past. Integrating elements of plot, character, imagery, and digression associated with his

[114] Albouy likewise perceives in the text, which he considers after *MIS* to be 'le plus *riche* des roman hugoliens', a 'cohérence à tous les niveaux' ('Présentation', 26).

earlier texts, Hugo uses metaphoricity—metaphors for metaphor—as part of an overdetermined universe where everything refers to and becomes everything else. Yet this stunning *mise en abyme*, whereby *L'Homme qui rit* both reflects its predecessors and subsumes them in a more complex system, goes even further. The scattered references to *Quatrevingt-Treize*, a text that Hugo had announced as early as 1862 but that appeared only in 1874, also gesture towards a glorious future, both artistic and revolutionary.

Hugo's ambitions—as apparent here as ever—do not just bracket his place in French literary history but extend to the international scene as well. After all, his novel perpetuates the French–English sociopolitical parallels developed in *Les Travailleurs de la mer*, a clue that the two works serve similar aims, including offering his own rendition of some of Great Britain's most celebrated classics. In the last section of this chapter, we will examine the writer's bid for immortality by contending with another of his earliest English 'ancestors', John Milton.

MILTON IN HUGO

The presence in *Les Travailleurs de la mer* of a Shakepearean pre-text prompts further scrutiny of *L'Homme qui rit* for a similar literary dialogue. That Hugo's narrative is set in seventeenth-century England again points to the island nation as a possible source of inspiration, and the Restoration background brings Milton immediately to mind. In researching and composing his narrative, Hugo would have thought many times about the author of the great epic poem *Paradise Lost*—who had, in 1660, been imprisoned for his writings as a republican propagandist under Cromwell.[115] Like Milton, Hugo aspired to be the Homer or Vergil of his age.[116] Both authors were also viewed by some contemporaries as literary relics, Milton under the English Restoration and Hugo under the Second Empire, even as they were producing their most celebrated works.[117] In the light of these congruencies, Dea's prescient blindness would constitute an obvious reference to the blind Milton, who also figures in *William Shakespeare* as one of a long line of visionary writers claimed by Hugo as

[115] See Christopher Hill, *Milton and the English Revolution* (New York: Viking, 1977), 356, and David Loewenstein, *Milton's* Paradise Lost (Cambridge: Cambridge University Press, 1993), 18.

[116] See John Leonard, 'Introduction', in John Milton, *Paradise Lost* (London: Penguin, 2000), p. ix.

[117] See Laura Lunger Knoppers, *Historicizing Milton: Spectacle, Power, and Poetry in Restoration England* (Athens: University of Georgia Press, 1994), 4, and Loewenstein, *Milton's* Paradise Lost, 19.

his predecessors. In fact, Hugo mentions Milton twenty times in his 1864 essay (as opposed to 100 times for Shakespeare, its putative subject). Clearly, the English poet was very much present in his reflections during the 1860s. Vying with the Bard for the honour of being England's preeminent poet, Milton would be a worthy touchstone, in addition to Shakespeare, against which the mature Hugo could measure his own achievements. Although Hugo scholarship has established the novelist's early familiarity with and allusions to Milton's work, the connections between *Paradise Lost* and *L'Homme qui rit* have thus far been unexplored. To elucidate their intertextuality, I look first at the young Hugo's exposure to *Paradise Lost* and identification with the blind English poet, then at his later affinities with Milton as a republican rebel, and lastly at specific features common to their visions in *Paradise Lost* and *L'Homme qui rit* of diabolic plots, primordial chaos, the Parliament of Hell, and alternative futures—features that seek to educate both Milton's and Hugo's readers in discerning their own historical destiny.

'Je serai Milton ou rien . . . '

Though Milton's reputation in England suffered in the century following his death, it was revived by such Romantic poets as William Blake (1757–1827), George Gordon, Lord Byron, and Percy Bysshe Shelley through their admiration for the 'sublime' figure of Satan, whom they took to be the hero of *Paradise Lost.*[118] In France, Jacques Delille's (1738–1813) rhymed verse rendition of Milton's blank verse work appeared in 1804–5. Chateaubriand had also read and begun translating *Paradise Lost* into French prose during his exile in England in the 1790s—a project that he would not complete and publish until 1836. But the young Hugo would probably have read Chateaubriand's chapter-long discussion in *Le Génie du Christianisme* (1802) of the 'beautés supérieures' of *Paradise Lost*, and perhaps even his earlier poem, 'Milton et Davenant' (1797).[119]

[118] Loewenstein, *Milton's* Paradise Lost, 59.

[119] François-René de Chateaubriand, *Le Génie du Christianisme* (Paris: Firmin Didot, 1858), 184. Moreover, in 1823 Hugo's oldest brother, Abel (1798–1855), published in the *Tablettes romantiques* a prose 'fragment' entitled *Milton*, the hero of which was the elderly poet (see Albouy, *La Création mytholoque*, 128 n. 63; Jean Gillet, 'Milton dans *Cromwell*', in A. R. W. James (ed.), *Victor Hugo et la Grande-Bretagne* (Liverpool: Francis Cairns Publications, 1986), 39; and Jacques Seebacher, 'Comment peut-on être Milton?', in Jacques Blondel (ed.), *Le* Paradis perdu *1667–1967* (Paris: Minard, 1967), 248). It is worth noting that, in Chateaubriand's poem, the republican Milton and the royalist Davenant save each other's lives under Cromwell and Charles II, respectively; Abel instead depicts Davenant asking that Milton be spared, whereas Victor has Milton attempting to rescue Davenant in his 1827 play *Cromwell*. See also Jean Gillet, *Le* Paradis perdu *dans la*

More importantly, Hugo knew Milton beyond just the second-hand opinions of others. Albouy cites solid evidence, for example, not only that the young poet read Delille's translation of *Paradise Lost*, but also that Miltonian echoes pervade his work from the outset: 'l'abbé Grillet aperçoit, dans les *Odes [et Poésies diverses]*, dès 1822, quelques réminiscences du *Paradis perdu*, traduit par Delille. Milton figure dans le drame de *Cromwell*, et, en 1834, Hugo transforme son article de *La Muse [française]* (May 1824) sur l'*Eloa*, de Vigny, en une étude du *Paradis perdu*'.[120] Hugo's admiration for and sense of literary competition with Milton thus dates back to the beginning of his career as a poet, critic, novelist, and playwright. Jacques Seebacher ventures that: 'Pour Hugo, qui avait voulu être "*Chateaubriand ou rien*", le génie et l'originalité consistent peut-être en une imitation de soi-même au travers des autres, et spécialement de Milton.'[121] In any event, Hugo's deep identification with the English poet was perhaps sealed by troubles with his vision in his youth. As early as 1824, when he began an intermittent twenty-five-year struggle with eye diseases to which 'he at times felt... he would lose his sight',[122] he compared himself 'à Homère, à Milton, à Ossian et à tous ces sublimes aveugles qui ont chanté' (ii. 1440; 15 May 1824 letter to Saint-Valry). Many years later, in 'Du génie', a fragment originally destined for *William Shakespeare*, he recalls in familiar terms another attack on his vision in 1828: 'Et voilà que je me mis à espérer que je serais peut-être un jour aveugle comme Homère et comme Milton,' because, he explains, physical debilitations in great artists 'semblent un signe d'élection. Etre foudroyé, c'est être prouvé titan' (xii. 412).[123] As Paulson points out, the early reference to Titans, which 'implies participation in the struggle of generations, the symbolic Oedipal rivalry', suggests a poet embroiled in 'rivalry with his ancestors'[124]—even, I would venture, at the end of an immensely distinguished career.

littérature française de Voltaire à Chateaubriand (Paris: Klincksieck, 1975), 503–23, 560–78, regarding Delille's translation of Milton's poem and Chateaubriand's account of *Paradise Lost* in *Le Génie du Christianisme*, respectively.

[120] Albouy, *La Création mythologique*, 128; see also *OC* v. 146–7. For additional reflections on the literary relations between Hugo, Delille, and Milton, see esp. Barrère, *Victor Hugo à l'œuvre*, 75; Seebacher, 'Comment peut-on être Milton?', 242; Gillet, 'Milton dans *Cromwell*', 40, 47 n. 5; and Marie-Élisabeth Bougeard-Vetö, *Chateaubriand Traducteur: De l'exil au* Paradis perdu (Romantisme et Modernités, 91; Paris: Champion, 2005), 309 n. 7.

[121] Seebacher, 'Comment peut-on être Milton?', 241.

[122] Paulson, *Enlightenment*, 182.

[123] See Jean Gaudon, *Le Temps de la contemplation*, 37, 424 n. 54, and Brombert, *Victor Hugo and the Visionary Novel*, 78.

[124] Paulson, *Enlightenment*, 183.

While the arc of his republican life comes to resemble more and more Milton's political rise and fall, Hugo's maturing creative powers likewise lead to late masterpieces such as *Les Contemplations* and *Les Misérables*. In this way, the English poet's work returns to the fore during exile in the Channel Islands. Already in his 1826 preface to the *Odes et ballades*, Laurence Porter contends, Hugo 'no longer casts a nostalgic backward glance at the Ancien Régime . . . a political system from which he is coming to wish himself free'.[125] The following year, Hugo anticipates in *Cromwell* 'l'ébranlement de ses certitudes royalistes'[126]—to be abrogated in full with the July Revolution.[127] During political exile under the Second Empire, the Miltonian reverberations begin to multiply. For instance, in *La Fin de Satan*, his unfinished epic poem begun in 1854 and abandoned in 1862, Hugo takes up the story of the fallen angel previously recounted by Milton and Vigny and then, in *La Chute d'un ange* (1838), by Lamartine. Now Hugo himself is a 'fallen angel'—having rebelled against Napoléon III's imperial reign.[128] The resonances of a poetic life that had come full circle, from royalist accuser to republican outlaw, from Milton's political antithesis to his latter-day counterpart, extend, I argue, beyond *La Fin de Satan* to *L'Homme qui rit* as well. The two 'revolutionary prose writer[s]' end up with similarly prophetic world views—and with the continued courage to 'attack tyranny' in the present age.[129]

Despite the genre differences between *L'Homme qui rit* and *Paradise Lost*, similarities between the two works abound. Each was composed and published under the threat of censorship by a government hostile to the author's republican affinities. 'Not being able to say certain things directly, Milton would expect his reader . . . to be alert to hints, to allusions . . . to analogies, to perhapses'[130] that linked his moral tale to the current political

[125] Porter, *The Renaissance of the Lyric*, 87.

[126] Gillet, 'Milton dans *Cromwell*', 47.

[127] See Seebacher, 'Comment peut-on être Milton?', 243–6.

[128] Ironically, Hugo's exile parallels the fate of Napoléon I–Satan, 'captif suprême | Sur un rocher' (ii. 15), in an early poem, 'Buonaparte' (*Odes et poésies diverses*), that is packed with Miltonian imagery. Gillet points out the correspondences for Hugo between Napoléon, Satan, and Cromwell ('Milton dans *Cromwell*', 46–7), remarking elsewhere that the Milton of *Cromwell* appears as 'une sorte de prophète biblique épris de liberté avant tout' (*Le* Paradis perdu, 620 n. 92)—another example of Hugo's imagination leading his politics while he was still an *ultra* (see *EN* 20–1, 56–7, 156–8, 195–6). Finally, we might add that, according to some interpretations of *Paradise Lost*, Satan is faced with 'an infinite fall through an infinite abyss' (Leonard, 'Introduction', xix), much as he is in *La Fin de Satan*. See also Max Milner's observation that Hugo, like Milton, 'fait de la chute de Satan un drame du retrait de la lumière' ('Le Satan de Milton et l'épopée romantique française', in Jacques Blondel (ed.), *Le* Paradis perdu *1667–1967* (Paris: Minard, 1967), 238).

[129] Loewenstein, *Milton's* Paradise Lost, 13, 119.

[130] Hill, *Milton and the English Revolution*, 405; see also 404, 407, and Sharon Achinstein, *Milton and the Revolutionary Reader* (Princeton, NJ: Princeton University Press, 1994) 173, 177, 201.

scene. More formally, both *L'Homme qui rit* and *Paradise Lost* are epic in scope, with sweeping temporal vistas that provide the occluded subtext about contemporary events with a historical frame. Both also display dramatic features, not just in the overall confrontation between good and evil but in a multitude of monologues and of dialogues between and among the prime players.[131] Finally, the *mélange des genres* in Hugo and Milton alike draws on sublime and grotesque imagery—often figured spatially along the vertical axis—to depict the conflict of ethical forces. Despite the different eras, nations, and cultures that separate poem and novel, their cosmic scale constitutes a key shared signature.

Such general resemblances do not, of course, suffice to bind the two texts into a dialogic relationship. Nor does the fact that the narrator of *L'Homme qui rit* mentions Milton twice within just a few chapters at the beginning of Part Two, first to satirize the rage under Charles II for Dryden—at the expense of Shakespeare and of 'l'auteur du *Paradis perdu*' (xiv. 137)—and second to remark that Lord David belonged to a club founded by Swift, 'en remplacement de la Rota, fondée par Milton' (xiv. 149). The seventeenth century throws out the older generation, denying an 'anxiety of influence'; the nineteenth century remembers its ancestors, but acknowledges them only indirectly. To tease out Hugo's deeper homage to Milton, one must examine more specific aspects of plot and character. Since *Paradise Lost* is loosely based on the account of man's fall in Genesis, it is essential to identify characteristics of *L'Homme qui rit* that point, beyond Hugo's acquaintance with the Bible, to some degree of familiarity with Milton's interpretation of the same primary source. Among the most salient features held in common, in my view, are the portraits of Satan and Barkilphedro; the temptation of Adam and Gwynplaine, respectively, by Eve and Duchess Josiane; the role of Chaos; the notion of a 'Parliament of Hell'; and the vision of future history. In the rest of this section, I illuminate the extraordinary literary affinities between Milton and Hugo.

Reading Villainy, Rewriting (Future) History

As we have observed in our study of Barkilphedro, for whom '[nuire], c'est jouir' (xiv. 161), personal pleasure for Hugo's villain resides in destroying the pleasure of others. He is, like Milton's Satan, a creature who conceals 'Deep malice . . . couched with revenge' (IV. 123).[132] The connection with

[131] For Laura Knoppers, Milton's poem 'links theatricality with Satan, who has a full complement of props, costumes, scenery, and dramatic ploys' (*Historicizing Milton*, 36).

[132] John Milton, *Paradise Lost*, ed. John Leonard (London: Penguin, 2000), 77; see also 118 (ll. 665–6). References in the text to *Paradise Lost* (hereafter *PL*) are to book and line.

Satan is further reinforced by Barkilphedro's status as an 'êtr[e] cach[é] et vénéneux' (xiv. 162), an 'âm[e] reptil[e]' (xiv. 157), a 'bêt[e] plat[e]' (xiv. 163) motivated by envy (xiv. 162)—not of God's elevation of his son in Heaven but of the high-born and well-off. He, not Gwynplaine, is the true grotesque of Hugo's narrative, another trait shared with Satan, who is reduced to a 'monstrous serpent on his belly prone' (X. 514) at the end of *Paradise Lost*.[133] Barkilphedro targets Josiane as his object of vengeance, ruining Gwynplaine and Dea's quiet 'éden' (xiv. 189) in the process. Satan aims to destroy Adam and Eve's 'private, domestic joy' in their earthly garden in order to 'surpass | Common revenge, and interrupt [God's] joy | In our Confusion' (II. 370–2) and to 'regain joy for himself'.[134] Both delight in others' ruin.

Each malefactor is also a master of rhetoric who effectively manipulates others. Milton sets elaborate scenes in Heaven, Hell, and Eden where Satan twists logic and duels verbally with others to attain his own ends, a much greater role than that assumed by the Devil in Genesis. A 'sly hypocrite', Satan 'Once fawned, and cringed, and servilely adored | Heav'n's awful Monarch' (IV. 957, 959–60)—an obvious prototype for Barkilphedro's unctuous character. When Barkilphedro whispers in Queen Anne's ear, as Napoléon III presumably whispers in Queen Victoria's, he recalls Satan's sly insinuations, hypocritical nature, and politically savvy discourse throughout *Paradise Lost*.[135] While railing against God's tyranny, Satan is revealed as the true tyrant, much as Barkilphedro sees himself as victim, rather than victimizer.[136] And when Satan attempts to return in triumph to a Hell restored to joy, only to encounter instead 'A dismal universal hiss, the sound | Of public scorn' (X. 508–9), the analogy between the loss of Paradise in Milton and that of the Second Republic in Hugo becomes clear. 'The Satanic restoration is revealed as false, transient, and perverted—a pointed figure for the contemporary

[133] See Knoppers, *Historicizing Milton*, 109.

[134] Knoppers, *Historicizing Milton*, 82, 80.

[135] See David Loewenstein, *Representing Revolution in Milton and his Contemporaries* (Cambridge: Cambridge University Press, 2001), 204–5, 226.

[136] Michael Bryson contends that, while 'Milton uses Satan to critique tyranny', he 'merely sets himself up as an alternate monarch, another tyrant, another king' (*The Tyranny of Heaven: Milton's Rejection of God as King* (Newark: University of Delaware Press, 2004) 109; see also Achinstein, *Milton and the Revolutionary Reader*, 203–4, and Loewenstein, *Milton's* Paradise Lost, 63–4)—in other words, that even God the supreme ruler enters into Milton's global condemnation of royalism. We cannot know if Hugo read *PL* in this way. However, we have already projected a parallel reading of *HQR*, whereby Barkilphedro's despotism constitutes an attack on the autocratic institutions not only of the English Restoration but also of the Second Empire.

political scene [of the English Restoration]'[137] that in turn figures the Second Empire in *L'Homme qui rit.*

In Genesis, Satan tempts Eve with a fruit (traditionally, an apple)—and the promise of divine knowledge. In *Paradise Lost*, the temptation scene is a drawn-out affair, where Satan, in his serpentine disguise and through 'a rhetorical tour de force',[138] offers a wide range of arguments geared towards breaking down Eve's initial scepticism and resistance to disobeying God's command. In *L'Homme qui rit*, Barkilphedro never crosses paths with Dea, so the innocent 'Eve' (xiv. 190) of the edenic Green Box escapes a direct assault by this diabolic schemer. Instead, Barkilphedro sets up Josiane's encounter with Gwynplaine, the rightful owner of Corleone House, who will then be ensnared in the Duchess's evil web.[139]

The Miltonian overtones are established at several points in the seduction scene where, we have seen, Josiane appears first as 'Ève' (ii. 7. 3; xiv. 308) and then as 'Satan' (ii. 7. 4; xiv. 313). That her bedroom is a 'grotte de mirroirs' (xiv. 309) alludes to Eve's initial, narcissistic gaze in *Paradise Lost* into the 'crystal mirror' (iv. 263) of a lake, before she is divinely guided to meet her mate and to throw off self-love for mutual devotion.[140] Like Satan, Josiane knows how to use words and appearances to sway others, and her efforts to captivate Gwynplaine run the gamut of persuasive strategies. Satan, for example, flatters Eve for her 'celestial beauty', maintaining that she deserves to be seen 'A goddess among gods, adored and served | By angels numberless, thy daily train' (ix. 540, 547–8).[141] And he claims that this 'Goddess humane,' along with Adam, will 'pu[t] off | Human, to be as gods' (ix. 732, 713–14) by attaining to the superior knowledge of good and evil bestowed by the forbidden fruit. Josiane likewise deals from a position of 'masculine' power in relation to Gwynplaine's 'feminine' status as her lower-class prey. Previously perceived as a

137 Knoppers, *Historicizing Milton*, 92; see also 87.

138 Loewenstein, *Representing Revolution*, 210.

139 It is significant that Barkilphedro's temptation of Gwynplaine with an array of material goods, much as Jesus is tempted by Satan, echoes the basic plot of Milton's *Paradise Regained*, published in 1671 (see e.g. Knoppers, *Historicizing Milton*, 140–1, and Robert Thomas Fallon, *Divided Empire: Milton's Political Imagery* (University Park: Pennsylvania State University Press, 1995), 167–9). Whether Hugo was acquainted with this sequel to *PL*, which Chateaubriand mentions briefly in *Le Génie du Christianisme*, either through his own youthful readings or, later in life, through François-Victor's, is as yet to be determined. See also Robert Couffignal's analysis of Hugo's debt to Milton in 'Le Sacre de la femme' (1858) in terms of 'l'intensité de la lumière, le "*décor brodé au petit point*", l'innocence de l'amour charnel' ('Le *Paradis perdu* de Victor Hugo à Pierre-Jean Jouve', in Jacques Blondel (ed.), *Le* Paradis perdu *1667–1967* (Paris: Minard, 1967), 253–4).

140 See Diane Kelsey McColley, *Milton's Eve* (Urbana: University of Illinois Press, 1983), 74–85.

141 See Loewenstein, *Milton's* Paradise Lost, 113.

'déesse' by both Ursus (xiv. 230) and Gwynplaine (xiv. 240), she repeats the metaphor when she tells him, 'Ton approche fait sortir l'hydre de moi, déesse. Tu me révèles ma vraie nature' (xiv. 316). To persuade the young man that her inaccessibility is just an illusion, she brings herself down to his monstrous level—a witty inversion of Satan's argument in *Paradise Lost.* She is, tellingly, Gwynplaine's 'miroir' (xiv. 316), yet another allusion to Eve's original self-centred developmental stage. Given this elaborate scene, we must conclude that Josiane's multi-pronged approach to seduction corresponds more closely to the campaign against Eve by Milton's antagonist than to Satan's easy conquest in Genesis (3:1–5).

But the Satanic figures of Josiane and Barkilphedro are not the only points of comparison with Milton's great work. The overdetermination in *L'Homme qui rit* of the notion of chaos—as a play within the narrative and a state to be vanquished both morally and aesthetically—suggests that its importance derives from the signal role of Chaos in *Paradise Lost.* Mentioned in the first sentence of Milton's poem, where 'the heav'ns and earth | Rose out of Chaos' (I. 10), Chaos initially appears as the raw matter used by God for his Creation. It is also the 'gloomy deep' (I. 152), the place of 'utter darkness' (I. 72) into which Satan and the other rebel angels are plunged after they lose their battle in Heaven, God having already transformed its lowest reaches into the prison-like Hell.[142] This 'dark immeasurable abyss' (VII. 211) thus corresponds spatially to the infinite regressions of the mirrored *mises en abyme* in Hugo's novel.[143]

Here Satan, 'like a weather-beaten vessel' amid the 'elements | In mutiny' (II. 1044, 925–6), serves as an early version of the storm-tossed *Matutina*. At the same time, Chaos in Milton is personified, along with Night, 'The consort of his reign' (II. 963); the source of all discord and disjunction, the two 'hold | Eternal anarchy, amidst the noise | Of endless wars, and by confusion stand' (II. 895–7).[144] Ursus likewise embodies 'les forces féroces de la nature, les faims inconscientes, l'obscurité sauvage' in his play, a nightly spectacle staged in the dark of 'le chaos combattant l'homme' (xiv. 198). In each case, the idea not just of turmoil but also of ceaseless strife pervades the depiction of chaos. And in each, hope arrives,

[142] See Leonard, 'Introduction', 292, 295. Gillet notes that, for Delille, 'le premier péché devient surtout rébellion' (*Le* Paradis perdu, 518)—a reflection of his monarchic views, which would have corresponded to the young Hugo's as well.

[143] The 'dreary, barren landscape' (Loewenstein, *Milton's* Paradise Lost, 72) of Milton's Hell adds the horizontal axis of wasteland imagery to the vertical axis of apocalyptic imagery in the poem. We have seen that Hugo combines the negative and positive sublime in *HQR* as well.

[144] See Fallon, *Divided Empire*, 84, 116, and Neil Forsyth, *The Satanic Epic* (Princeton, NJ: Princeton University Press, 2003), 116.

metaphorically, in the form of light. In *L'Homme qui rit*, the 'lumière' (xiv. 198) that suddenly appears, personified by Dea, is that of 'l'esprit' (xiv. 199) awaking to full consciousness. In *Paradise Lost*, Adam first learns that it is God's 'Word, begotten Son' (vii. 163), by whose command 'light | Ethereal... | Sprung from the deep' (vii. 243–5) in the Creation; after the fall, he is shown a vision of the Son's redeeming sacrifice, which he considers a goodness 'more wonderful | Than that which by creation first brought forth | Light out of darkness' (xii. 471–3). For both Hugo and Milton, the *fiat lux* implies not mechanical production but morally purposeful creativity.[145] Given Chaos's lament to Satan that his realm has been severely reduced, 'Encroached' (ii. 1001) by God's carving out Hell below and earth and sky above, it is no coincidence that Hugo represents his own cogent act of Creation out of disparate and antithetical entities in and through the idea of *Chaos vaincu*.[146]

In addition to *Chaos vaincu*, Hugo's treatment of the House of Lords in *L'Homme qui rit* stands as a striking *mise en scène* of the confrontation between ravening appetites and higher consciousness/conscience. As the sole voice raised against the self-centred peers, Gwynplaine re-enacts the scene in *Paradise Lost* where the angel Abdiel alone stands against the archangel Lucifer–Satan in his bid to overthrow God.[147] Withdrawing

[145] The evolution from the material to the spiritual in *Chaos vaincu* reflects the angel Raphael's explanation to Adam that, in God's universe, 'body up to spirit work[s]' (v. 478). See Loewenstein, *Milton's* Paradise Lost, 96, 98, 103.

[146] Milton critics consider the 'Pontifical', 'high arched... bridge | Of length prodigious' (x. 313, 301–2) forged over Chaos by Sin and Death for easy passage from Hell to earth to refer, for the republican poet, to Satan's 'imperial kingship' and 'the Renaissance revival of triumphal architecture and pageantry' by the Caroline court (Stevie Davies, *Images of Kingship in* Paradise Lost*: Milton's Politics and Christian Liberty* (Columbia: University of Missouri Press, 1983), 95, 111); cf. Knoppers, *Historicizing Milton*, 98–9, 105–9. Hugo would have drawn a similar analogy between this construct, the Satanic 'false emperor' (Davies, *Images of Kingship*, 98) otherwise known as Napoléon III, and the architecture of the Second Empire.

[147] Loewenstein's argument that the character of Abdiel 'captures the spirit of seventeenth-century resistance writing and its radical Protestant roots, while he stimulates debate in Heaven about the nature of its politics and laws' (*Representing Revolution*, 226; see also 237), evokes Hugo as well in his roles both as a leftist representative in a conservative National Assembly under the Second Republic and as a republican outlaw resisting in multiple genres the illegitimate reign of Louis-Napoléon. Just as Milton discovered that the leaders of the seventeenth-century revolution against the British monarchy 'prefer[red] their own ambitions to the country's interest' (Achinstein, *Milton and the Revolutionary Reader*, 205; see also 269), the President of the Second Republic betrayed Hugo's trust and the nation's laws with his *coup d'état*. The novelist invests Gwynplaine, then, with his own lived experience while modelling the protagonist on Abdiel, who 'joins... the Old Testament succession of single just men, defenders of God against a corrupt multitude' (Marshall Grossman, *'Authors to Themselves': Milton and the Revelation of History* (Cambridge: Cambridge University Press, 1987), 97). See also Stanley Eugene Fish, *Surprised by Sin: The Reader in* Paradise Lost (London: Macmillan, 1967) 182–4.

to the 'Mountain of the Congregation' (V. 766) where his palace is located, the wily fiend turns his legions against the Father and his newly anointed Son by embracing a policy 'similar to that adopted by Parliament in the early stages of the civil war'.[148] Thus does Milton sketch the origins of the Parliament of Hell—a literary trope of the period 'that carried specific political meanings'[149]—so vividly depicted in book II. Only the seraph Abdiel attempts to dissuade Satan and his minions by disputing him point by point. Like Gwyplaine's impassioned plea for social justice before the other lords, Abdiel's 'zeal | None seconded, as out of season judged, | Or singular and rash' (V. 849–51). Both characters are plainly the odd ones out in their opposition to the powers that be. The reader can also detect the arrogance of Hugo's aristocrats when the 'haughty' (V. 852) Satan famously contends,

> We know no time when we were not as now;
> Know none before us, self-begot, self-raised
> By our own quick'ning power... (V. 859–61)

Why should either dark angels or self-satisfied nobles yield ground to anyone or accept a change in status, when they think they are their own authors and guides?

Gwynplaine, of course, argues that all, including the rich, are subject to forces larger than themselves, that no one is immune to a reversal of fortune. Abdiel, too, fearlessly responds to Satan, 'I see thy fall | Determined,' since God's wrath will bring 'His thunder on thy head, devouring fire' (V. 878–9, 893). In so doing, Abdiel 'give[s] Satan and the rebel angels a crucial opportunity to reform their dangerous political course'.[150] In *L'Homme qui rit*, Gwynplaine's courageous prediction of social turmoil transforms Milton's divine judgement from above into exploding rage from the impoverished classes below. And, as with Abdiel, Gwynplaine's lonely crusade in Hugo's version of the Parliament of Hell encounters an abundance of 'hostile scorn' (V. 903) when the lords cruelly mock both message and messenger. If, then, as Fallon asserts regarding *Paradise Lost*, 'the most comprehensive description of human government in the poem is the regime of Hell itself',[151] Hugo's infernal House of Lords indicts the failure not only of English institutions in Milton's century and the next but also of government in mid-nineteenth-century France.

[148] Fallon, *Divided Empire*, 123.
[149] Achinstein, *Milton and the Revolutionary Reader*, 198; see also 179–81.
[150] Loewenstein, *Representing Revolution*, 228.
[151] Fallon, *Divided Empire*, 110; see also 71.

Gwynplaine's speech in the House of Lords highlights a final feature common to *Paradise Lost* and *L'Homme qui rit*—namely, the visionary evocation of future history. Hugo's deformed hero predicts the cataclysms to come that will restore social justice in England—and beyond. Among the aspects of humanity's future that the angel Michael reveals to Adam and Eve before they are expelled from the Garden of Eden, one finds similarly apocalyptic images, particularly those of the Flood and of the destruction of Nimrod's Tower of Babel. The latter episode portrays Nimrod, 'Of proud ambitious heart', as a Satanic figure who hunts 'With war and hostile snare such as refuse | Subjection to his empire tyrannous' (xii. 25, 31–2), and thus as another exemplar for Hugo's elaboration of Barkilphedro-Napoléon III. The 'evil age of Nimrod-Satan'[152] corresponds, in Hugo's system, to the English Restoration–French Second Empire. In *Paradise Lost*, Nimrod's hubris in aiming to build 'A city and tow'r, whose top may reach to Heav'n' invites God's 'derision' and punishment in the form of linguistic confusion, so that the building is 'left | Ridiculous, and the work Confusion named' (xii. 44, 50, 61–2). Although Barkilphedro survives untouched in *L'Homme qui rit*, we have seen that Gwynplaine's prophesy regarding society's underdogs is aimed, not at his villainous counterpart, but at an entire social structure in danger of being toppled.[153]

The model for the radical reversal envisioned by Gwynplaine can be discerned in Milton's account of Noah and the destruction of humankind in the Deluge.[154] Unlike the original description of Noah's antediluvian existence in Genesis 6, the 'reverend sire' in *Paradise Lost* assumes the role of a prophet, attempting to turn his revelling compatriots from their riotous ways:

> he oft
> Frequented their assemblies, whereso met,
> . . . and to them preached
> Conversion and repentance . . . (xi. 720–4)

[152] David Loewenstein, *Milton and the Drama of History* (Cambridge: Cambridge University Press, 1990), 109; see also 110 and Marshall Grossman, *'Authors to Themselves'*, 168–71.

[153] Hugo may well have seen in Napoléon III a Nimrod figure, given the emperor's ambitious building projects in the French capital. It is clear, for example, from the critique in *Les Misérables* of the Haussmanisation of Paris (see *FT* 97–8, 203–4) that the writer was bitterly opposed to the sweeping urban reconstruction agenda of the Second Empire. See Jean Gaudon's discussion of Nimrod's role in *FS* as the 'anti-*Plein ciel*' (*Le Temps de la contemplation*, 287; see also 311).

[154] Marshall Grossman points out that Raphael's earlier account to Adam of the war in Heaven introduces 'mobility, upward and downward, into the spatial architecture of providence' (*'Authors to Themselves'*, 93), an essential feature of *HQR* as well.

In other words, Noah provides the mould for Gwynplaine, not just because of his preaching but also because his words fall on deaf ears. Each is a 'righteous man or saint [depicted] as a stranger within his own land', a political exile like Hugo and Milton themselves.[155] The resonances of this episode in *Paradise Lost* with the scene in the House of Lords in *L'Homme qui rit* are perpetuated by the mode of punishment to be visited on the unrepentant. Michael reveals to Adam that, the ark aside, all the habitations

> Flood overwhelmed, and them with all their pomp
> Deep under water rolled; sea covered sea,
> Sea without shore; and in their palaces
> Where luxury late reigned, sea-monsters whelped
> And stabled... (XI. 748–52)

Such portentous, apocalyptic imagery with all of its vatic overtones sounds very much like the Hugo of 'Plein mer', *Les Travailleurs de la mer*, and *L'Homme qui rit*. From the horrific fate of *Leviathan*, to that of Clubin, to that of the *Matutina*, respectively, the triumph of the wicked quickly reverses into a trip to the bottom of the sea. Similarly, in Gwynplaine's entreaty to the other peers, the haves end up in the deep, their solid existence ending 'en submersion' (xiv. 354); the 'naufrage' of the poor entails their own 'engloutissement' (xiv. 351)—perhaps even as a tasty morsel in some 'sea-monster's' belly. Once again, Hugo's text recalls Milton's, providing an updated version of the 'one just man' pitted against the multitudes.

Gwynplaine tries, like the prophets in *Paradise Lost*, to 'renovate human history',[156] a role assumed by the visionary Milton and Hugo as well. Though both poets have fallen on 'evil days' (VII. 25–6) that have exiled them from the political scene and frustrated 'the progressive historical process',[157] both hope for a positive reversal of history from current decline to new sociopolitical advances. The 'promised new paradise in England'[158] after the Revolution and in France under the Second Republic may have been lost only temporarily. Not until *Quatrevingt-Treize*, however, does Hugo abandon the Miltonian shifts in fortune echoed in

[155] Loewenstein, *Milton and the Drama of History*, 104; see also 106. According to Loewenstein, the Flood 'demolish[es] a dissolute culture which, at least from Milton's historical "prospect", looks much like the world of Laudian and Restoration England'—a perspective assumed by Hugo in the 'demolition of triumphs, festivals, pomp, and palaces' (*Milton and the Drama of History*, 107) in his fictive world and the Second Empire alike.

[156] Loewenstein, *Milton and the Drama of History*, 103.

[157] Loewenstein, *Milton and the Drama of History*, 97; see also 104.

[158] Loewenstein, *Milton's* Paradise Lost, 18.

L'Homme qui rit—those of 'the bleak, cyclical patterns of tragic history' that 'vacillate between periods of progress and decline'—to imagine a different, more redemptive configuration for history's uneven itinerary.[159]

In *Paradise Lost*, Adam learns that 'he must be able to envision alternative futures as the putative consequences of alternative choices'.[160] Milton's poem encourages the reader to do so as well, to understand that what happens in the here and now will affect subsequent events and to imagine a more just form of government than the current royalist regime. In *L'Homme qui rit*, Hugo returns to Milton's age in a similar attempt to persuade his readers to reject autocracy—whether that of monarchy or empire—by giving 'historic particulars mythic resonance'.[161] Adam sees future history unfold, with all its ups and downs, in the larger context of the cosmic struggle between good and evil. Hugo's readers travel to another country in another century, where the confrontation between material and spiritual impulses provides new insights into their own age. In each case, the text unveils ugly realities behind shiny surfaces, including the hypocrisy and self-serving rhetoric of those in power and their sycophants. From this perspective, both *Paradise Lost* and *L'Homme qui rit* foster their readers' ability to discern their own place in history, to distinguish truth from falsehood in the present, and to dream of a better future.[162] The overlapping temporal frames—the mark of visionary narratives—work in opposite directions towards similar ends. As Christopher Hill concludes about Milton's outlook: 'The Golden Age lies not in the past, but in the future of men and women who understand their destiny. *Paradise Lost* is a poem about the education of humanity'.[163] So is *L'Homme qui rit*.

Despite the political setbacks for the French nation, Hugo's text provides a template for future progress to his own 'fit reader',[164] transcending the 'anxiety of influence' by offering a modern, *French* response to his predecessor's epic work. Hugo's prodigiously fertile poetic imagination

[159] Loewenstein, *Milton and the Drama of History*, 94, 113; see also 114–16. Gwynplaine's meandering in the desert during the blizzard thus repeats Milton's view of history as 'decline, repetition, and labyrinthine wandering' (Loewenstein, *Milton and the Drama of History*, 123).

[160] Marshall Grossman, *'Authors to Themselves'*, 93.

[161] Loewenstein, *Representing Revolution*, 240; see also 225, 231.

[162] See esp. Achinstein, who argues that 'Milton summons readers to become more keenly aware of their susceptibility to political deception. Milton aimed to promote readerly skills as a means for English citizens to regain the individual freedoms that had slipped through the revolutionary leaders' fingers' (*Milton and the Revolutionary Reader*, 202; see also 222–3 and Loewenstein, *Milton and the Drama of History*, 108).

[163] Hill, *Milton and the English Revolution*, 393.

[164] The term refers to the prayer of Milton's narrator that he will 'fit audience find, though few' (vii. 30), and is used throughout Milton scholarship.

defends him from being 'absorb[ed] . . . into his precursor',[165] instead subsuming Milton's work and incorporating its power into his own reading of history—just as Gilliatt–Hugo introjects the force of the tempest/*The Tempest* in *Les Travailleurs de la mer*. Like *Paradise Lost*, *L'Homme qui rit* seeks 'to create an order of historical meaning'[166] amid the chaos of lived experience—a concern that, we shall see, pervades *Quatrevingt-Treize* as well. By grasping in *L'Homme qui rit* Hugo's pedagogical impulse as recuperated from Milton, the reader sees in the nineteenth-century revolutionary writer a person who is surprisingly receptive to lessons from the past and who seeks to pass them on as a precious heritage to the modern world. This pedagogical impulse is also evident in *Quatrevingt-Treize*, where the fate of France's youngest citizens hangs in the balance.

[165] Weiskel, *The Romantic Sublime*, 203.
[166] David Quint, *Epic and Empire: Politics and Generic Form from Virgil to Milton* (Princeton, NJ: Princeton University Press, 1993), 44.

4

Romanticism and Utopia: *Quatrevingt-Treize* and Endless Revolution

While the 'Reliquat' of *Quatrevingt-Treize* dates back to the early 1840s, it contains reflections on the Convention nationale (1792–5) and its heroes rather than a detailed project for the novel. The book's storyline—and its place in Hugo's projected trilogy on '*l'Aristocratie*[,] *la Monarchie*[,] [et] *Quatrevingt-treize*' (xiv. 27)—remained undeveloped until 1862, following the publication of *Les Misérables.* Hugo first mentions his forthcoming novel by name that year in a letter to Paul Meurice (dated 18 October 1862; xii. 1198), and begins researching in earnest its historical background. Indeed, since the second volume of the three-part series was never written, *Quatrevingt-Treize* assumes even greater importance as the sequel and end point of the world vision presented in its predecessor.[1] Having covered the first (and to considerable extent the second) subject in *L'Homme qui rit*, Hugo followed through with a meditation on the third, despite the fall of his arch-enemy Napoléon III in the interim. The novel's focus on the French Revolution and Terror clearly targets more than the eradication of the Second Empire.

Officially announced in 1867, the book has as its immediate catalysts the capture of Napoléon III by the Prussians at the Battle of Sedan, the instauration of the Third Republic, and Hugo's glorious return to France in 1870—followed in 1871 by an aborted term as a legislator, the death of his older son Charles (1826–71), and the bloody insurrection of the Paris Commune. Dubbed 'l'Année terrible' in an eponymous collection of

[1] From the power of the lords to the divine right of kings to the Revolution and its aftermath, Hugo's projected triptych would highlight the evolution of authority up to the nineteenth century. The suppression of the second volume on monarchy, however, suggests that its real target was that contemporary form of absolutism, the Second Empire. In the wake of 1870, the book was no longer needed. But after the Commune, the third volume was. According to Guy Rosa, 'abandonnant sa trilogie, Hugo se mettait en mesure d'avoir sur la Terreur et la Commune un regard prospectif et non plus rétrospectif. Il pouvait les confronter non au passé, mais à l'avenir' ('Présentation', to Victor Hugo, *Quatrevingt-Treize*, in *Œuvres complètes*, 18 vols (Paris: Le Club Français du Livre, 1967–70), xv. 232). Cf. Roman, *Victor Hugo et le roman philosophique*, 434–5.

poetry (1872), the year 1871 tested Hugo's profoundest beliefs in human progress. The trials continued into 1872 as well. In February, his daughter Adèle returned from a decade-long descent into madness in the Americas and was committed to a mental care facility a month after his own defeat in the national legislative elections.[2] *Quatrevingt-Treize* thus emerges from the ashes of its author's most intimate personal and political dreams. Hugo's return to Guernsey in August 1872 to write it signals a rejection of the motherland, still unable to complete delivery of the Revolution of 1789, still fraught with the violence of revolt and oppression of 1793.[3] At the same time, the novelist's 'wind', so vital to the elaborate rhythms and matrices of both *Les Travailleurs de la mer* and *L'Homme qui rit*, appears somewhat diminished in his new work. *Les Travailleurs de la mer* runs to about 240 pages in the *Œuvres complètes,* and *L'Homme qui rit*, 355 pages; *Quatrevingt-Treize* takes up only 220 pages or so. Is Hugo's inspiration, perhaps, beginning to go dry? Judging by the novel's highly favourable popular reception at the time, one would think not. The steady stream of scholarly studies since the 1980s devoted to the novel suggests that, even today, it merits serious attention. The appearance of *Quatrevingt-Treize* in 2002 on the reading list for the *agrégation* (state advanced-level teachers' qualifying examination) in French literature further underscores its relevance to a new generation of readers.

As we have seen, Hugo was inspired early in his career by both Chateaubriand and Sir Walter Scott to transport his reader to other times and other places. In *Bug-Jargal*, he followed Chateaubriand to the French colonies, in this case the Greater Antilles in 1791, then produced several historical novels in the mode of Scott, setting *Han d'Islande* in seventeenth-century Norway and *Notre-Dame de Paris* in late-medieval Paris. Thus, whereas the

[2] His only surviving child, François-Victor, was also ill during this period with tuberculosis, dying suddenly in Dec. 1873, six months after Hugo had completed his novel and only two months before its publication in Feb. 1874. Cf. Michel Granet, 'L'Idéologie de la révolution chez V. Hugo à travers sa trilogie incomplète, *L'Homme qui rit/La Monarchie/Quatre-Vingt-Treize*', in Anne-Marie Amiot (ed.), *Idéologies hugoliennes*, Actes du Colloque Interdisciplinaire, 23–25 May 1985 (Nice: Serre, 1985), 27.

[3] Cf. Rosa's explanation of the writer's new retreat to Guernsey: 'Pourvoyeur à l'histoire du sens que ses actes n'y auraient pas eu, Hugo participe à la Commune en écrivant *Quatrevingt-Treize* dans l'exil retrouvé' ('"Quatrevingt-treize" ou la critique du roman historique', *Revue d'Histoire Littéraire de la France*, 75 (1975), 343). Priscilla Parkhurst Ferguson likewise considers the link for Hugo between the Terror of 1793 and 'l'Année terrible' of 1871, remarking that 'the novelist's political problem was to refurbish the ideal of the Revolution by incorporating 1793 in an interpretation that would transcend the ideological divisions of the present' ('*Quatrevingt-treize*: Turning the Terror to Account', in Robert T. Denomme and Roland H. Simon (eds), *Unfinished Revolutions: Legacies of Upheaval in Modern French Culture* (University Park: Pennsylvania State University Press, 1998), 71).

temporal frames of the three historical novels shift ever more backwards in time, the geographical backdrop moves progressively closer to home. Is a similar inverse relation to be found among the four last historical narratives? Though most of *Les Misérables* centres on nineteenth-century Paris, critics have demonstrated its extensive eighteenth-century prehistory.[4] Moreover, Hugo stages a number of crucial scenes, notably Jean Valjean's encounter with Bishop Myriel and his rebirth many years later as Monsieur Madeleine, in the provincial towns of Digne in the south and Montreuil-sur-mer in the north of France, respectively. Most of the novel's exoticism resides therefore in its moderate displacement from the here and now of urban/Parisian France in the 1860s.

The last three novels likewise envision some form of *ailleurs*, given the exotic background of the 1820s Channel Islands for *Les Travailleurs de la mer*, of late-seventeenth- and early-eighteenth-century England for *L'Homme qui rit*, and of late-eighteenth-century Brittany for the opening and closing books of *Quatrevingt-Treize*, with the middle book taking place in Paris. In other words, the overall spatial trajectory of all four texts moves first from the provinces towards the Parisian centre (*MIS*), then to the Channel Islands (*TM*) and beyond, from the southern British coast to London (*HQR*), and back towards Paris via the north-western provinces, before returning to Brittany/Vendée (*QVT*). In contrast with the earlier series of narratives, however, the apogee of the temporal trajectory is congruent with its spatial counterpart in *L'Homme qui rit*, which marks the farthest point in space and time alike in the later narratives. The other three works occupy for the most part the relatively restricted terrain between the 1790s and the 1830s. From a wider standpoint, it is startling to encounter in the end point represented by *Quatrevingt-Treize* a return to the revolutionary period depicted in Hugo's first narrative, *Bug-Jargal*. What sense one might make of such intricate choreographies within and between the novels remains, of course, to be seen.

At the very least, the emphasis on France's revolutionary past ties *Quatrevingt-Treize* to *Les Misérables*, where a large part of the storyline is devoted to Marius' republican friends in *les Amis de l'ABC* and to their subsequent martyrdom on the 1832 Parisian barricades in a failed revolution. One need not look very far to find parallels between the visionary leader Enjolras in the earlier novel and the idealist hero of *Quatrevingt-Treize*, Gauvain—who also contains elements of the merciful and self-sacrificing Jean Valjean. The continued elaboration of the personality traits associated with these characters will enrich our study of Hugo's

[4] See esp. Yves Gohin, 'Une histoire qui date', in Anne Ubersfeld and Guy Rosa (eds), *Lire* Les Misérables (Paris: José Corti, 1985), 31.

last novel. At the same time, the revolutionary referents in *Quatrevingt-Treize* can be considered not only to 'preface' the many reflections on revolution in *Les Misérables* but also to 'realize' the prophetic warnings that Gwynplaine issues in *L'Homme qui rit* during post-Restoration England. In examining *Quatrevingt-Treize*, we will determine whether Hugo shifts positions regarding the role of revolution in effecting historical progress after the 1871 Commune. Finally, the intense use of metaphorical language in *Les Travailleurs de la mer* to figure Gilliatt's sublime feats in the face of raging seas and skies has its counterpart in the abundant nature imagery in *Quatrevingt-Treize*, a feature of *Les Misérables* as well—but one that is largely missing from *L'Homme qui rit*. *Quatrevingt-Treize* therefore shares important features with the previous three novels, as if it were entering, perpetuating, and perhaps redirecting an ongoing conversation.

Although the historical dimensions of these narratives have been amply discussed in the critical literature, our analysis of the intertwining of metaphor and mimēsis in *Les Travailleurs de la mer* and *L'Homme qui rit* has filled a scholarly gap—and uncovered an additional angle of approach to *Quatrevingt-Treize*: the role in Hugo of the French provinces and fringes per se. Considered most broadly, the margins of France stretch in Hugo's fiction as far as Saint-Domingue, but his interest in the later novels resides geographically closer, in the locales that lie between the centre—that is, Paris—and the *other* Other, Great Britain. While Priscilla Parkhurst Ferguson finds that 'the opposition Paris–France generates the entire novel',[5] I argue that these two poles represent but half the configuration of geographical and political tensions in the text. Our study up to now has demonstrated that England serves as an important subtext to *Les Travailleurs de la mer* and *L'Homme qui rit*, not only as both the twin and contrary of France, but also through the artistic models offered by Shakespeare, on the one hand, and Milton, on the other. The same is true of *Quatrevingt-Treize*. For example, as with the lengthy preface to *Les Travailleurs de la mer* on the Channel Archipelago and the extended discussions of English culture, politics, and mores in *L'Homme qui rit*, the discourse in *Quatrevingt-Treize* pertaining to Brittany points in multiple directions. Viewed microscopically, the region presents a formidable natural, cultural, and political barrier to outside forces. Viewed telescopically, however, it links warring forces in a joint venture that transcends immediate events. In this way, the tension between the urban hub and the exotic periphery in Hugo's last novel not only replays that between England and France. It also gestures past the real, the historical, and the

[5] Ferguson, '*Quatrevingt-Treize*', 72.

natural towards the timeless and the ideal. Once again, historical refiguration and metaphorical redescription are intimately connected—a relationship in *Quatrevingt-Treize* that we shall explore through the novel's utopian and dystopian discourse.

By the same token, the looming presence of Great Britain beyond the basic storyline of *Quatrevingt-Treize* suggests the possibility of an English literary parallel, in the mould of Shakespeare and Milton for the two previous narratives, with Hugo's new historical novel. This time, the literary parallel is Charles Dickens, who had published *A Tale of Two Cities* (1859) in French as *Paris et Londres en 1793* (1861) only a year before Hugo announced his forthcoming trilogy. Though the personal relations between Dickens and Hugo, based on their encounter in January 1847, were fleeting, their literary dialogue extended over several decades. As his biographer John Forster reports, Dickens called upon his eminent French contemporary at his home in the Place Royale, and their meeting was, for Dickens, most satisfactory. Hugo received him

> with infinite courtesy and grace . . . and talked of his childhood in Spain, and of his father having been Governor of the Tagus in Napoléon's wars; spoke warmly of the English people and their literature; and [discussed contemporary music and theatre]. To Dickens he addressed very charming flattery, in the best of taste; and my friend long remembered the enjoyment of that evening.[6]

To all appearances, it was the auspicious beginning of a long friendship between two of the foremost novelists of their day. Ten years Hugo's junior, Dickens had been deeply influenced by *Le Dernier Jour d'un condamné* and *Notre-Dame de Paris*.[7] The francophilia of this 'Français naturalisé, et Citoyen de Paris'[8] answered Hugo's *literary* appreciation in the 1820s and 1830s of Scott, Byron, Milton, and Shakespeare and, perhaps, of Dickens's own popular renown in the following decade. Their personal relationship nevertheless did not last. The evidence indicates that they never saw each other again or corresponded. The Revolution of 1848 and the political changes leading up to the *coup d'état* of 1851 kept Dickens out of France. When he returned to his adopted country in 1853—and for many years thereafter, till his death in 1870—Hugo was no longer there.[9]

[6] John Forster, *The Life of Charles Dickens*, ed. A. J. Hoppé, i (London: Dent, 1966), 451–2.

[7] See Richard Maxwell, 'City Life and the Novel: Hugo, Ainsworth, Dickens', *Comparative Literature*, 30 (Spring 1978), 157, 169–70, and Kenneth Ward Hooker, *The Fortunes of Victor Hugo in England* (New York: Columbia University Press, 1938, 93).

[8] Quoted in Forster, *The Life of Charles Dickens*, 450.

[9] See Floris Delattre, *Dickens et la France* (Paris: Gamber, 1927), 5, 26.

And yet, the affinities explored in their one encounter do not evaporate during the many years of Hugo's exile, with the case of *A Tale of Two Cities* and *Quatrevingt-Treize* being particularly intriguing. It is impossible to know whether *A Tale of Two Cities* reached Hugo before 1862 either in Mme Loreau's translation or through the mediation of François-Victor, who had been assisting his father since 1855 in understanding the English masters. Still, the testimony of the date '1793' in Dickens's translated title is most suggestive, and the international dimension stressed in both versions of the book's name may likewise re-emerge in the genesis of *Quatrevingt-Treize*.

More readily demonstrable, and thus more significant for a discussion of the two works, are their formal and thematic conjunctions: both are historical novels in the best tradition of the authors' common ancestor, Sir Walter Scott;[10] both deal with the French Terror via the epic struggles of nation and generation; both abound in characters with either doubles or split identities; both satirize not only revolutionary excess but also the shortcomings of their own era; both end on the scaffold with a utopian vision of the future. Moreover, these extensive *correspondances* intersect, from one standpoint, in the portrayal by both Hugo and Dickens of the competitive/cooperative relations between England and France—a *topos* previously explored in our discussion of *L'Homme qui rit*. Despite these striking similarities, 'dont les choix formels et l'arrière-plan appellent la comparaison', according to Dominique Peyrache-Leborgne,[11] the two works are rarely discussed in tandem in the critical literature—a lacuna begging to be filled. To do so is to provide insights into Hugo's rivalry with his famous contemporary as he sought to assure his literary legacy.

[10] Hugo, of course, took up the challenge of Scott in France from the outset of his career. In 1838, Dickens's novels were first translated into French and, according to M. G. Devonshire: 'As early as 1849, after the appearance of *David Copperfield*, the French had decided that Dickens was Scott's successor [in England]' (*The English Novel in France, 1830–1870* (London: University of London Press, 1929), 327). The echoes between Dickens's description of *A Tale of Two Cities* in a letter to Forster, dated 25 Aug. 1859, and Hugo's 1822 account of *HI* are striking. The latter, we will recall, is conceived as 'un long drame . . . dans lesquels les descriptions suppléaient aux décorations et aux costumes. Du reste tous les personnages se peignaient par eux-mêmes' (ii. 1168). Dickens later outlines his own enterprise in much the same terms: 'I set myself the task of making a *picturesque* story . . . with characters true to nature, but whom the story should express, more than they should express themselves, by dialogue' (quoted in Delattre, *Dickens et la France*, 176; cf. 37–8). See also Shaw, *The Forms of Historical Fiction*, for a comparison of Hugo and Dickens (esp. p. 110) and of each with Scott; and Andrew Sanders, 'Dickens's French Historical Novel', in Sylvère Monod (ed.), *Charles Dickens et la France: Colloque International de Boulogne-sur-Mer, 3 juin 1978* (Lille: Presses Universitaires de Lille, 1979), 63, 65–6.

[11] Dominique Peyrache-Leborgne, 'Roman historique et roman-idylle chez Dickens et Hugo: *A Tale of Two Cities* et *Quatrevingt-treize*', *Dalhousie French Studies*, 36 (1996), 51.

The novel's affiliation with *A Tale of Two Cities* becomes clearer after we unravel the web that links Paris, Brittany, and Great Britain not only with each other but also with Hugo's much wider meditation on the forces of disjunction and the political ideal. To this end, I begin by showing how the geographic tensions operate in *Quatrevingt-Treize*, looking at the repetition of several key ideas from the earlier essay on the Channel Archipelago, as well as at the double identity of Brittany as both a barrier and a nexus. I then analyse the corresponding dramatic tensions between Hugo's warrior protagonists—the royalist Marquis de Lantenac, his republican grandnephew Gauvain, and the former priest Cimourdain, who raised Gauvain as the family tutor—before turning to the discourse of the ideal that emanates from all these oppositions and connections. Finally, I explore the kinship of *Quatrevingt-Treize* and *A Tale of Two Cities*, and so of Hugo and Dickens, by examining the series of echoing structures in both novels.

FORCES OF UNION AND DISUNION IN 1793

Almost from the outset of *Quatrevingt-Treize*, the reader is struck by a number of allusions to its companion texts, *Les Travailleurs de la mer* and *L'Homme qui rit.* The first chapter of the second book, for instance, begins by referring to 'ce qui se passait dans l'Archipel de la Manche' in spring 1793, 'au moment où la France [est] attaquée à la fois à toutes ses frontières' (xv. 295). Transported to the far side of the Channel from the locus of Gilliatt's and Gwynplaine's adventures, the reader anticipates other possible nods to the earlier texts—and soon finds them. Not only does this book on 'La Corvette *Claymore*' (I. 2) in the English fleet display the same extensive knowledge of seafaring vocabulary that one finds in *Les Travailleurs de la mer.* The ship also wends its way through the same landmarks between Jersey and Guernsey, notably 'les Hanois et les Douvres' (xv. 297), as Gilliatt's little boat on its rescue mission. When the war vessel finds itself threatened with a 'naufrage' (xv. 305), because it is taking on water and dodging a number of dangerous reefs in the dark after the cannon episode, the reader makes a further connection with the terrifying shipwreck scene at the beginning of *L'Homme qui rit.* In like manner, the pressure of English politics on French events recalls the scathing indictment of the British aristocracy in the same novel. Finally, just as Hugo's preface to *Les Travailleurs de la mer* on 'L'Archipel de la Manche' introduces the reader to the exotic flora, fauna, and culture of the Channel Islands, the first part of *Quatrevingt-Treize* transports the reader to a strange world closer to home. The novel thus joins the 'Archipelago' in blending Barthes's two kinds of realism, so that 'la queue fantasmatique de la "réalité"' is conjoined with 'l'intelligible du "réel"'.[12] As we observed in our study of *Les Travailleurs de la mer*, Hugo uses the alien universe of his 'Archipelago' to guide the reader towards a new perception of France itself. The metaphorical statements that portray the islands in idyllic, utopian terms serve the ends of mimetic reconstruction through comparison with the absent homeland.[13] We shall see that the exotic assumes similar dimensions in *Quatrevingt-Treize* in the portrayal of Brittany, the wild land a few miles away in France. The geographical tensions in the text are repeated in the forces of disunion within and between opposing camps, while the equivocal status of Brittany as both French and Other points to the reconciliation of opposites at multiple levels of the narrative.

Paris, Bretagne, la Grande-Bretagne: Hugolian Exotica

Brittany's double identity is signalled from the outset, when Part I of the novel, 'En Mer', begins not at sea but on land: 'Dans les dernier jours de mai 1793, un des bataillons parisiens amenés en Bretagne par Santerre fouillait le redoutable bois de la Saudraie en Astillé' (xv. 287). Situated between the English Channel, which protects it from foreign invasion, and the French political centre in Paris, the royalist province is menaced as the story opens by the intrusion of the Revolutionary Army. While part of the *patrie*, it is a *pays* unto itself, as Michelle Fléchard, the nursing mother discovered in the bushes by the soldiers and whose first language is not French (xv. 290), explains. 'Vous êtes de France, moi je suis de Bretagne,' she tells her interrogator, Sergeant Radoub. 'Ce n'est pas le même pays' (xv. 290). Little wonder that another soldier dubs the natives 'des iroquois de la Chine' (xv. 292)—they might as well be in a far-off country.

Indeed, the exotic qualities of Brittany reside in both its terrain and its inhabitants. The region's unfriendly geographic features—thick forests and brushwood (xv. 288), quicksand along the shore (xv. 318), and a labyrinthine topography 'où les armées républicaines se perdaient' (xv. 331)—render it virtually impenetrable to outsiders. Furthermore, its strange human culture, where the natives dress like wild men (xv. 332–3), sleep in hollow tree trunks (xv. 393), hide underground (xv. 319), and speak French, if at all, infused with linguistic oddities (xv. 293, 328), guarantees

[12] Barthes, *Le Plaisir du texte*, 74.

[13] Or, as Laforgue puts it, 'l'archipel de la Manche, terre pour ainsi dire franco-anglaise, constitue un lieu privilégié pour appréhender d'Angleterre la Révolution française' ('La Révolution française', 128).

that the Republican soldiers will feel *dépaysés*.[14] They have unwittingly become travellers in both space and time. The forest is 'the emblem of the feudal past—dark, threatening, local'.[15] The implicit connivance of nature and denizens to drive out the Revolutionary Army early in the storyline becomes explicit in Part III, 'En Vendée', which devotes its first six chapters to this symbiotic relationship. Here Hugo depicts in detail the confrontation between 'la révolution française' and the Breton peasant, 'ce sauvage grave et singulier... vivant de lait et de châtaignes... ayant sur le dos un veste de cuir... tatouant ses habits comme ses ancêtres les Celtes avaient tatoué leur visages, respectant son maître dans son bourreau, parlant une langue morte' (xv. 388). His slave mentality that defends the oppressor against the liberator is as impervious to new ideas as the forest is to strangers. Like denizen, like habitat. The contained resembles the container: 'Rien de plus sourd, de plus muet et de plus sauvage que ces inextricables enchevêtrements d'épines et de branchages; ces vastes broussailles étaient des gîtes d'immobilité et de silence' (xv. 389), we learn, as the description of the forest as a secret city of underground dwellers simultaneously points to the deaf and mute 'hommes enfouis' (xv. 391) in its crypts. Evoking Michelle Fléchard's earlier embrace of the concrete *pays* over the abstract *patrie*, the text indicates that the dispute of 'paysans contre patriotes' is that of 'l'esprit local contre l'esprit central' (xv. 396), of the reactionary Breton margin against the progressive Parisian centre.

But the *otherness* of Brittany derives from more than just its geographic isolation and the primitive habits and ultraconservative mindset of the native population, because the region is not as insulated from the outside as it first appears. While constituting a solid barrier to the spread of Republican ideals from within France, it fails to avert foreign aggression from the sea—much to the dismay of the revolutionaries. In fact, although Brittany is closed off to the interior, the Bretons are on the verge of opening its coastline to their royalist allies. The threat to the new Republic is therefore multiple. According to Hugo's Robespierre: 'Vendéens et Anglais, c'est Bretagne avec Bretagne. Les hurons du Finistère parlent la même langue que les topinambous de Cornouailles... Quand l'insurrection paysanne sera complète, la descente anglaise se fera' (xv. 353–4). The ancient, fraternal alliance of Brittany and Great Britain, based on shared

[14] The odd language in Bretagne contains some foreign elements. For instance, the peasants at one point cry 'Hurrah!', and the narrator adds that 'ces cris anglais sont fort usités sur la côte bretonne-normande, en commerce perpétuel avec les îles de la Manche' (xv. 333). In the references to both the English expression and the Channel Islands, one can detect elements of *HQR* and *TM*, respectively, seeping into *QVT*.

[15] David Denby, 'Civil War, Revolution and Justice in Victor Hugo's *Quatrevingt-treize*', *Romance Studies*, 30 (1997), 10.

linguistic and cultural origins, threatens not just the integrity but also the survival of the young Republic. England is the nation to which nobles like the Marquis de Lantenac have fled and from which they will undoubtedly return with an army of foreign invaders—to be joined by their loyal Breton subjects: 'Lantenac n'avait qu'une pensée: s'emparer d'un point du littoral, et le livrer à Pitt' (xv. 405; see also 397, 401, 410, 426, 468, 470), accompanied by a trained army of 20,000 Englishmen.[16]

The marquis's connection to England is so disturbing that his great-nephew Gauvain, who commands the revolutionary troops sent to quash the Breton rebellion, no longer considers him to be French. The young captain condemns him outright: 'Lantenac est un étranger... Lantenac appelle les Anglais. Lantenac c'est l'invasion. Lantenac est l'ennemi de la patrie' (xv. 418). Instead of appearing to Gauvain as a worthy ancestor, Lantenac is a mortal enemy, both personal and political. Thus, 'le duel entre lui et moi ne peut finir que par sa mort, ou par la mienne' (xv. 418), Gauvain declares, just as France and Britain are lined up for a bloody confrontation. To face this familial foe in a 'guerre à la mort' (xv. 400) is, for Gauvain, to wage civil war in miniature in order to prevent the greater evils engendered by the gruesome consequences of an English incursion: 'Lantenac ne se reposerait pas tant qu'il n'aurait point réalisé ce plan exécrable, poser, comme un couvercle de tombe, la monarchie sur la république et l'Angleterre sur la France... la vie de Lantenac... c'était le débarquement des Anglais, le recul de la révolution, les villes saccagées, le peuple déchirée' (xv. 487). Lantenac's very existence represents, for Gauvain, a deadly peril not only for the republican form of government but for national sovereignty itself. The dangers inherent in 'Angleterre et France mêlées' (I. 2. l), the title of an early chapter, are to be avoided at all costs. Danton's extended argument with Robespierre in Part II, 'A Paris', concludes with much the same point: 'le danger est un cercle et nous sommes dedans. A l'extérieur la coalition, à l'intérieur la trahison' (xv. 354). The novel itself can be read as an elaboration on this double danger, with England standing throughout as the ominous power propelling from the wings the counter-revolutionary forces of *la Vendée* occupying centre stage.

In a vivid illustration of Hugo's dramatic imagination, the text sets up a series of spatial oppositions that feed into the overall storyline about civil discord. The trinity of Marat, Danton, and Robespierre, located in the

[16] The proliferation of references to William Pitt the Younger underlines the metonymic relation of the British Prime Minister to the English nation and its very real menace to the fledgling French Republic. Cf. Sheila Gaudon, who underscores the distinction for Hugo between the British people and their untrustworthy government—'l'Angleterre hypocrite, perfide, punique' ('Anglophobie?', 58)—represented by Pitt.

French capital, occupies one pole of tension and power; that of Cimourdain, Gauvain, and Lantenac, who struggle ideologically and militarily in far-off Brittany, occupies the other. By the same token, the dichotomy between government and region, Paris and Brittany, and, by extension, France and England carries a temporal dimension as well. In conflicting with national interests, Breton resistance to change pits the past against the future. The stakes are high. The subject of extended discussions in the novel between Cimourdain and Gauvain, on the one hand, and between Gauvain and Lantenac, on the other, the conception of and adherence to different time frames passionately engage all three protagonists. As in theatrical dialogue, the apparently static exchanges move the action along, again displacing it temporally from a beginning to a dénouement. That both ends of the story take place in the Breton forest creates a circular closure, as if history, too, were perhaps not linear but cyclical in nature. How one can arrive at such a relatively harmonious point from distinctly discordant origins is the focus of the next two subsections.

Struggle and Strife in the New Republic

As we have observed, the antithetical pairings in *Quatrevingt-Treize* of geographical entities is closely related to divergent social and political allegiances—allegiances that have already caused national strife and that now threaten war with England. Domestic conflict is everywhere present in the text, simmering not only in the tensions among its protagonists, but also in the dominant images of death and dismemberment. The patterns of civil war in the characters' moral dilemmas emerge in familial confrontations. Not only must Gauvain oppose the repressive politics of his forebears; he must risk rejection by the one he has chosen as a father-figure. Cimourdain ends by immolating his spiritual son on the altar of the guillotine, with no divine intervention to stay his hand. Gauvain is beset by disorder during his moral crisis at the close of the narrative. The pressures of dissolution on the individual both from within and without seem overwhelming. The common fate of martyrs, regicides, medieval prisoners, and traitors to the Revolution—masks assumed, at one time or another, by Gauvain—is to be torn to pieces, that is, to be devoured by the carnivorous forces of disunity that haunt human history. Much of the novel is therefore shaped around a series of grotesque figures and themes associated with civil war. The singularity of the 'mass atrocities and exterminations of... the Terror in France' (*MHF* 331) yields a wealth of striking scenes and imagery. Monsters lurk where one least expects them. It is all very well for the narrator to maintain in 'A Paris': 'Etre un membre de la Convention, c'était être une vague de l'Océan... La force d'impulsion venait d'en haut' (xv. 379). In 'En Mer' and 'En Vendée', Paris and its principles are less the centre of the universe than the creation of Satan himself.

In an early episode on the *Claymore*, for example, a runaway cannon wreaks havoc on the boat and its occupants. The ship is torn apart by both the mindless forces unleashed within and the relentless pressures from without: 'Un canon qui casse son amarre devient brusquement on ne sait quelle bête surnaturelle. C'est une machine qui se transforme en un monstre... C'est l'entrée en liberté de la matière; on dirait que cet esclave éternel se venge' (xv. 302). The machine's false autonomy is manifest in its erratic 'méandres' (xv. 302) that make stopping it so difficult. The cannoneer attempts to arrest his careening weapon that opens gash upon gash in the flanks of the vessel as, beneath them, 'le flot, aveugle, dirigeait le combat' (xv. 304). Designed to protect the ship in battle, the cannon now creates breaches in the ship's hull and tears apart the crew members who get in its way: 'Les quatre roues passaient et repassaient sur les hommes tués, les coupaient, les dépeçaient et les déchiquetaient' (xv. 303)—not unlike the atrocities of war enacted on land at that very moment. The fissures and divisions opened by the out-of-control machine serve as metaphors for struggle and warfare, tropes also developed in *Les Misérables*.[17] For Suzanne Guerlac as well, 'the conflict between part and whole has larger significance in *Quatrevingt-treize*. It figures the very structure of civil war.'[18] The description of the loose cannon at the beginning of *Quatrevingt-Treize* parallels that of Waterloo in *Les Misérables* as a paradigm for conflict and disjunction. Ravaged internally by civil war and externally threatened by the monarchies of Europe, France may be in no better shape than the hapless *Claymore*—a ship of state equally at sea.[19]

[17] See *FT* 291–2. Cf. Donald Aynesworth regarding the connection between the cannon and Lantenac: 'A prodigy of improvisation, the very motion of the cannon is prototypical of the potential for anarchy inherent in the strategy—the practice of secrecy and surprise—of guerrilla warfare. The place of the "carronade" in the ship is thus precisely analogous to that of the Marquis in the Vendée and of the latter in France itself. Each is the enemy within' ('Anonymity, Identity, and Narrative Sovereignty in *Quatrevingt-Treize*', *Kentucky Romance Quarterly*, 29/2 (1982), 202).

[18] Suzanne Guerlac, 'Exorbitant Geometry in Hugo's *Quatrevingt-treize*', *MLN*, 96 (May 1981), 861.

[19] Cf. Sandy Petrey's remark that 'the shifting support furnished the cannon by the sea is analogous to that given the ship of state by historical change' (*History in the Text:* Quatrevingt-treize *and the French Revolution* (West Fayette, IN: Purdue University Press, 1981), 90). Brombert likewise comments on the 'extended metaphor comparing the Convention to a stormy sea': 'The great actors of the Revolution may think that they shape events; they are in reality acted upon' (*Victor Hugo and the Visionary Novel*, 221)—not unlike the cannon moved by the rolling waves under the *Claymore*. For Hugo's use of the ship metaphor in *TM*, see Ch. 2 above.

And that is only the beginning. Once Lantenac has made his secret landing in Brittany to rouse the locals, only to discover that the Convention has declared him a wanted man, the locus of physical destruction shifts implicitly from the brute maiming force of the cannon to the cleaving gesture of the guillotine. The cannon seems to possess 'une âme de haine et de rage', to be a 'cécité' with eyes, a giant 'sauterelle' or 'tigre' (xv. 305) ready to pounce on its prey; the guillotine rigidly and coldly executes the will of some human beings to dismember others by separating their heads from their bodies. The menace of the mechanical 'monstre de bois' (xv. 505) looms over the entire text, most especially in Parts II and III. In 'Magna testantur voce per umbras' (II. 2. 2; 'He bears witness with a loud voice amid the shadows') and 'Tressaillement des fibres profonds' (II. 2. 3), for example, Marat, Danton, and Robespierre reveal their ruthless approach to assuring the success of the new French Republic. Marat illustrates his belief that 'le danger est partout, et surtout au centre' by predicting that 'Robespierre fera guillotiner Danton' (xv. 357)—a prediction that Hugo's reader knows to have become true. At the same time, Marat rues 'le démembrement' (xv. 357) of the nation in general, torn between various regional and governmental factions and undermined by military treason (by Dumouriez, who fled to Belgium when he was recalled to Paris) and retreat (by Custine, who was subsequently guillotined). What is needed, he claims, is 'l'unité' (xv. 357), but plainly he is not the one to forge harmonious union.[20]

When Cimourdain joins the three revolutionary heads to receive their orders as a delegate of the Comité de salut public, Robespierre specifies that Lantenac is to be declared 'hors la loi' and that 'il faut le guillotiner' (xv. 362), to which the priest readily agrees. Cimourdain is then drawn into a discussion with Marat about what he would do if a revolutionary leader freed a royalist leader. His response, 'Je serais de l'avis de Léchelle, je le ferais fusiller,' echoes the desire of the army's commander-in-chief, but Marat offers another choice, 'Ou le guillotiner' (xv. 364). Again Cimourdain acquiesces, only to learn to his dismay that the young commander in question is his beloved Gauvain. On the face of it, these exchanges between Cimourdain, Robespierre, and Marat appear merely to lay out the legal justifications for executing either Lantenac, as an enemy of the state, or Gauvain, as a traitor to his duty. But the scene also reveals Cimourdain's intransigence in carrying out the letter of the (revolutionary) law, much as Javert inflexibly adheres to the legal status quo in *Les*

[20] Like ancient historians, Hugo '[does] not hesitate to place in the mouths of [his] heroes invented discourses'—a staple of historical fiction. Modern historians, on the other hand, 'no longer permit themselves these fanciful incursions' (*TN* iii. 186).

Misérables.[21] Their relation suggests that the priest may not be able to recognize the superior ethos represented by Gauvain's 'clémence' (xv. 364; see also xv. 413, 417, 430). From this point the promising young warrior's fate is sealed.

Intimations of the inevitable dénouement of the novel recur in 'La Mère' (III. 4)—especially in 'La mort passe' (III. 4. 1) and 'Une méprise' (III. 4. 4)—where Michelle Fléchard's wanderings through forests and villages in an effort to find her children intersect with and eventually parallel the travels of the guillotine destined for the fortified rebel tower of la Tourgue. In one town, she encounters the guillotine by chance, then takes a second route through the woods to reach their common goal. At that point, a brief but significant episode takes place, when a group of Breton royalists hiding in the forest attempts to ambush the party transporting the guillotine for Lantenac's execution. Ending up instead with the ladder meant to rescue the child hostages, which they mistakenly believe is for 'l'escalade de la Tourgue', they declare their prize 'égal' (xv. 451) to the guillotine as a viable military target.[22] The revolutionaries, of course, await both the ladder and the guillotine, but by the time the latter arrives, they must use it to execute Gauvain rather than Lantenac. And, of course, the guillotine integrates 'une échelle' (xv. 505) as part of its construction, creating a hybrid of the two vertical objects. For Radoub, who sits on the military tribunal charged with judging Gauvain and who votes to acquit, it makes no sense 'si l'on guillotine les gens parce qu'ils ont fait de bonnes actions' (xv. 498), in this case either Lantenac or Gauvain. To do so is to descend

[21] Umberto Eco declares that 'we would call [Cimourdain] a police commissioner today' ('Excess and History in Hugo's *Ninety-Three*', in Franco Moretti (ed.), *The Novel: Forms and Themes*, ii (Princeton, NJ: Princeton University Press, 2006), 275). Pierre Campion sees the character as 'un complexe de la raison, du droit et de l'efficacité . . . de la conviction et de la responsabilité, d'une pitié humaine qui tournerait à l'inhumanité' ('Raison de la littérature: *Quatrevingt-treize* de Victor Hugo', *Romantisme*, 124/2 (2004), 111). And Piroué declares him 'un faible à force d'orgueil intellectuel' (*Victor Hugo romancier*, 93). See also *FT* 80–8, and Roche, *Character and Meaning*, 88.

[22] 'Ordered independently by Gauvain and Cimourdain, [the] delivery and appearance [of the ladder and guillotine] are confused. They reflect the contrary forms of the Republic and the opposing views of the world espoused by Gauvain and Cimourdain; more generally, they reflect the mysterious rapport between good and evil' (James F. Hamilton, 'Terrorizing the "Feminine" in Hugo, Dickens, and France', *Symposium*, 48/3 (Fall 1994), 207) in the text. Cf. Ferguson's argument that 'the mobility of this instrument of the Revolution translates perfectly the mobility of the Revolution itself, an idea that can take hold anywhere. Modernity and the Revolution are rendered by movement' ('*Quatrevingt-Treize*', 78–9). As noted in our analysis of *TM*, revolutionary movement in Hugo is also equated with metaphoricity—an idea that dates back to his portrait in *NDP* of the gypsy Esmeralda, whose song—'volatile, insaisissable, indestructible'—figures the 'révolution mère' (iv. 141) occasioned by the invention of the printing press. Her transformation in turn of the grotesque Quasimodo into a sublimely mobile *deus ex machina* allies the bell-ringer with the people's eventual triumph over oppression in 1789 (see *EN* 189–92).

into savagery: 'Alors mangeons-nous les uns les autres,' he declares; 'nous nous abrutissons à la fin' (xv. 498–9). The reference to cannibalism, a staple of Hugo's *imaginaire* found throughout his works, stands as the definitive verdict on the use of violence in the name of the law. Recalling the novelist's indictment of capital punishment forty-five years earlier in *Le Dernier Jour d'un condamné*, the guillotine's 'son de ferraille' and 'grincement métallique' (xv. 489) align the machine with humanity's most inhumane practices.

Not coincidentally, the text juxtaposes the monstrous creation of the French Revolution with its feudal counterpart, the ancestral tower known as la Tourgue—'abréviation paysanne, [qui] signifie la Tour-Gauvain' (xv. 423)—where the final battle between royalists and republicans takes place. Along with interspersed allusions in the novel to the guillotine, one finds repeated references to the torments once inflicted in the deepest recesses of la Tourgue. Here, the first thing one notices is the vertical furrows in the walls, excavated long ago by two wheels: 'Jadis, aux temps féodaux, c'était dans cette chambre que se faisait l'écartèlement, par un procédé moins tapageur que les quatre chevaux... On attachait à chacune de ces roues un bras et une jambe du patient, puis on faisait tourner les deux roues en sens inverse, ce qui arrachait l'homme. Il fallait de l'effort' (xv. 422; see also 492, 506). As in the secretive torture of Esmeralda in the crypt of the Palais de Justice in *Notre-Dame de Paris*, no one hears the screams. The resulting amputations are at least if not more barbarous than those effected by the guillotine. That one must exert considerable 'effort' to dismember another underscores the willfulness involved. The conscious choices of both ancient and revolutionary justice meet in the showdown between guillotine and keep, a 'battle' no less crucial than the one between Gauvain's and Lantenac's troops.

The confrontation is set up from the beginning of the narrative when, just before the incident with the cannon, two royalists on the *Claymore* discuss the necessity for vengeful violence against the revolutionaries. The cycle of brutality, driven by ancient antipathies, seems inexorable: 'Les régicides ont coupé la tête à Louis XVI, nous arracherons les quatre membres aux régicides' (xv. 301). Injustice is countered by injustice; reprisals beget reprisals. 'The worst [of all the ancient passions] is vengeance... which makes both partners in hatred wrong.'[23] Indeed, medieval justice is still alive and well among those who continue to adhere to the monarchy in the wake of 1789. The very real threat of being punished by such outmoded means in present-day France is reiterated in 'A Paris' when Marat mocks Robespierre's

[23] Pierre Saint-Amand, 'Hot Terror: *Quatrevingt-treize*', *SubStance*, 86 (1992), 70.

obsessive attention to appearance: 'tu n'en iras moins place de Grève . . . ', he declares, 'et tu es tiré à quatre épingles en attendant que tu sois tiré à quatre chevaux' (xv. 360). The typical Hugolian pun uses the square number four and the verb 'tiré' (*pulled* or *drawn*) to indicate extreme neatness, on the one hand, and extreme messiness, on the other. Yet, beneath the gallows humour, the menace to those who fail to deliver a powerful new nation is patent. If Gauvain and Cimourdain had not vanquished Lantenac and his followers at la Tourgue, they might well have been drawn and quartered, whether by horses or on relentless machinery, in the scenario for an alternative ending. Gauvain's death on the guillotine is, ironically, the one originally reserved for Lantenac.

The two specific agencies of dismemberment, both ancient and modern, participate in an even wider thematics of disjunction, of which just a few examples will suffice. In their first meeting during the night-time battle in the streets of Dol, Lantenac laments missing when he shoots at his great-nephew: 'un peu plus bas, j'avais la tête' (xv. 408). One need not use a guillotine to 'behead' the enemy. Later on, Lantenac's lieutenant, the hideous l'Imânus, displays a better aim when he shoots one of the attacking Revolutionary Army soldiers in la Tourgue: 'La balle avait crevé l'œil et traversé la tête' (xv. 467). In both cases, the royalists symbolically take their revenge on the 'vieille seigneurie . . . décapitée' (xv. 493) by the opposition. Some injuries are inflicted lower down on the body, as when l'Imânus himself has 'le ventre . . . fendu de part en part' (xv. 467), a point reiterated when Radoub proclaims: 'Je me risque. C'est égal, je viens toujours d'en éventrer un' (xv. 468). Whether slicing off heads or gutting the enemy, the gestures are savage in the extreme. Body wounds likewise appear on la Tourgue, long ago 'fendue par [une] explosion . . . et la déchirure praticable qui servait de brèche . . . ressemblait plutôt au coup de lance qui perce qu'au coup de hache qui entaille' (xv. 458). The metaphorical depiction of the tower affiliates it not just with past assaults but also with the one about to take place, the setting of the battle encapsulating the carnage about to take place. After all, the royalists expect that, in the end, 'on se hacher[a]' (xv. 453) in ferocious hand-to-hand battle. The multiple allusions to the *hache* or 'H'—Hugo's signature pun since *Han d'Islande*, reiterated in the form of Notre Dame Cathedral and in the shape of the wrecked *Durande* in the Douvres—certainly recall similar techniques from the earlier works. Thus, like the cathedral in *Notre-Dame de Paris*, the architectural focus of *Quatrevingt-Treize* at once contains and reflects the dramatic tensions and actions that surround it.[24] But the self-reference of ripping and

[24] See *EN* 165–77, 184–5, 191–4, 202–3. Mary Anne O'Neil asserts that, together with the ragtag Vendean army, with its forest 'maze of secret passages for the rebellious peasants

piercing may carry more personal meaning for the author as well. The *déchirure* in la Tourgue later colours Michelle Fléchard's anguished cry for her imperilled children, experienced by Lantenac as 'on ne sait quoi d'inarticulé et de déchirant' (xv. 475), with the poet's own wrenching loss of several offspring.

Finally, the famous rending in 'Le Massacre de Saint-Barthélemy' (III. 3) of the pages depicting the saint's martyrdom assumes new meaning when read in the light of the other disjunctions in the text. The allusion in the chapter title to the horrendous 1572 massacre during the French Wars of Religion (1562–98) alerts the reader straight away to the episode's connection to the broader motif of civil strife. The terrible specter of *sparagmos*—'that is, cannibalism, mutilation, and torture'[25]—that haunts Hugo's narrative is nowhere more vivid than in this scene of wanton destruction by the three little Fléchards abandoned in the ancestral library attached to la Tourgue. Part of a three-story structure spanning a nearby ravine in the forest, the library played an essential role in Gauvain's childhood education by Cimourdain: 'les souvenirs domestiques de Gauvain étaient là ... les fatalités tortueuses de la vie l'amenaient à attaquer, homme, cette muraille vénérable qui l'avait protégé enfant' (xv. 430). For now, it protects the Fléchard children as well, and they are ready to pursue knowledge in a way appropriate to their age. After waking from a nap while the epic battle between revolutionaries and royalists rages around them, the young hostages amuse themselves by exploring their unfamiliar surroundings.[26] The discovery of the priceless medieval illuminated manuscript on a lectern in the centre of the room leads to wholesale devastation.

The 'carnage' begins when four-year-old René-Jean tears the page on display: 'cette déchirure de saint Barthélemy se fit de travers ... il laissa dans le livre tout le côté gauche avec un œil et un peu de l'auréole du vieil évangeliste apocryphe' (xv. 440). In other words, the injuries that the little boy inflicts on the saint foreshadow those of l'Imânus's victim, who likewise loses an eye and much of his head. The child's innocent crime against art resembles and contrasts alike with the crimes against humanity that result from civil war. René-Jean's eighteen-month-old sister Georgette immediately rips the page he gives her into pieces, 'si bien que

and traps for the revolutionary soldiers', the tower represents 'a Gothic Terror ... that threatens the forward motion of civilization with fear and prejudice' ('Classical Terror/ Gothic Terror: Victor Hugo's *Quatrevingt-treize*', *Poetica*, 39–40 (1993), 265, 266).

[25] Frye, *The Anatomy of Criticism*, 222.

[26] In a text full of ironies, one of the most notable is that Lantenac and his adherents are holding royalist children captive.

l'histoire pourrait dire que saint Barthélemy, après avoir été écorché en Arménie, fut écartelé en Bretagne' (xv. 440). Once again, the children repeat at their own level the gestures of adults, both the feudal lords who quartered their victims in la Tourgue in the past and the royalist adherents who harbour similar intentions regarding their Republican enemies. Gaps—the necessary condition for Hugo's 'poetics of transcendence'—abound.

The entire manuscript passes through the three children's eager hands as, 'joyeux, éperdus, triomphants, impitoyables, déchirant les estampes, balafrant les feuillets, arrachant les signets, égratignant la reliure, décollant le cuir doré, déclouant les clous . . . déchiquetant le texte auguste . . . riants, féroces, les trois anges de proie s'abattirent sur l'évangéliste sans défense' (xv. 441). Undoing step by step the process used to construct the beautiful and irreplaceable book, they indulge in many of the actions associated in the text with other agents.[27] From 'la Tourgue . . . balafrée' (xv. 421) to the cannon wheels that 'déchiquetaient' (xv. 303) the sailors on the *Claymore*, to the 'balafre' (xv. 411) earned by Cimourdain when he takes a blow meant for Gauvain, to Radoub, 'égratigné à l'épaule' (xv. 462) in the fight in the tower, to 'le peuple déchirée' (xv. 487) between British and French armies, to the 'évangiles déchirés' (xv. 316), according to Lantenac, by impious republicans—the novel offers a constellation of images that reflect the havoc wreaked by the children in the library. Much as *Chaos vaincu* constitutes a *mise en abyme* of *L'Homme qui rit*, 'Le Massacre de Saint-Barthélemy' concentrates the violence and brutality of the French Terror in *Quatrevingt-Treize* into a single scene—but one purged of the divisive partisanship of the adult characters. The episode thus briefly interrupts 'le cadre terrible de l'action pour en suggérer l'inanité et le scandale'.[28] The children's mock epic replies to the grotesque slaughter that surrounds them.

Perhaps Robespierre best captures the essence of civil war as portrayed in the novel when he tells Danton: 'La guerre étrangère, c'est une écorchure qu'on a au coude; la guerre civile, c'est l'ulcère qui vous mange le foie' (xv. 353). A kind of monstrous self-cannibalization, it consumes the host from within. This reflexive aspect of domestic warfare mirrors the *vivandière*'s assertion, in the introductory chapters, that her job is to provide something to drink 'quand on se mitraille et qu'on s'assassine' (xv. 292).[29]

[27] Like Lethierry's steamboat in *TM*, the manuscript represents a unique *œuvre* for which there is no substitute, and so, of incalculable value.

[28] Peyrache-Leborgne, 'Roman historique', 61; see also 62–3.

[29] According to Charles Nunley, both the *vivandière* and Michelle Fléchard 'fulfill similar functions: while Fléchard nurses her young, the *vivandière* "nurses" wounded soldiers' ('(En)gendering Terror: Women and Violence in *Quatrevingt-treize*', in John

For all their vaunted rhetoric, the two opposing camps are, from her perspective, simply engaged in mutually assured destruction. The storyline supports her view when Lantenac persuades the sailor Halmalo not only not to kill him for having ordered his brother executed for dereliction of duty in the cannon episode, but also to serve as the marquis's emissary to raise the call to insurrection throughout Brittany: 'en guerre civile, c'est la pire qui est la meilleure. La bonté d'une guerre se juge à la quantité de mal qu'elle fait' (xv. 321), Lantenac intones, fully embracing the general conflagration and seducing Halmalo to participate in it as well. Though he is a hero in his own mind, the noble's affiliation with Satan from the viewpoint of the revolutionaries is supported by his own actions and words.

What might the worst be in matters of internecine conflict? Certainly, Hugo's novel highlights the plight of innocent (and non-partisan) women and children, like the Fléchards, from beginning to end.[30] But the damage occurs, not just on the civil level, with the French killing the French, but also within families, as both siblings and generations turn against each other. As Isabel Roche observes, 'familial connections [in *Quatrevingt-Treize*] are constantly sacrificed on both sides for the greater good of the war'.[31] The term 'fratricide' first appears in the text when Danton intercedes in an argument between Marat and Robespierre, pleading, 'il ne faut pas de fratricide . . . il ne faut pas de lutte entre deux hommes qui servent le peuple' (xv. 359). In this way, the dispute between national leaders appears as a model for the *frères ennemis* motif related to civil war. In designating Marat as the aggressor 'Caïn' (xv. 360), Danton's character reminds the reader that the two sides of the French conflict are not equally guilty. It is therefore no surprise that Gauvain links the royalists' cause, and hence Lantenac, with 'la guerre civile, le talion, l'affreuse logique des représailles, le meurtre, le carnage, le fratricide, la rage, la rancune, toutes les gorgones' (xv. 483). The fratricides are not the revolutionaries seeking to impose a new order on society but the resentful reactionaries who cling to the past and aim to exact vengeance for perceived injustices. Eliminating Lantenac therefore means, for Gauvain, ending 'la lutte fratricide, la guerre bestiale' (xv. 487), as well. Despite the possible Oedipal overtones of the situation, Gauvain focuses on the wider implications for the French

T. Booker and Allan H. Pasco (eds), *The Play of Terror in Nineteenth-Century France* (Newark: University of Delaware Press, 1997), 37). See also James Hamilton, 'Terrorizing the "Feminine"', 205.

[30] Although Michelle Fléchard's spouse fought and died for the royalist cause, she herself is intent only on her children and completely uninterested in political matters.

[31] Roche, *Character and Meaning*, 157.

nation rather than on any personal vendetta that might be involved in their conflict.

Cimourdain, too, underlines the familial aspects of the domestic French war, but from a different angle. In learning that Gauvain intends to have Lantenac executed if he is caught, the priest remarks, 'c'est plus que la guerre dans la patrie, c'est la guerre dans la famille. Il le faut, et c'est bien. Les grands rajeunissements des peuples sont à ce prix' (xv. 400). For Cimourdain, the new ideas largely associated with the younger generation are destined to triumph in this epic struggle. Yet this intellectualization of history ignores the tragic details. For example, the chapter title 'Plus quam civilia bella' (III. 2. 1; xv. 399; 'Wars more than civil'), picks up a theme previously developed in the scene on the *Claymore*, where it is clear that the war that lies ahead is more (or less) than 'civil'. Indeed, it goes so far as to 'divise[r] l'humanité sur elle-même'.[32] The issue, though, is neither fratricide nor parricide but filicide. One of the boat's passengers, the comte du Boisberthelot, defends the worthiness of some members of the bourgeoisie in his exchange with another nobleman: 'Il y a pourtant dans ce tiers état . . . des gens estimables. Tenez, par exemple, ce horloger Joly . . . pendant que le père sert dans les blancs, le fils sert dans les bleus. Rencontre. Bataille. Le père fait prisonnier son fils, et lui brûle le cerveau' (xv. 299). The tale of the father killing his son because of their political differences is rendered even more ghastly by the notion that such an act could elevate the humble watchmaker in the count's esteem. But the royalists are desperate and prepared to transcend the general fratricide of civil war by killing, if necessary, their own offspring. In the late eighteenth century, Cronus continues to devour his young.

When Cimourdain later hears from an innkeeper that 'un ci-devant qui est pour la république se bat contre un ci-devant qui est pour le roi . . . Et le curieux, c'est que les deux ci-devant sont deux parents' (xv. 400), the potential replay of the watchmaker's tale forecasts the impending confrontation between Lantenac and Gauvain.[33] The real horror, here too, is the possibility of filicide. Lantenac's claim to Halmalo that, 'de même que j'ai fait fusiller ton frère, je ferais fusiller mon fils' (xv. 317) reveals the ruthlessness that steadies his arm in Dol, when he shoots to kill his great-nephew (and thus his symbolic son) in their first military engagement. The text makes it plain that the conflict is Oedipal. As he prepares to encounter Gauvain in the little town, Lantenac fumes: 'Quelle idée a-t-il d'être

[32] Campion, 'Raison de la littérature', 110.

[33] Guerlac likewise considers this anecdote to be 'the story of *Quatrevingt-treize* . . . in miniature' (*The Impersonal Sublime*, 20). See also Roman, *Victor Hugo et le roman philosophique*, 571–2.

jacobin? ce Gauvain! ce polisson! son héritier, car le marquis n'avait pas d'enfants, un petit-neveu, presque un petit-fils!—*Ah!* disait ce quasi grand père, *si je mets la main dessus, je le tue comme un chien!*' (xv. 404). By being a relative ('ce Gauvain'), and a close one at that ('presque un petit-fils'), Gauvain attracts the special ire of his ancestor. Once again, the older generation has no compunction about slaying the younger one, in a tragedy of mythical proportions.[34] The danger for Gauvain exists in his own camp as well, given Cimourdain's instructions from Paris. Obviously, republican 'fathers' are willing to execute their own 'sons', a situation even more horrible than the unintended parricides committed by family members fighting on opposing sides. During Gauvain's trial, one of the judges cites a Roman precedent from the year 414, when 'Manlius fit mourir son fils pour le crime d'avoir vaincu sans son ordre... La pitié peut avoir les proportions d'un crime' (xv. 498). Rather than serving as an example to the younger generation—a metonymical function—the older generation makes an example of those who fail to live up to its particular notion of law, duty, and/or discipline.

From a wider perspective, then, the war-torn nation serves as an organizing metaphor for Hugo's text, where buildings, bodies, families, regions, and even books are divided against themselves. The moral equivalent, a warring conscience, plays a prominent role in *Les Misérables*, where Jean Valjean must repeatedly unravel the dilemmas that confront him in his quest for redemption.[35] The epicentre of the ex-convict's internal battles, 'Une Tempête sous un crâne' (I. 7. 3), serves as a template not just for Gwynplaine's stricken conscience in *L'Homme qui rit* but also for Gauvain's deliberations in 'Gauvain pensif' (III. 6. 2) about whether to save Lantenac's life. The choice is difficult. Although the marquis has thrown away his escape from la Tourgue in order to rescue the Fléchard children from the burning library, to liberate him is to perpetuate the war that weighs on the entire country. The trial within begins:

> Gauvain subissait un interrogatoire.
> Il comparaissait devant quelqu'un.
> Devant quelqu'un de redoutable.
> Sa conscience.

[34] Lantenac's fulminations against his great-nephew are strongly reminiscent of the royalist ancestor Gillenormand's rantings in *MIS* about Marius' republicanism (see esp. xi. 514–16). In so far as Gillenormand largely plays a comic role in the earlier novel (see *FT* 73–5), we might view this scene in *QVT* as mixing both genres and messages: Lantenac's views, though laughable, can easily lead to tragic consequences.

[35] See *FT* 143–54.

> Gauvain sentait tout vaciller en lui. Ses résolutions les plus solides, ses promesses les plus fermement faites, ses décisions les plus irrévocables, tout cela chancelait dans les profondeurs de sa volonté. (xv. 483)

Before the young captain is tried before a revolutionary tribunal, he must first adjudicate a situation in which he himself, as both a member of Lantenac's family and the royalist leader's sworn enemy, is involved. His internal polarization, combined with the menace of the guillotine, leaves little hope for integrity.

Apparently, Lantenac has endured a similar internal struggle in deciding to abandon his bid for freedom—at least, Gauvain imagines his great-uncle's conflict in trying to resolve his own:

> Jamais, dans aucun combat, Satan n'avait été plus visible, ni Dieu.
> Ce combat avait eu pour arène une conscience.
> La conscience de Lantenac.
> Maintenant il recommençait, plus acharné et plus décisif encore peut-être, dans une autre conscience.
> La conscience de Gauvain.
> Quel champ de bataille que l'homme! (xv. 484)

Having associated the division in Jean Valjean's conscience with the Battle of Waterloo in *Les Misérables*,[36] Hugo draws on the same treasury of images in *Quatrevingt-Treize* to describe Gauvain's dilemma in terms of the internecine war in which he is engaged. In both novels, the writer's 'new kind of epic' involves internal rather than external combat.[37] Opposed to Lantenac in their military clashes, Gauvain now finds himself confronting the man in his mind as well. Through these two inner voices, Gauvain argues with himself about the alternative courses of action. Can he allow the enemy to occupy the higher moral ground? To do so is to lose his revolutionary cause, at least symbolically. 'Et Lantenac transfiguré ne transfigurerait pas Gauvain!' (xv. 485), he wonders. The metonymical contagion of one conscience by another—not unlike Bishop Myriel's infection in *Les Misérables* by the Conventionnel G. (and of Jean Valjean by Myriel)[38]—must be doubled by huge changes in the realm of action. Otherwise, Gauvain thinks, 'L'homme du passé irait en avant, et l'homme de l'avenir en arrière!' (xv. 485). If Lantenac can sacrifice himself to save the little Fléchards, should Gauvain not follow the ancestral example by

36 See *FT* 191.

37 Brombert, *Victor Hugo and the Visionary Novel*, 218. Cf. Guerlac, who perceives in Gauvain's dilemma 'a kind of résumé of the novel', one that reflects 'all the major issues with which [it] has been concerned' ('Exorbitant Geometry', 869)—in other words, yet another *mise en abyme* of the text.

38 See *FT* 128–30.

sacrificing himself in turn? The schism in his country replays itself in his head as he tries to see where the good resides: 'Deux abîmes s'ouvraient devant Gauvain. Perdre le marquis? ou le sauver? Il fallait se précipiter dans l'un ou dans l'autre' (xv. 488). Whereas Javert is confronted with the oxymoronic 'gouffre en haut' (xi. 915) of Jean Valjean's sublime ethos, Gauvain is left to puzzle, 'Lequel de ces deux gouffres était le devoir?' (xv. 488).[39] At some point, he must choose one gulf or the other and hurl himself, body and soul, into it. Either way, he will heal his split conscience, even if one route dictates that he will die in the process, thereby completing the arc of the novel's 'poetics of transcendence'.

The role of Britain and France in this decision is vital, for Gauvain's quandary involves the relationship between the two countries. Because of his uncle's association with the English, we have seen, Gauvain considers him an 'étranger' (xv. 418). After reintegrating himself, however, into the family of man, Lantenac no longer seems alien to Gauvain and must therefore be saved. Yet England remains outside this magic sphere, rendering the choice impossible: as noted earlier, Gauvain must prevent Lantenac from imposing 'la monarchie sur la république et l'Angleterre sur la France. Sauver Lantenac, c'était sacrifier la France' (xv. 487). Oscillating between the contradictory demands of his conscience, Gauvain suddenly shifts into the imperative mood: 'Alors c'est bien. Va, fais les affaires des Anglais. Déserte. Passe à l'ennemi. Sauve Lantenac et trahis la France' (xv. 488). And this is, finally, the command that he obeys, if we are to believe his apparent confession before the military tribunal: 'J'ai oublié les villages incendiés, les champs ravagés, les prisonniers massacrés, les blessés achevés, les femmes fusillées, j'ai oublié la France livrée à l'Angleterre; j'ai mis en liberté le meurtrier de la patrie. Je suis coupable' (xv. 497). One might infer that Gauvain has promoted familial over political concerns, that the mortal opposition of England and France no longer interests him per se.

The cannon's blood bath, the confrontation of man-made implements of destruction, the dismemberment of human bodies, the mutilation of the Saint-Barthélemy manuscript, Gauvain's divided loyalties and conscience—all are emblems of the savage disjunctions, personal, familial, and civil, that operate in *Quatrevingt-Treize*. While they suggest a deeply dystopian outlook, the novel defies such simplistic interpretations. If one reconsiders, for example, the episode of the ladder and the guillotine, which turn out to be metaphorically interchangeable, it appears to carry more weight than the amount of textual space devoted to it would indicate. Repeated allusions to both devices through the rest of the storyline suggest

[39] Cf. Laforgue, 'La Révolution française', 135 n. 73.

that one needs to look closer. For, in addition to the overarching thematics of disjunction in the text that we have just examined, Hugo develops a parallel thematics of unity and connectedness. From this perspective, guillotines and ladders encapsulate the tension between splitting and conjoining, respectively. The gaps engendered by war are wounds that may somehow be healed. As I shall show, the forces of union in the text are also important thematic and structural elements.

Doubles, Twins, and Triplicates

My reading of the opening scenes in *Quatrevingt-Treize* has demonstrated that the spatial oppositions associated with Brittany and Paris, on the one hand, and with England and France, on the other, prepare a larger meditation on the discordant relations that permeate the text. A more attentive reading, however, reveals that the ambiguous status of Brittany as both French and non-French instantiates the multiplication of identities in the novel. Some involve double or even triple identities; some, paired objects or characters.[40] Above all, through the relations of 'parents' and 'children', Hugo suggests some final reconciliation of all these opposites.

In the introductory chapters, for example, the *Claymore* on which Lantenac reaches Brittany's shores 'était monté par un équipage français mais faisait partie de la flotille anglaise' (xv. 295). Both French and English, the 'strangely double nature' of the vessel noted by Guerlac[41] is matched by that of its mysterious passenger, who wears a traditional two-sided vest that can offer 'le côté velu ou le côté brodé' (xv. 296) and who can be distinguished by his 'habits de paysan, mains d'aristocrate' (xv. 297). The reference to the same person in the chapter title, 'Noblesse et roture mêlées' (I. 2. 3), echoes the mixing of England and France on the boat itself. That the man with the dual identity—'gentilhomme en France, mais prince en Bretagne' (xv. 298)—is betrayed by a double agent is merely icing on the doppelgänger cake. The subsequent mention of a second royalist double agent, 'Encore un des nôtres qui était des leurs' (xv. 300), complains Boisberthelot, along with Lantenac's charge soon thereafter to Halmalo to disguise himself as a republican in order to incite the Breton royalists to rebel, underscores the slipperiness of identities in Hugo's narrative. Even the enemy troops are surprisingly intermingled, with a host of 'bourgeois' commanding the royalists and of 'nobles' at the

[40] Cf. Rosa's analysis of what he calls 'la double appartenance' of the main characters in the novel and its relation to Scott's method of character development ('Présentation', 235). Cf. also Roman, *Victor Hugo et le roman philosophique*, 258–63.

[41] Guerlac, 'Exorbitant Geometry', 858.

head of the revolutionaries (xv. 299). If 'each side of the conflict contains the other within itself', as Guerlac argues regarding the novel's metaphysical stakes, it is not just because 'the terms of the war are . . . not stable'.[42] Rather, the shared identities in the text point to Hugo's use of poetic discourse to create a metaphorical redescription of the way in which we view the world, past as well as present. To 'se[e] the similar in the dissimilar' is to perform a 'semantic operation' that simultaneously 'opposes and unites identity and difference' (*RM* 6, 196). Hugo's double agents and characters who cross class lines enter into the system of categorical transgressions that define metaphor.

Inanimate objects, too, fall into this thematics of double identities. We have already mentioned the mistaken identification of the rescue ladder and the guillotine, but it also turns out that there are two critical ladders in the text: the one intercepted and burned by the Breton peasants hiding in the forest and another one, which makes its appearance much later, housed in the library in la Tourgue. The first is metaphorically replaced at the scene of the battle, then, not only by the guillotine, but also by the second rescue ladder that is deployed from up above, rather than from down below. When Lantenac returns to the scene of the crime—the arson he had ordered to destroy the library with its young hostages—he performs in a spatially inverse mode the salvific act that the ladderless revolutionaries cannot. 'En descendant cette échelle qui le rendait à ses ennemis, et qui, échelle de sauvetage pour les autres, était pour lui échelle de perdition' (xv. 484), he invests the second ladder with yet another identity, since he considers that it will serve to lose him even as it serves to save the children. And yet, from Gauvain's perspective, the ladder is the means to his great-uncle's salvation.

The two-sidedness of the ladder can be found in other objects as well. For instance, the episode of the unfettered cannon, 'une machine qui se transforme en un monstre' (xv. 302), reiterates the trope through metaphorical analogy. The instrument of human will and the untamed beast are one and the same. The use of metaphor operates elsewhere in the text, too, to open new perspectives on the material world. Thus, the comparison between 'une tour en rase campagne' and 'un navire en pleine mer' (xv. 454) alludes to both la Tourgue and the *Claymore*, while playing on the contrast between the horizontal and vertical planes. The correspondence between tower and vessel recurs when the narrator points out the extreme ferocity that marks both 'les rencontres de sapeurs dans les galeries couvertes quand la contre-mine vient couper la mine' and 'les boucheries à

[42] Guerlac, 'Exorbitant Geometry', 859.

la hache sous les entreponts des vaisseaux qui s'abordent dans les batailles navales' (xv. 459). In this way, the beginning and end of the novel achieve a certain balance, if not parity, as the unnarrated last stand of the severely disabled *Claymore* can be traced in the revolutionaries' fight to enter la Tourgue through the gash in its side. It is doubtless no accident that Lantenac, who manages to escape from the first disaster, thanks to Halmalo, also ends up escaping from the second, again through Halmalo's agency. In any case, this final battle site for revolutionaries and royalists is depicted, like the cannon and the rescue ladder, as binary in nature: 'La Tourgue avait son côté sauvage, la tour, et son côté civilisé, la bibliothèque' (xv. 430). The vertical tower, where men were once tortured, and the horizontal library, where the wisdom of the ages is preserved, represent terror and transcendence, two aspects of the experience of the sublime described by Weiskel.[43] By the same token, the *côté sauvage* and the *côté civilisé* of la Tourgue are allied with Lantenac and Gauvain, respectively, at least until the marquis transcends his brutal past in the novel's dénouement.[44] Lantenac's change of heart in the book 'In dæmone Deus' (III. 5; xv. 473; 'God in the Demon') reiterates the duality of the tower, itself the double of the *Claymore*.

Most striking, however, is the proliferation in the novel's characters of multiple identities. Many of these assume the form of gender blending or 'sexual ambivalence'.[45] At the outset, the *vivandière* declares herself to be 'une bonne femme et un brave homme' (xv. 292), thereby transcending any one sexual identity, and she is not the only character to do so. Similarly, the beggar Tellmarch, who ministers to the near-dead Michelle Fléchard after the massacre at the Herbe-en-Pail farm where the Bonnet-Rouge battalion had camped, considers her physical and emotional distress 'avec des pensées de femme' (xv. 415). The first physical description of Gauvain indicates that this 'âme héroïque et innocente', transfigured in conflict by the sword in his hand, sports 'cet air effeminé qui dans la bataille est formidable' (xv. 493). Though perhaps consonant with his 'feminine' tendencies towards clemency, the trait reappears in the final depiction of Gauvain, as he mounts the guillotine: 'Son cou blanc faisait songer à une femme, et son œil héroïque faisait songer à un archange' (xv. 508). The young man is, like the *vivandière* and the generous beggar, both masculine *and* feminine, his forceful heroism conjoined with more feminine qualities.

[43] See esp. Weiskel, *The Romantic Sublime*, 83–106.

[44] For James Hamilton, 'Tower and *châtelet* coexist as complementaries—angry phallus and protective womb' ('Terrorizing the "Feminine"', 206; see also 208)—projections, I would add, of the different ethical worlds of the two members of the Gauvain family who confront each other at the ancestral home.

[45] Brombert, *Victor Hugo and the Visionary Novel*, 211.

Such gender *mélanges* in *Quatrevingt-Treize* extend to the realm of parenting as well. Radoub, with his 'effrayante face velue, hérissée et fauve' (xv. 294), initially appears under the 'masculine' sign, which soon involves assuming responsibility for the Fléchard brood. When little Georgette at her mother's breast looks at him and smiles, he sheds a 'feminine' tear and declares: 'Camarades, de tout ça je conclus que le bataillon va devenir père. Est-ce convenu? Nous adoptons ces trois enfants-là' (xv. 294). The sergeant's devotion to his adopted children drives much of the storyline, as he fights to liberate the small hostages from la Tourgue in ways that Michelle Fléchard, were she present (and even when she eventually shows up), never could. Once they are rescued and the family reunited, Radoub remains 'près des enfants et de la mère, presque aussi maternal qu'elle' (xv. 481). Replacing the mother in the battle for the children's lives, Radoub displays a double parental role, one at once paternal and maternal.[46] Likewise, given the textual emphasis on Michelle Fléchard's instinctive motherhood and blind but relentless search for her three small children, it is significant that Cimourdain's unwavering political certitude is characterized as 'la *flèche* qui ne voit que le but et qui y va' (xv. 347; emphasis added) and that his love for Gauvain is not strictly paternal. 'L'esprit allaite; l'intelligence est une mamelle,' we learn. 'Il y a analogie entre la nourrice qui donne son lait et le précepteur qui donne sa pensée. Quelquefois le précepteur est plus père que le père, de même que souvent la nourrice est plus mère que la mère' (xv. 349–50)—a comparison repeated three paragraphs later. Contrary to Umberto Eco's view regarding Cimourdain that 'Hugo never conjures up a passion that is anything other than the total identification of a man—chaste because of his faith and later because of his revolutionary fervour—with spiritual fatherhood',[47] the text stresses the man's spiritual *motherhood*. As with Jean Valjean's nurturing maternal love for Cosette in *Les Misérables*,[48] the priest metaphorically replaces Gauvain's missing mother, taking her place in his young charge's life.

The point is reinforced in the dénouement, when Cimourdain gazes upon Gauvain as he sleeps in his cell the night before his execution: 'une mère regardant son nourrisson dormir n'aurait pas un plus tendre et plus inexprimable regard' (xv. 501). The analogy between the learned priest and the nursing mother invests Cimourdain's love for Gauvain with much

[46] According to James Hamilton's Jungian analysis, 'Radoub and his men become nurturing, protective, surrogate fathers. In contrast, Lantenac counterfeits paternity by taking the three children by force as hostages' ('Terrorizing the "Feminine"', 205)—hardly a paternal posture.

[47] Eco, 'Excess and History in Hugo's *Ninety-Three*', 275.

[48] See *FT* 79, 139–41.

the same power while subtracting nothing from his basic masculinity. Hugo structures his plot so that, just as Michelle Fléchard recovers her offspring, Cimourdain loses his. The emotional repercussions of this tragedy for Cimourdain, who does not betray his feelings when he carries out the duties imposed on him by the Revolutionary Comité de salut public, is thus amply prepared by the dramatization of the mother's despair and anguish throughout the novel. Through their androgynous features, Radoub and Cimourdain join Jean Valjean and Gwynplaine as *both/and*—that is, metaphorical—propositions.

For those characters whose complexity leads to internal divisions—a trait previously noted in Gauvain—the text offers additional modes of identity expansion. The young hero's dialogue with himself in 'Gauvain pensif', for example, shows that his self-concept as a member of Lantenac's family conflicts with his self-concept as a revolutionary who above all espouses the family of man. That he is able to reconcile the two aspects of his split conscience by performing his duty sequentially, first to Lantenac, as his saviour, then to the French nation, as its 'chose de la loi', points to their integration at another level. Cimourdain is also two men, 'un homme tendre et un homme sombre' (xv. 412), the one attached to Gauvain and the other to revolutionary ideals. He, too, resolves his (presumed but unvoiced) psychological clash between both imperatives in a sequential manner, by executing first Gauvain, then himself. In so doing, he transcends the gap that has opened between them.

When one adds the viewpoint of the royalists, Cimourdain's selves continue to subdivide. To himself, he is 'le représentant de la loi' and 'le commissaire de la Révolution'; to l'Imânus and his colleagues, he is 'un rénégat' and 'un apostat', not to mention 'le démon' (xv. 456). From the perspective of his enemies, the former priest is another person altogether. To Cimourdain's further claim, 'Je suis votre frère,' l'Imânus replies, 'Oui, Caïn' (xv. 457)—the same designation that Danton uses for Marat. In this way, the text not only reveals differences within similarities; it also subtly interlaces disparate characters. Hugo's skill as a dramatist is manifest in such dialogues, both inner and outer, and it can be discerned in passages that do not involve two human interlocutors as well. Thus, even at the micro level, one finds odd 'conversations', like Michelle Fléchard's cry into the deserted forest, 'Y a-t-il quelqu'un ici?', which is answered by the 'coup de tonnerre' (xv. 452) of cannon fire; or the 'son de clairon' exchanged with the 'son de trompe' (xv. 456) before the battle; or 'le tonnerre assaillant' of the Revolutionary Army replying to 'le tonnerre embusqué' (xv. 459) of their foes in la Tourgue; or the 'coup de pistolet' that responds at the end to the executioner's 'coup de hache' (xv. 509). In each case, the non-human counterparts are metonymies for either the royalist or revolutionary forces, which in principle are diametrically opposed. At the same time, the echoing repartees within the manifold dialogues forge links between the antithetical forces in the novel.

The pattern of creating analogies between extremes recurs in instances of twinning, as when the inflexible Lantenac meets his polar opposite, the merciful beggar Tellmarch: 'Un homme était là dans les haies, de haute taille comme lui, vieux comme lui, comme lui en cheveux blancs, et plus en haillons encore que lui-même. Presque son pareil' (xv. 327). Apparent differences are erased by their common identity as elderly men in need. The point is emphasized when Tellmarch remarks to his guest, 'Nous voilà frères, monseigneur. Je demande du pain, vous demandez la vie. Nous sommes deux mendiants' (xv. 328), and they eat the same loaf of bread and drink water from the same pitcher.[49] Their relationship prefigures the intricate pairing of Lantenac and Gauvain, who, though on opposite sides of the political spectrum, share the same ancestor and end up fighting in the tower bearing the family name: 'La Tour-Gauvain avait une destinée étrange: un Gauvain l'attaquait, un Gauvain la défendait' (xv. 430). But it is Gauvain, the aggressor, who resided there happily as a child and who harbours real attachments to the place, whereas Lantenac, the defender, spent most of his life at Versailles. The tension between the two relatives (and two generations) is not, therefore, that of genuine contraries. For the peasants, their conflict represents 'la guerre de saint Michel contre Belzébuth'; the innkeeper, however, sees things differently, as he tells Cimourdain, 's'il y a un diable, c'est bien Lantenac, et s'il y a un ange, c'est Gauvain' (xv. 401).[50] The shifting and even reversible identities obfuscate the nature of both men. From antithetical they become interchangeable, a basically metaphorical function. As in *L'Homme qui rit*, the 'excess of endless reversals'[51] that overflows the novel's emplotment leads to a more highly integrated order.

In the same vein, Gauvain and Cimourdain may disagree about the republican ideal without losing their fundamental accord: 'C'était comme une âme coupée en deux, et partagée' (xv. 417). As one divided soul, they are both separate and united. Their dissociation centres principally on their approach to securing the nation. Because Cimourdain espouses 'la république de la terreur' and his protégé, 'la république de la clémence', they attempt to conquer la Vendée by 'la rigueur' and 'la douceur'

[49] The two fighters in *HQR*, we will recall, display the same unifying gesture.

[50] Like Cimourdain, then, Gauvain is associated with Michelle Fléchard, whose first name is a homonym in French for the archangel Michael (*Michel*) and whose last name, evoking arrows, suggests militancy in the service of the good.

[51] Eco, 'Excess and History in Hugo's *Ninety-Three*', 283; see also 280–2.

(xv. 416), respectively. Yet both subscribe unequivocally to a republican form of government. The two sides of one 'soul' are mediated by a common identity, just as Cimourdain and Lantenac, who oppose each other politically, share an inflexible allegiance to rules and principles: 'ces deux hommes, le marquis et le prêtre, étaient jusqu'à un certain point le même homme. Le masque de bronze de la guerre civile a deux profils, l'un tourné vers le passé, l'autre tourné vers l'avenir, mais aussi tragique l'un que l'autre' (xv. 429). The two older men both subscribe to perpetuating internal strife in their country in the name of a social ideal. They are a matched pair, 'terrible contre terrible' (xv. 363), as Cimourdain describes it—the one as ruthless as the other. They are as much equivalents as rivals. According to the narrator, '[ces] deux hommes... étaient égaux dans la balance de la haine... Chacun de ces deux hommes était, pour le camp opposé, le monstre' (xv. 429). Though mortal ennemies, they both demonstrate monstrous qualities for their adversaries, to the point that they are, in fact, metaphorical twins. If their 'ideological positions become equidistant in the equilibrium of the Terror',[52] it is because bringing opposites into proximity is an important mark, we have seen, of metaphorical statements. When Cimourdain offers himself in exchange for the marquis at la Tourgue, proclaiming, 'Deux hommes sont de trop, Lantenac pour nous, moi pour vous' (xv. 457), he stresses their interchangeability. More surprising yet, after the marquis has rescued the children in the library, Cimourdain seizes him, Javert-like, by the collar and declares, 'Je t'arrête'—to which Lantenac replies, 'Je t'approuve' (xv. 480). Having listened to his own conscience, Lantenac has already arrested himself. The seeming gaps between each set of characters are thus bridged when viewed from a different perspective.

Their points of consonance are again in evidence when the text weaves multiple strands between the antagonistic views represented by Lantenac, on the one side, and by Cimourdain and Gauvain, on the other. When the narrator describes the events of July 1793, he points to striking resemblances between royalists and revolutionaries: 'Pas de grâce! Pas de prisonniers! était le cris des deux partis' (xv. 426). The two sides are equally merciless, a recurring motif in the text. Through the mediating function of metaphor, the opposing camps of ferocious royalist and republican leaders share in a third identity as 'hyène contre hyène' (xv. 301; see also 383).[53] Fearing that the Revolution might abort in its early years, Cimourdain wants it to be sufficiently horrible to 'jeter aux démons la lueur infernale,

[52] Saint-Amand, Hot Terror', 70.

[53] This rapaciousness is, in turn, reflected in the chief instrument of justice, the guillotine, a notion that dates back to *DJC* (see *EN* 115, 119).

et leur rendre terreur pour terreur' (xv. 346). France's violent history requires a violent response, thereby assuring the self-similarity, the recursion, of past and present. Following the model of *L'Homme qui rit*, temporal dimensions overlay each other in multi-level symmetries. From this perspective, the guillotine and la Tourgue, whose juxtaposition we have examined above, share a common denominator despite their origins in different centuries: 'Un monstre de pierre faisait pendant au monstre de bois' (xv. 505). Both modes of delivering death and terror are grotesque.[54] And, despite the show of force from the French republicans, the Bretons reply in kind. In their labyrinthine forest, the passage of the Revolutionary Army gives birth to radical resistance, since, 'sous la pression de ce pied gigantesque, la révolution, jaillissait la guerre civile' (xv. 390). Action evokes reaction, to the point that the two enemy camps are linked symbiotically. The same point is made when the narrator depicts the clashing forces as 'la terreur répliqua[nt] à la terreur' (xv. 393), carnage invoking more carnage. Cause and effect become confused as each incident incites another in a vicious cycle of violence in which both sides are both assailed and assailants.[55]

Finally, one might observe that Brittany, as depicted in *Quatrevingt-Treize*, is not truly the antithesis of Paris, given the use of similar imagery to describe the two landscapes. For instance, Danton says that Marat is a 'reptile' who lives in a 'cave' (xv. 359; see also 358, 360), like the Bretons-'reptiles' (xv. 389) in their underground refuges; the chapter on 'Les rues de Paris dans ce temps-là' (II. 1. 1) reveals a post-Revolutionary Paris nearly as exotic to Hugo's reader as Bretagne (xv. 341–4); and the ensemble of constructs housing the Convention turn out to be as convoluted and as 'violent, sauvage... farouche' (xv. 371) as the Breton countryside. Through images of caves and labyrinths, the two antagonistic parts of France are brought into a relation of parity. This is, of course, the structure of metaphor: two terms compared through a shared attribute. Because metaphor 'presents two ideas at once... both tenor and vehicle in interaction', it is defined not as the '[semantic] clash itself, but rather [as]

[54] Yves Gohin likewise notes that, 'au moment où [Hugo] tend à opposer... la guillotine à la Tourgue, il en vient à faire apparaître davantage en quoi elle lui ressemble' ('Alternance et adhérance des contraires dans *Quatrevingt-Treize*', in J. A. Hiddleston (ed.), *Victor Hugo,* Romancier de l'abîme*: New Studies on Hugo's Novels* (Oxford: European Humanities Research Centre, 2002), 157).

[55] Rosa approaches this notion of the novel's recursive structure when he asserts that the work constitutes 'un discours unifié, où le général est de même essence que le particulier, le collectif de même nature que l'individuel, l'histoire du même ordre de réalité que le fictif' ('"Quatrevingt-treize"', 336).

its resolution' (*RM* 81, 190). Both twinned and dual identities in the novel imply some point of consonance or congruity.[56]

The two-sidedness and binary tensions originally associated with Brittany in the text thus give way to more complicated figures, including what we might call tripartite identities. The first number associated with a geometric figure, the triangle, the digit three has a held mystical significance from antiquity, and Hugo taps into this common ground. Most obviously, the 'trois têtes dans un bonnet' (xv. 294) of the Fléchard children adopted by the 'bataillon du Bonnet-Rouge' foreshadow the three heads of government ruling from Paris, themselves compared with the three judges of the underworld in 'Minos, Éaque et Rhadamante' (II. 2. 1). Or, as Marat tells Danton and Robespierre: 'Nous sommes les trois têtes de Cerbère' (xv. 357), one of which, so they claim, speaks, one roars, and all three bite. The mythic dimensions of the revolutionary leaders—at least in their own minds—counterbalance the small lives of the 'trois enfants-Jésus' (xv. 476) held hostage in la Tourgue, who achieve a symbolic significance of their own. Through their extreme youth and exemplary innocence, the little Fléchards are juxtaposed with the sly and powerful potentates at the triple head of the government. So, even though Danton, Marat, and Robespierre play signal roles in the centre of Hugo's narrative, Georgette, René-Jean, and Gros-Alain occupy much more important roles in the novel as a whole, not just as the Bretons' hostages but also as emblems of the nation's future. We shall explore the children's role in greater detail in the following section.

The importance in *Quatrevingt-Treize* of the number three—a feature of *Notre-Dame de Paris* as well[57]—creates recurrent rhythms and patterns that help to structure the novel's internal geometry. Not unexpectedly, the text yields a shower of entities and phenomena, beyond the Fléchard children and the Parisian triumvirate, that bear triple identities. For instance, the crew on the *Claymore* has 'le triple fanatisme du navire, de l'épée et du roi' (xv. 295); the royalist leader bears three titles as 'le marquis de Lantenac, vicomte de Fontenay, prince en Bretagne' (xv. 315; see also 332); the *Convention nationale* is composed of 'la Montagne . . . la Gironde . . . la Plaine' (xv. 374); Michelle Fléchard instinctively gives the little buckwheat loaf she gets from a kind peasant woman to the 'trois petits enfant déguenillés et pieds nus' (xv. 450) she meets on her way to la Tourgue; Gauvain's dilemma presents itself as a dreadful crossroads where

[56] Guerlac's observation that, 'although Hugo is infamous for his antitheses, it is striking how often he provides them with an armature, a central structure which holds the opposites together while keeping them apart' ('Exorbitant Geometry', 867; see also Brombert, *Victor Hugo and the Visionary Novel*, 219–20, 224–5), in fact describes this metaphorical process.

[57] See *EN* 198.

the 'trois idées suprêmes de l'homme, l'humanité, la famille, la patrie' (xv. 488) confront each other; and the three judges that Cimourdain foresees making up the court martial for Lantenac (xv. 481) instead preside at Gauvain's trial (xv. 496)—a variation on the underworld magistrates ruling in Paris. But perhaps the most interesting three-sided figure is the 'objet triangulaire' (xv. 489), or 'triangle . . . en fer' (xv. 505), of the guillotine blade. Like the threat of capital punishment in *Le Dernier Jour d'un condamné*, this image hangs over the entire narrative—until it hangs over Gauvain at the end.

Hugo adds a host of more complicated triangular/triangulated figures as well, drawing on the ancient notion of the number three as a term that unites, resolves, or harmonizes opposites. Just as twinning interweaves antagonistic forces and characters, triangles in the text often consist of two different or separated units that are mediated by a third, thus bringing them into a relation of parity. From a spatial viewpoint, this spanning function involves filling a gap—an operation associated in *Les Misérables* with both Jean Valjean and metaphorical patterns.[58] We shall see such patterns emerge in *Quatrevingt-Treize* as well. To be sure, some geographical arrangements in the novel appear to echo each other. Thus, the position of the doomed *Claymore* 'entre l'écueil démon et la flotte fantôme' (xv. 309), Scylla and Charybdis, structurally repeats other configurations: for example, the Bretons caught 'entre deux feux' (xv. 463) in Dol; the threatened 'république entre deux feux' (xv. 322)—that of the continental armies, on the one hand, and of the Bretons and English, on the other; and Brittany strategically located between Paris and London—that is, between republican France and monarchist England. This paradigm reveals double dangers for the boat, the royalist rebels, the Republic, and the province, respectively—not unlike some unfortunate head trapped between the chopping block and the falling blade of the guillotine.

In particular, Brittany, we have noted, is of capital importance to the new French Republic because of its long coastline. Instead of protecting France's western flank, however, the Atlantic Ocean brings the British military through Lantenac's agency. The marquis undercuts the nation's defensive posture of leaning back against the sea because of his unique ties with England: 'un homme allait lui jeter le pont, un homme allait lui tendre la main . . . un homme allait crier: Angleterre, prends la France!' (xv. 486), Gauvain agonizes in his dilemma. One person suffices to bring the two separate nations into physical contact. But Lantenac is not the only intercessory agent. While he aims to 'ouvrir la porte à Pitt', Gauvain

[58] See *FT* 294–5.

inversely 'repousse Lantenac dans l'intérieur et les Anglais dans la mer' (xv. 401). In other words, he interposes himself between Lantenac and the English invaders.[59] In either filling gaps or standing between opposing forces, the two sworn enemies once again demonstrate their (familial and metaphorical) filiation.

At the same time, physical intervention by a person or object is sometimes the key to salvation. Because Tellmarch insists on defining himself simply as 'un pauvre'—neither 'dans la loi' nor 'hors la loi' (xv. 328)—rather than as a royalist or a republican, he generously extends assistance to both sides. 'Homme de la charité et du rêve',[60] he transcends political interests. First, he takes in the fugitive Lantenac, knowing him to be 'le seigneur' of the domain of which he himself is 'le mendiant' (xv. 327), a point of commonality in their twinning. Then he takes in the badly wounded Michelle Fléchard and nurses her back to life. The compassionate beggar's counterpart, then, is the *vivandière*, '[qui] verse à boire à tout le monde . . . Aux blancs comme aux bleus' (xv. 292), since death has equal claims on them all.

The pattern extends to the main characters in the narrative as well. Cimourdain throws himself between Gauvain and the murderous Vendean recruit in Dol, taking the saber blow meant for his spiritual 'son'. Lantenac ends up passing the Fléchard children from the burning library in la Tourgue to the Republican soldiers on the ladder below. The rescue ladder that he puts out of the window into the ravine constitutes 'une communication . . . établie entre la salle incendiée [de la bibliothèque] et la terre' (xv. 479); it connects the hell of the fire above with the heaven of the untouched forest floor. For James Hamilton, 'mythically, the ladder not only rejoins family members [restoring the three children to Mother Fléchard] and a divided self [reconnecting Lantenac with the feeling part of himself, the anima], it restores universal order by reconciling the opposites of air and earth, fire and water/milk'.[61] Through its deployment,

[59] In Dol, Gauvain employs the opposite strategy, trapping the 5,000 Vendean fighters between 1,200 revolutionary soldiers and a small band composed of himself and nineteen other recruits, who surprise and rout the enemy with the illusion of a large charging force from the rear (xv. 409–10). Cf. Guerlac's comment that 'this ambush from behind repeats the structure of surprise attack from within, established in the cannon episode' (*The Impersonal Sublime*, 25)—as we have seen, a typically Hugolian technique of self-similar patterns. Whereas Grant considers that 'Gauvain never descends into any hell' (*The Perilous Quest*, 237) in the novel, I agree with Claudie Bernard's argument that, 'pour remédier à l'écrasement des siens [à Dol], Gauvain n'hésite pas à descendre dans "l'enfer", condition d'une remontée triomphante' (*Le Chouan romanesque: Balzac, Barbey d'Aurevilly, Hugo* (Paris: Presses Universitaires de France, 1989), 176).

[60] Peyrache-Leborgne, 'Roman historique', 60.

[61] James Hamilton, 'Terrorizing the "Feminine"', 207.

Michelle Fléchard, who awaits 'au pied de l'échelle' in the ravine, is 'jetée sans transition de l'enfer au paradis' (xv. 479), mentally ascending along the vertical axis of the salvation offered to her hostage children. The means of 'communication' along which Lantenac physically descends after the children's rescue elevates him symbolically and, in so doing, fosters a sublime moment for the mother as well, as the two metaphorically switch places with each other on the top and the bottom of the ladder. When Gauvain subsequently gives his cape to Lantenac so the latter can leave his prison cell unchallenged, a similar exchange occurs. As the young captain explains at his court martial, by means of his coat '[Lantenac] est sorti à ma place et je suis restée à la sienne' (xv. 496): the humble vestment operated the metaphorical substitution of one man for the other.

The many resonances between Lantenac's and Gauvain's characters as both twinned and intermediary agents suggest that their pairing, along with those of Gauvain and Cimourdain and of Cimourdain and Lantenac, is part of a more complicated geometrical figure. Since each is connected to the other two, all three are triangulated, a technique used in *L'Homme qui rit* as well. Rosa formulates the relationship somewhat differently—'Chaque personnage est donc le terme de deux couples dont chacun est contradictoire et qui restent entre eux antithétiques'[62]—while yet conserving the essentially triangular structure. This relationship can be seen, for instance, in the reflection that Cimourdain's 'destin avait cela d'étrange qu'il était entre deux Gauvain, l'un dont il voulait la mort, l'autre dont il voulait la vie' (xv. 453). The priest thus constitutes one side of a triangle of which Gauvain and Lantenac constitute the other two. Connected to the marquis by his penchant for rules and dogma, Cimourdain shares as well in Gauvain's republican idealism. The first intersection is oriented towards the authoritarian past, principally represented by Lantenac; the second towards the democratic future, principally represented by Gauvain. But the three little Fléchards also enter into this configuration through their 'bégaiement', since 'le berceau a un Hier de même que la tombe a un Demain; ce demain et cet Hier amalgament dans ce gazouillement obscur leur double inconnu' (xv. 435). The point of contact between Yesterday and Tomorrow, the children mediate history through their rapturous sense of the present—a sense expressed not only in their 'babbling' but also in their wondrous exploration of the library and its treasures.

They join with Lantenac in mediating Gauvain's perception of his mission, leading to his fateful decision to free the marquis. The young

[62] Rosa, 'Présentation', 247; see also 249–5, and Roman, *Victor Hugo et le roman philosophique*, 564–5.

hero confesses at his military trial that 'une bonne action, vue de trop près, m'a caché cent actions criminelles; d'un côté un vieillard, de l'autre des enfants, tout cela s'est mis entre moi et le devoir' (xv. 497). Accepting responsibility for the eclipse of his duty because of the children's rescue by his great-uncle, Gauvain is ready to die. Still, one might well wonder if he regrets his action—that is, if he truly renounces his behaviour, or if instead he assumes it as a badge of honour. Does Lantenac's single salvific deed outweigh, for Gauvain, his many criminal deeds? If so, the act of saving children must in and of itself carry special sociopolitical resonances. The following section explores the crucial role of the little Fléchards in marrying historical refiguration and metaphorical redescription in the text.

SUBLIME DISCOURSES

As we have seen, the reconciliations in *Quatrevingt-Treize* of antitheses on yet another plane subtly undermine the novel's dominant images of *sparagmos* associated with civil war. A battery of strategies counters the portrayal of centrifugal, divisive forces with more subtle centripetal conjunctions between them. Through metaphorical redescription, Hugo weaves analogical relations between the various antithetical poles in his text, which end up resembling each other as much as they at first seemed to differ. Along with his paired or triangulated locales and characters, more abstract gaps and disjunctions—generational, historical, and ideological—resolve themselves in striking ways. To illuminate these connections, we shall examine the parental and filial bonds among the different generations in the story and their relation to an implicit ethical and political hierarchy. We shall also elucidate how nature models alternative realities.

From the Real to the Ideal

If we consider the characters in the narrative by age, for example, we see four living generations—an unusual number. According to Ricoeur, historians use the 'succession of generations' to create a 'network of contemporaries, predecessors, and successors' (*TN* iii. 109), and Hugo has envisioned such a network. Lantenac, the great-uncle, is the oldest character in the novel, followed by Cimourdain, Gauvain's father-figure, then by the thirty-year-old Gauvain (Marat, Danton, and Robespierre are also in their thirties), and finally by the three little Fléchards. The most dramatic tension between the different age groups is doubtless that between the children and Lantenac, who takes them as hostages, uses them as pawns in his showdown with the Revolutionary Army, and orders them sacrificed to the royalist cause in the ensuing inferno in la Tourgue. A stereotypical kindly ancestor he is not. At the opposite end of the spectrum, the children's mother is, not surprisingly, maternal love incarnate: 'cette mère, c'était la maternité; tout ce qui résume l'humanité est surhumain' (xv. 475). The intensity of Michelle Fléchard's parental instincts elevates her to mythic status. Yet, as our analysis has shown, Cimourdain is equally devoted to his protégé, Gauvain: 'Cimourdain était le Pygmalion d'une âme. Un esprit peut avoir un enfant. Cet élève, cet enfant, cet orphelin, était le seul être qu'il aimât sur la terre' (xv. 350; see also 430, 453, 459). The implication is that, like Michelle Fléchard, he would do whatever was necessary to preserve his 'progeny'.

Radoub, too, is parentally dedicated to saving the battalion's adopted children. When he begs Gauvain to let his troops lead the forces attacking la Tourgue—'Et puis, voyez-vous, mon commandant, dans cette tour, il y a nos mômes. Nous avons là nos enfants, les enfants du bataillon, nos trois enfants... Et voici ce que dit le bataillon: nous voulons que les mômes soient sauvés, ou être tous tués' (xv. 456)—he and his men exhibit the same fervour as the biological mother. Feelings this strong run counter to the divisive forces in the text, reconstituting fractured biological families with families of choice. Lantenac does not hesitate to try to kill his only 'héritier' (xv. 404), and so to destroy the last (metonymic) link between the Gauvain generations. Gauvain, along with Radoub, transcends the lack of shared relations to think of others as part of a larger human kinship. He explains his reputation for clemency to Cimourdain as a form of principle: 'Je ne fais pas la guerre aux femmes... Je ne fais pas la guerre aux vieillards... Je ne fais pas la guerre aux enfants' (xv. 417). If soldiers are legitimate targets, civilians are to be spared, even those complicit in rebellion. Capturing his relations with Michelle Fléchard, Lantenac, and the Fléchard children, respectively, in a *mise en abyme* of Hugo's narrative, Gauvain intends not to defend ideas, as would an 'homme politique' (xv. 417), but the people who are often sacrificed to those very abstractions.

His links with other generations are again evident in his concerns about the library in la Tourgue: 'il y avait les archives de la famille... brûler ces archives, c'était attaquer ses pères... Peut-être son propre berceau, à lui Gauvain, était-il dans quelque coin du grenier de la bibliothèque' (xv. 430). Not only is he loath to 'attack his (fore)fathers', however symbolically; he also reveals an affiliation with the little Fléchards, who are barely out of the 'cradle' themselves. As Victor Brombert rightly asserts, the library is 'a sacred repository of the past, as well as a transmitter of a spiritual legacy affecting the future'.[63] That Georgette soon awakens in her 'berceau' (xv. 435) recalls the bed that Gauvain once occupied and suggests that she is, by extension, his sibling (or daughter) in the human family.

In this way, the establishment of generational bonds in *Quatrevingt-Treize* extends beyond the realm of character development to embrace ideological issues as well. When Cimourdain asks Gauvain in the dénouement to whom he would entrust a child in his ideal world, the young man replies: 'D'abord au père qui l'engendre, puis à la mère qui l'enfante, puis au maître qui l'élève, puis à la cité qui le virilise, puis à la patrie qui est la mère suprême, puis à l'humanité qui est la grande aïeule . . . Chacun de ces degrés . . . est un des échelons de l'échelle qui monte à Dieu' (xv. 503). In an astonishing *tour de force*, Hugo recapitulates much of the novel in Gauvain's vision of human relations in the as-yet-unrealized Republic, including the vertical axis and connecting function of the ladder featured in the climactic scene at la Tourgue. Although biological fathers are absent in the text (except in ancillary tales), Michelle Fléchard, Cimourdain, and Paris fulfil the functions of *mère*, *maître*, and *cité*, respectively. Moreover, the point about the supreme motherhood of the *patrie* has already been made by Cimourdain, in his exhortation to the rebels in the tower to surrender, when he tells them: 'Oui, vous êtes mes frères . . . D'ailleurs, est-ce que nous n'avons pas tous la même mère, la patrie?' (xv. 457). Despite the masculine etymology of *patrie*, the feminine gender of the term puts it, for Hugo, in the camp of 'motherland' rather than 'fatherland'—thus concretely grounding the abstract notion of France itself in the impassioned affections and fostering activities of Radoub, Cimourdain, and Michelle Fléchard. From this perspective, the young mother's allegiance to *pays* over *patrie* in the opening pages of the novel places her in the camp of those as yet unenlightened by the idea of a nurturing nation. Finally, the *grande aïeule* associated here with *humanité* most closely corresponds in the novel to the oldest character, Lantenac—perhaps the least humanitarian of its protagonists. And so another puzzle presents itself to the reader: how is the treacherous and intransigent royalist forebear transfigured, in the eyes of Gauvain, into a champion of humanity?

The answer, I think, lies in how ethical relations are depicted in the text. After all, the notion of a hierarchical arrangement, or 'échelle qui monte à Dieu', of people and institutions responsible for raising children evokes the same spatial configuration in the rescue of the Fléchard children from la Tourgue: 'vingt hommes accoururent . . . et en un clin

[63] Brombert, *Victor Hugo and the Visionary Novel*, 217.

d'œil ils s'étagèrent du haut en bas, adossés aux échelons... Cela fit sur l'échelle de bois une échelle humaine' (xv. 479). In each case, a human ladder that stretches upwards proves essential to securing the future of children. Hugo's development of moral hierarchies in his previous fiction, especially *Bug-Jargal*, *Notre-Dame de Paris*, and *Les Misérables*,[64] suggests that a similar ethical order, corresponding to different notions of justice, may be operating in *Quatrevingt-Treize* as well. Certainly, Lantenac's early role as judge and jury to Halmalo's hapless brother and the requisite trial scene of melodrama at the end[65] point more generally to the ways in which societies address issues of fairness, equity, and human rights. The various characters' responses to these issues at the heart of the conflict between royalists and republicans in the novel also help to define their relative moral standing.

One immediate observation is that there is no quintessential villain in *Quatrevingt-Treize* in the mould of a Musdoemon, a Biassou, a Thénardier, a Clubin, or a Barkilphedro—that is, a character who aims to dupe others for his own personal gain. Like the typical *trompeur trompé*, the Bretons exhibit cognitive limits, but they are not malicious for the sake of malice. Early on, the narrator explains their myopia as unenlightened 'conscience' (both consciousness and conscience) made unhealthy because of their relative isolation: 'le désert est parfois malsain à la conscience peu éclairée; la conscience peut être géante, cela fait Socrate et Jésus; elle peut être naine, cela fait Atrée et Judas. La conscience petite est vite reptile' (xv. 395). At the lowest rung of ethical awareness, one finds the reptilian, Satanic mindset of a traitor–Judas or a power-hungry fratricide–Atreus. While the text portrays the Vendean insurrection as sheer folly—'l'absurdité en rut'—and moral chaos—'sans calcul, sans stratégie, sans chef, sans responsabilité... essai inconscient de parricide' (xv. 397)—it insists on the peasants' basic selflessness. If their cause is 'se suicidant pour des absents, dévouée à l'égoïsme' (xv. 397), the egotists are the largely absent nobles glad to have others fight in their stead. Because of the Bretons' intense loyalty, the struggle of 'l'idée locale contre l'idée universelle', of 'paysans contre patriotes' (xv. 395), is not merely egocentric. Peasants with long-standing grievances against church and state alike are willing to forgive all and to die 'pour le seigneur, le curé et le roi!' (xv. 292). Although they seem both credulous and short-sighted from one perspective, their devotion and self-sacrifice make them worthy of respect—and perhaps honour—from another.

[64] See *EN* 64–97, 172–7, 181–4, and *FT* 16–186.

[65] See Brooks, *The Melodramatic Imagination*, 31–2, 45.

The same can also be said of Lantenac's battle for power against the revolutionaries. For this author of civil strife does not doubt, until the very end of Hugo's novel, that he is its hero. His strict moral code, like Javert's, does not recognize the validity of any ethos outside established law and order. The problem is that the system to which he cleaves was abolished by the Revolution and no longer legally exists. The conventional mentality, most recently skewered in *L'Homme qui rit*, assumes that whatever is, is right. Lantenac can be considered ultra-conventional, since he thinks that whatever was, was right. As he describes himself to Gauvain: 'ça croit en Dieu, ça croit à la tradition, ça croit à la famille, ça croit à ses aïeux, ça croit à l'exemple de son père, à la fidélité, à la loyauté, au devoir envers son prince, au respect des vieilles lois, à la vertu, à la justice; et ça vous ferait fusiller avec plaisir' (xv. 491). He genuinely believes that he has returned to Brittany 'pour faire le bien' (xv. 330)—a claim that temporarily reassures Tellmarch—and that it is the revolutionaries, not he and his supporters, who are betraying France. Throughout Part I of *Quatrevingt-Treize*, others admire the marquis's sense of virtue and justice: he is no common 'hors la loi' (xv. 326, 328, 362). Even Halmalo, who wants to avenge his brother's death by killing Lantenac, ends by accepting that the noble's value system is superior to his own. Without the reader's privileged knowledge that history did not vindicate those values, one would have to await the brutal conclusion of 'En Mer', with the massacre he leads at the Herbe-en-Pail farm, to realize that Lantenac could not possibly be the principal hero of Hugo's story.[66]

Indeed, until the battle at la Tourgue, it is hard to conceive that he is a hero at all. Normally read as occupying the lowest rung of Hugo's hierarchy of protagonists, Lantenac is known to the locals to be 'sans miséricorde' (xv. 405), and he gives ample proof of his ruthlessness when he has his soldiers shoot the *vivandière* and Michelle Fléchard and take the three children hostage; or when he tries to kill his great-nephew in Dol; or when he implicitly approves of l'Imânus' plan to set the library on fire with the children inside should they fail to hold back the revolutionary soldiers.[67] And yet, compared to the twisted l'Imânus—'le barbare' among

[66] I refer here to the modern reader, since, according to Hooker, the impact of *QVT* in England in the nineteenth century took quite a different turn: 'Hugo attempted to make the Republicans Cimourdain and Gauvain his heroes, yet Lantenac, their enemy, became the English hero of the book, and in spite of this reversal the English greatly enjoyed the performance as a whole' (*The Fortunes of Victor Hugo in England*, 192).

[67] The marquis projects, as Roman notes, 'l'image du Dieu de l'Ancien Testament, celui de la faute et de la vengeance' (*Victor Hugo et le roman philosophique*, 442). Lantenac sees himself 'on God's side fighting a holy war against Satanic revolution', in Grant's view; but, because of his order to shoot a mother, he has committed a sin on the order of the

'les sauvages' (xv. 405)—Lantenac seems almost civilized; compared to 'les absents' who let peasants defend their aristocratic privileges, he is supremely courageous. He also exhibits considerable 'générosité' (xv. 465) by allowing his wounded men to escape from la Tourgue before he takes his turn. Though ferocious to his enemies, Lantenac inspires his band of rebels in the siege of the tower: 'Le marquis, infatigable, robuste comme un jeune homme, soulevant des poutres, portant des pierres, donnait l'exemple, mettait la main à la besogne, commandait, aidait, fraternisait, riait avec ce clan féroce, toujours le seigneur pourtant, haut, familier, élégant, farouche' (xv. 433). Cast from the same physical pattern as the vigorous Jean Valjean, who carries Marius, unconscious, through the Paris sewers at the age of sixty-three, Lantenac shows his 'fraternal' side as well. But, whereas the sublime ex-convict embodies above all a metaphorical principle, the marquis has, like Javert, a more metonymical function.[68] He not only believes in the 'exemple' (xv. 491) of his father; he also supplies an 'exemple' for others to follow, as the peasant crew's 'guide et maître' (xv. 433) who points the way and imposes his will, and as 'L'Ancêtre' (III. 7. 1) who has a living lineage in Gauvain.

Equally inflexible and ferocious, Cimourdain nonetheless adheres to a different set of rules and principles than Lantenac—not to maintain the status quo for a privileged few but to construct a viable republic for all citizens. In his view, the Revolution is 'sans pitié pour [le vieux monde]' (xv. 418), just as the royalists are for the new one. The priest aims to destroy the past; the noble, to destroy the present. In the book (II. 1) and chapter (II. 1. 2) 'Cimourdain', the reader learns that Gauvain's former tutor is one of those men 'qui ont en eux une voix, et qui l'écoutent' (xv. 417; see also xv. 500). He is a man of high, though rigid, conscience. As such, he is, like Lantenac, capable of being 'le plus fraternel des hommes' (xv. 417), tending to the wounded, caring for the sick, moved by barefoot children, giving all he has to the poor. He is also known as '"le féroce"' (xv. 417; see also 453) in the exercise of his duty—a term previously associated with the marquis (xv. 310, 363). The narrator stresses the consequences of Cimourdain's austere behaviour: 'Les sévères sont des infortunés; qui voit leurs actes les condamne, qui verrait leur conscience les absoudrait peut-être' (xv. 429). By his terrible acts, Cimourdain parallels Lantenac, while his selfless motives, in contrast with those of the marquis, exculpate him.

Still, the man is not infallible. Along with Javert, Cimourdain believes that one must, at all costs, carry out the letter of the law, crying 'Force à la

comprachicos' 'sin against a child' in *HQR* and 'will have to expiate his crime' (*The Perilous Quest*, 228).

[68] See *FT* 169–73, 100–2.

loi!' (xv. 508) when Gauvain's troops protest their leader's death sentence. He also shares the policeman's desire for absolute certitude, replacing 'la raison par la logique' (xv. 347). David Denby goes so far as to see in the priest 'a kind of Stalinist *avant la lettre*',[69] while Victor Brombert remarks on his 'incorruptible "commissar" mentality'.[70] In *Les Misérables*, logic implies the geometric space of straight lines and symmetry;[71] the same is true in *Quatrevingt-Treize* as well: 'En révolution rien de redoutable comme la ligne droite. Cimourdain allait devant lui, fatal' (xv. 347). Of course, his rectilinear certitude makes him fatal to others rather than to himself. He fits right in, then, with the revolutionary leadership in Paris, ensconced in a hall in the Tuileries: 'Tout cet ensemble était violent, sauvage, régulier. Le correct dans le farouche; c'est un peu toute la révolution . . . Les bâtisseurs de ce temps-là prenaient le symétrique pour le beau' (xv. 371). The architecture of the Convention nationale reflects its logical but savage approach to imposing a new social order.[72]

That said, Cimourdain is not simply a composite of Gauvain, Lantenac, and Javert. He also resembles Claude Frollo, the ascetic archdeacon in *Notre-Dame de Paris*, who has an adopted son (Quasimodo), is allied with symmetry and linearity, and inexorably pursues his own ends.[73] Cimourdain's character likewise contains some echoes of Enjolras in *Les Misérables*, through his uncompromising virtue and commitment to the republican cause: 'Cimourdain était sublime; mais sublime dans l'isolement, dans l'escarpement, dans la lividité inhospitalière; sublime dans un entourage de précipices. Les hautes montagnes ont cette virginité sinistre' (xv. 349). The vertical axis, the sublime attitude, the virginal passion—all recall imagery associated with the heroic Enjolras.[74] At the same time, terms such as 'inhospitalière', 'précipices', and 'sinistre'—terms that pertain neither to Enjolras nor to Javert—recycle elements of the equally chilly Claude Frollo and of Duchess Josiane in *L'Homme qui rit*. In sum, the priestly personage of *Quatrevingt-Treize* constitutes a complex amalgam of

[69] Denby, 'Civil War, Revolution and Justice', 12.

[70] Brombert, *Victor Hugo and the Visionary Novel*, 214.

[71] See *FT* 95–100.

[72] O'Neil considers that this 'unstable' quality of the neoclassical edifice 'suggests repression', and hence 'a type of evil that threatened the First French Republic from its incipience. This Classical Terror is a psychic rigidity, an excessive reliance upon reason, a bloodthirstiness that runs counter to the Hugolian notion of the true movement of history' ('Classical Terror/Gothic Terror', 262, 264)—and that also characterizes Cimourdain. Saint-Amand comments on the geometrical lines of the Tuileries housing the Convention, too, noting that 'as a group and as passions, [the Convention] tears apart the very place that shelters it . . . The Convention is antithetical to measured action, it is stormy, an active reservoir of antagonisms' ('Hot Terror', 68). See also Nunley, '(En)gendering Terror', 42.

[73] See *EN* 180–4.

[74] See *FT* 133–4, 249.

other Hugo characters with either authoritarian tendencies (Frollo, Javert, Josiane, Lantenac) or republican aspirations (Enjolras, Gauvain). Within the novel, he occupies the pivotal point between Lantenac's backward orientation and Gauvain's utopian agenda, between ultra-conventionality and radical social inventiveness.

In 'Les deux pôles du vrai' (III. 2. 7), the contrast between Gauvain's and Cimourdain's conceptions of their mission appears as a clash of principles, one of which seems destined to triumph in Brittany: 'deux formes de la république étaient en présence, la république de la terreur et la république de la clémence, l'une voulant vaincre par la rigueur et l'autre par la douceur. Laquelle prévaudrait?' (xv. 416). Cimourdain aims to impose the full force of the decrees he carries from Paris—that is, to apply them universally; Gauvain prefers to vanquish through persuasion, by demonstrating through pity and compassion the moral superiority of republicanism. Responding to the priest's contention that the Revolution will one day justify the Reign of Terror, Gauvain argues: 'Liberté, Egalité, Fraternité, ce sont des dogmes de paix et d'harmonie. Pourquoi leur donner un aspect effrayant? Que voulons-nous? conquérir les peuples à la république universelle... Pas plus que les oiseaux, les peuples ne sont attirés par l'épouvantail' (xv. 419). The ability to put himself, empathetically, in the place of others—a trait particular to Jean Valjean as well[75]—stokes Gauvain's clemency and testifies to his powerful imagination. By juxtaposing his point of view with Cimourdain's, Hugo enables the reader to distinguish between the two higher levels of ethical reasoning beyond Lantenac's, just as he illuminates the moral hierarchy represented by Javert, Enjolras, and Jean Valjean in *Les Misérables*.[76]

This process of differentiation is heightened in the dénouement when Cimourdain visits Gauvain in the dungeon of la Tourgue the night before the young man's execution. Acknowledging that he owes the moulding of his soul to his old tutor, Gauvain declares: 'J'étais né noué. Les préjugés sont des ligatures, vous m'avez ôté ces bandelettes, vous avez remis ma croissance en liberté, et de ce qui n'était déjà plus qu'une momie, vous avez refait un enfant. Dans l'avorton probable vous avez mis une conscience. Sans vous, j'aurais grandi petit. J'existe par vous' (xv. 501). The knots, ligatures, and mummy wrappings all convey the metonymical

[75] See *FT* 155–6.

[76] While James Hamilton considers 'the best educated and most conscious [characters in *QVT*], Cimourdain and Lantenac' to be 'evil' ('Terrorizing the "Feminine"', 207), I see them both as defending moral values that are less inclusive and progressive than Gauvain's. Cf. Roman's argument that all three characters, acting by the light of their individual conscience, 'se révèlent... capables d'agir contre leur intérêt' (*Victor Hugo et le roman philosophique*, 445).

attachments to Gauvain's noble past that Cimourdain had severed by instilling a conscience free of class prejudice.

The references to Gauvain's childhood are crucial here because they connect him implicitly to the little Fléchards, with all their unrealized potential. To grow up should not mean to shrink—a theme that reappears at several junctures in the text. Indeed, Lantenac accuses Gauvain of taking the inverse path to adulthood laid out by Cimourdain. 'En grandissant, vous avez trouvé moyen de vous rapetisser,' the noble charges his republican heir, who has strayed from 'l'honnêteté' (xv. 493) by destroying the past. To be 'des hommes nouveaux' is thus, for Lantenac, to become 'petits' (xv. 494). But Gauvain has already fought this battle with his great-uncle in his moral dilemma:

> Répondre à un acte généreux par un acte sauvage!
> Donnez ce dessous à la révolution!
> Quel rapetissement pour la république!
> ... Quoi! Ne pas lutter de magnanimité! Se résigner à cette défaite, étant les plus forts ... et de faire dire qu'il y a, du côté de la monarchie, ceux qui sauvent les enfants, et du côté de la république, ceux qui tuent les vieillards! (xv. 485)

The notions of thriving and shrivelling applied both to Gauvain's education and to the reputation of the new Republic are again linked to the fate of children. How might they best be elevated to the stature of republican citizens?

In their final encounter, Gauvain and Cimourdain debate the nature of the republic for which they both strive, thereby revealing important points of contention. Their divergent perspectives also replay the 'rebound-effect of the future on the past' observed in *L'Homme qui rit*, enabling the reader to see all of history, including the present, as a work-in-the-making: 'Knowing that people of the past formulated expectations, predictions, desires, fears and projects is to fracture historical determinism by retrospectively reintroducing contingency into history' (*MHF* 381, 382). For the former priest, 'la république de l'absolu' follows the crisp outlines of a mathematical model, aiming for 'le définitif, c'est-à-dire le droit et le devoir parallèles, l'impôt proportionnel et progressif... le nivellement, aucune déviation, et, au-dessus de tout, cette ligne droite, la loi' (xv. 502). Returning to the vocabulary of geometric space (*parallèles, proportionnel, ligne droite*), the text underscores Cimourdain's rule-bound concept of fair government. The social harmony he seeks is, he maintains, that of algebra, and he dreams of 'l'homme fait par Euclide' (xv. 502). Such fearful symmetries might well, as Mary Anne O'Neil suggests, lead to 'a new age of repression'.[77]

[77] O'Neil, 'Classical Terror/Gothic Terror', 271.

Gauvain, on the contrary, opposes the urge to 'mettre tout en équilibre', since there would be no place in such a system for 'le dévouement, le sacrifice, l'abnégation, l'entrelacement magnanime des bienveillances, l'amour' (xv. 502). Here, the word 'entrelacement' suggests a kind of web in which human relations are intertwined, rather than programmed, through mutual commitment and self-sacrifice. That man should, for Gauvain, be 'fait par Homère' (xv. 502) completes the contrast between his poetic, Romantic ideal and the geometric, neoclassical ideal espoused by Cimourdain—a relation previously elaborated in both *Notre-Dame de Paris* and *Les Misérables*.[78] Gauvain explains to his adoptive father: 'Au-dessus de la balance, il y a la lyre. Votre république dose, mesure et règle l'homme; la mienne l'emporte en plein azur; c'est la différence entre un théorème et un aigle' (xv. 502). Cimourdain is the only major character in the novel not to undergo a life-changing 'transfiguration'. Like the Revolution he incarnates, he lacks for Hugo 'de l'imagination politique et morale—poétique—qui inventerait la résolution sans terreur des servitudes anciennes'.[79] Geometric thinking helps humanity create an orderly, but static social environment; poetic thinking enables people to mount the vertical axis of imaginary vision, to capture through a transcendent leap (*aigle, l'emporte en plein azur*) a sense of the dynamic whole in which all are harmoniously interwoven.[80] Higher than Cimourdain's *summum bonum* of 'la justice', which is based on '[le] droit strict', the governing principle in Gauvain's 'république de l'idéal' is 'l'équité' (xv. 502). The tension is therefore not so much between 'cold rationality and humanitarian sentiment',[81] masculine and feminine principles, but between the two characters' equal passion for competing notions of human potential.[82]

As their discussion evolves, Gauvain proceeds ever deeper into his visionary state, seeing a world not just where the poor are helped, but where poverty is eliminated altogether, where nature is harnessed for food and energy for all, where men and women serve each other in a relation of

[78] See *EN* 196–206, and *FT* 191–3, 259–63, 321.

[79] Campion, 'Raison de la littérature', 112; see also Rosa, 'Présentation', 258–9.

[80] According to Brombert, Gauvain's retrieval of poetry through the lyre also 'retrieves past culture... through a reference to the Homeric epic. His prison vision harmonizes future and past, thus canceling the temporal antagonism preached by Revolutionary doctrinaires' (*Victor Hugo and the Visionary Novel*, 223). I would stress here the bridging function of metaphorical imagination in forging this relation of concord between past and future.

[81] James Hamilton, 'Terrorizing the "Feminine"', 209.

[82] Or, as Ferguson aptly observes, 'the debate that makes *Quatrevingt-treize* a novel of and for the 1870s, is not the victory of the republic, which is assured, but the nature, and hence the course, of that republic... the legitimacy of the Third Republic lies in its rejection of Cimourdain's republic of the sword and in its acceptance of Gauvain's republic of the spirit' ('*Quatrevingt-treize*', 76–7).

'égalité' (xv. 503). Rather than look to the past or the present, one must, he believes, follow the dictum: 'Toujours en avant... Regardons toujours du côté de l'aurore, de l'éclosion, de la naissance' (xv. 503). The more Gauvain speaks like a prophet, the more Cimourdain listens intently: 'Les rôles étaient intervertis, et maintenant il semblait que c'était l'élève qui était le maître' (xv. 504). The reversal of roles along the vertical plane not only signals Gauvain's ethical ascendency; it also refers to the issue of education. In the light of the imperative to focus on 'dawn', 'hatching', and 'birth', the larger question of the future of France's children is obviously back in play. Gauvain tells Cimourdain about the difference between their two utopias, 'Vous voulez la caserne obligatoire, moi, je veux l'école. Vous rêvez l'homme soldat, je rêve l'homme citoyen. Vous le voulez terrible, je le veux pensif. Vous fondez une république de glaives, je fonde... Je fonderais une république d'esprits' (xv. 504). The educational reform instituted in the wake of the 1848 Revolution is presented from the standpoint of the past, as a lost utopian dream of the First Republic. By schooling all of France's children, including those of peasants like Michelle Fléchard, the nation will be able to continue to 'move forward' through the well-formed minds of its citizenry. Gauvain's faith in universal education—one of Hugo's most fervent causes[83]—reminds the reader that the ability to enjoy novels such as this one was not always a given. But, under the Republic, some espoused literacy and individual reflection as basic human rights, rights for which they were willing to fight and die. In a poignant shift in tenses, Gauvain first claims that he 'is founding' a 'republic of minds'. Then he remembers that he is about to be executed and indicates that he 'would found' one—if he could.

Perhaps Gauvain's character is especially anointed to carry this message because of its curiously child-like nature. When we first encounter the young captain, we learn that he has 'une encolure d'Hercule, l'œil sérieux d'un prophète et le rire d'un enfant' (xv. 403). The first is manifested by his heroics in battle; the second in his political vision; the third, more indirectly, in the scene in the library with the small hostages: 'Le rire de Georgette fit rire René-Jean, et le rire de René-Jean fit rire Gros-Alain' (xv. 437). Unlike Danton's roaring laughter and Marat's ironic smile in 'A Paris' (Robespierre, it turns out, is capable of neither expression), the children's laugher is pure, infectious joy. Meandering among the books that Gauvain once read at Cimourdain's knee, they seem to follow dreams of their own: 'Georgette [n'entendait pas ses frères], et les ondulations de sa voix semblaient moduler le bercement d'un rêve. Ses yeux grands

[83] See Rosa, 'Présentation', 239, 255.

ouverts regardaient en haut, et étaient divins; quel que soit le plafond ou la voûte qu'un enfant a au-dessus de sa tête, ce qui se reflète dans ses yeux, c'est le ciel' (xv. 436). Beneath the sentimentalized view of children and the suggestion that their young souls were recently in heaven, the passage develops links with Gauvain through terms like 'bercement' (which recalls his 'berceau'), 'rêve'/'yeux grands ouverts' (his visionary qualities), 'en haut' (his association with verticality), and 'divin' (his embrace of the 'haute loi divine de pardon, d'abnégation, de rédemption, de sacrifice' (xv. 485)). A similar lexical field appears as well in the dénouement, when Gauvain tells Cimourdain that he absolves the present moment, trusting in his conscience and in a higher power: 'Gauvain leva le doigt au-dessus de sa tête. Cimourdain suivit du regard la direction de ce doigt levé, et, à travers la voûte du cachot, il lui sembla voir le ciel étoilé' (xv. 504). The repetition of 'au-dessous de sa tête', 'voûte', and 'ciel' once again weaves subtle connections between Gauvain and the next generation.[84]

The library occasions additional parallels with Gauvain. When Gros-Alain unearths a dusty doll's cart in a corner, the narrator remarks that it was perhaps 'un des hochets avec lesquels avait joué Gauvain enfant' (xv. 439). Like the books and the cradle, the reminder of the soldier's own childhood highlights his alliance with the pure, unprejudiced perspective of the little Fléchards. This perspective is evidenced, for example, in the children's reaction to a woodlouse they spy creeping across the floor:

> Gros-Alain l'aperçut et cria:
> —Une bête.
> René-Jean accourut.
> Gros-Alain reprit:
> —Ça pique.
> —Ne lui fais pas de mal, dit René-Jean.
> Et tous deux se mirent à regarder ce passant. (xv. 437)

Through the use of short exchanges that are offset typographically, Hugo dramatizes the boys' reaction to the bug. In spite of their imminent delight in ripping up the Saint-Barthélemy manuscript, they display a startling respect for real life, even the lowliest of creatures. Such clemency is, we have seen, Gauvain's hallmark. In this way, the text suggests that a

[84] Eco reinforces this interpretation when he observes that 'the recurrent motif of the three children accompanies the tormented adventures of Gauvain, who in the name of kindness and mercy submits to the punishment he has brought on himself. Both motifs cast a ray of hope on a future that can only be ushered in through human sacrifice' ('Excess and History in Hugo's *Ninety-Three*', 276).

proper education would nurture those innate tendencies towards benevolence while curbing any urges towards wanton destruction or violence.[85]

At the same time, the expression '[ce] passant', used throughout *Les Misérables* to designate both Jean Valjean and the narrator,[86] carries special resonances in Hugo related not only to the transitory nature of life but also to the shifts involved in the process of transfiguration. The notion of transfiguration, already observed with regard to Lantenac and Gauvain alike as they surpass themselves to attain superhuman heroic status, finds a minor, comic echo in Georgette's efforts not to cry when she falls down. Told by René-Jean that she is too big to do so, she replies, 'J'ai grande'; the narrator then comments, 'Et sa grandeur la consola de sa chute' (xv. 439). Enacting in miniature the moral courage of the adult characters in the novel, the toddler demonstrates the consolatory power of achieving a higher state of being. As Lantenac descends the rescue ladder to certain death at the hands of his enemies after saving the children, 'il se fit autour de cet homme qui arrivait d'en haut un recul d'horreur sacré comme autour d'une vision . . . à chaque pas qu'il faisait vers ces hommes dont les prunelles effarées se fixaient sur lui dans les ténèbres, il semblait plus grand' (xv. 480).[87] The heroic stature of the marquis confers on him a quasi-divine aura (*horreur sacré, prunelles effarées*) and genuine greatness (*grand*), as opposed to his prior self-aggrandizement as lord and master of the region.

In his final encounter with Cimourdain, Gauvain expresses a similar goal of surpassing (one's) nature: 'Soyons la société humaine. Plus grande que la nature,' he declares. 'Si vous ajoutez quelque chose à la nature, vous serez nécessairement plus grand qu'elle; ajouter, c'est augmenter; augmenter, c'est grandir. La société, c'est la nature sublimée' (xv. 504). To grow up, to transcend one's instincts, to partake of a sublime/sublimated state—all are communicated by the notion of 'grandir' in Hugo's text, and all are implicated in the relations between the children, Gauvain, and Lantenac. Vital to understanding these relations is Gauvain's conception of 'la société humaine', one both human (by definition) and humane (through its institutions), in the wake of Lantenac's salvific gesture in

[85] The scene therefore serves as a variation on Gauvain's final dialogue with Cimourdain, which champions 'a republic based on education, not militarism' (Denby, 'Civil War, Revolution and Justice', 15).

[86] See *FT* 210, 271.

[87] The aggrandizing technique, which recalls the projection of Bug-Jargal's 'ombre colossal' (ii. 666) just before his kingly stature is revealed, highlights Hugo's visual imagination. One finds the same cinematic effect in André Malraux's *La Condition humaine* (1933), when Katow goes to his heroic death. When he approaches the headlight of the train where he will be burned alive, 'la silhouette de sa tête se perdait au plafond' (*La Condition humaine* (Paris: Gallimard, 1972), 252).

rescuing the Fléchard children. For, as the young hero claims, 'Lantenac transfiguré' (xv. 485) had to transfigure him as well, to alter his already nonconformist outlook about treating the enemy with mercy rather than revenge.

A rereading of the rescue scene and of Gauvain's subsequent musings casts new light on the question of causality. As noted earlier, Lantenac believes firmly in the metonymical idea of providing examples, which take the form not just of devoting his own energy and devotion in the service of a royalist ideal, but also of punishing those who, like Halmalo's brother, err in their own duty, or who are simply fighting on the other side. Thus, when Halmalo asks how he will know where to rejoin 'monseigneur', the marquis replies that he will be easy to find: 'Avant huit jours on parlera de moi, je ferai des exemples, je vengerai le roi et la religion' (xv. 322).[88] Lantenac's ethics of retribution and narrow focus on his anti-revolutionary agenda would seem to preclude being able to step back and see others from a non-political angle. Still, when he hears Michelle Fléchard's anguished pleas for help as he escapes from la Tourgue, he makes a radical leap into Gauvain's ideal nation by recognizing the innocence and humanity of his little peasant hostages and by rushing to save them. To do so is not only to risk his own life but, more significantly for the marquis, to abandon his political aims.

Lantenac's about-turn, his 'geste d'humanisation',[89] follows several movements. First, he is transfixed by Michelle Fléchard's cry, with its 'on ne sait quoi d'inarticulé et de déchirant' (xv. 475), upon perceiving her children in the flaming tower. The cry, we have seen, embodies the tearing and dismemberment of the French body politic, in which Lantenac is fully engaged.[90] But then the mother names her offspring—'Mais mes enfants

[88] The members of the Comité de salut public are similarly obsessed with punishing perceived traitors among the army leaders. 'Il faut des exemples' (xv. 355; see also 382), fumes Danton, after enumerating a long list of supposed offenders. And Cimourdain aims to behead Lantenac on the grounds of the ancestral home, 'afin que la demeure féodale vît tomber la tête de l'homme féodale, et que l'exemple fût mémorable' (xv. 453). The equal ferocity of the opposing sides is again manifest.

[89] Campion, 'Raison de la littérature', 110.

[90] 'The cry then, in all its phonic presence, is the voice of nature itself, nature—or maternity—as voice, an irreducible reality beyond which, Hugo would seem to be saying, one cannot go' (Jeffrey Mehlman, *Revolution and Repetition: Marx/Hugo/Balzac* (Berkeley and Los Angeles: University of California Press, 1977), 57). According to Aynesworth, Lantenac 'obeys the call of maternal instinct still more decisively than did Halmalo the voice of a man who spoke "comme le bon Dieu"' ('Anonymity, Identity, and Narrative Sovereignty', 205). Primal maternal instinct trumps the marquis's capacity for deceptive theatrics. I do not agree, however, with Aynesworth's discernment of an 'elliptical transference of conscience from the peasant to the aristocrat' ('Anonymity, Identity, and Narrative Sovereignty', 205), since Michelle Fléchard is plainly a creature of limited reflection and intellect. Rather, her anguish serves to awaken Lantenac's own conscience that till then had been

vont brûler! Ah! voilà une chose! Georgette! mes enfants! Gros-Alain, René-Jean! . . . Qui donc a mis mes enfants là!' (xv. 475)—rendering concrete what until then had been, for the noble, an abstract crime. For he was the one who had put the children in such terrible danger. The indirect accusation is soon reiterated, when Michelle Fléchard repeats each of the children's names and laments: 'Qu'est-ce qu'ils ont fait, ces innocents-là! moi on m'a fusillée, eux on les brûle! qui est-ce donc qui fait ces choses-là! . . . Vous voyez bien que je suis leur mère. Ce qui se passe dans ce temps-ci est abominable' (xv. 476). Although Lantenac had had her shot, the peasant woman now appears before him as a mythical figure, 'transfigurée en euménide . . . pren[ant] les proportions épiques du désespoir' (xv. 475). Her questions, punctuated as exclamations, accumulate, seeking to identify who would shoot a woman and burn her 'innocent' children. In effect, she humanizes the little hostages, thereby evacuating their symbolic value for Lantenac. His pawns are suddenly revealed as real children, with their own short—and potentially horrendous—history. He, too, understands that the events of 'this era' approach the unspeakable. As the children continue to sleep while the fire rages around them, the narrator declares that 'un tigre eût pleuré de voir ces roses dans cette fournaise et ces berceaux dans ce tombeau' (xv. 476). Beneath the vivid antithetical imagery and sentimentalized portrait of innocence in peril, we see that the 'tiger' is Lantenac himself—since the scary scenario of 'la mise en liberté du tigre' (xv. 487) later contemplated by Gauvain, a scenario even more deadly to the French ship of state than the 'entrée en liberté' (xv. 302) of the cannon/'tigre' (xv. 305) to the *Claymore*, occasions its own ethical storm.

Does Lantenac, then, cry before the wrenching spectacle that confronts him? The text again fails to relay his thoughts or feelings, but his miraculous appearance soon thereafter at the locked door to the library with the missing key and his dramatic plunge within, 'la tête haute' (xv. 477), suggests at the very least that he has found a higher good to pursue than returning the monarchy to power. When the toddler Georgette smiles at him, 'cette conscience si haute et si obscure eut l'éblouissement de l'innocence' (xv. 479), and his wet eyes witness at last to his emotion. Again, the text stresses the children's innocence and purity, communicated through a trusting smile. In an earlier description of Georgette and her brothers as they sleep following the 'massacre of Saint-Barthélemy', the narrator remarks that 'ils faisaient des songes de paradis qui se reflétaient sur leurs bouches en vagues sourires . . . ils étaient ceux que

slumbering under a multitude of dogma that justified the use of unconscionable means to royalist ends.

toutes les langues humaines appellent les faibles et les bénis, ils étaient les innocents vénérables' (xv. 442). They still inhabit a blissful utopia, as yet unspoiled by an awareness of the vicious factional tensions forging history around them.[91]

In principle, victory should follow 'la loi du plus fort', and Lantenac should simply sacrifice the peasant children to his political goals. But, as Gauvain later reflects, something utterly unexpected happens: 'la force des faibles était intervenue' (xv. 483). The three abandoned children, 'orphelins, seuls, bégayants, souriants', overwhelm all the calculations of 'l'antique férocité féodale', with its arrogant superiority complex, just by being so young: 'car celui qui n'a pas vécu encore n'a pas fait le mal, il est la justice, il est la vérité' (xv. 483–4). Those who are so inexperienced as to be free of evil personify what is just, fair, and true. With their 'songes de paradis'—dreams of a better world—the little Fléchards represent the nation's future—that is, the stakes for which both sides are at war.[92] Like the youngsters in Paris stumbling over *Ça ira*, 'ces petits enfants, c'était l'immense avenir' (xv. 344). As such, Lantenac now realizes, their lives must at all costs be preserved, no less by the royalists than by the revolutionaries. In the epic battle of moral values, 'cette toute-puissance, l'innocence' thus defeats 'l'énorme légion des crimes' (xv. 484) of those waging a merciless war. Along with Gilliatt doing battle with the 'legions' of natural forces arrayed against him on his atoll, Georgette, René-Jean, and Gros-Alain triumph over massive aggression by diverting it into another path altogether.

Gauvain considers Lantenac to have undergone a kind of conversion experience that turns his 'crimes' born of narrow self-interest into '[son] dévouement . . . son abnégation stoïque, son désintéressement superbe' (xv. 488)—marks in Hugo of ethical sublimity. Lantenac surpasses the historical moment by proving that 'au-dessus des royautés, au-dessus des révolutions, au-dessus des questions terrestres, il y a . . . la protection due aux faibles par les forts, le salut dû à ceux qui sont perdus par ceux qui sont sauvés, la paternité due à tous les enfants par tous les vieillards' (xv. 488). Recasting the thematics of parents and children that permeates his text,

[91] Peyrache-Leborgne maintains that Lantenac abandons the royalist cause because he is 'touché par cette incarnation de la Grâce—les enfants' ('Roman historique', 64)—whereas I see the mother's cry as also alerting him to their existence as flesh and blood. For Eco, the 'excessiveness [of their childish games] notifies us that . . . we are dealing not with an individual story but with the tragedy of an actant who may not have been redemptive but was at least benevolent: Innocence' ('Excess and History in Hugo's *Ninety-Three*', 292). My analysis demonstrates the redemptive side as well of the children's innocence, which, in converting Lantenac, echoes Gauvain's own salvific function.

[92] Cf. Brombert, *Victor Hugo and the Visionary Novel*, 208, and Roman, *Victor Hugo et le roman philosophique*, 437.

Hugo identifies a universal human law that transcends partisanship by countering the law of the jungle. The true 'force des faibles' is that they are, indeed, 'vénérables'—even more so than the elderly, who are duty-bound ('due . . . par tous les vieillards') to safeguard all members of the youngest generation as fervently as their own children. The use of religious vocabulary (*salut*, *perdus*, *sauvés*) recalls the notion of venerability while elevating all-embracing 'paternité' to a sacred imperative.

At this point, Lantenac finally comes into his own as a legitimate hero. Transcending his archaic concepts of honour and patriotism, which have led him into crimes against humanity, the marquis signals for Gauvain the genuine healing that comes when dogma gives way to a higher sense of right and wrong. 'Et l'on pouvait dire: Non, la guerre civile n'existe pas, la barbarie n'existe pas, la haine n'existe pas, le crime n'existe pas, les ténèbres n'existent pas; pour dissiper ces spectres, il suffit de cette aurore, l'enfance' (xv. 484), the young man observes. Although Lantenac had earlier rejected the idea of republican confraternity, he redeems himself both *paternally* and *humanly* when he recognizes that, in some way, the children in jeopardy are *his*. Like metaphor itself, recognition 'elevat[es] two impressions to the level of essence, without abolishing their difference' (*TN* ii. 149). In this case, the marquis perceives something of himself in the Other—and of the Other in himself. His revised sense of right and wrong entails a heightened sense of self, since recognition involves a self-reflective 'movement that carries self-esteem toward solicitude and solicitude toward justice' (*OA* 296). Suddenly, Gauvain can no longer take the man for his ethical inferior. Worse yet, Lantenac might in fact be his moral superior, having not only demonstrated Gauvain's hallmark 'pitié' (xv. 416) but also rejected his long-standing commitment to partisan aims.[93] If Gauvain fails to address the unexpected shift in hierarchy, 'l'homme des barbaries et des superstitions ouvrirait des ailes subites, et planerait, et regarderait ramper sous lui, dans de la fange et dans de la nuit, l'homme de l'idéal! Gauvain resterait à plat ventre dans la vieille ornière féroce, tandis que Lantenac irait dans le sublime courir les aventures!' (xv. 485). The risk is that the ethical sublime and grotesque will be permanently inverted, that Gauvain will prove unworthy of the ideals that impel him.

Lantenac's conversion before 'l'éblouissement de l'innocence' (xv. 479) thus constitutes for Gauvain an 'éblouissement . . . [de] la grande lueur éternelle' (xv. 483) that converts—or 'transfigures'—him in turn. Viewed

[93] My interpretation of Lantenac's character diverges from Roche's view that the marquis is not 'truly transfigured' because his decision to free the children 'does not in any way alter his system of beliefs or, consequently, his future actions in the war' (*Character and Meaning*, 98).

in the dazzling light of a universal value, Gauvain's use of warfare, that 'vieille ornière féroce', to engender a better world pales in comparison with Lantenac's renunciation of violence, however temporary. 'Lantenac s'était racheté de toutes ses barbaries par un acte de sacrifice. En se perdant matériellement il s'était sauvé moralement; il s'était refait innocent' (xv. 488) in his great-nephew's eyes. He has assumed the sacred quality of the children he rescued.[94] As a result, Gauvain is diverted from realizing his own political objectives that require him to execute Lantenac in order to save the Republic. Now that 'Lantenac venait de rentrer dans l'humanité, Gauvain allait, lui, rentrer dans la famille' (xv. 486) by rejecting the fratricide of civil war. Neither, in other words, is still *engagé* in the political moment. Rather, they have both vaulted to another mode of thinking, one where the welfare of individuals supersedes the will to establish a specific form of government. In this way, Hugo uses the familial relationship between the two characters to 'poin[t] to the larger importance of human, fraternal connection and to its supremacy to collective political and historical action'.[95] The cessation of hostilities in the name of royalism or republicanism, on the other hand, means that the once crucial issue of an English invasion evaporates, in the end, for each heroic character. The juxtaposition of English and French is reconciled in their common foundation in 'l'humanité'.

Gauvain's 'confession' to the military tribunal must therefore be read ironically, since he has done no less than follow the metonymical example of his now genuinely noble forebear by choosing people over politics. He, too, has forgotten wrongs to avenge and governments to support because his 'république de l'idéal' depends more on the moral autonomy of individuals than on legal prescriptions, like Cimourdain's 'république de l'absolu' (xv. 502). He has come full circle, granting clemency to his familiar adversary, Lantenac, as he once did to strangers. The generational and ideological gap between them resolves itself through the notion of 'humanity' that transcends any particular historical point in time. Sandy Petrey has amply shown that the pastoral discourse in the text gestures towards the timeless realm of nature, where historical tensions yield to higher harmonies.[96] But, just as 'historical time . . . mediates between lived time and cosmic time', Hugo's historical fiction uses 'procedures of connection . . . that assure the reinscription of [phenomenological existence] on [the rhythms of the natural universe]' (*TN* iii. 99; see also

[94] I thus concur with Petrey that the 'novel is in fact dominated by innocence' (*History in the Text*, 50).

[95] Roche, *Character and Meaning*, 158.

[96] See esp. Petrey, *History in the Text*, 35–50.

109).[97] Cyclical time stands not so much in opposition to linear or historical time as in metaphorical relation—one of Hugo's 'procedures of connection'—as one strategy of renewing the idea of what is humanly possible.

The terms that describe this natural backdrop to the book's dramatic action therefore point equally to the human realm, especially to the little Fléchards and their semi-utopian 'songes de paradis' (xv. 442). From this perspective, Georgette's dazzling smile for Lantenac both recalls Gauvain's bedazzlement by 'la force des faibles' (xv. 483) and announces 'l'éblouissement éternel' (xv. 507) of nature itself. That the three small hostages hear in the 'confusion de bruits farouches' of the roaring battle around them 'une sorte d'harmonie' (xv. 438) not only indicates their closeness to 'l'harmonie qui se dégage de la douceur colossale des choses' in the wild Breton countryside, where 'tout aimait tout' (xv. 442). It also prepares the reader for the subtext of the execution scene at the end, where Gauvain dies on a splendid spring day, with its 'gamme harmonieuse' of greenery and 'groupes d'arbres fraternels' (xv. 507) that give lessons in peace and concord to warring humans. Such imagery gives new meaning to Gauvain's argument that society is 'la nature sublimée' (xv. 504). Nor are we far here from Hugo's description of the Channel Islands in the preface to *Les Travailleurs de la mer* or the evocation in 'Foliis ac frondibus' (*MIS* IV. 3. 3) of Cosette's fecund, harmonious, confraternal garden on the Rue Plumet.[98] Tellingly, the revolutionary leader's 'doux sourire' (xv. 501) as he evokes for Cimourdain his ideal republic, '[qui met] tout en harmonie' (xv. 502), becomes a 'sourire continué' (xv. 508) as he mounts the scaffold. Returning once again to Gauvain's child-like traits, the dénouement invests him with the innocence of the redeemed ancestor who has provided the model for a superior moral order.[99]

[97] Cf. Ferguson's argument that one way is which Hugo 'attains the distance from the ordinary that [his politics of transcendence] require' is 'by "naturalizing" social and political phenomena' ('*Quatrevingt-treize*', 72–3; see also 75). Cf. also Gohin's comments, in 'Alternance et adhérance', 158–60, on the role of nature in the text, particularly as 'l'accomplissement du bien absolu' (p. 159).

[98] See *FT* 305–6. Hugo's sensuous descriptions of nature in both *MIS* and *QVT* evoke the representations in *PL* (see esp. book VII) of the 'fecundity and energy associated with divine creation' (Loewenstein, *Milton's* Paradise Lost, 107–8).

[99] It is noteworthy that Radoub's despair at Gauvain's trial—'Je veux mon chef! Il me faut mon chef!' (xv. 449)—echoes Michelle Fléchard's as she pleads for her children—'Je veux mes enfants, il me faut mes enfants!' (xv. 476)—and that both faint when the fate of their loved one(s) has been decided, for better or worse. Through this analogy, one might argue that Lantenac's gesture, by symbolically saving his own 'son', makes him doubly worthy of Gauvain's reciprocal act of generosity. Their rivalry thus becomes one of emulation in the service of 'l'absolu humain' (xv. 483). Derek J. Turton similarly concludes that 'both men rise above their duty to be united in the common cause of humanity'

By grounding his novel in recognizable generational patterns of conflict and reconciliation, Hugo enables the reader to understand both the relations between his protagonists' divergent ethical positions and the educational power of exemplary behaviours that challenge and transform those stances. In this way, the ideal in *Quatrevingt-Treize* is firmly anchored in the real. The book itself might be considered an instructional manual about the different levels of human consciousness (and conscience) that represent increasingly more integrative notions of fairness, justice, and social harmony. From clan to country to ideal nation to humanity—the progression entails inhabiting ever wider frames of reference for resolving dilemmas and making judgements. The narrative loop that begins and ends in nature likewise points towards alternative modes of being, the better 'to raise [our historical condition] to the level of historical consciousness' (*TN* iii. 102). The *ailleurs* of the historical past thus intersects with that of utopian discourse within both a pastoral frame and an idealized future.[100] The ways in which Hugo refigures history in the text to conform to a poetic vision of human relations—a vision that revisits the tensions between England and France as well—is the subject of the following subsection.

True and False Utopias

In our study so far, we have seen that Brittany exists in *Quatrevingt-Treize* as more than a real place. The site that links royalists and revolutionaries, Britain and France, it is also a symbolic space, one where strife and competition resolve into cooperative relations. The echoing patterns of plot, character, and description point towards the France of the future—a future that is yet to be forged in the aftermath of the failed insurrection of the 1871 Commune. Amid the many strategies for creating unity in diversity, we have observed that the use of doubles and twinning reveals underlying points of congruity between apparent dichotomies. Equally important are triadic structures, with Lantenac, Cimourdain, and Gauvain forming, on the one hand, a hierarchy of moral and political values and, on the other, a grouping of Janus-figures linked to and dependent upon

('Symbolic Confrontation in Hugo's *Quatrevingt-treize*', *Revue de l'Université d'Ottawa*, 44/3 (July–Sept. 1974), 374).

[100] According to Eco, 'the tragic and romantic magic of *Ninety-three* lies in bringing together on the same playing field the reasons of history and the reasons of various single morals, to measure the constant fracture between politics and utopia' ('Excess and History in Hugo's *Ninety-Three*', 293). This fracture, in our reading, is figured by the images of disjunction in the novel essential to Hugo's 'poetics of transcendence', as well as by the tensions between the politically expedient Cimourdain and the idealistic Gauvain.

each other. As noted above, this configuration recurs in the three leaders directing the government and in the little Fléchards who inspire others to transcend their limitations. It reappears in the Revolutionary ideal of 'Liberté, Egalité, Fraternité', as well as in the tripartite structure of *Quatrevingt-Treize* itself. All these elements participate in a system of triads that subverts the novel's superficial dualism and suggests the possibility of a more richly harmonious order through an ethos that elevates people—that is, *l'humanité*, over politics. Rather than presenting 'mutually exclusive visions of historical and pastoral discourse',[101] the novel employs the natural world as a metaphorical redescription of how history *should* operate.

History in *Quatrevingt-Treize* thus assumes a complex role, whereby the characters are rooted in a particular place and time that both perpetuate traces of the past and aim towards an as-yet-unfulfilled future that also affects the reader's present. Hugo's display of historical consciousness, 'for which every past that is retained can be set up as a quasi-present endowed with its own retrospections and anticipations, some of which belong to the [retained] past of the actual present' (*TN* iii. 32), requires the reader to reflect on the here and now. Where, in these enormous temporal vistas, can human progress be perceived—if at all? After all, 'the allegories that Hugo draws between different events (1650, 1789, [1793], 1871) suggest . . . that history is a pointless repetition of horrors'.[102] As with *Les Misérables*, Hugo treats his text as fertile ground for recuperating lost strands of history and interweaving them with better-known events and concepts. Like the real corvette *Vengeur*, the fictional *Claymore* is destined to sink in battle, 'mais la gloire l'a ignoré. On n'est pas héros contre son pays' (xv. 318). The invented boat, which mirrors a real one, is 'recuperated' by the historical novelist.[103] Cimourdain, too, is treated as a historical figure, even though 'personne aujourd'hui ne sait son nom. L'histoire a de ces inconnus terribles' (xv. 349). Once again, the writer rescues a tiny portion of the past from oblivion, restoring the lost significance for his reader. He also details ethnographically the primitive mindset and lifestyle of those who inhabit 'La Vendée' (III. 1) at the turn of the previous century; and he conjures up a verbal confrontation between the three members of the Comité de salut public that begs the question of which

[101] Petrey, *History in the Text*, 47; see also 100.

[102] Timothy Raser, 'Revolution and Aesthetics in Hugo's *Quatrevingt-treize*', *L'Esprit Créateur*, 29/2 (1989), 51.

[103] As Raser points out, however, the *Claymore* 'was the name of the gunship used by the Commune against Versailles in 1871' (Revolution and Aesthetics', 60 n. 3)—further evidence that the historical referents in the text are largely concerned with contemporary events.

political faction is the most brutal and self-deluded. The multiple references to even earlier historical personages—Plato, Draco (xv. 346), Dante, Vergil (xv. 439), Æschylus (xv. 458), Homer (xv. 475, 502), Euclid (xv. 502)—highlight the epic and mythical dimensions of the battle for France's heart and soul.

Among the narrator's historical references, the pre-Revolutionary period mentioned most frequently is the Middle Ages. Lantenac may well belong to 'cette race d'hommes de guerre du dix-huitième siècle' (xv. 433); but what he represents is a thoroughly entrenched feudal era that began with the Fall of Rome. Allied with La Tourgue, in which are condensed 'quinze cents ans, le moyen âge, le vasselage, la glèbe, la féodalité' (xv. 506; see also 430–1, 488), the Breton noble is targeted for a death replete with symbolism, whereby the 'demeure féodale' will witness the fall of the head of 'l'homme féodal' (xv. 453). And Cimourdain is not the only character to note the irony in his plans for executing the enemy leader. In his moral dilemma, Gauvain ponders the appropriateness of 'l'homme féodal' awaiting punishment in 'l'oubliette féodale' (xv. 486) of the ancestral tower. One might say that Lantenac's end will enact poetic justice. That his local supporters sport the kind of animal-hair helmet worn by 'les rois de Bretagne au sixième siècle et les paysans au dix-huitième siècle' (xv. 450) merely accentuates the ridiculously reactionary perspective of the royalist faction.

Against this pernicious past are arrayed the revolutionary forces in the novel. As 'l'homme en qui se concentrait cette gerbe de fléaux qu'on nomme le passé' (xv. 487), Lantenac carries most of the textual burden for the repressive sociopolitical system to which the Breton rebels, in their unenlightened existence, wish to return. In his view, 'les progrès' inaugurated by the Revolution are completely illusory, since 'l'on extermine en masse tout le passé, depuis la Bastille jusqu'à l'almanach. On remplace les saints par les légumes... Voilà qui était beau et noblement ordonné; vous l'avez détruit' (xv. 493). The grotesque, pedestrian ideas of the republican 'bêtes brutes' (xv. 494) have replaced the sublime beauties of neoclassical monarchic order. The revolutionaries, of course, look at the situation in reverse. Pitting the guillotine against the Breton 'bastille' (xv. 320; see also 505) la Tourgue, that emblem of feudal power, the narrator considers the two 'monstre[s]' (xv. 505) comparable in eliciting terror. Though analogous, however, the constructs are not equal, because the first embodies the past and the second the present.

The same can be said of Lantenac and Cimourdain, who share similar traits but different allegiances. So, if 'Cimourdain, c'est-à-dire 93, tenait Lantenac, c'est-à-dire la monarchie' (xv. 486), then the act of condensing in the guillotine 'une année, 93' (xv. 506), effectively transforms the guillotine into a personification of the priest, just as the ancient keep personifies Lantenac. In the juxtaposition of the two structures, one generation picks up where the other leaves off: 'La toute-puissance déchue avait l'horreur de la toute-puissance nouvelle. L'histoire criminelle considérait l'histoire justicière. La violence d'autrefois se comparait à la violence d'à présent' (xv. 506). An updated version of the competition between architecture and printing in the famous chapter 'Ceci tuera cela' (V.2) in *Notre-Dame de Paris*,[104] the Oedipal struggle between succeeding generations, one devoted to immutable social forms and the other to rapid change, suggests that the 'son'—in this case, the Republican priest—is destined to triumph over the 'father'—the royalist forebear. In earlier years, we are told, Cimourdain 'haïssait le présent, et il appelait à grands cris l'avenir' (xv. 346). Now that the present of the *ancien régime* has become the past and his dream of a Republican future, the new present, 'l'histoire justicière' includes a sweeping judgement not just on individuals but on the entire period that came before.[105]

From the reference point of 'la patrie', which is variously described as having been 'adopté[e]' (xv. 346) by Cimourdain and as 'la même mère' (xv. 457) and 'la mère suprême' (xv. 502) for everyone, those who cling instead to the regional ideal of 'le pays' are '[des] ennemis' (xv. 364; see also 418). In contrast, the values of the Republican state are *Liberté, Égalité, Fraternité*. While not legally formulaic, this three-pronged social ideal helps determine which actions and attitudes advance and which impede the moral development of the fledgling nation. In its role as an educational manual, *Quatrevingt-Treize* might be expected to project examples, both positive and negative, of the values trifecta. The novel begins, for instance, with the horrifying 'entrée en liberté de la matière' (xv. 302; see also 304) when the loosed cannon takes over the *Claymore*. Despite the language of autonomy—left momentarily alone, 'elle était livrée à elle-même. Elle était sa maîtresse, et la maîtresse du navire. Elle pouvait en faire ce qu'elle voulait'—the trembling crew's 'épouvante' (xv. 303) signals the presence of an evil force that will choose to work ill for them and their vessel. The cannon's false self-rule parallels the eruption of the national subconscious in the form of the guerilla-like Bretons seeking independence from the Republic. What they fail to perceive is that they are not their own 'maîtres' but the subjects of others who do not have their interests in mind. If the unleashed matter can be considered 'cet esclave

[104] Cf. Eco, 'Excess and History in Hugo's *Ninety-Three*', 278.
[105] The inverse takes place within the text, since, '"lecteurs" avant nous, les personnages déchiffrent leur présent comme un passé à partir de leur futur, c'est-à-dire de notre présent' (Bernard, *Le Chouan romanesque*, 217).

éternel qui se venge' (xv. 302), the implication is that the royalist vassals are just 'slaves' whose revenge is wholly misdirected.

By the same token, one can read the proliferation of double agents in Part I of the novel as so many instances of false confraternity. And, despite the fact that Lantenac 'fraternisait' with his band in preparing for battle in la Tourgue, he is 'toujours le seigneur' (xv. 433)—a further mark of his followers' true servitude. Finally, Hugo's narrative provides several examples of depraved equality. Thus, the multiple resemblances between the opposing forces, resemblances that brand them both as 'hyènes' (xv. 301) and as purveyors of 'terreur' (xv. 346, 393), testify to a pernicious *Égalité*. Rather than model exemplary behaviours, the two sides compete to commit the worst atrocities. Their 'égalité d'acharnement' (xv. 403) may be heroic in war; for the young Republic, it is morally deadly. This interpretation of the twinning in the text between royalists and revolutionaries explains Lantenac's ironic comments in la Tourgue regarding the enemy's overwhelming numbers: 'Tuer dehors est inutile. Ne tuez que dedans. Dedans, l'égalité se refait'; and he adds, laughing, 'Egalité, Fraternité' (xv. 454). For both camps to be equally equipped for carnage makes a mockery of both ideals.

Though it is tempting to conclude that the royalists alone are incapable of living up to Republican ideals, closer examination implicates most of the Republican characters themselves in producing mere simulacra of the standards to which they supposedly adhere. One can be stuck in the present as well as in the past. Gauvain's declaration to Cimourdain that 'Liberté, Egalité, Fraternité, ce sont des dogmes de paix et d'harmonie' (xv. 419) provides to Hugo's own 'histoire justicière' (xv. 506) the guidelines for assessing progress in each area. 'If actual history follows an intelligible course'—one where revolution is considered not to retard but to accelerate progress—'then the [historical or fictive] narrative we make of it may claim to equate itself with this meaning' (*TN* iii. 210). The verdict rendered by the novel is that the revolutionaries themselves often fail to understand the ramifications of their goals. In the initial portrait of Cimourdain, for example, the narrator remarks that the priest believed, 'dans son ingénuité implacable, que tout est équité au service du vrai' (xv. 348), that believing in something true makes one's actions just. As with all fanatics, the ends justify the means, however brutal. One can further detect the circularity (if not self-delusion) in reasoning that, because one possesses the (one and only) truth, one cannot but embrace the highest form of justice. For Cimourdain, then, the Revolution is a bloody but necessary operation to extirpate the 'gangrène'–'tyrannie' that threatens his nation's integrity: 'Elle mutile, mais elle sauve' (xv. 418), he tells

Gauvain. The hangman is a physician, one that works through disjunctions rather than harmonies.

It is no surprise that Cimourdain's inflexible approach to shaping the new nation is shared by Marat, Danton, and Robespierre. While authentic revolution strives for release from the vicious patterns of the past, *Quatrevingt-Treize* depicts what happens when this impulse becomes reified by the authoritarian structures of a falsely fraternal state. Can replacing Marat's notion of 'unité' (xv. 357) entail anything more than rigid conformity? Between the horror of anarchic chaos and civil war and the terror of citizen clones, there must be another alternative. For the post-Revolutionary France of Hugo—including his present-day world—lacks what Fredric Jameson refers to as 'the *utopian imagination*, the imagination of otherness and radical difference'.[106] In perhaps his supreme act of clemency, Gauvain tells Cimourdain that he absolves 'le moment présent' because it is a tempest, and 'une tempête sait toujours ce qu'elle fait' (xv. 504; see also 380). At first, it seems as if the young man is forgiving his mentor for sentencing him to death, but then it is obvious he is also referring to the violence of the Revolution itself, including the Reign of Terror. He is able to embrace 'ce qui est' (xv. 504) without losing his dream of another mode of being. 'D'ailleurs, que m'importe la tempête, si j'ai la boussole, et que me font les événements, si j'ai ma conscience!' (xv. 504), he tells Cimourdain. He can ride above the storm—and thus above history itself—because he has the unerring aid of his internal 'compass'. Like Jean Valjean, Gauvain has internalized a universally valid code of conduct that does not depend on the relative circumstances of one era or another.[107]

Given the failures of '93—that is, of the novel's present—what should *Liberté, Égalité, Fraternité* look like? Lantenac himself provides an instance of the first during the fire. According to Gauvain's deliberations, 'il avait, volontairement, spontanément, de sa pleine préférence, quitté la forêt . . . la sécurité, la liberté, pour rentrer dans le plus effroyable péril' (xv. 484), not only by rushing into the inferno in the library, but also by descending the ladder into the hands of his enemies. Though the marquis loses his 'liberté' in the sense of freedom from constraint, he exercises a more genuine form of freedom through his choice of heroic action (*volontairement, de sa pleine*

[106] Fredric Jameson, 'Progress versus Utopia', *Science-Fiction Studies*, 9/2 (July 1982), 153.

[107] As Gohin puts it, 'Explicitement, la morale individuelle est préférable à la raison d'État' ('Alternance et adhérance', 211). By following the voice of conscience, Gauvain need not fear death—indeed, he can die happy and fulfilled as a human being. Cf. Ricoeur's comment on stoicism in Heidegger 'that makes resolution in the face of death the supreme test of authenticity' (*TN* iii. 254).

préférence, *effroyable péril*) over self-preservation. Gauvain highlights this exercise of free will by further reflecting that: 'Le marquis de Lantenac avait eu le choix entre la vie d'autrui et la sienne; dans cette option superbe, il avait choisi sa mort' (xv. 484). The ability to apply one's own judgement to a situation and to select an appropriate response—one that poses no harm to others—is emblematic of civil liberty. In recognition of his great-uncle's adherence to conscience rather than to self-interest or royalist dogma, Gauvain cannot, he believes, do any less. After all, 'en pareil cas, abdication, c'est complicité' (xv. 485). The loaded notion of 'abdication', here as in *Les Misérables*, concerns self-rule—that is, the autonomy that informs both the Republic and its citizens.[108]

To assert this freedom, Gauvain liberates Lantenac in a stunning *coup de théâtre*. When the imprisoned ancestor ends his anti-Republican diatribe by declaring, 'Qu'est-ce que cela me fait? Je suis mort', Gauvain replies, 'Vous êtes libre' (xv. 494); and when Cimourdain discovers that the marquis is missing from his cell, Gauvain repeats, 'Il est libre' (xv. 496). Jean Valjean uses precisely the same words, 'Vous êtes libre' (xi. 859), in releasing Javert at the barricades instead of executing him on behalf of the young insurgents. In Hugo's moral imagination, the ultimate revolutionary gesture is to free not oneself but one's enemies. While the expression in *Quatrevingt-Treize* refers literally to Lantenac's release from the tower dungeon, it also carries a figurative meaning—that he is a free agent, empowered by Gauvain to continue to follow his own conscience, wherever it may lead. The man's earlier crimes are simply forgotten, to remain unavenged. Such forgetfulness is, for Ricoeur, an essential element of what he calls the work of forgiveness, which restores the guilty person 'to his capacity for acting, and action . . . to its capacity for continuing' (*MHF* 493). In a way, Lantenac not only precedes but also succeeds Gauvain, who, we will remember, was 'né noué' by prejudice before Cimourdain had 'remis [s]a croissance en liberté' (xv. 501). In the end, the young hero walks to the guillotine 'librement. Il n'avait pas de cordes ni aux pieds ni aux mains' (xv. 508). For the death freely offered, he has transcended all partisanship, his eyes fixed on a *different* future. The ancestor, meanwhile, goes on.

Gauvain has also adopted, I would argue, a variation on the aim of *Fraternité* in the larger idea of *Humanité*. His analogue, the generous

[108] See *FT* 199. Cf. O'Neil's perceptive analysis of the novel's dénouement in the light of the Arthurian Grail legends, particularly with regard to Gawain/Gauvain's exploits and to Lantenac as a healed Fisher King: 'A true knight, who has become the champion of the stranger, the orphan, the poor . . . Lantenac offers, ironically, a better example of a leader contributing to the triumph of the People than the revolutionary Cimourdain' ('Classical Terror/Gothic Terror', 267, 269).

beggar Tellmarch, gives an early example of the protagonist's embrace of all humans when, in wondering why he had saved the merciless Lantenac, tells himself, 'Parce que c'est un homme' (xv. 414). Clearly, the sense of the term in this context is 'human being'—a sense reinforced when Tellmarch muses, regarding the fate of Michelle Fléchard, that 'avoir sauvé cette mère le consolait d'avoir sauvé ce marquis' (xv. 414). As much a member of humanity as the noble, the peasant woman is at least as worthy of salvation. Equally significant, Gauvain, unlike Cimourdain, never calls anyone 'frère'. His eyes are on a broader swath of the population, as evidenced by his views—examined above—on educating children and elevating the status of women. So, when Lantenac saves the Fléchard children, those observing from below see 'un homme... là-haut, un homme... dans la salle de la bibliothèque, un homme... dans la fournaise' (xv. 479). The repetition of the word 'homme' carries a literal meaning, of course, but it also emphasizes the man's humanity. For this reason, Gauvain can later reflect that, through Lantenac's unanticipated act, 'un héros sortait du monstre; plus qu'un héros, un homme' (xv. 485), in other words, someone fundamentally connected to other members of the human race. In a novel that begins with an emphasis on the exotic, 'the notion of humanity has the effect of lessening, to the point of eliminating, the otherness that is at the root of [the diversity of persons]'; relations of power, which exploit such alterity, give way to the Golden Rule (*OA* 223). Colonization, from this perspective, is unthinkable.

What Gauvain learns, then, from the ancestor's example is that the absolute to which he had adhered as a republican was in fact only relative: 'Un absolu supérieur venait de se révéler. Au-dessus de l'absolu révolutionnaire, il y avait l'absolu humain' (xv. 483). He is converted, like Javert, by the revelation of a more complex moral order and a higher good. Forging such universal ties is, in Gauvain's view, a vital goal that has not yet been accomplished by either the Revolution or the Reign of Terror: 'Chaque siècle fera son œuvre,' he tells Cimourdain in their final conversation, 'aujourd'hui civique, demain humaine' (xv. 503). Tomorrow will be better than today; progress does not come all at once but evolves over time. Like the construction of the eponymous cathedral in *Notre-Dame de Paris*, where 'chaque flot du temps superpose son alluvion, chaque race dépose sa couche... chaque individu apporte sa pierre' (iv. 95; see also 144), the future nation is a work of faith for those labouring in the present. In a strange way, a full embrace of 'la grande aïeule' (xv. 503)—humanity—is a task to be passed on to the next generation, and perhaps beyond. In a parallel to the relations between Gauvain and Lantenac, 'the tie between futureness and pastness is assured by a bridging concept, that of being-in-debt'; future generations assume this debt that 'marks [their] dependence on the past in terms of heritage' (*MHF* 363). The metonymical link of a shared legacy also serves to mediate between individual differences that might initially divide a nation's citizens, much as we earlier discerned that divergent aspects of the novel are drawn into a relation of parity by a third, intermediary entity.

The idea of *Égalité* takes centre stage as Gauvain prepares to die. In his exchange with Cimourdain, he begins by acknowledging the priest's role in bringing him into a relation of parity with others: 'Je n'étais qu'un seigneur, vous avez fait de moi un citoyen; je n'étais qu'un citoyen, vous avez fait de moi un esprit' (xv. 501). Ironically inverting social ranks, he was elevated from being 'only' a lord to the plenitude of citizenship, on an equal level with everyone else. Moreover, at the same time that his tutor equipped him 'pour aller dans la réalité humaine', he gave Gauvain the spiritual and intellectual tools 'pour aller au-delà' (xv. 501). Mimēsis and poiēsis conjoin in his sense of being both grounded in reality and capable of pushing into unknown realms. He is fit for both 'la vie terrestre' and 'la vie céleste' (xv. 501), ready to live and to die—as well as to aspire to a more utopian world. We should especially note here that 'aller au-delà' is not the same as 'aller dans l'au-delà', that going beyond entails an exploration of human frontiers, as it did in *Les Travailleurs de la mer*.

When Cimourdain and Gauvain debate their divergent interpretations of the social ideal, several crucial aspects of the concept of 'equality' emerge. The priest, for instance, believes in giving everyone 'ce qui lui revient', the soldier, 'ce qui ne lui revient pas', which he defines as 'l'immense concession réciproque que chacun doit à tous et que tous doivent à chacun, et qui est toute la vie sociale' (xv. 502). The economic and legal language (*doit, doivent, concession*) implies that the flow of gracious compromises and concessions from individuals to the collective whole and from the collective whole to individuals ensures that the coffers of good will remain full. All of this, Gauvain readily admits, takes place outside any system of 'justice' because it involves 'équité' (xv. 502)—fairness based on the perceived equality (*réciproque*) of large and small entities. When he presents his corollary dream of equality of the sexes, Cimourdain protests that 'les deux êtres sont divers,' to which Gauvain replies, 'J'ai dit l'égalité. Je n'ai pas dit l'identité' (xv. 503). Taking particular aim at the definition of equality as 'identité' in Cimourdain's 'république de l'absolu' (xv. 502), Hugo suggests that the geometrically correct political state would end up being totalitarian. By sacrificing his adopted child to that ideal, Cimourdain demonstrates that he has lost sight of the Republic that *could be* through serving the one that now *is*. Utopia must, as Jameson remarks, be radically *other*.[109]

For Hugo, then, the vengeful exchanges of 'hyène contre hyène' (xv. 301) and 'terreur pour terreur' (xv. 346) yield to a superior form of reciprocity—the essentially metaphorical structure of Gauvain's 'égalité', whereby individual identities are retained and enhanced rather than effaced. Cimourdain's ideal of mathematical equivalence is trumped by his pupil's dream of metaphorical parity.[110] In this analogical paradigm, Gauvain can switch places with his great-uncle in prison—'il est sorti à ma place et je suis resté à la sienne' (xv. 496)—and the faithful Radoub can volunteer in turn to substitute his own head on the guillotine. 'Je vote pour qu'on me coupe la tête à sa place' (xv. 499), the sergeant declares as his way of pushing for acquittal. As the comic rejoinder to Gauvain's tragic confession, the notion of replacing someone in death finds an additional echo in the execution scene, when a grenadier points to the guillotine and asks, 'Reçoit-on des remplaçants pour ça? Me voici' (xv. 508). An important *topos* in Hugo that recalls Jean Valjean's role in *Les Misérables* and that dates back to his earliest works, the theme of the substitute saviour is closely linked, for the writer, to the transformational power of metaphor.[111]

The process of transfiguration is, we have seen, central to *Quatrevingt-Treize*, especially Lantenac's conversion that metonymically engenders a change of heart in Gauvain as well. The monstrous ancestor becomes a hero—'ce n'était plus un tueur que Gauvain avait devant lui, mais un sauveur' (xv. 485)—saving himself, too, along the way. When Gauvain reflects that 'le porte-glaive s'était métamorphosé en porte-lumière. L'infernal Satan était redevenu le Lucifer céleste' (xv. 488), he once again links

[109] It is no coincidence that the pathologically clement Gauvain fervently pursues the ethical principle of 'équité' or 'égalité' in the realm of social justice or that he focuses on the universal of 'l'humanité'. According to Ricoeur, '*Equality*... *is to life in institutions what solicitude is to interpersonal relations*... Justice... adds to solicitude, to the extent that the field of application of equality is all of humanity' (*OA* 202). Gauvain's conception of the ideal state is thus presented not so much as superior to Cimourdain's but as 'radicalement différente, comme d'un autre ordre' (Gohin, 'Alternance et adhérance', 169).

[110] Thus, metaphor for Hugo, as for Ricoeur, 'reveals something concerning the scope of equivalence that distinguishes it from mathematical equality' (*RM* 206). Cf. James Hamilton's conclusion regarding *QVT*: 'Only by letting go of power through compassion can the hero hope to transcend the polarities of an impossible situation and arrive at a synthesis on a higher level' ('Terrorizing the "Feminine"', 214).

[111] See *FT* 147, 155, and *EN* 107–8. In Ricoeur's formulation,'the commandment to love one's enemies begins by breaking the rule of [tit-for-tat] reciprocity and requiring the extraordinary' (*MHF* 482). When Jean Valjean saves Javert from death on the barricades or Gauvain frees his political enemy and takes his place on the scaffold, they signal a moral order centred on clemency rather than the talion.

religious and sociopolitical imagery. Indeed, he interweaves the two, since the 'glaive' is a symbol of justice and 'lumière' is associated with the issue of education, which plays a critical role in the novel. Even the terms 'infernal' and 'céleste' can be applied, beyond their biblical allusions, to dystopian and utopian representations. We should therefore not be surprised to discover metaphorical language used to describe Gauvain's dream of a better future. He exclaims to Cimourdain on the eve of his execution:

> Non, non, non, plus de parias, plus d'esclaves, plus de forçats, plus de damnés! je veux que chacun des attributs de l'homme soit un symbole de civilisation et un patron de progrès; je veux la liberté devant l'esprit, l'égalité devant le cœur, la fraternité devant l'âme . . . Plus d'homme reptile. Je veux la transfiguration de la larve en lepidoptère; je veux que le ver de terre se change en une fleur vivante, et s'envole. Je veux . . . (xv. 504)

The novel's closing utopian vision expresses Gauvain's will, not just to change the world, but to see it, metaphorically, *otherwise*. In a reprise of the republican aims of *Liberté, Égalité, Fraternité*, his aspirations for the future turn these three human 'attributes' into 'symbols' of civilization and 'patterns' for progress.

The abstract language conceals a larger message, however. The closing image in Part II of revolutionaries battling royalists—'Sauvagerie contre barbarie' (xv. 383)—yields in Part III to one of a polity concerned with values of the mind, heart, soul. The reptilian 'conscience petite' (xv. 395) of those obsessed with secretive hide-outs (or politics) gives way to a soaring, open-air existence (*lepidoptère, s'envole*). Because failing to liberate Lantenac would have meant, to Gauvain's mind, that '[il] resterait à plat ventre dans la vieille ornière, tandis que Lantenac irait dans le sublime courir des aventures' (xv. 485), the marquis appears as the first 'larva' in the text to have exited his chrysalis and flown off—with the 'transfigured' Gauvain soon to follow. When the young hero lapses into silence, he enters into the sublime by transcending speech, experiencing like the poet himself 'the *ecstatic* moment of language—language going beyond itself' (*RM* 249)—as it reaches other spheres of meaning.[112] Because 'the incantatory effect of the rhetoric that activates the speaker's vision of the future signifies the priority of poetry over politics',[113] the text here

[112] In yet another connection between Gauvain and the little Fléchards, the children's 'bégaiement' (xv. 435), whereby speech hesitates in its beginnings, finds its counterpart in the visionary's inability to complete his thought in words.

[113] Aynesworth, 'Anonymity, Identity, and Narrative Sovereignty', 212.

surpasses its origins as a historical novel about France's political past to leap into the realm of lofty, but largely unspeakable, futuristic revelations.

Projecting in his own actions his vision of a new world order where *Liberté, Égalité, Fraternité* find their highest modes of expression, the political 'prophète' (xv. 403) Gauvain exemplifies the ideal citizen of a Republic that does not yet exist, but towards which everything is tending. At the same time, it is significant that the revolutionary leader does not reject his entire past in order to advance towards the future. Unlike Cimourdain, Gauvain 'can envisage the future because he has retrieved the spiritual legacy of the past'.[114] True to the structure of other Hugo narratives, where the younger generation thrives when it combines continuity and originality, metonymical and metaphorical axes,[115] Gauvain accepts his heritage by internalizing aspects of both of his father figures. To introject the father is, for Weiskel, to surmount terror—in this case the Terror—by expanding one's psychic resources, metaphorically substituting 'a "power within" for the external power'.[116] Along with Cimourdain's fervent commitment to the French Republic, he emulates Lantenac's capacity for heroic sacrifice and self-reinvention.[117] Tradition, both received and transmitted, joins metaphor as a dialectic 'of the near and the far, the familiar and the alien, of temporal distance and the fusion of the horizons of the past and the present without confusing them' (*TN* iii. 228). Despite the antithesis in the text between past and present, the two time frames are reconciled in and through Gauvain as equally necessary for future progress. In Gauvain's words:

> Ce que la révolution fait en ce moment est mystérieux. Derrière l'œuvre visible il y a l'œuvre invisible. L'une cache l'autre. L'œuvre visible est farouche, l'œuvre invisible est sublime. En cet instant, je distingue tout très nettement. C'est étrange et beau. Il a bien fallu se servir des matériaux du passé. De là cet extraordinaire 93. Sous un échafaudage de barbarie se construit un temple de civilisation. (xv. 501–2)

From the vantage point of impending death, Gauvain can grasp what was previously obscured—the whole trajectory of history. The 'matériaux du passé', embodied by Lantenac, mix with 'cet extraordinaire 93', embodied

[114] O'Neil, 'Classical Terror/Gothic Terror', 271.

[115] See *EN* 42–4, 55–7, 193, 200–4, and *FT* 123, 137–8, 234.

[116] Weiskel, *The Romantic Sublime*, 95.

[117] Roman notes that, paradoxically, Gauvain represents 'les valeurs chevaleresques de ses ancêtres' even better than Lantenac: 'La fidélité à l'esprit du passé n'est réelle que si elle est vécue en fonction du progrès et tient compte du présent. Vivre l'Histoire sera dès lors reconnaître sa filiation mais refuser la sclérose de la tradition' (*Victor Hugo et le roman philosophique*, 437).

by Cimourdain, to forge the sublimely civilized work of the future. The structure of Gauvain's insight reconfigures his earlier claim that Lantenac's rescue of the Fléchard children eclipsed his own duty towards the Republic. In this revised schema, the savage, visible work is civil war, including Gauvain's role in the Revolutionary Army, and the sublime, invisible work is the awakening of Lantenac's humanity and, subsequently, of Gauvain's conversion to pacifist utopianism. The temporary shock of French slaughtering French eclipses the permanent shifts in attitudes and beliefs from which new laws and institutions will emerge. Temples of civilization are, like cathedrals, built one stone at a time.

The importance of assuming an inclusive if not omniscient historical perspective becomes clear when we consider the dangers of short-sightedness. The narrator remarks about the experience of the Convention:

> Ce qui échappait aux contemporains, c'était précisément sa grandeur; on était trop effrayé pour être ébloui . . . ce qui est trop haut, un génie aussi bien qu'une montagne, une assemblée aussi bien qu'un chef-d'œuvre, vus de trop près, épouvantent . . . On s'essouffle aux escarpements, on glisse sur les pentes, on se blesse à des aspérités qui sont des beautés . . . l'ascension terrifie autant que la chute. De là plus d'effroi que d'admiration. On éprouve ce sentiment bizarre, l'aversion du grand. On voit les abîmes, on ne voit pas les sublimités; on voit le monstre, on ne voit pas le prodige. (xv. 367)

Recalling the description of Cimourdain as 'sublime dans l'isolement, dans l'escarpement, dans la lividité inhospitalière' (xv. 349), the passage employs the vertical axis to depict the psychological effect of volatile events when viewed too closely.[118] The fear of being harmed overcomes the desire for glory—an astute observation—to the point that one loses all appreciation for what has been achieved or for where one is headed. Risk avoidance trumps the pursuit of additional gains. Like Cimourdain, the Convention's pivotal role as the site where past and future meet turns it into an 'inhospitable' environment. To reach the peak for an awe-inspiring 360-degree temporal panorama, one must conquer 'escarpements . . . pentes . . . aspérités'. The latter cannot simply be banished or repressed, because they constitute essential elements of both 'l'œuvre visible' and 'l'œuvre invisible'. By remembering and surmounting the harshness of past and present alike, Cimourdain's 'république de la terreur' can some day become Gauvain's 'république de la clémence' (xv. 416). If 'without memory . . . there is no principle of hope' (*TN* iii. 258), Hugo's

[118] If 'tout le mouvement du texte est ascendant, qui commence à la mer et au naufrage, et s'achève sur un envol' (Meschonnic, *Pour la poétique IV*, 199), it is a movement mediated by all three protagonists.

examination of France's past provides keys to a constructive view of the future.[119]

The 'clarté d'aurore [qui] grandissait' (xv. 505) in Gauvain's meditative eye thus reflects a future equally personal and collective. The notion of expansion, previously discerned in the text in relation to both growing up and sublimation, signals the transcendent moment of the hero's approaching death. Although Gauvain does not specifically tie England and France together in his view from the scaffold, the two-faced nature of all three protagonists provides an analogue for the inseparability of these 'twin' countries. By the same token, the strange alliance fostered by civil war between Bretons and France's traditional enemies adumbrates a world where alien 'brothers' can live together in concord. Lantenac's remark to Gauvain that 'le génie de la France est composé du génie même du continent' (xv. 493) extols the human variety and interdependence that the grand-nephew cherishes as well. Moreover, the invisible work of progress has, at least briefly, transfigured Lantenac into the generous Gauvain and Gauvain into the citizen of a future Republic at harmony with itself and with other nations. When Gauvain chooses to perpetuate this system of interchangeability by replacing his symbolic 'father' in death, he again affirms the primacy of metaphorical parity over mathematical equivalence.

His victory over the undifferentiated world of 'identité' revered by Cimourdain is figured in the novel's final image. When Cimourdain shoots himself at the moment of Gauvain's execution, 'ces deux âmes, sœurs tragiques, s'envolèrent ensemble, l'ombre de l'une mêlée à la lumière de l'autre' (xv. 509). Gauvain meets death accompanied by the spiritual 'sister' who had opposed his embrace of the enemy in life. There can be no continued opposition where the deepest love and respect are concerned. Their 'discordant concordances', to use Ricoeur's term, are resolved on yet another level. Or, as Bernard Leuilliot interprets the novel's concluding image, 'la thèse et l'antithèse, entre lesquelles le dogmatisme oblige à choisir, font peut-être, en réalité, système'.[120] This dynamic system—the 'interdependence of opposites' illustrated, for James Hamilton, by the same scene[121]—is, in fact, that of tenor and vehicle. Within the exotic bounds of Brittany that open and close Hugo's narrative, England and France, here and there, then and now, I and thou, become metaphorical

[119] For Shaw, this shining future represents both a synthesis of past antithetical entities and the diametric opposite of that past: 'The opposition between revolution and royalism which dominates much of the novel has . . . been largely superseded by an opposition between both and the future' (*The Forms of Historical Fiction*, 111).

[120] Leuilliot, 'La Loi des tempêtes', 92.

[121] James Hamilton, 'Terrorizing the "Feminine"', 214.

siblings across time and space. Spatial exoticism in *Quatrevingt-Treize* thus reveals its poetic function, that of imagining a temporal *ailleurs*—a true utopia in the still unevolved future. In this way, the novel connects '[temporal] difference pushed to the point of... temporal exoticism' (*TN* iii. 146) with both present and future time, just as metaphor bridges the 'distance' between two apparently unrelated terms. In the final section of this chapter, I turn to that future, now Hugo's present, to probe the writer's reflections on contemporary political and literary history, including the textual dialogue with his English 'twin', Charles Dickens.

POLITICAL AND LITERARY DIALOGUES

By setting his story not only in the historical, 'exotic' past but also in a region of the country unfamiliar to most readers, Hugo develops dazzling congruities between space and time that leave open the question of the present. The readers' displacement to a defamiliarized version of France allows them to look at their own world afresh. As in *L'Homme qui rit*, Hugo's narrative about the Reign of Terror shows the past as 'a space of experience open to a horizon of expectation' (*TN* iii. 227) in order to stimulate thinking about where we are and where we are headed. To what extent, then, does *Quatrevingt-Treize* address the here and now? And in what ways does it distinguish itself from Dickens's recent work on the same historical period—and on similar issues? After looking at the portrait that emerges in Hugo's text of mid-nineteenth-century France, we will examine the echoes of Dickens's earlier narrative. In so doing, we can more easily identify the distinctive qualities of Hugo's poetic vision and prose style.

Waking Dreamscapes

It is impossible to mistake the irony of Gauvain's final, visionary speech in the light of the bloody events and reactionary politics surrounding the conception of *Quatrevingt-Treize*.[122] Could anyone who had lived through the 1848 Revolution, the Second Empire, or the Paris Commune believe that the young hero's utopia of equity, harmony, and humanity had at last been realized, albeit several generations later? The genesis of the novel amid civil disarray and imperial rule closely allies the historical past portrayed in the narrative with contemporary events. In this way, Hugo

[122] Gauvain here recalls Enjolras's evocation of France's glorious future from atop the barricades (v. 1. 5)—another dream that remains unfulfilled in 1874.

aligns his own lived existence with his nation's long-term trajectory. According to Ricoeur, lengthy time spans can 'act as a screen hiding the time that we are. This disastrous consequence can be avoided only if an analogy is preserved between the time of individuals and the time of civilizations: the analogy of growth and decline, of creation and death, the analogy of fate' (*TN* i. 224). The interplay within *Quatrevingt-Treize* between growing children and static elders—itself a metaphor for the triumph of the new Republic over a calcified monarchy—extends to the tension between the time of the novel and that of the writer (and beyond, to that of the reader). An omniscient narrator, Hugo at times moves forwards, 'considering the present from the point of view of the anticipation of a remembered past' (*TN* ii. 94). That the writer chose to compose his work in Guernsey suggests, moreover, that the textual tie between England and France refers as much to the present as to the Reign of Terror. For Hugo, one must seek unity and happiness, if only for a while, *elsewhere*—whether on his gentle isle or between the pages of a good tale well told.

Occasionally, the text alludes to the author's present, sometimes more directly than others. Indeed, one might say that, like Proust, Hugo ably uses 'prolepsis within a globally retrospective narrative... Some prolepses take a particular line of action to its logical conclusion, to the point of rejoining the narrator's present' (*TN* ii. 83).[123] We have seen, for example, that the Convention is difficult to apprehend and appreciate when viewed close up. It should be contemplated, not by 'myopes', but by 'aigles'—such as the genius–author: 'Aujourd'hui', the narrator declares, '[la Convention] est en perspective, et elle dessine sur le ciel profond, dans un lointain serein et tragique, l'immense profil de la révolution française... C'est par la Convention que s'ouvrit la grande page nouvelle et que l'avenir d'aujourd'hui commença' (xv. 367). The future that is today owes its existence to this monumental undertaking, this 'premier avatar du peuple' that proclaimed the First Republic on a fall equinox, 'sous [le] signe de l'Egalité et de la Justice' (xv. 367). Reminding his reader about the nation's daring origins, Hugo also inserts an implicit question about the fate of justice and equality in 'l'avenir d'aujourd'hui.' At the time of the events in his narrative, the revolutionaries were convinced that

[123] Gérard Genette's comment that the narrator of *À la recherche du temps perdu* (1913–27) 'never ceases to hold all of its places and all of its moments, to be capable of establishing a multitude of "telescopic" relations among them' (*Narrative Discourse: An Essay in Method*, trans. Jane E. Lewin (Ithaca, NY: Cornell University Press, 1983), 78) can also be applied to Hugo's 'bird's-eye view' of French past, present, and future history. Cf. Ricoeur's observation that 'history... functions in turn as an eyepiece, a microscope, or a telescope' (*MHF* 211).

people in the future would appreciate their sacrifices. In his verbal jousting with l'Imânus before the battle at la Tourgue, Cimourdain maintains: 'Vous saurez plus tard, ou vos enfants sauront, ou les enfants de vos enfants sauront que tout ce qui se fait en ce moment se fait par l'accomplissement des lois d'en haut, et que ce qu'il y a dans la Révolution, c'est Dieu' (xv. 457). Here the text skips forwards a few generations—roughly to the mid-1860s, when Hugo and other exiled republicans indeed saw in the Revolution of 1789 the fulfilment of divine law. Because 'the present is both what we are living and what realized the expectations of the remembered past' (*TN* iii. 35), current events are loaded with significance and value judgements that witness to historical memory.

For this reason, negative images of the future can also be detected in the text, as when the narrator describes the chaining of republican prisoners—a version of a scenario depicted in *Le Dernier Jour d'un condamné* (ch. 13) and *Les Misérables* (IV. 3. 8) as well—who are then executed en masse: 'On adossait la chaîne à une fosse creusée et l'on fusillait; les fusillés tombaient dans la fosse parfois vivants; on les enterrait tout de même. Nous avons revu ces mœurs' (xv. 393). The horror not just of mass executions but of being buried alive (suffocation being Hugo's nightmare ending par excellence) has been perpetuated into modern times. When the narrator distinguishes between mountain insurgents like the Swiss and forest insurgents like the Vendeans several pages later, he targets his own era even more specifically: 'L'un combat pour l'humanité, l'autre pour la solitude; l'un veut la liberté, l'autre veut l'isolement; l'un défend la commune, l'autre la paroisse. Communes! communes! criaient les héros de Morat... La montagne est une citadelle, la forêt est une embuscade; l'une inspire l'audace, l'autre le piège' (xv. 395). While the Swiss assume characteristics of the revolutionaries (*humanité*, *liberté*), the term 'communes' is startling in its triple usage, including once with capital letters—plainly a reference to the leftist Paris Commune and its struggle with the more politically moderate provisional government in Versailles. The ambush theme previously associated with such villains as Clubin and the octopus in *Les Travailleurs de la mer* and Barkilphedro in *L'Homme qui rit* thus vilifies not only the counter-revolutionary Bretons but also Thiers's merciless forces. Likewise, the term 'audace', so prominently featured in both 'Plein ciel' and *Les Travailleurs de la mer* to extol the heroic exploration of human limits, returns here in a political context—one that points to the failed democratic socialist experiment of the Communards. If, as Jameson maintains, science fiction enables readers to '[apprehend] the present as history' by '[dramatizing their] incapacity to imagine the future',[124] the historical novel instead focuses on the past in order to shine a critical light on contemporary issues. For Hugo, the moment to establish 'la république de la clémence' (xv. 416) glimpsed long ago in a still-awaited future cannot come too soon. The Terror of 1793 is yet to be redeemed in 1874.[125]

Is historical progress possible, then, in Hugo's opinion? One might expect that recent events in his life would undercut any sense of optimism about humanity's direction. Moreover, the very emphasis on utopian vision in the text might, according to Ricoeur, signal an essential pessimism: 'The idea of progress which still bound the past to a better future . . . tends to give way to the idea of utopia as soon as the hopes of humanity lose their anchorage in acquired experience and are projected into an unprecedented future' (*TN* iii. 215). Gauvain's dreams are, in this scenario, symptomatic not only of the character's anxiety about the misdirected Revolution but also of Hugo's misgivings about his own era. And yet, the text offers another reading altogether. Renewing a basic theme in *Les Misérables*, the narrator of *Quatrevingt-Treize* claims that apparent setbacks may in reality advance the cause of *Liberté, Égalité, Fraternité*: 'en démontrant la nécessité de trouer dans tous les sens la vieille ombre bretonne et de percer cette broussaille de toutes les flèches de la lumière à la fois, la Vendée a servi le progrès. Les catastrophes ont une sombre façon d'arranger les choses' (xv. 397). Catastrophes unleash an abundance of light-emitting gaps (*trouer*, *percer*) that illuminate—and so eliminate—their sources. By rudely interrupting any halt in progress, including reactionary civil wars, revolution for Hugo allows progress to unfold by reconnecting present and future.[126] History can then march on in a more orderly fashion (*arranger les choses*). Michelle Fléchard pursues her children by instinct, but 'toujours en avant' (xv. 420), just as Gauvain declares his thought to be: 'Toujours en avant' (xv. 503). In keeping with Gilliatt's survival on his reef, both hope and will power are essential to their efforts.

Nevertheless, one need not necessarily go forwards in the straight line traced by Cimourdain's linear understanding of progress. The direct connecting function of ladders in the novel is paralleled by the more indirect linking of la Tourgue's 'escalier en colimaçon' (xv. 424), whose spiral form is mentioned ten more times in the text. Not all paths forwards

[124] Jameson, 'Progress versus Utopia', 153.

[125] In effect, according to Guerlac, Hugo 'manipulat[es] the aesthetic terms of tragedy, terror and pity' in the text in order to 'champio[n] amnesty for the Communards' ('Exorbitant Geometry', 872, 874). Cf. also Petrey's account of Hugo's complicated relation to the Commune, as well as his argument that Gauvain's nation lies outside not just France but all human history (*History in the Text*, 99–119, 30).

[126] See *FT* 216–17, 222–3, 297–8.

are undeviating. Michelle Fléchard's route is full of false turns: 'Elle prit d'abord le sentier qu'il fallait, puis celui qu'il ne fallait pas, et elle finit par se perdre... Approchait-elle du but?... Elle était dans la Voie Douloureuse, et elle sentait l'accablement de sa dernière station' (xv. 452). Assuming the outlook of a Roman Catholic from Brittany, the narrator assimilates the suffering mother with the Mater Dolorosa following the Stations of the Cross in order to deepen empathy for her character. Her circuitous trajectory, a two-dimensional spiral, does not betray her instincts and leads her to her children at the moment she is about to drop from exhaustion. Gauvain's more evolved conscience/consciousness is similarly recursive. In his moral dilemma, '[il] subissait ces spirales vertigineuses de l'esprit revenant sur lui-même, qui font la pensée pareille à la couleuvre' (xv. 488). The multi-layered spirals wind not through space but through time as the young hero seeks his way through a challenging problem. Like Jean Valjean, who combines Javert's straight-arrow morality with Thénardier's sneaky serpentine ways, Gauvain follows a purposively winding mental itinerary that captures all possible angles of the situation before making his decision to spare Lantenac.[127] More importantly, 'the spatial perspective... serves as a metaphor for all the other expressions of point of view', including the 'temporal plan[e]' (*TN* ii. 94); space in the text operates both literally and analogically, allowing the reader to think about the more abstract fourth dimension in relatively concrete terms.

The implication of the shower of helical imagery in *Quatrevingt-Treize* is that, for Hugo, history likewise pursues an indirect route towards its teleologically necessary republican goals. The 'disturbing tension between progress and recurrence, between concepts of linear and cyclical history', discerned by Brombert[128] yields to a totalizing pattern that resolves the antinomy. The recursive path of history may seem at times to lead backwards. Yet the cycles that loop over each other are not two- but three-dimensional, moving in an upward spiral.[129] In this way, the spatially configured *mises en abyme* in 'L'Archipel de la Manche' and *L'Homme*

[127] See *FT* 174–5, 184–5. Allied with the notion of serpentine wiles, l'Imânus provides an example of an ethos (or politics) in thrall to false reasoning: 'C'était un cœur plein d'aboutissements tortueux, porté à tous les dévouements, enclin à toutes les fureurs. Raisonnait-il? Oui, mais comme les serpents rampent; en spirale' (xv. 405). With both Gauvain and l'Imânus, as with Jean Valjean and Thénardier in *MIS*, Hugo illustrates 'the major contribution of fiction to philosophy' hailed by Ricoeur, notably 'the exploration of the nonlinear features of phenomenological time' (*TN* iii. 132).

[128] Brombert, *Victor Hugo and the Visionary Novel*, 207.

[129] Cf. Bernard, who sees in the 'Massacre de Saint-Barthélemy' the liquidation of the children's 'tradition sanguinaire et au fond illégitime', and so, in the pattern of bits of paper carried off in the wind, the 'points de suspension mystérieux mais prometteurs qui prolongent la spirale ascendante de l'Histoire' (*Le Chouan romanesque*, 214).

qui rit, along with the overlapping time frames in the latter, are seconded by nested temporal patterns in *Quatrevingt-Treize.* Historical self-similarity—the sense that events are just repeating themselves—is, then, an illusion, because each iteration contains an element of progress over the previous one. Like Gauvain's final apprehension of Lantenac's contribution to future history, the present makes use of 'les matériaux du passé' (xv. 501) in a different context, thereby giving birth to new attitudes and institutions. Such an explanation of recurring tyranny, whether in the form of monarchy or of empire, as well as of subsequent revolutions and other manifestations of civil discord, fosters continued hope for a better future. The nonlinear dynamics of history are full of potential surprises. If the model reader, for Hugo, was both 'someone reading in 1874' and 'the future reader',[130] his novel aims to reshape far more than attitudes towards contemporary events. Gauvain's vision at the end of the narrative—in a recognizable historical past—is that of Hugo himself for the years to come. It is up to the reader to judge if both will have died in the service of an impossible dream.

Fraternal Visions in *Quatrevingt-Treize* and *A Tale of Two Cities*

Hugo's emphasis in the text on all-inclusive spatial and temporal perspectives also discloses his conception of the work itself. The novelist's comments, discussed above, about the terrors of being too close to unstable circumstances—'ce qui est trop haut, un génie aussi bien qu'une montagne, une assemblée aussi bien qu'un chef-d'œuvre, vus de trop près, épouvantent . . . On . . . voit le monstre, on ne voit pas le prodige' (xv. 367)—apply to his narrative as well. The obvious self-reference (*génie*, *chef-d'œuvre*, *monstre*, *prodige*) suggests that Hugo draws not just on French historical 'materials' but also on those of his own literary past. In considering the writer's work from a limited perspective, some might experience 'ce sentiment bizarre, l'aversion du grand'; with time, however, its 'sublimités' (xv. 367) should be more amply foregrounded, dominating the literary landscape.

This notion of literary pre-eminence, along with the twinning in the text of France and Britain as political entities, points towards the relations between Hugo and his English counterpart, Charles Dickens. As with Shakespeare and Milton, whose works help to illuminate *Les Travailleurs de la mer* and *L'Homme qui rit*, we can see in *Quatrevingt-Treize* reflections

[130] Eco, 'Excess and History in Hugo's *Ninety-Three*', 291.

of Dickens's *A Tale of Two Cities*, a hugely successful narrative likewise set during the Reign of Terror. 'By the time of [Dickens's] death, [*A Tale of Two Cities*] was well on the way to being established as one of his most extensively published as well as most popular works.'[131] A celebrated writer in the same mould as Hugo, Dickens produced one bestseller after another and was known to millions of readers in the Anglophone world—and beyond. On the global stage of the early 1860s, when Hugo conceived the story line of *Quatrevingt-Treize* just after publishing *Les Misérables*, no one competed better for the limelight than Dickens. Both authors shared deft emplotments, melodramatic flourishes, concern for *les misérables*, and use of both idealized and grotesque characters. Both aspired to be the heir of Sir Walter Scott. That Dickens was considered the literary successor of Sir Walter Scott in Great Britain could not have escaped Hugo's notice, given François-Victor's dedication to English literary studies beginning in the 1840s and his subsequent translation of Shakespeare's complete works. Still, Dickens's stature as a novelist could not, in my view, have evoked the same anxiety of influence as that exerted on Hugo by epic poets (Homer, Vergil, Dante, Milton), poet-novelists (Scott), or poet-dramatists (Shakespeare).[132] Not only had these other rivals or *frères ennemis* survived, to varying degrees, a longer test of time; they also occupied an important place in the poet's *imaginaire* as fundamentally analogical thinkers. In *Quatrevingt-Treize*, I argue, Hugo exploits his familiarity with Dickens as his literary *Other*, the better to showcase the originality of his own art.[133] In the analysis that follows, I discuss those aspects of *A Tale of Two Cities* that served Hugo's purposes before highlighting a number of significant differences between the two works.

A Tale of Two Cities resembles *Quatrevingt-Treize* in important structural and thematic ways. The historical setting, paired characters and countries, generational conflict, sociopolitical satire, and visionary discourse—all

[131] Colin Jones, Josephine McDonagh, and John Mee, 'Introduction: *A Tale of Two Cities* in Context', in Colin Jones, Josephine McDonagh, and Jon Mee (eds.), *Charles Dickens,* A Tale of Two Cities *and the French Revolution* (Chippenham: Palgrave Macmillan, 2009), 4.

[132] Unlike either Milton or Shakespeare, Dickens merely dabbled in poetry—a distinction that sets him apart from the genealogy of visionary poets and prophets claimed by Hugo in *WS*.

[133] Sadrin argues convincingly that Hugo had already referred obliquely to Dickens while in exile, leaving 'traces' or 'reminiscences' of *Great Expectations* (1860–1) in *L'Homme qui rit*. In the critic's view, Hugo would have read Dickens in translation, since he would not have wanted to be 'ignorant of the greatest English novelist of his age'. The two texts share a number of salient features, including an 'inaugural gibbet scene', and both respond to 'a common source of inspiration' ('"In the Name of the King"', 224, 223, 224), Mary Shelley's *Frankenstein*. In neglecting to mention François-Victor's extensive knowledge of English literature, Sadrin misses another possible source for his father's familiarity with Dickens's works.

contribute to the intertexual dialogue. In each narrative, the reader encounters a nation *in extremis*. If Hugo's ship of state is at sea, Dickens's France in 1793 is threatened by an infernal 'deluge from below'.[134] But in Dickens's version of the Reign of Terror, the English are eager not to invade their neighbouring country but to ease the distress of the French. The role of geography is therefore less strategic than social. In Hugo, the English use of the Channel poses an enormous threat to the new Republic. In Dickens, the opposition between France and England is accentuated by the sojourns back and forth across the Channel by many of the protagonists—Dr Manette, the Tellson's banker Mr Lorry, Charles and Lucie Darnay, and Sidney Carton—who cannot help but prefer the relative freedom and order of English society to the chaos and tyranny of France. Critics see Darnay and Carton as two halves, as two potentialities, of the same being.[135] Yet the theme of divided identities extends much further.[136] The epic struggle between Gauvain and his patrician patriarch, for instance, is also figured in Darnay's rejection of his own aristocratic heritage, as incarnated in his wicked uncle the Marquis St Evrémonde. The son of Evrémonde's twin brother, Charles bears an especially weighty legacy. By renouncing 'his country, his property and his family name', Darnay 'deal[s] a fatal blow to his uncle, his family and the repugnant values of the past'.[137] At the same

[134] Charles Dickens, *A Tale of Two Cities*, ed. Edward Wagenknecht (New York: Random House, 1967), 288; hereafter *TTC*. All references to Dickens's novel in the text will be from this edition. Cf. Taylor Stoehr's remarks on imagery in Dickens that might well apply to the *Claymore*: 'The motion of the lamps seems like the swaying of ship-lanterns at sea, which in turn reminds us of tempest, sea, and crew (connection by contiguity) and from these we are referred back again metaphorically to the state of France, its being at sea and in danger of tempest' (*Dickens: The Dreamer's Stance* (Ithaca, NY: Cornell University Press, 1965), 62–3).

[135] The point is a staple of Dickens criticism. See, e.g., Alexander Welsh, *The City of Dickens* (Oxford: Clarendon Press, 1971), 130; Lawrence Frank, 'Dickens' *A Tale of Two Cities*: The Poetics of Impasse', in Michael A. Cotsell (ed.), *Critical Essays on Charles Dickens's* A Tale of Two Cities (New York: G. K. Hall, 1998), 128–31; Albert D. Hutter, 'Nation and Generation in *A Tale of Two Cities*', *PMLA*, 93 (May 1978), 455; John Gardiner, 'Dickens and the Uses of History', in David Paroissien (ed.), *A Companion to Charles Dickens* (Malden, MA: Blackwell, 2008), 254; and Catherine Waters, *Dickens and the Politics of the Family* (Cambridge: Cambridge University Press, 1997), 147.

[136] Jean-Pierre Vernier rightly notes that: 'Toute l'intrigue... repose sur l'utilisation du double et du masque, procédé qui n'a rien d'exceptionnnel mais qui permet à Dickens de créer de nombreuses variations fort complexes à différents niveaux' ('Lecture de *A Tale of Two Cities*', in Sylvère Monod (ed.), *Charles Dickens et la France: Colloque International de Boulogne-sur-Mer, 3 juin 1978* (Lille: Presses Universitaires de Lille, 1979), 72; see also 70–1). Paul Davis interprets the text similarly: 'Reading *A Tale of Two Cities* calls for double vision, for England is implicit in the images of France, characters divide within themselves or mirror others, the present lingers as a palimpsest in the annals of the past' ('A Tale of Two Cities', in David Paroissien (ed.), *A Companion to Charles Dickens* (Malden, MA: Blackwell, 2008), 414; see also 420).

[137] Frank, 'Dickens' *A Tale of Two Cities*', 114.

time, these negative paternal influences are supplanted in both works by the more powerful and positive perspective of a good 'father'—that is, of Manette and Cimourdain.[138] Gauvain's identification with the 'transfigured' Lantenac, on the other hand, rewrites the relations between Darnay and Evrémonde, who presents no redeeming qualities. The complex interlacing of the characters of Hugo's (great-)uncle and nephew is, in Dickens, much more dichotomous.

Like Lantenac, Dr Manette is presented in 'Recalled to Life', the opening section of Dickens's own tripartite book, with all the fanfare of a chief protagonist. Even near the novel's close, the celebrated martyr of the Bastille views himself as the saviour of his son-in-law, a moral victor in his own right: 'He had accomplished the task he had set himself, his promise was redeemed, he had saved Charles. Let them all lean upon him' (*TTC* 305). His division between sanity and madness is doubled by Carton's divided loyalties and split personality and by Charles's shared identity with both Carton and Manette himself. For Paul Davis, the use of split characters, replications, and doubles in the text makes it 'difficult to decide just who is the hero of the story'[139]—a tactic we observed at the beginning of *Quatrevingt-Treize* as well. Darnay thus pleads with Lucie's father for her hand by depicting himself as a kindred spirit:

> Like you, a voluntary exile from France; like you, driven from it by its distractions, oppressions, and miseries; like you, striving to live away from it by my own exertions, and trusting in a happier future . . . Not to divide with Lucie her privilege as your child, companion, and friend; but to come in aid of it, and bind her closer to you, if such a thing can be' (*TTC* 142–3)[140]

Instead of being structured around one very simple case of double identity, *A Tale of Two Cities* discloses the proliferation of paired characters also central to *Quatrevingt-Treize*.[141] Moreover, as with Hugo, it is through

[138] According to Frank, Darnay 'meets in Manette the father he might have chosen for himself' ('Dickens' *A Tale of Two Cities*', 119).

[139] Davis, 'A Tale of Two Cities', 420. See also Simon Petch, 'Economies of Love and Law in *A Tale of Two Cities*', in Penny Gay, Judith Johnston, and Catherine Waters (eds), *Victorian Turns, NeoVictorian Returns: Essays on Fiction and Culture* (Newcastle upon Tyne: Cambridge Scholars, 2008), 75.

[140] Cf. Michael Hollington's hypothesis that the theme of exile in Dickens's text reflects the writer's 'painful separation from his wife . . . in 1858, which can be seen . . . as a kind of voluntary self-exile, or banishment into exile, or both . . . Metaphorically at least he had become a version of the figure we find imprinted at the heart of *A Tale of Two Cities*, a wanderer and exile from felicity' ('The Losing Game: Exile and Threshold in *A Tale of Two Cities*', *Cahiers victoriens et édouardiens*, 51 (2000), 191).

[141] Petch uncovers several instances of triangulation in Dickens's novel, 'most obviously in the Carton–Darnay–Lucie relationships, and most powerfully in the intensely configured triangle, modelled on the triadic structure of the trust . . . formed by the agreement between

the relations of 'parents' and 'children' that Dickens suggests some final reconciliation of all these opposites.

But the quest for unity is hampered here, too, by powerful forces of disjunction. Again, there is a monster of sterility—the guillotine—to confront and vanquish. Looming over Dickens's novel, this barren, bloodthirsty presence captures the vengeful spirit that permeates the revolutionaries' notion of justice. It is a spirit no more enlightened than that of the aristocrats they seek to overthrow. The gluttonous marquis, rumoured to be 'rather rapidly swallowing France' (*TTC* 110), meets a vampire's end when he is driven 'fast to his tomb' (*TTC* 137) with a stake/dagger through the heart. Unsatisfied, the populace continues to arm itself 'in hunger and revenge' (*TTC* 227), and the revolutionaries crowd the courtrooms with 'life-thirsting, cannibal-looking, bloody-minded [jurymen]' (*TTC* 334). Foreshadowing Hugo's image of the self-consuming civil war, Dickens uses the 'metaphor of cannibalism'[142] to depict the revolutionaries' devolution. Even the crowd's old hero, Dr Manette, realizes that, in the right circumstances, they would gladly 'rend him to pieces and strew him over the streets' (*TTC* 303). This rapaciousness is, in turn, reflected in their chief instrument of justice: 'All the devouring and insatiate Monsters imagined since imagination could record itself, are fused in the one realization, Guillotine' (*TTC* 390). For both Hugo and Dickens, the trope of primitive justice, of vengeance, is *sparagmos*: dismemberment and radical disjunction. Lantenac the 'tigre' (xv. 488) meets his match in the 'tigress' (*TTC* 381), Madame Defarge.[143]

Dickens does not, like Hugo, repeat the patterns of civil war in moral dilemmas affecting his major characters. But these patterns emerge, as with *Quatrevingt-Treize*, in familial confrontations. Anticipating Gauvain, Darnay opposes an aristocratic uncle while potentially losing the support of his adopted father-figure in a court setting. Those who so ardently preach 'Liberty, Equality, Fraternity, or Death' in *A Tale of Two Cities* do

Lucie and Carton to keep Carton's secret' ('Economies of Love and Law', 75–6). Although less complicated than the triangulated relationship between the Janus figures of Gauvain, Cimourdain, and Lantenac, Hugo may have noticed the pattern in Dickens.

142 Waters, *Dickens and the Politics of the Family*, 134.

143 Like Hugo, Dickens witnessed public beheadings. He was, moreover, fascinated by violent death. John Carey reports that Dickens was drawn to public executions and that he 'never missed a human carcass if he could help it' (*The Violent Effigy: A Study of Dickens's Imagination* (London: Faber, 1973), 81; see also 20–2). According to Albert D. Hutter, the theme of mutilation in Dickens stands as a 'metaphor for social disintegration' ('Dismemberment and Articulation in *Our Mutual Friend*', in Michael Timko, Fred Kaplan, and Edward Giuliano (eds), *Dickens Studies Annual: Essays on Victorian Fiction*, xi (New York: AMS Press, 1983), 163). Cf. also James M. Brown, *Dickens: Novelist in the Market Place* (London: Macmillan, 1982), 122.

not hesitate to turn family members against each other to avenge past social wrongs through future generations of innocents. One might argue that the reconciliation of generations in Hugo through the character of Gauvain responds to Dickens's more sombre picture of 'the recurring struggle between generations, between fathers and sons'.[144] The judge presiding at Charles's trial tells Manette: 'If the Republic should demand of you the sacrifice of your child herself, you would have no duty but to sacrifice her' (*TTC* 335).[145] It is a sacrifice of biblical proportions, one that Abraham–Cimourdain carries out in Hugo's narrative. Similarly, it is possible to perceive in Sydney Carton's general disarray something like Gauvain's inner tumult during his moral dilemma. As part of their dramatic structure, both texts depict individuals under inner and outer pressure alike.

As in *Quatrevingt-Treize*, apparent oppositions prevail in the world where Manette, Darnay, and Carton struggle for dignity and survival. For Dickens, eighteenth-century England and France are pitted against each other, not so much as political antagonists, but as two antithetical social constructs and views of the future. Charles renounces his nationality and his birthright, declaring to his uncle that '[this] property and France are lost to me', that he will abandon this 'wilderness of misery and ruin' (*TTC* 132) to earn his own living in that 'Refuge' (*TTC* 133) he calls England. In a more comic vein, Lucie's guardian companion Miss Pross asserts her national virtue against the demonic Madame Defarge at the novel's close: 'You might, from your appearance, be the wife of Lucifer . . . Nevertheless, you shall not get the better of me. I am an Englishwoman' (*TTC* 386).[146] The moral battlelines are drawn in this symbolic 'confrontation between France and England',[147] with England clearly having the upper hand.

[144] Frank, 'Dickens' *A Tale of Two Cities*', 131.

[145] For the melodramatic aspects of this trial scene, see Sally Ledger, 'From the Old Bailey to Revolutionary France: The Trials of Charles Darnay', in Colin Jones, Josephine McDonagh, and Jon Mee (eds), *Charles Dickens,* A Tale of Two Cities *and the French Revolution* (Chippenham: Palgrave Macmillan, 2009), 82–3.

[146] Associated with Lucifer, Madame Defarge is a diabolical version of Lantenac, who in Gauvain's eyes is transformed from 'l'infernal Satan' to 'le Lucifer céleste' (xv. 488) when he saves the Fléchard childen. In *TTC,* her counterpart is plainly Lucie, who 'brings light to a dark, troubled world' (James Hamilton, 'Terrorizing the "Feminine"', 210). See also Davis, 'A Tale of Two Cities', 417–18; Doris Y. Kadish, *Politicizing Gender: Narrative Strategies in the Aftermath of the French Revolution* (New Brunswick, NJ: Rutgers University Press, 1991), 157; John Kucich, 'The Purity of Violence: *A Tale of Two Cities*', in Howard Bloom (ed.), *Charles Dickens's* A Tale of Two Cities (New York: Chelsea House, 1987), 65; John B. Lamb, 'Domesticating History: Revolution and Moral Management in *A Tale of Two Cities*', *Dickens Studies Annual,* 25 (1996), 234; and Waters, *Dickens and the Politics of the Family,* 125, 139).

[147] Waters, *Dickens and the Politics of the Family,* 141.

In particular, Dickens's constitutional monarchy represents the opportunity to engage, not in endless cycles of vengeance, but in ordinary business. While young Jerry Cruncher yearns to inherit his father's trade and Mr Lorry glories in the efficiency and respectability of Tellson's Bank, Charles Darnay is able to find work enough to support himself and his loved ones. 'Le business', by way of contrast, does not figure at all in Hugo's novel. Indeed, *Quatrevingt-Treize* deals almost exclusively in the clash of ideals and principles rather than the pragmatics of succeeding in daily life.

Yet the contrasts between the two countries in *A Tale of Two Cities* are, for the most part, superficial. Throughout the text, Dickens suggests that the world it portrays is but an analogue for mid-nineteenth-century England. 'It was the best of times, it was the worst of times,' he famously begins, a mixture of heaven and hell much 'like the present time' (*TTC* 3). The explicit reference to his own era boldly asserts a relationship that remains much more implicit in *Quatrevingt-Treize*. Dickens's derisive treatment of the revolutionaries is doubled by an even greater pity for what they suffered under the French monarchy. This contempt for anyone who knows neither love nor mercy culminates in the novel's closing plea for social reform to those inhabiting the here and now: 'Sow the same seed of rapacious licence and oppression over again, and it will surely yield the same fruit according to its kind' (*TTC* 391).[148] The prevailing notion of justice in Georgian England—'Whatever is, is right' (*TTC* 64)—finds its echo not only in the new French Republic (as depicted in both *A Tale* and Hugo's text) but also in the reality of Dickens's day. J. M. Rignall asserts, regarding Dickens's determinism, that 'the potential for violence is not confined to a savage past and an alien setting but lies very close to home... the violent continuum [of history] may not have expired with the Revolution'.[149] So, when the author castigates the French nobles' 'inhuman abandonment of consideration not easy to be understood in these days' (*TTC* 116) or sardonically enumerates the 'luxuries befitting the state of a marquis in a luxurious age and country' (*TTC* 127), he is

[148] Others have noted the comparison. See, e.g., Edward Wagenknecht, 'Introduction', in Charles Dickens, *A Tale of Two Cities* (New York: Random House, 1967), p. xvi; Andrew Sanders, 'Dickens's French Historical Novel', in Sylvère Monod (ed.), *Charles Dickens et la France: Colloque International de Boulogne-sur-Mer, 3 juin 1978* (Lille: Presses Universitaires de Lille, 1979), 63; Vernier, 'Lecture de *A Tale of Two Cities*', 73; and Brown, *Dickens*, 115–16. For Gardiner, Dickens's 'lack of social complacency' and 'view of what oppression can drive people to... might almost have been addressed to those politicians who had thrown out [Lord John] Russell's [1854] reform bill only a few years ago' ('Dickens and the Uses of History', 251).

[149] J. M. Rignall, 'Dickens and the Catastrophic Continuum of History in *A Tale of Two Cities*', *ELH* 51/3 (Autumn 1984), 581.

simultaneously judging Victorian England. Through the story of Darnay, that 'elegant translator' (*TTC* 138), the two times and places are made equivalent. The dual citizenship of Charles and Lucie and Dr Manette, who announce elements of Hugo's double agents studied earlier in this chapter, provides a bridge between past and present. The 'headlong, mad, and dangerous [footsteps]' (*TTC* 232) once associated with the far-off French throngs may soon be sounded by English crowds. The people's 'Ogreish' (*TTC* 66) fascination with capital punishment will doubtless lead them to re-enact the full-scale legal massacres of those earlier 'Ogre[s]' (*TTC* 378) called Jacques if social reforms are not forthcoming.[150] In short, Dickens uses the French past to comment on the English present; Hugo's optic remains focused on the parallels between past and present-day France alone, with hints of a wider European alliance further off in the future.

The process of differentiation and equalization, so crucial to *Quatre-vingt-Treize*, likewise operates in *A Tale of Two Cities* not only with nations but also with the novel's protagonists. Hugo's spurious confraternal state echoes the systematic loss of otherness observed in the revolutionaries' treatment of Charles Darnay, who is considered no different from any other aristocrat. Although he has generously returned to France to save another, he falls victim himself to those fanatically avenging the aristocrats' earlier inhumanities. To equate Darnay thus with his vicious uncle, his 'twin', is to trade genuine justice for a blindly mathematical formula. Cimourdain, we have seen, makes a similar error in embracing the ideal of 'identité' (xv. 503) over Gauvain's notion of 'équité' (xv. 502), whereby individuals can be simultaneously the same and other. Hugo's clones share a common ancestry with Dickens's, all, of course, named Jacques—or jackal, cousins to the ferocious warriors in *Quatrevingt-Treize*.

And what of the transfigurations of Lantenac and Gauvain and the metaphorical substitution of one for the other in the dénouement of Hugo's narrative? Such miraculous transformations pervade the ending of *A Tale of Two Cities* as well. In particular, Sydney Carton cancels Darnay's failed quest to acquit himself and his future race of the sins of his forefathers by rescuing Charles from prison and facing death in his

[150] Cf. Vernier, who sees in the self-sacrifice of Carton, 'le miroir de Darnay', a model for the relations between the two countries, whereby 'le sacrifice de la paix sociale en France peut éventuellement permettre à l'Angleterre d'éviter ce genre d'épreuve' ('Lecture de *A Tale of Two Cities*', 74). Jones, McDonagh, and Mee further stress the risk in 1859 posed by Napoléon III's 'aggressive foreign policy' of 'giving the British ruling classes a pretext to put reform on the shelf for a generation or more, as had been the case in the 1790s and 1800s' ('Introduction', 10).

place.[151] Chris R. Vanden Bossche confirms that Darnay is liberated 'through a substitution of likenesses analogous to the writer's device of metaphorical substitution'.[152] Carton's triumph, which parallels Mr Lorry's earlier rescue of Dr Manette, permits the continuation of the Manette–Darnay line through a male heir. Just as Manette has conquered his 'natural antipathy' (*TTC* 353) for the child of his mortal enemies, so does Carton transcend a destructive past for Lucie's sake. His symbolic castration by the *vagina dentata* of the guillotine paradoxically preserves his own fertility, too, both through the generations of Darnay children named after him and by the power that his story will have over their hearts and minds. (The notion of passing wisdom on, metonymically, to the next generation anticipates the role of education in *Quatrevingt-Treize*.) Carton's 'transcendent rebirth from dissipated wastrel to heroic human being'[153] prefigures Lantenac's moral rehabilitation in saving the Fléchard children. The derelict's replacement of his more radiant twin in Dickens is, moreover, inverted in Hugo into Gauvain's shining self-sacrifice for his redeemed ancestor, 'Lucifer'–Lantenac. Both writers, however, subscribe to a system of interchangeability, or metaphorical parity, over strict mathematical equivalence.

Thus, Gauvain's final dream of society's metamorphosis and his firm step on the way to the guillotine reflect the future envisioned by Sydney Carton from the scaffold. Here, as in *Quatrevingt-Treize*, the final chapter works toward the 'retournement théâtralisé de la catastrophe en vision rédemptrice et anti-tragique'.[154] What Carton beholds there is not merely his own survival in Lucie and Charles's offspring, but also the progress of all individuals in freedom and justice. His 'firstborn' will grow to be 'foremost of just judges and honoured men' (*TTC* 396) and the bearer of his legend.[155] But Carton's utopian dream reaches wider still to encompass the entire French nation and even his native England:

[151] The 'suicidal vengeance' (*TTC* 333) of the revolutionaries is reflected in their homicidal wish to 'change places' (*TTC* 382) with any who would send them to their death; Carton, on the other hand, chooses to die not as a suicide but as a participant in a higher order of exchange. His original wish to 'change places' (*TTC* 89) with Darnay because of his love for Lucie is completely, if not ironically, fulfilled.

[152] Chris R. Vanden Bossche, 'Prophetic Closure and Disclosing Narrative: The French Revolution and *A Tale of Two Cities*', *Dickens Studies Annual*, 12 (1983), 216.

[153] Arthur Rankin, '"Recalled to Life": Sacrifice and Renewal in *A Tale of Two Cities*', in Harold Bloom and Blake Hobby (eds), *Rebirth and Renewal* (New York: Chelsea House, 2009), 208.

[154] Peyrache-Leborgne, 'Roman historique', 64.

[155] Cf. Ledger's comment that 'the projected establishment of a just legal order beyond the pages of the novel and outside of its chronology... is consonant with Dickens's commitment to legal reform in the 1850s' ('From the Old Bailey to Revolutionary France', 84).

> I see a beautiful city and a brilliant people rising from this abyss, and, in their struggles to be truly free . . . I see the evil of this time and of the previous time of which this is the natural birth, gradually making expiation for itself and wearing out.
>
> I see the lives for which I lay down my life, peaceful, useful, prosperous and happy, in that England which I shall see no more. (*TTC* 396)[156]

Carton's 'prophetic' (*TTC* 395) eye sees that France's madness will, like Dr Manette's, eventually yield to unity and sanity. This new integrity invites an even more complex form of social synthesis. Earlier, Dickens hints that Tellson's, that place of 'High Exchange' (*TTC* 248), provides a model for international commerce and cooperation. Carton repeats this suggestion through his own 'high trade' in the realm of ethical action: as the worthy son of his father-figure, Mr Lorry, he points the way to a confraternity without borders.

Adopting the condemned seamstress as his 'sister' (*TTC* 374), he helps her meet death with the sympathy that must one day join their respective countries: 'these two children of the Universal Mother, else so wide apart and differing, have come together, on the dark highway, to repair home together' (*TTC* 394).[157] The final union or 'togetherness' in death of Carton and the French seamstress should, the text implies, incorporate the best of both their nations. As Albert D. Hutter notes, 'Dickens' use of doubles [including England and France] may suggest, not splitting, but reunifying something once divided or divisible'.[158] Like Carton, Gauvain

[156] Cf. Garrett Stewart's superb analysis of the 'closural pattern of rhythmic repetition' in this scene, as well as of the limits of Carton's vision to the 'time elapsed between the Revolution and Dickens's writing of the novel in the middle of the next century'. Hugo's prospective history, glimpsed through Gauvain, extends well beyond the writer's own lifetime; in Dickens, 'the authority of fiction, like the authority of [Carton's] deathbed revelation, is held to the precincts of retrospect' ('Death by Water in *A Tale of Two Cities*', in Howard Bloom (ed.), *Charles Dickens's* A Tale of Two Cities (New York: Chelsea House, 1987), 114, 115) . To this end, Haussmann's impressive work in the 1850s of transforming Paris, for Dickens, into 'the very quintessence of urban modernity' meant that '[a] New London could learn from the example of the New Paris which Sydney Carton had imagined on the scaffold' (Jones, McDonagh, and Mee, 'Introduction', 14, 15).

[157] For both novelists, the ideal world can at present be found only in the afterlife, so Gauvain and Carton must give their lives to inhabit it. Cf. F. S. Schwartzbach: 'The only way Carton can reach this other, visionary city [evoked earlier in the novel] is to die—it is a prevision of heaven' (*Dickens and the City* (London: Athlone, 1979), 178).

[158] Hutter, 'Nation and Generation', 455. I therefore disagree with Sylvère Monod's conclusion that: 'The *Tale* . . . cannot be said to closely unite and associate the two cities. It merely relates the story of an Anglo-French family, a story which is set first in England, and later in France' (*Dickens the Novelist* (Norman: University of Oklahoma Press, 1968), 466). Hugo himself often referred to the fraternal link between these two nations—joined in the European community—during his exile. See esp. the excerpts from his speeches and other writings in Jersey and Guernsey in Barrère, *Victor Hugo à l'œuvre*, 97–9.

meets death accompanied by a spiritual 'sister'—his beloved 'âm[e] ... sœu[r]' (xv. 509), Cimourdain. Both texts close, then, 'non sur le tragique de l'Histoire, mais sur un autre registre et un autre contexte, celui de l'envol, celui d'une transcendance où la violence et la mort n'ont enfin plus de prise'.[159] Death becomes the passage to another mode of being, one that resolves all discordances.

Despite these striking thematic and stylistic resemblances, the two novels work from different rhetorical angles. At the risk of oversimplification, Hugo's approach is fundamentally metaphorical while Dickens's is metonymical. That is, Hugo injects into his work poetic qualities and analogical intricacies that add a third dimension to Dickens's wonderfully dramatic narrative. Towards the end of *Quatrevingt-Treize*, for example, Cimourdain speaks of taming that wild beast, utopia: in this way, the careening cannon of Part I foreshadows the priest's claim that Gauvain's ideal lacks sufficient direction or principle. The son's poetic vision, as revealed in their final encounter, needs to be grounded in more prosaic considerations. In my view, this underlying disparity between two very similar voices marks the primary distinction between Hugo and Dickens as well. Dickens's text repeatedly stresses the importance of continuity—that is, of narrative, hypotactic, metonymical structures—whereas Hugo's focuses primarily on originality and innovation—that is, on poetic, paratactic, metaphorical structures. Dickens promotes legacies; Hugo champions disjunctions and displacements.

A *Tale of Two Cities* is bound together by Lucie's 'Golden Thread' (Book II), spun—metonymically—across time and space. Not only does she weave together several generations of men who see themselves in each other because of their love for her; she also supplies the male child—the dropped stitch, the missing link—required for perpetuating all these loved ones in the future.[160] Dickens's dominant image of Lucie's connective thread is in essence a metaphor about narrative. For him, the historical process is defined, like the novel itself, by 'its emphatic linearity, continuity, and negative teleology'.[161] The only way around such strict determin-

[159] Peyrache-Leborgne, 'Roman historique', 65.

[160] Cf. Stoehr: 'the principle of combination and connection that holds [the many details of the novel] together in their clusters and larger configurations is contiguity. Metonymically and anaphorically controlled patterns dominate the structure, keeping the materials ordered' (*Dickens*, 32). Lucie's role as Madame Defarge's counterpart extends to her weaving as well: 'angelic and fairylike in its transcendence of time and space, [it] overcomes the dark side of mythos as symbolized by Defarge's fellow hag and *tricoteuse*, "Vengeance"' (James Hamilton, 'Terrorizing the "Feminine"', 211). See also Lamb's discussion of Lucie's binding function ('Domesticating History', 233, 236, 240–1) as a force opposed, for Dickens, to revolutionary madness.

[161] Rignall, 'Dickens and the Catastrophic Continuum of History', 575; see also 576, 586.

ism, in Dickens, lies in the atemporal, utopian space of domestic felicity that binds 'revolutionary desire' through 'repetitive sameness'; historical forgetfulness substitutes the 'bourgeois myth of progress' for the terrifying spectre of chaotic 'revolutionary change'.[162] One escapes civil upheaval by upholding eternal familial values.

Quatrevingt-Treize portrays instead the radical gaps and discontinuities of transfiguration, ruptures through which *sparagmos* continues to dominate Hugo's novel even as it depicts reconciliation and transcendence. Without 'tearing apart... the sacrificial body' there can be no leap to a higher order of being.[163] Carton sees all plainly at the end and leaves an heir to bring his dream to fruition. The dénouement of Dickens's *Tale* thus 'reaffirms the supremacy of bourgeois values—class structure, gender roles, and absolute moral values'.[164] Gauvain rejects the status quo, lapsing into silence as the metaphors of transformation multiply, a vision passed on to no one—except, perhaps, the reader. As we hear (or overhear) the imaginary dialogue between Dickens and Hugo, it is Hugo who poses questions, and Dickens who offers answers. Dickens wraps complicated issues up neatly, even pragmatically; Hugo continues to disturb us. It is possible that Dickens's death on 8 June 1870—just a few months before the end of the Second Empire and Hugo's triumphant return to Paris—prompted Hugo to have this last word in their literary relationship while yet paying homage to his English 'sibling'. In any case, his novel, which he began drafting on 16 December 1872, responds amply to Dickens's negative depiction of the French Revolution by illuminating and dramatizing the less-well-known utopian impulses implicated in the Reign of Terror. Still, as a fundamentally *poetic* historical novelist, he did not need to survive Dickens to assert the freshness of his own confraternal vision.

* * *

Are poets necessary to the Republic of the future? When Hugo's narrator notes that, under the French monarchy, Cimourdain felt 'vaguement républicain... de la république de Platon peut-être, et peut-être aussi de la république de Dracon' (xv. 346), the reader is well prepared for the dénouement. An agent of Draconian methods to the end of realizing the

[162] Lamb, 'Domesticating History', 234, 236; see also Rignall, 'Dickens and the Catastrophic Continuum of History', 585.

[163] Frye, *The Anatomy of Criticism*, 148. In Frye, '*sparagmos*, or the sense that heroism and effective action are absent, disorganized or foredoomed to defeat, and that confusion and anarchy reign over the world, is the archetypal theme of irony and satire' (*The Anatomy of Criticism*, 192). In Hugo, however, such defeat may be illusory, signaling triumph on yet another level.

[164] James Hamilton, 'Terrorizing the "Feminine"', 212.

French Republic, the priest never manages to think outside the system he has helped to create so that it can continue to evolve. To the condemned Gauvain, he declares, 'Tu te perds dans le nuage,' adding: 'Poésie. Défie toi des poètes' (xv. 502)—an allusion to Plato's warning in the *Republic* (Book 10) that poiēsis, which elicits unreasonable judgements by confusing the emotions, must be censored, if not banned, in the ideal political state. For the philosopher, truth and therefore the good lie *elsewhere*.

But Gauvain supplies the exiled Hugo's rebuttal. After the young hero has outlined his dreams for harnessing nature to produce abundant food and energy, Cimourdain again comments, 'Te voilà en plein songe,' to which Gauvain replies, 'C'est-à-dire en pleine réalité' (xv. 503). In other words, through metaphorical redescription the poetic imagination serves a genuinely mimetic function. As Ricoeur argues: '*Mimêsis* is *poiêsis*, and *poiêsis* is *mimêsis*' (*RM* 39). To banish poetry is, in Hugo's opinion, to banish the future.

It is no accident, then, that nature plays such a large role in *Quatrevingt-Treize*. According to the novelist's system, the 'work of formation/transformation' (*TN* ii. 80) that characterizes nature and poetry alike must be infused into the sociopolitical realm as well. For this reason, Hugo plunges his readers into a metaphoricized version of the French nation's past, the better to stimulate their own quest for *another* world. Although he himself is hardly likely to live to see his vision fulfilled, he leaves his text, like a message in a bottle, for future generations to ponder and to hold up to their own reality. If the drowning *comprachicos* in *L'Homme qui rit* set adrift an avowal of their sins against humanity, Hugo uses his 'poetics of transcendence' to confess his faith, not in steady evolution, but in human progress through radical individual and social transformation, along with artistic and technological innovation. Today, Gauvain's schemes for vast sources of energy—wind, water, and geothermal power—are at last on the cusp of coming to fruition. His dream of universal peace and harmony is still the stuff of fiction.

Conclusion

In a career that spanned over sixty years and five genres (poetry, drama, fiction, political writings, and critical prose), Victor Hugo exploited an astonishingly rich array of images and arguments that engaged the turbulent politics and literary currents of the nineteenth century. His fiction continues to attract readers and critics throughout the world, underscoring the transnational and transhistorical impact of his largely *poetic* reflections on the inseparable connections between individual and collective striving. If great works are 'those that never cease decontextualizing and recontextualizing themselves in the most diverse cultural circumstances' (*TN* iii. 179), then *Les Travailleurs de la mer*, *L'Homme qui rit*, and *Quatrevingt-Treize* must be considered among Hugo's *chefs d'œuvre*.

Hugo's later novels also pose exciting responses to the question of creativity and generativity in what is normally one's *troisième âge*—in this case the author's seventh and eighth decades. Like Beethoven's last quartets, the works of Hugo's mature years stand as monumental achievements. Examining Hugo's entire trajectory as a novelist enables us to see both cumulative change and the development of his literary identity. While Harold Bloom, W. Jackson Bate, and others have studied the sense of rivalry and 'the anxiety of influence' experienced by our very best authors, Hugo's writings help us to understand not just aspirations but strategies. In his poetic universe, the works interanimate each other, finally merging into one gigantic, socially engaged *œuvre*.

Key to this enormous literary creation is the notion of living history, communal as well as personal, a notion that plays to the elderly Hugo's strengths: his broad experience as a writer, citizen, family man, and statesman and his largely optimistic outlook. For such an artist, ageing does not entail despondency. Like his previous narratives, the later fiction reveals an arsenal of rhetorical and literary tactics for recuperating the past in order to shape the present, but with distinctly futuristic overtones. 'To think of history as one is to posit the equivalence between three ideas: one time, one humanity, one history . . . Without memory . . . there is no principle of hope' (*TN* iii. 258). Hugo's use of memory in the historical novel thus corresponds to Ricoeur's notion of heritage as 'enabl[ing] us to see how every turning backwards comes from a resoluteness . . . turned toward the future' (*TN* iii. 74). To recuperate the past is to illuminate and expand one's identity in preparation for moving forwards. Progress does not spring up *ex nihilo*. At the same time, Hugo would say, without metaphor we cannot imagine our past, envision our future, or judge either in relation to a political ideal. In their function as dynamic, semantic operations, his metaphorical statements point beyond themselves to the real as a kind of mimēsis. Poetic fiction is, for him, inseparable from historical fiction.

The enormous popular success of *Les Misérables* in effect granted Hugo licence to draw on nineteenth-century French history in order to suggest a path towards better days. Instead of repeating a simple formula for success, however, each novel after *Les Misérables* explores new potential for poetic discourse to effect social reform. Each novel is an experiment, not a part of a series like Scott's Waverley novels or Balzac's *Comédie humaine*. Moving from French to British history in *Les Travailleurs de la mer* and *L'Homme qui rit*, then back to royalist Brittany in *Quatrevingt-Treize*, Hugo envelops more places and centuries in his meditation on *universal* history. And, just as his use of metaphor allows an exchange between alien ideas, his historical reconstructions of the Channel Islands, the English post-Restoration period, and the French Terror enable readers to enter the imaginative space of past eras, to interpret them analogically in relation to the present, and to consider alternative futures. Ricoeur frames the temporal relationships nicely: 'On the one hand, the historical present is, in each era, the final term of a completed history, which itself completes and ends history. On the other hand, the present is, again in every era . . . the inaugural force of a history that is to be made' (*TN* iii. 239–40). Uniting utopian thought, dramatic emplotment, historical contexts, and poetic expression, *Les Travailleurs de la mer*, *L'Homme qui rit*, and *Quatrevingt-Treize* offer not just engaging epic tales but also complex paradigms for contemplating social equity and justice in the light of models of metaphorical parity.

In this way, Hugo's 'poetics of transcendence'—his quest for transcendent harmony beyond apparent discontinuities—is closely allied with both the logical clashes resolved by metaphor and Ricoeur's 'discordant concordances' that reconcile different perceptions of past, present, and future. Social disharmony, apocalyptic vision, the tensive quality of metaphor whereby disparate terms become equal—all contribute to Hugo's Romantic sublime. The notion of a geometry of chaos dates back to at least *Notre-Dame de Paris*, where the Romanesque foundation that underlies the Gothic cathedral represents Hugo's conception of his own fictive enterprise. The image of the spider, recycled from Frollo to Esmeralda to Quasimodo, repeats the effect of his textual web, whose transformative alchemy changes opposites into metaphorical equivalents. In *Les Misérables*, the motifs are layered in multidimensional, self-similar designs, so that even small details reflect and evoke the larger enterprise. Similarly, Hugo figures transcendence in his last three novels though elaborate verbal networks, where space and time intersect, and where metaphorical (lyrical) and metonymical (narrative) patterns reinforce each other. Appearing in ever more intricate configurations, these multi-level repetitions also incorporate features from his own earlier fiction. The patterns create the effect of spatial *mises en abyme*, ones doubled by spiralling temporal cycles that hold the promise of progress, despite occasional relapses into tyranny or social disorder. In salvaging his nation's *political* past—from the horrors of monarchic government in *L'Homme qui rit* to the origins of the Republic in *Quatrevingt-Treize*—Hugo also renews his own *creative* history and looks ahead to future glories on both counts.

As a young man, Hugo had dreamed of vying with Chateaubriand, Sir Walter Scott, and his own contemporaries for literary glory. At the end of his long career, he claimed the privilege of ranking with the most celebrated writers of Western literature. Hugo's major accomplishment was to become both the national poet *and* the Victorian Sage of France: he was its 'great man of letters', a kind of Thomas Carlyle, Charles Dickens, John Ruskin, and Alfred, Lord Tennyson—with elements of William Wordsworth, George Gordon, Lord Byron, and William Blake—rolled into one. In the twentieth century, Alexandr Solzhenitsyn might be considered his peer in the area of prose fiction. Still, one is hard pressed to identify a poet–novelist–playwright–essayist with a similar readership or unity of vision across time and genres.

Hugo was clearly aware of his *singularité*, so much so that, far from shrinking from any 'anxiety of influence', he fully embraced the concept within an international context. Indeed, one might conclude from our analysis of *Les Travailleurs de la mer*, *L'Homme qui rit*, and *Quatrevingt-Treize* that he purposely sought English exemplars of the genres in which he shone—Shakespeare for theatre, Milton for epic poetry, Dickens for socially conscious fiction—the better to pay homage to his various counterparts by having them live on as subtexts in his own work. 'L'intertextualité', Anne Ubersfeld maintains, 'n'est ni un rapport originel ou causal, ni une imitation, elle est une transformation. Lire un livre dans un autre livre . . . [c'est] voir ce que devient le livre dans l'œuvre d'autrui: quelles images, venues d'ailleurs, *membra disjecta*, accouchent d'autres images.'[1] Thus, while Hugo appropriates resources and elements supplied by other writers, the artistry is very much his own. His literary allusions constitute a mode of dialogue, of literary familiarity and camaraderie, rather than an expression of creative apprehension.

At the same time, the novelist's aim to compete not only with renowned contemporaries like Charles Dickens but also with the greatest writers of history—Vergil, Dante, Shakespeare, Milton—indicates far more than the presence of a powerful ego. It is not enough to imagine a vision of national history—one must also create a vision of the future, a collective destiny. Hugo's *œuvre* documents the ferocious trajectory of his ambition to make an indelible mark on the universe, to be remembered and celebrated in succeeding centuries for speaking truth to power, for being a prophetic voice. His deployment of self-similar motifs invites the reader to read through the many layers to glimpse the larger meaning. But Hugo's journey is not static, merely reflecting the self reflecting other selves in a supreme form of *l'art pour l'art*. Instead, it takes him into the future and into the transnational, where his audience is legion. He became one of the most widely translated, most widely read, authors of all times because he crafted his fiction to be both timely and timeless, historical and universal.

His final works thus position him, Janus-like, between his predecessors and his literary heirs. The singularly Hugolian synthesis of ethics and aesthetics, philosophy and poetics, aims to capture all reality, however disparate, chaotic, or fleeting, and to transform it into finely structured verbal constellations that stimulate the reader's sense of what *could* be. While these literary webs are beautiful in and of themselves, their political import indicates the seriousness of Hugo's endeavour. The seemingly infinite recursions are designed to persuade his readers, to lure them into the seductively haunting *mises en abyme* of his verbal constructs and turn their complacent attitudes topsy-turvy. For Hugo, believing is seeing, and he works relentlessly to create powerful, unforgettable visual images that convey equally powerful ideas.

The open-ended closures of the later novels assume fresh significance from this perspective, since they provide the last 'notes' on which Hugo's massive orchestrations end. Whether one interprets them tragically or comically, genuinely happy endings for Hugo's *readers* require that they become socially involved, mobilizing their imagination of alternative futures in order to continue the poet's struggles against political oppression. Like Milton, he employs tactics to develop 'readerly skills' in his compatriots, to

[1] Ubersfeld, *Paroles de Hugo*, 66.

create 'revolutionary reader[s] ... well armed to see through the manipulations of ... politicians'.[2] His fictive conjurations seek to expose the illusory nature of political propaganda and extremism, as well as other sham discourses, the better to counter them. Hugo challenges us as readers, critics, and citizens to engage with his works in our own times—and to hear the urgency of his voice.

* * *

My debt to Ricoeur in elucidating Hugo's work is obvious, and I suggest that this approach can be used to reconsider other authors as well. The conjunction of metaphorical redescription and historical refiguration provides, at the least, a model for exploring the prose fiction of other nineteenth-century French poets—for instance, Alfred de Vigny's *Cinq-Mars* (1825), Alfred de Musset's *Confession d'un enfant du siècle* (1836), or Théophile Gautier's *Mademoiselle de Maupin* (1835), *Le Roman de la momie* (1858), and *Le Capitaine Fracasse* (1863). Looking further abroad, one might turn to earlier narratives like Goethe's *Die Leiden des jungen Werthers* (1774) and *Wilhelm Meisters Lehrjahre* (1795–6) or Sir Walter Scott's two dozen volumes of historical fiction, given each writer's extensive poetic career and influence on the young Hugo. The intensely metaphorical language of Herman Melville's *Moby-Dick* (1851) invites scrutiny as well, especially since Melville was also a poet, though not known as such until after his death. The novels of William Faulkner, who published four collections of poetry in his lifetime (two others appeared posthumously), and of Vladimir Nabokov, who wrote hundreds of poems in Russian, might also lend themselves to a Ricoeurian reading. Such a reading could even be applied to non-poets—for instance, to the lyrical novels of Saul Bellow and William Styron.

Research along these lines should yield new insights into the peculiar qualities of poetic prose and, in the case of writers with a historical bent, into the relationship between metaphor and mimēsis. How unusual is the interweaving of both modes of analogical thinking found in Hugo's later fiction? Are the depictions of space and time equally extensive in other authors; are they equally subject to stunning *mises en abyme*? My guess is that the union in Hugo of lyrical and narrative discourse, of the 'power of redescription' and 'mimetic power', provides a unique model for the ways in which 'fiction makes use of history [to refigure time]' (*TN* iii. 181). As non-realist works of art apparently unconcerned with 'reflecting [the current] epoch', *Les Travailleurs de la mer*, *L'Homme qui rit*, and *Quatrevingt-Treize* illustrate Ricoeur's definition of 'true mimesis of action'

[2] Achinstein, *Milton and the Revolutionary Reader*, 222, 225.

(*TN* iii. 191). One might even claim that, by commenting indirectly on the present through representations of past and future history—representations that marry masterful plotting developments with unusually figurative language—Hugo's mimetic art rivals, if not surpasses, that of literary realism. Through his *poetic* historical narratives, he provides not only signature works but also some of the greatest *realist* novels of his day.

* * *

Two thousand years ago, Callimachus, a distinguished Greek critic, librarian, and author living in what is now Libya, offered what has become a famously pithy statement about lengthy tomes—*mega biblion, mega kakon* (a long book, a great evil). We could apply his maxim not just to the present volume but also to the challenge of considering Hugo's last three novels through the lens of his earlier works. I have argued that Hugo created and sustained a deeply metaphorical dialogue among his own writings—narrative, poetic, dramatic, political, and philosophical—as well as among the works of his literary rivals, living and dead, in the Western literary tradition. His intertextual credentials, in short, have been impeccable. The recurrent themes, *topoi*, and character types found in individual novels enable a larger, richer discourse about past and present relevant not only to France but to all nations. The remarkable consistency of his vision and passions throughout five decades explains the coherence of his aesthetics and politics. At the same time, we should recognize Hugo's vibrant capacity for reinvention, for continuous experimentation with mixing genres, especially the fusion of figurative language and historical fiction. The multi-level symmetries that structure the elaborate patterns, voices, and dynamics within and among the late novels carry the union of geometry and poetry first expounded in *Notre-Dame de Paris* to marvellously daring—and dazzling—extremes. For the *resolute* reader or critic, these works offer an extraordinary epic adventure.

Select Bibliography

Achinstein, Sharon, *Milton and the Revolutionary Reader* (Princeton, NJ: Princeton University Press, 1994).

Albouy, Pierre, *La Création mythologique chez Victor Hugo* (Paris: José Corti, 1963).

——'Présentation', to Victor Hugo, *L'Homme qui rit*, in *Œuvres complètes*, ed. Jean Massin, 18 vols (Paris: Le Club Français du Livre, 1967–70), xiv. 5–26.

——'Hugo, ou le Je éclaté', *Romantisme*, 1–2 (1971), 53–64.

Armstrong, Marie-Sophie, 'Hugo à l'aire Saint-Mittre: Zola et la problématique de la propriété littéraire', *French Review*, 76/2 (Dec. 2002), 346–57.

Aynesworth, Donald, 'Anonymity, Identity, and Narrative Sovereignty in *Quatrevingt-Treize*', *Kentucky Romance Quarterly* 29/2 (1982), 201–13.

Ballestra-Puech, Sylvie, '"Car Dieu, de l'araignée, avait fait le soleil": Métamorphoses d'Arachné chez Victor Hugo', in Dominique Peyrache-Leborgne and Yann Jumelais (eds), *Victor Hugo ou les frontières effacées* (Horizons Comparatistes; Nantes: Pleins Feux, 2002), 107–22.

Barrère, Jean-Bertrand, 'Victor Hugo et la Grande-Bretagne', *Revue de littérature comparée*, 28 (1954), 137–67.

——*Victor Hugo à l'œuvre: Le Poète en exil et en voyage* (Paris: Klincksieck, 1970).

——'Victor Hugo et le franglais', in A. R. W. James (ed.), *Victor Hugo et la Grande-Bretagne* (Vinaver Studies in French, 3; Liverpool: Francis Cairns Publications, 1986), 15–22.

Barthes, Roland, *Le Plaisir du texte* (Paris: Seuil,1973).

Baudelaire, Charles, 'Victor Hugo', in *L'Art romantique*, ed. Henri Lemaitre, in *Curiosités esthétiques et* L'Art romantique (Paris: Garnier, 1962), 729–43.

Baudouin, Charles, *Psychanalyse de Victor Hugo* (Paris: Armand Colin, 1972) (first pub. 1943 by Éditions du Mont-Blanc, Geneva).

Bernard, Claudie, 'Le Supplément contractuel: Lecture de *Quatrevingt-treize* de Victor Hugo', *Romanic Review*, 75 (1984), 335–55.

——'"Les Travailleurs de la mer" et le travail du texte', *Letteratura francese contemporanea le correnti d'avanguardia*, 7/17 (1986), 31–47.

——*Le Chouan romanesque: Balzac, Barbey d'Aurevilly, Hugo* (Paris: Presses Universitaires de France, 1989).

Bloom, Harold, *The Anxiety of Influence: A Theory of Poetry* (New York: Oxford University Press, 1973).

Bougeard-Vetö, Marie-Élisabeth, *Chateaubriand Traducteur: De l'exil au* Paradis perdu (Romantisme et Modernités, 91; Paris: Champion, 2005).

Brombert, Victor, *Victor Hugo and the Visionary Novel* (Cambridge, MA: Harvard University Press, 1984).

Brombert, Victor, 'Ma destinée: "L'ordre, c'est le délire"', in Jacques Seebacher and Anne Ubersfeld (eds), *Hugo le fabuleux: Actes du Colloque de Cerisy, 30 juin–10 juillet 1985* (Paris: Seghers, 1985), 224–38.

Brooks, Peter, *The Melodramatic Imagination: Balzac, Henry James, Melodrama, and the Mode of Excess* (New Haven, CT: Yale University Press, 1976).

Brown, James M., *Dickens: Novelist in the Market Place* (London: Macmillan, 1982).

Brunet, Étienne, *Le Vocabulaire de Victor Hugo*, i (Paris: Champion-Slatkine, 1988).

Bryson, Michael, *The Tyranny of Heaven: Milton's Rejection of God as King* (Newark: University of Delaware Press, 2004).

Çambel, A. B., *Applied Chaos Theory: A Paradigm for Complexity* (San Diego, CA: Academic Press, 1993).

Campion, Pierre, 'Raison de la littérature: *Quatrevingt-treize* de Victor Hugo', *Romantisme*, 124/2 (2004), 103–14.

Carey, John, *The Violent Effigy: A Study of Dickens's Imagination* (London: Faber, 1973).

Charles, David, *La Pensée technique dans l'œuvre de Victor Hugo: Le Bricolage de l'infini* (Paris: Presses Universitaires de France, 1997).

Chateaubriand, François-René de, *Le Génie du Christianisme* (Paris: Firmin Didot, 1858) (first pub. 1802).

Cobb, Noel, *Prospero's Island: The Secret Alchemy at the Heart of* The Tempest (London: Coventure, 1984).

Couffignal, Robert, 'Le *Paradis Perdu* de Victor Hugo à Pierre-Jean Jouve', in Jacques Blondel (ed.), *Le* Paradis Perdu *1667–1967* (Lettres modernes; Paris: Minard, 1967), 251–74.

Dällenbach, Lucien, *Le Récit spéculaire: Essai sur la mise en abyme* (Paris: Seuil, 1977).

Danton, Georges, 'Sur un nouvel impôt et de nouvelles levées', in *Discours civiques de Danton*, ed. Hector Fleishmann (Paris: Fasquelle-Charpentier, 1920).

Davies, Stevie, *Images of Kingship in* Paradise Lost*: Milton's Politics and Christian Liberty* (Columbia: University of Missouri Press, 1983).

Davis, Paul, 'A Tale of Two Cities', in David Paroissien (ed.), *A Companion to Charles Dickens* (Blackwell Companions to Literature and Culture, 51; Malden, MA: Blackwell, 2008), 412–21.

Delattre, Floris, *Dickens et la France* (Paris: Gamber, 1927).

Denby, David, 'Civil War, Revolution and Justice in Victor Hugo's *Quatrevingt-treize*', *Romance Studies*, 30 (1997), 7–17.

Devonshire, M. G., *The English Novel in France, 1830–1870* (London: University of London Press, 1929).

Dickens, Charles, *A Tale of Two Cities*, ed. Edward Wagenknecht (New York: Random House, 1967) (first pub. 1859).

Eco, Umberto, 'Excess and History in Hugo's *Ninety-Three*', in Franco Moretti (ed.), *The Novel: Forms and Themes*, ii (Princeton, NJ: Princeton University Press, 2006), 274–94.

Fallon, Robert Thomas, *Divided Empire: Milton's Political Imagery* (University Park: Pennsylvania State University Press, 1995).

Ferguson, Priscilla Parkhurst, '*Quatrevingt-treize*: Turning the Terror to Account', in Robert T. Denomme and Roland H. Simon (eds), *Unfinished Revolutions: Legacies of Upheaval in Modern French Culture* (University Park: Pennsylvania State University Press, 1998), 66–80.

Fish, Stanley Eugene, *Surprised by Sin: The Reader in* Paradise Lost (London: Macmillan, 1967).

Forster, John, *The Life of Charles Dickens*, ed. A. J. Hoppé, i (London: Dent, 1966) (first pub. 1872–4).

Forsyth, Neil, *The Satanic Epic* (Princeton: Princeton University Press, 2003).

Foucault, Michel, *Discipline and Punish: The Birth of the Prison*, trans. Alan Sheridan (New York: Pantheon Books, 1977); orig. pub. as *Surveiller et Punir* (Paris: Gallimard, 1975).

Fowler, Elizabeth, 'The Ship Adrift', in Peter Hulme and William H. Sherman (eds), The Tempest *and its Travels* (Philadelphia: University of Pennsylvania Press, 2000), 37–40.

Frank, Lawrence, 'Dickens' *A Tale of Two Cities*: The Poetics of Impasse', in Michael A. Cotsell (ed.), *Critical Essays on Charles Dickens's* A Tale of Two Cities (Critical Essays on British Literature; New York: G. K. Hall, 1998), 111–32. From *American Imago*, 36 (1979), 214–44.

Friedemann, Joë, '*L'Homme qui rit* ou les voix du silence', in Dominique Peyrache-Leborgne and Yann Jumelais (eds), *Victor Hugo ou les frontières effacées* (Horizons Comparatistes; Nantes: Pleins Feux, 2002), 197–210.

Frye, Northrop, *The Anatomy of Criticism* (Princeton, NJ: Princeton University Press, 1957).

Fukuyama, Francis, *The End of History and the Last Man* (New York: Free Press, 1992).

Gardiner, John, 'Dickens and the Uses of History', in David Paroissien (ed.), *A Companion to Charles Dickens* (Blackwell Companions to Literature and Culture, 51; Malden, MA: Blackwell, 2008), 240–54.

Gaudon, Jean, *Le Temps de la contemplation: L'Œuvre poétique de Victor Hugo des* Misères *au* Seuil du gouffre *(1845–1856)* (Paris: Flammarion, 1969).

——'"L'Homme qui rit" ou la Parole impossible', *L'Information littéraire*, 35/5 (1984), 197–204.

——'Les Vicissitudes du savoir', in Guy Rosa (ed.), L'Homme qui rit *ou la parole-monstre de Victor Hugo* (Paris: SEDES, 1985), 25–34.

Gaudon, Sheila, 'Anglophobie?', in A. R. W. James (ed.), *Victor Hugo et la Grande-Bretagne* (Vinaver Studies in French, 3; Liverpool: Francis Cairns Publications, 1986), 53–73.

Genette, Gérard, *Narrative Discourse: An Essay in Method*, trans. Jane E. Lewin (Ithaca, NY: Cornell University Press, 1983); orig. pub. as *Nouveau Discours du récit* (Paris: Seuil, 1980).

Gélineau, Alain-René, *Victor Hugo et l'expérience de la transcendance* (Paris: Argel, 1984).

Georgel, Pierre, 'La "figure" de Victor Hugo: Les images', in Pierre Georgel (dir.), *La Gloire de Victor Hugo* (Paris: Éditions de la Réunion des musées nationaux, 1985), 64–157.

Gerstman, Gayla, 'The Mastery of Language and Language of Mastery in Victor Hugo's *L'Homme qui rit*', in Carrol F. Coates (ed.), *Repression and Expression: Literary and Social Coding in Nineteenth-Cenury France* (Studies on Themes and Motifs in Literature, 22; New York: Peter Lang, 1996), 81–7.

Gillet, Jean, *Le* Paradis perdu *dans la littérature française de Voltaire à Chateaubriand* (Paris: Klincksieck, 1975).

——'Milton dans *Cromwell*', in A. R. W. James (ed.), *Victor Hugo et la Grande-Bretagne* (Vinaver Studies in French, 3; Liverpool: Francis Cairns Publications, 1986), 39–48.

Gleick, James, *Chaos: Making a New Science* (New York: Viking, 1987).

Gleizes, Delphine, 'Les Paradoxes de la cave pénale: De quelques représentations carcérales dans l'œuvre de Victor Hugo', *Romantisme*, 126/4 (2004), 17–28.

Gohin, Yves, 'Introduction' [to *Les Travailleurs de la mer*]', in Victor Hugo, *Notre-Dame de Paris: 1482* et *Les Travailleurs de la mer*, ed. Jacques Seebacher and Yves Gohin (Paris: Pléïade-Gallimard, 1975), 1257–90.

——'Une histoire qui date', in Anne Ubersfeld and Guy Rosa (eds), *Lire* Les Misérables (Paris: José Corti, 1985), 29–57.

——'Alternance et adhérance des contraires dans *Quatrevingt-Treize*', in J. A. Hiddleston (ed.), *Victor Hugo,* Romancier de l'abîme*: New Studies on Hugo's Novels* (Legenda/Research Monographs in French Studies; Oxford: European Humanities Research Centre, 2002), 156–78.

Granet, Michel, 'L'Idéologie de la révolution chez V. Hugo à travers sa trilogie incomplète, *L'Homme qui rit/La Monarchie/Quatre-Vingt-Treize*', in Anne-Marie Amiot (ed.), *Idéologies hugoliennes*, Actes du Colloque Interdisciplinaire, 23–25 May 1985 (Nice: Serre, 1985), 19–30.

——'La Mise en abyme de l'aventure et de l'écriture dans *L'Homme qui rit*', in Guy Rosa (ed.), L'Homme qui rit *ou la parole-monstre de Victor Hugo* (Paris: SEDES, 1985), 47–53.

Grant, Richard B., *The Perilous Quest: Image, Myth, and Prophecy in the Narratives of Victor Hugo* (Durham, NC: Duke University Press, 1968).

——'Victor Hugo's *Les Travailleurs de la mer*: Towards an Epic Synthesis', *L'Esprit créateur*, 16/3 (Fall 1976), 231–46.

Grossman, Kathryn M., *The Early Novels of Victor Hugo: Towards a Poetics of Harmony* (Histoire des idées et critique littéraire, 241; Geneva: Librairie Droz, 1986).

——*Figuring Transcendence in* Les Misérables*: Hugo's Romantic Sublime* (Carbondale: Southern Illinois University Press, 1994).

——'Nouer, dénouer, ouvrir: La Fin des *Misérables*', in Pierre Laforgue (ed.), *Pratiques d'écriture: Hommage à Jean Gaudon* (Bibliothèque du XIXe siècle; Paris: Klincksieck, 1996), 227–41.

Grossman, Marshall, *'Authors to Themselves': Milton and the Revelation of History* (Cambridge: Cambridge University Press, 1987).

Guerlac, Suzanne, 'Exorbitant Geometry in Hugo's *Quatrevingt-treize*', *MLN*, 96 (May 1981), 856–76.

——*The Impersonal Sublime: Hugo, Baudelaire, Lautréamont* (Stanford, CA: Stanford University Press, 1990).

Hamilton, Donna B., *Virgil and* The Tempest*: The Politics of Imitation* (Columbus: Ohio State University Press, 1990).

Hamilton, James F., 'Terrorizing the "Feminine" in Hugo, Dickens, and France', *Symposium*, 48/3 (Fall 1994), 204–15.

Hiddleston, J. A., 'Suicide in the Novels of Victor Hugo', in J. A. Hiddleston (ed.), *Victor Hugo,* Romancier de l'abîme*: New Studies on Hugo's Novels* (Legenda/Research Monographs in French Studies; Oxford: European Humanities Research Centre, 2002), 196–211.

Hill, Christopher, *Milton and the English Revolution* (New York: Viking, 1977).

Hollington, Michael, 'The Losing Game: Exile and Threshold in *A Tale of Two Cities*', *Cahiers victoriens et édouardiens*, 51 (2000), 189–205.

Hooker, Kenneth Ward, *The Fortunes of Victor Hugo in England* (New York: Columbia University Press, 1938).

Hugo, Adèle, *Victor Hugo raconté par un témoin de sa vie: 1802–juin 1821*, in Victor Hugo, *Œuvres complètes*, ed. Jean Massin, i (Paris: Le Club Français du Livre, 1967), 829–991.

Hugo, François-Victor, trans., *Œuvres complètes de W. Shakespeare*, 18 vols. (Paris: Pagnerre, 1859–72).

Hugo, Victor, *Œuvres complètes*, ed. Jean Massin, 18 vols (Paris: Club Français du livre, 1967–70).

Hugo, Victor-Marie, *Œuvres complètes*, ed. Paul Ollendorff and Albin Michel, 46 vols (Paris: Imprimerie nationale, 1904–52).

Hutter, Albert D., 'Nation and Generation in *A Tale of Two Cities*', *PMLA*, 93 (May 1978), 448–62.

——'Dismemberment and Articulation in *Our Mutual Friend*', in Michael Timko, Fred Kaplan, and Edward Giuliano (eds), *Dickens Studies Annual: Essays on Victorian Fiction*, xi (New York: AMS Press, 1983), 135–75.

Jackson, William J., *Heaven's Fractal Net: Retrieving Lost Visions in the Humanities* (Bloomington: Indiana University Press, 2004).

James, Tony, *Dream, Creativity, and Madness in Nineteenth-Century France* (Oxford: Clarendon Press, 1995).

Jameson, Fredric, *Marxism and Form: Twentieth-Century Dialectical Theories of Literature* (Princeton, NJ: Princeton University Press, 1971).

——'Progress versus Utopia', *Science-Fiction Studies*, 9/2 (July 1982), 147–58.

Jones, Colin, McDonagh, Josephine, and Mee, Jon, 'Introduction: *A Tale of Two Cities* in Context', in Colin Jones, Josephine McDonagh, and Jon Mee (eds), *Charles Dickens,* A Tale of Two Cities *and the French Revolution* (Palgrave Studies in Nineteenth-Century Writing and Culture; Chippenham: Palgrave Macmillan, 2009), 1–23.

Kadish, Doris Y., *Politicizing Gender: Narrative Strategies in the Aftermath of the French Revolution* (New Brunswick, NJ: Rutgers University Press, 1991).

Kant, Immanuel, *Critique of Judgment*, trans. J. H. Bernard (New York: Hafner, 1968); orig. pub. as *Kritik der Urteilskraft* (1790).

Kessler, Joan C., 'Babelic Ruin, Babelic "Ebauche": An Introduction to a Hugolian Problematic', *Stanford French Review*, 7/3 (Winter 1983), 285–99.

Knoppers, Laura Lunger, *Historicizing Milton: Spectacle, Power, and Poetry in Restoration England* (Athens: University of Georgia Press, 1994).

Kucich, John, 'The Purity of Violence: *A Tale of Two Cities*', in Howard Bloom (ed.), *Charles Dickens's* A Tale of Two Cities (Modern Critical Interpretations; New York: Chelsea House, 1987), 57–72. From *Dickens Studies Annual* 8 (1980), 119–37.

Laforgue, Pierre, 'Le Romanesque et l'écriture de l'histoire dans *L'Homme qui rit*', in Guy Rosa (ed.), L'Homme qui rit *ou la parole-monstre de Victor Hugo* (Paris: SEDES, 1985), 231–50.

——'La Révolution française vue d'Angleterre', in A. R. W. James (ed.), *Victor Hugo et la Grande-Bretagne* (Vinaver Studies in French, 3; Liverpool: Francis Cairns Publications, 1986), 121–36.

——*Victor Hugo et* La Légende des siècles: *De la publication des* Contemplations *à l'abandon de* La Fin de Satan *(avril 1856–avril 1860)* (Orléans: Paradigme, 1997).

——'Réalité, possible et chimère, dans *Les Travailleurs de la mer*', in Michel Viegnes (ed.), *Hugo et la chimère* (*Recherches & Travaux*, 62/Revue de UFR de Lettres Classiques et Modernes; Grenoble: ELLUG/Éditions littéraires et linguistiques de l'Université de Grenoble, 2003), 49–71.

Lamb, John B., 'Domesticating History: Revolution and Moral Management in *A Tale of Two Cities*', *Dickens Studies Annual*, 25 (1996), 227–43.

Ledger, Sally, 'From the Old Bailey to Revolutionary France: The Trials of Charles Darnay', in Colin Jones, Josephine McDonagh, and Jon Mee (eds), *Charles Dickens,* A Tale of Two Cities *and the French Revolution* (Palgrave Studies in Nineteenth-Century Writing and Culture; Chippenham: Palgrave Macmillan, 2009), 75–86.

Leonard, John, 'Introduction', in John Milton, *Paradise Lost* (London: Penguin, 2000), pp. ii–xli.

Lestringant, Frank, 'L'"Archipel de la Manche", ou l'Insulaire de Hugo', *Studi francesi*, 47/2 (2003), 267–74.

Leuilliot, Bernard, 'La Loi des tempêtes', in Jacques Seebacher and Anne Ubersfeld (eds), *Hugo le fabuleux: Actes du Colloque de Cerisy, 30 juin–10 juillet 1985* (Paris: Seghers, 1985), 84–97.

——'L'Histoire réelle telle qu'en Shakespeare', in A. R. W. James (ed.), *Victor Hugo et la Grande-Bretagne* (Vinaver Studies in French, 3; Liverpool: Francis Cairns Publications, 1986), 141–59.

——'Introduction', in Victor Hugo, *Quatrevingt-Treize* (Paris: Livre de Poche, 2001), 7–43.

Loewenstein, David, *Milton and the Drama of History* (Cambridge: Cambridge University Press, 1990).

——*Milton's* Paradise Lost (Cambridge: Cambridge University Press, 1993).

——*Representing Revolution in Milton and his Contemporaries* (Cambridge: Cambridge University Press, 2001).

Lowrie, Joyce O., *Sightings: Mirrors in Texts—Texts in Mirrors* (Amsterdam: Rodopi, 2007).

McColley, Diane Kelsey, *Milton's Eve* (Urbana: University of Illinois Press, 1983).

Malraux, André, *La Condition humaine* (Folio, 1; Paris: Gallimard, 1972) (first pub. 1933).

Mandelbrot, Benoit B., *The Fractal Geometry of Nature* (San Francisco, CA: W. H. Freeman, 1982).

Massin, Jean (ed.), *Œuvres complètes* by Victor Hugo, 18 vols (Paris: Le Club Français du livre, 1967–70).

Maurel, Jean, *Victor Hugo philosophe* (Paris: Presses Universitaires de France, 1985).

Maurois, André, *Olympio, ou la vie de Victor Hugo* (Paris: Hachette, 1954).

Mauron, Charles, 'Les Personnages de Victor Hugo: Étude psychocritique', in Victor Hugo, *Œuvres complètes*, ed. Jean Massin, 18 vols (Paris: Le Club Français du Livre, 1967–70), ii, pp. i–xlii.

Maxwell, Richard, 'City Life and the Novel: Hugo, Ainsworth, Dickens', *Comparative Literature*, 30 (Spring 1978), 157–71.

—— *The Mysteries of Paris and London* (Charlottesville: University Press of Virginia, 1992).

Mehlman, Jeffrey, *Revolution and Repetition: Marx/Hugo/Balzac* (Berkeley and Los Angeles: University of California Press, 1977).

Meschonnic, Henri, *Pour la poétique IV: Écrire Hugo* (Paris: Gallimard, 1977).

Miller, J. Hillis, 'The Problematic of Ending a Narrative', *Nineteenth-Century Fiction*, 33 (June 1978), 3–7.

Millet, Claude, '*Les Travailleurs de la mer* de Victor Hugo: Un roman d'amour', *Romantisme*, 115 (2002), 13–23.

Milner, Max, 'Le Satan de Milton et l'épopée romantique française', in Jacques Blondel (ed.), *Le* Paradis Perdu *1667–1967* (Lettres modernes; Paris: Minard, 1967), 219–40.

Milton, John, *Paradise Lost*, ed. John Leonard (London: Penguin, 2000) (first pub. 1667).

Monod, Sylvère, *Dickens the Novelist* (Norman: University of Oklahoma Press, 1968).

Montier, Jean-Pierre, 'Le "Finale" des *Travailleurs de la mer*: Horizon et limite du texte romanesque', *Littérature*, 135 (2004), 3–23.

Morisot, Jean-Claude, 'Le Frénétique et le quotidien: Hugo, Zola et le "rire de force"', *Nineteenth-Century French Studies*, 18/3–4 (Spring–Summer 1990), 474–81.

Moutet, Muriel, 'Concentration et dissolution du moi dans *Moby Dick* et *Les Travailleurs de la mer*', in Dominique Peyrache-Leborgne and Yann Jumelais (eds), *Victor Hugo ou les frontières effacées* (Horizons Comparatistes; Nantes: Pleins Feux, 2002), 367–83.

Nash, Suzanne, 'Transfiguring Disfiguration in *L'Homme qui rit*: A Study of Hugo's Use of the Grotesque', in Robert L. Mitchell (ed.), *Pre-text, Text, Context: Essays on Nineteenth-Century French Literature* (Columbus: Ohio State University Press, 1980), 3–13.

Neefs, Jacques, 'Penser par la fiction (*Les Travailleurs de la mer*)', in Jacques Seebacher and Anne Ubersfeld (eds), *Hugo le fabuleux: Actes du Colloque de Cerisy, 30 juin–10 juillet 1985* (Paris: Seghers, 1985), 98–107.

Noetinger, Élise, 'La Sinistre Beauté du masque: Étude de *L'Homme qui rit* de Victor Hugo', *French Studies*, 53/4 (Oct. 1999), 405–16.

——'L'Art du costume: *L'Homme qui rit* ou le drame de l'apparence', in J. A. Hiddleston (ed.), *Victor Hugo,* Romancier de l'abîme*: New Studies on Hugo's Novels* (Legenda/Research Monographs in French Studies; Oxford: European Humanities Research Centre, 2002), 137–55.

Nunley, Charles, '(En)gendering Terror: Women and Violence in *Quatrevingt-treize*', in John T. Booker and Allan H. Pasco (eds), *The Play of Terror in Nineteenth-Century France* (Newark: University of Delaware Press, 1997), 35–44.

O'Neil, Mary Anne, 'Classical Terror/Gothic Terror: Victor Hugo's *Quatrevingt-treize*', *Poetica*, 39–40 (1993), 259–73.

Paris, Bernard J., '*The Tempest*: Shakespeare's Ideal Solution', in *Bargains with Fate: Psychological Crises and Conflicts in Shakespeare and his Plays* (New York: Plenum, 1991), 261–77.

Paulson, William R., *Enlightenment, Romanticism, and the Blind in France* (Princeton: Princeton University Press, 1987).

——'L'*Anankè* des choses: Capitalisme et sacrifice dans *Les Travailleurs de la mer*', in David Ellison and Ralph Heyndels (eds), *Les Modernités de Victor Hugo* (Transatlantique, 1; Paris: Presses de l'Université de Paris-Sorbonne, 2004), 27–40.

Petch, Simon, 'Economies of Love and Law in *A Tale of Two Cities*', in Penny Gay, Judith Johnston, and Catherine Waters (eds), *Victorian Turns, NeoVictorian Returns: Essays on Fiction and Culture* (Newcastle upon Tyne: Cambridge Scholars, 2008), 68–77.

Petrey, Sandy, *History in the Text:* Quatrevingt-Treize *and the French Revolution* (West Fayette, IN: Purdue University Press, 1981).

Peyrache-Leborgne, Dominique, 'Victor Hugo et le sublime: Entre tragique et utopie', *Romantisme*, 82 (1993), 17–29.

——'Roman historique et roman-idylle chez Dickens et Hugo: *A Tale of Two Cities* et *Quatrevingt-treize*', *Dalhousie French Studies*, 36 (1996), 51–67.

——'Le Héros sublime dans *Titan* et *L'Homme qui rit*: D'une mythologie des belle-âmes aux fantastiques chimères', in Patrick Marot (ed.), *La Littérature et le sublime* (Toulouse: Presses Universitaires du Mirail, 2007), 305–36.

Piroué, Georges, *Victor Hugo romancier, ou les dessus de l'inconnu* (Paris: Denoël, 1964).

——*Lui, Hugo* (Paris: Denoël, 1985).

Porter, Laurence M., *The Renaissance of the Lyric in French Romanticism: Elegy, 'Poëme' and Ode* (French Forum Monographs, 10; Lexington, KY: French Forum, 1978).

——*Victor Hugo* (Twayne's World Authors Series, 883; New York: Twayne, 1999).

Quint, David, *Epic and Empire: Politics and Generic Form from Virgil to Milton* (Princeton, NJ: Princeton University Press, 1993).

Rankin, Arthur, '"Recalled to Life": Sacrifice and Renewal in *A Tale of Two Cities*', in Harold Bloom and Blake Hobby (eds), *Rebirth and Renewal* (Bloom's Literary Themes; New York: Chelsea House, 2009), 201–9.

Raser, Timothy, 'Revolution and Aesthetics in Hugo's *Quatrevingt-treize*', *L'Esprit Créateur*, 29/2 (1989), 50–61.

Revol-Marzouk, Lise, *Le Sphinx et l'Abîme: Sphinx maritimes et énigmes romanesques dans* Moby Dick *et* Les Travailleurs de la mer (Grenoble: ELLUG/Éditions littéraires et linguistiques de l'Université de Grenoble, 2008).

Richer, Jean, 'Grands transparents dans *Les Travailleurs de la Mer*', in Anne-Marie Amiot (ed.), *Idéologies hugoliennes*, Actes du Colloque Interdisciplinaire, 23–5 May 1985 (Nice: Serre, 1985), 107–11.

Ricoeur, Paul, *The Rule of Metaphor: Multi-Disciplinary Studies of the Creation of Meaning in Language*, trans. Robert Czerny (London: Routledge & Kegan Paul, 1978); orig. pub. as *La Métaphore vive* (Paris: Seuil, 1975).

——*Time and Narrative*, trans. Kathleen McLaughlin Blamey and David Pellauer, 3 vols (Chicago, IL: University of Chicago Press, 1984–8); orig. pub. as *Temps et récit* (Paris: Seuil, 1983–5).

——*Oneself as Another*, trans. Kathleen Blamey (Chicago, IL: University of Chicago Press, 1992); orig. pub. as *Soi-même comme un autre* (Paris: Seuil, 1990).

——*Memory, History, Forgetting*, trans. Kathleen Blamey and David Pellauer (Chicago, IL: University of Chicago Press, 2004); orig. pub. as *La Mémoire, l'histoire, l'oubli* (Paris: Seuil, 2000).

Rieben, Pierre-André, *Délires romantiques: Musset, Nodier, Gautier, Hugo* (Paris: José Corti, 1989).

Rignall, J. M., 'Dickens and the Catastrophic Continuum of History in *A Tale of Two Cities*', *ELH*, 51/3 (Autumn 1984), 575–87.

Robb, Graham, *Victor Hugo: A Biography* (New York: W. W. Norton, 1997).

Roche, Isabel, *Character and Meaning in the Novels of Victor Hugo* (Purdue Studies in Romance Literatures, 38; West Lafayette, IN: Purdue University Press, 2007).

Roman, Myriam, *Victor Hugo et le roman philosophique: Du 'drame dans les faits' au 'drame dans les idées'* (Paris: Honoré Champion, 1999).

——'Les Îles anglo-normandes: Insularité et communauté dans *Les Travailleurs de la mer*', in Lumilla Charles-Wurtz (ed.), *Victor Hugo 6: L'Écriture poétique* (Lettres modernes; Caen: Minard, 2006), 223–40.

Rosa, Guy, 'Présentation', to Victor Hugo, *Quatrevingt-Treize*, in *Œuvres complètes*, ed. Jean Massin, 18 vols (Paris: Le Club Français du Livre, 1967–70), xv. 229–60.

——'"Quatrevingt-treize" ou la critique du roman historique', *Revue d'histoire littéraire de la France*, 75 (1975), 329–43.

——'Critique et autocritique dans *L'Homme qui rit*', in Guy Rosa (ed.), L'Homme qui rit *ou la parole-monstre de Victor Hugo* (Paris: SEDES, 1985), 5–23.

Sadrin, Anny, '"In the Name of the King": From Dickens's *Great Expectations* to Hugo's *L'Homme qui rit*', *Dickens Quarterly*, 18/4 (Dec. 2001), 217–25.

Saint-Amand, Pierre, 'Hot Terror: *Quatrevingt-treize*', *SubStance*, 86 (1992), 61–72.

Sainte-Beuve, Charles Augustin, *Mes Poisons* (Paris: José Corti, 1988) (first pub. 1926).

Sanders, Andrew, 'Dickens's French Historical Novel', in Sylvère Monod (ed.), *Charles Dickens et la France: Colloque International de Boulogne-sur-Mer, 3 juin 1978* (Lille: Presses Universitaires de Lille, 1979), 61–8.

Schor, Naomi, *George Sand and Idealism* (New York: Columbia University Press, 1993).

Schwartzbach, F. S., *Dickens and the City* (London: Athlone, 1979).

Seebacher, Jacques, 'Comment peut-on être Milton?', in Jacques Blondel (ed.), *Le* Paradis Perdu *1667–1967* (Lettres modernes; Paris: Minard, 1967), 241–50.

——'Introduction', in Victor Hugo, *Châtiments. La Conscience. La Vision de Dante* (Paris: Garnier-Flammarion, 1970).

Shakespeare, William, *La Tempête*, trans. François-Victor Hugo, in *Œuvres complètes de W. Shakespeare*, 18 vols (Paris: Pagnerre, 1859–72), ii.

Shaw, Harry E., *The Forms of Historical Fiction: Sir Walter Scott and his Successors* (Ithaca, NY: Cornell University Press, 1983).

Spevack, Marvin, *The Harvard Concordance to Shakespeare* (Cambridge, MA: Harvard University Press, 1973).

Stephens, Bradley, 'Victor Hugo: *État présent*', *French Studies*, 63/1 (2009), 66–74.

Stewart, Garrett, 'Death by Water in *A Tale of Two Cities*', in Howard Bloom (ed.), *Charles Dickens's* A Tale of Two Cities (Modern Critical Interpretations; New York: Chelsea House, 1987), 107–20. From *Death Sentences: Styles of Dying in British Fiction*. Cambridge, MA: Harvard University Press, 1984.

Stoehr, Taylor, *Dickens: The Dreamer's Stance* (Ithaca, NY: Cornell University Press, 1965).

Tennyson, Alfred Lord, 'Ulysses', in *Selected Poetry*, ed. Norman Page (London: Routledge, 1995).

Thomas, John Heywood, *L'Angleterre dans l'œuvre de Victor Hugo* (Paris: A. Pedone, 1934).

Turton, Derek J., 'Symbolic Confrontation in Hugo's *Quatrevingt-treize*', *Revue de l'Université d'Ottawa*, 44/3 (July–Sept. 1974), 373–83.

Ubersfeld, Anne, *Paroles de Hugo* (Paris: Messidor, 1985).

Vanden Bossche, Chris R., 'Prophetic Closure and Disclosing Narrative: The French Revolution and *A Tale of Two Cities*', *Dickens Studies Annual*, 12 (1983), 209–21.

Vergil, *The Aeneid*, trans. Sarah Ruden (New Haven, CT: Yale University Press, 2009).

Vernier, Jean-Pierre, 'Lecture de *A Tale of Two Cities*', in Sylvère Monod (ed.), *Charles Dickens et la France: Colloque International de Boulogne-sur-Mer, 3 juin 1978* (Lille: Presses Universitaires de Lille, 1979), 69–76.

Wagenknecht, Edward, 'Introduction', in Charles Dickens, *A Tale of Two Cities* (New York: Random House, 1967), pp. iv–xviii.

Waters, Catherine, *Dickens and the Politics of the Family* (Cambridge: Cambridge University Press, 1997).

Weiskel, Thomas, *The Romantic Sublime: Studies in the Structure and Psychology of Transcendence* (Baltimore, MD: Johns Hopkins University Press, 1976).

Welsh, Alexander, *The City of Dickens* (Oxford: Clarendon Press, 1971).

——'Opening and Closing *Les Misérables*', *Nineteenth-Century Fiction*, 33 (June 1978), 8–23.

Wheeler, Richard P., 'Fantasy and History in *The Tempest*', in Nigel Wood (ed.), *The Tempest* (Theory and Practice Series; Buckingham: Open University Press, 1995), 127–64.

Wulf, Judith, 'Chimère et référence dans *L'Homme qui rit*', in Michel Viegnes (ed.), *Hugo et la chimère* (*Recherches & Travaux,* 62/Revue de UFR de Lettres Classiques et Modernes; Grenoble: ELLUG/Éditions littéraires et linguistiques de l'Université de Grenoble, 2003), 59–71.

——'"Rabâchage" et formation du sens romanesque chez Victor Hugo', in Nigel Harkness et al. (eds), *Visions/Revisions: Essays on Nineteenth-Century French Culture* (French Studies of the Eighteenth and Nineteenth Centuries, 14; Oxford: Peter Lang, 2003), 225–39.

Index